Renovating Holiness

Edited By
Josh Broward and
Thomas Jay Oord

SacraSage

www.renovatingholiness.com

SacraSage Press
Nampa, Idaho

Elevate Faith, a Division of Elevate Publishing www.elevatepub.com
Boise, Idaho

ISBN 978-1937498658

PRINTED IN THE UNITED STATES OF AMERICA

PRAISE FOR *RENOVATING HOLINESS*

This is an important book, and this is the right time for it to be published. Most of us would agree that an essential aspect of Christian discipleship is holiness of heart and life. But for many, the message has often been confusing, and for some, it seemed to lack credibility. This has especially been true as we have attempted to communicate the message of holiness across international and generational cultures. The authors of these essays represent voices from younger generations and diverse cultural perspectives. They give us an honest response as to how the message of holiness has been heard . . . and often dismissed. These emerging global leaders offer thoughtful words of hope. They interpret the biblical holiness message in ways that can be embraced and embodied in a diverse world that is both pre-Christian and postmodern. I highly recommend this book.

Ron Benefiel, Dean of the School of Theology and Christian Ministry, Point Loma Nazarene University

The reexamination of biblical holiness is the right—and responsibility—of the church in every generation, not for the purpose of compromise or change, but reaffirmation. Such a study, engaging international and intergenerational scholars at all levels of the church, has the potential to re-invigorate our belief in the centrality of the scriptural call to live Christlike in the church and world. This liberating truth, often obscured by antiquated language, would be restated in fresh lively thought forms and expressions understood by the current generation. I commend Oord and Broward whose work can mark the beginning of this much-needed discourse.

Jim L. Bond, General Superintendent Emeritus, Point Loma Nazarene University President Emeritus

It is high time for my generation (the Boomers) to listen carefully. We have been the presenters most of the time. The younger holiness crowd may recapture the passion and essence of the holiness message. This collection of reflections and challenges gives me hope that a core Biblical message has champions. I love the questioning, the honesty, the mixture of great scholarship and personal experience. My ears are on.

Dan Boone, President, Trevecca Nazarene University

Praise for Renovating Holiness

Renovating Holiness invites you to put your feet under a round table and to engage in dialog with a host of conversation partners. There will be times when you will say "wow" and times you might say "whoa." But you will encounter thoughtful ideas and make new friends as you read. Pull up your chair, listen to voices from around the world, and gain insights from a new generation of leaders. And be willing to think again how we preach, teach, and live the holiness message.

Randall J. Craker, Superintendent,
Northwest District Church of the Nazarene

When a theological claim encounters an experiential crisis, the result is either abandonment or reformulation. Out of their personal experiential crisis and that of their peers, the contributors to this volume have refused to abandon their heritage but are seeking a reformulation that reflects both truth and relevance.

H. Ray Dunning, Professor of Theology Emeritus,
Trevecca Nazarene University

Tom and Josh have gathered an incredibly diverse and representative collection of essays and essayists to rethink, renew, and renovate the central theme of the sacred Scriptures—holiness. Is there anything that we need more than this in the Church of the Nazarene? And is there anything we need more than to offer the Church universal? I think not.

Brad Estep, Pastor,
Kansas City First Church of the Nazarene

Challenging, thought provoking, and highly commendable! Josh Broward and Tom Oord have brought over 100 writers from all continents together to discuss holiness from their biblical perspective. The book will be an excellent tool for leaders as they struggle with the challenge of transferring the message of holiness to over 150 countries with dozens of languages and cultures.

Hermann Gschwandtner,
South Asia Field Strategy Coordinator

We have quested after the unity and diversity of the Wesleyan Holiness. This book could reveal the trial and triumph of our Nazarene heritage. This book shows our church's flavor, our color, and our aroma—within the contemporary church and also looking into the future.

Churlhee Amos Hahn, Chairperson of the Nazarene Heritage Academy,
Korean Nazarene University

Praise for Renovating Holiness

Renovating Holiness is an incredibly ambitious project that delivers on its promise. The scope and the depth of this volume are exceptional and noteworthy. The editors have assembled some of the best and the brightest Gen X and Millennial leaders of the global Church of the Nazarene, and the book offers the reader more than 100 compelling essays. At a time when the denomination is searching to understand its holiness history and to move forward in meaningful ways, this book stands at the cusp of a new century. It very well may be the transitional tour de force that re-invigorates holiness theology into the future.

Diane Leclerc, Professor of Historical Theology,
Northwest Nazarene University

Holiness—at its core—is about change, so any time we talk about how to change and how God is working among us to change us into the image of Christlikeness, that's a good thing. As a Nazarene pastor, I deeply appreciate this conversation and where it will take us.

Scott Marshall, Lead Pastor,
Real Life Community Church of the Nazarene

These younger voices are candid about the need to improve the way holiness is understood within the Church of the Nazarene. Their criticisms are surprisingly frank. Yet they remain hopeful, contextualizing the message for the millennial generation and in global cultures. Holiness for these young leaders is more than a private religious experience. It is communal and unapologetically activist. Holiness in these essays is a worldview affecting all of life, pointing to the possibilities of personal and social transformation.

Tom Nees,
President, Leading to Serve, Inc.,
Former Director of Nazarene Compassionate Ministries

Millennials and Xers are hungry for honest and authentic dialogue about the big issues facing our Church. They want to have their voices heard. More importantly, they want to make a difference not only in the Church but also in the real worlds where they live. This book offers the rest of us the opportunity truly to listen.

Dana Preusch, Director of the Center for Pastoral Leadership,
Nazarene Theological Seminary

Acknowledgements

We would like to express our thanks to several people who have played key roles in helping move this project forward.

- Thanks to all 100+ contributors. This is really your book, not ours.

- Thanks to the people of Northwest Nazarene University and Duneland Community Church for allowing Tom and Josh to invest time in *Renovating Holiness*.

- Thanks to Dorothy Bullon and Julia Ciupek Reed for assisting with translations.

- Thanks to Rick Edwards, Melissa Swearingen Watson, Sarah Broward, and Joy Henley (www.inkstainedediting.com) for proofreading the final manuscript.

- Thanks to David Brush (www.davidbrush.com) for setting up our website: www.renovatingholiness.com.

- Thanks to the people at Elevate Publishing for bringing this book to print.

- Thanks to all of the people who have offered your encouragements along the way. We pray that this book starts a conversation that helps us all.

We dedicate this book to . . .

all members of the Church of the Nazarene around the world who have scratched their heads in confusion about the doctrine of holiness,

all who have struggled with the doctrine as a whole and specifically with the ways we have so often misinterpreted it,

all who have wondered if they still have a place in the Church of the Nazarene despite their doubts or disagreements about entire sanctification,

all who have left the Church of the Nazarene specifically because of the way the doctrine of entire sanctification has been mishandled. (We are entirely sorry.)

We offer this book in the hope that . . .

we will take steps toward figuring this out together,

we will reform what needs reforming and carry forward all that should be carried forward,

we will acknowledge that the Church of the Nazarene is a big tent and holiness a broad theme, with room for many perspectives.

we will become more like Jesus individually and together, as we engage this process of discussion, exploration, and renovation.

Table of Contents

[Note: Each author's country of origin and country of residence are listed in brackets].

Table of Contents

Table of Contents

Table of Contents

Table of Contents

Table of Contents

Table of Contents

INTRODUCTION

Embracing Renovation
Josh Broward

Imagine that you have just inherited your grandparents' house. The only condition for inheritance is that you have to actually live in the house. Your grandparents, whom you loved dearly, had lived in the same house for sixty years. This simple abode holds an infinite amount of family memories . . . and dust.

You are thrilled to be entrusted with the task of tending the family's treasure of history and memory. Yet if you are going to live there, you'll have to make it your own. The vinyl armchair still permanently imprinted with the shape of your Grandpa's posterior is not something to keep for posterity's sake. Although the massive old TV—the kind that came in its own cabinet—faithfully cranked out *Wheel of Fortune* at 6:30 for decades, it too will have to go.

But the furniture is just the beginning, the whole interior desperately needs updating. The foot-wide pink flowers on the bathroom wallpaper may have been "snazzy" in the 70's, but now they just feel like Pepto Bismol had a fight with the Easter Bunny. New paint is a must in every room, but under the stained and faded carpets you discover a hidden treasure of long buried yet indestructible oak flooring. With a little elbow grease, those will shine in all their ancient glory.

However, we haven't even started talking about the real improvements. The windows leak like a sieve. Maybe that's why Grandma always had that nappy afghan and two cats on her lap! The wood furnace is literally a firetrap. And there's a spongy spot on the floor near the back porch where water has been seeping in every good rain.

The kitchen and dining room were designed for a time when meals were formal affairs with fine china. Your family prefers an open kitchen/dining/living room so that the hosting area can be expanded easily. Some walls will have to go.

Grandpa saved a lot of money by doing the work himself when he added the extra bedroom in '69, and he saved money again when he built "Grandpa's Workshop" in '83. But the additions are showing their age, especially around the seams where the ceiling is turning brown because of leaks.

Don't get me wrong. You're grateful for the house and all of the family heritage that goes with it. It's just that Grandma and Grandpa didn't notice their house

1

deteriorating at roughly the same rate as their bodies. They didn't really mind that wonky faucet in the bathroom because they had lived with it for 30 years. But if you are going to live there, you'll have to bring the house into the 21st century. Your challenge is to reshape the family history to be a working home for your family.

This is essentially the challenge facing us younger members of the Church of the Nazarene. We have inherited a doctrine of sanctification that our grandparents built. Our spiritual grandfathers and grandmothers were certainly faithful in their time, and we owe them a debt of gratitude. That they have willed their theological home to us is surely more than we deserve.

But they didn't seem to notice the radical changes happening in the world while they carried on with church as usual. Their language doesn't work in today's world. Their thought structures feel cramped in some places and leaky in others.

If we are actually going to live in this theological house with our family and our children, renovation is a must. And I don't just mean some new furniture and a little paint. We need some sledgehammers and some heavy machinery. We'll need to dig up parts of the yard and rent a dumpster.

However, all of this change is not a sign of disloyalty or disrespect. We are not being unfaithful to the legacy of those who came before, nor are we rejecting their hard work. We are faced with three choices:

1. Live with an obsolete and uncomfortable theological house and manage the resentment and hang-ups that engenders.
2. Move out and leave all our traditions behind.
3. Renovate the whole structure to keep what is best and to carry it forward into a new era for our friends and children.

In the Church of the Nazarene, it seems as though the majority of Gen-X have chosen *Option 1: Uncomfortable Resentment*. That hasn't gone well. Many of our pastors have stopped talking about or even caring about holiness. "Doctrine of Holiness" is one of the most dreaded classes in the curriculum at many of our schools. One of my peers relayed stories of how his friends baldly lied about their experiences with entire sanctification in their ordination interviews simply to tell the interviewers "what they wanted to hear."

A frighteningly large majority of Millennials have opted for *Option 2: Moving Out*. This has meant leaving nearly everything Nazarene behind, sometimes even leaving Christianity behind. As Grant Miller points out in his essay, holiness churches have fared the worst among all Christian groups. We are losing our youth and young adults—and fast. Our theological house doesn't fit our family, and our family is leaving.

This book is a call to embrace and to empower *Option 3: Renovation*. Our house has good bones. The fundamental structures of our tradition are strong and well built. The Church of the Nazarene has reached into centuries and millennia past for bricks and beams of substance and depth. This house is worth saving. This house is worth living in. This house can help us raise our families well.

Therefore, this house is worth renovating. Even more, renovation is a moral obligation and a dynamic privilege. If we want our family to stay here and to thrive here, the house must change. That is not negotiable. The only other option is a dying house inhabited by increasingly aged and lonely people, where young people only come for visits on holidays.

In truth, we—not only the contributors in this book, but also all leaders in the Church of the Nazarene—agree that renovation is an absolute necessity for the Church of the Nazarene. We love our denomination, and we want our denomination to thrive in our rapidly changing world. In our moments of greatest honesty, we know that refusing to change is choosing to die.

But, oh, what to change? And how? And when? And at what pace? And what must never change? Our answers to these questions differ. Here we debate. These are the great questions of our era. We must ask these questions openly and honestly. We need all our voices—young, middle aged, and old—for these questions.

In the Church of the Nazarene, however, this conversation has been dominated by the older voices that hold the seats and pulpits of power. The difficult truth is that our official conversations about the future of our church have been too old, too white, too male, and too American. The younger and varied voices have been welcomed only when they were harmonious with the perspectives of those in power. When our younger leaders have suggested more radical changes or raised difficult questions or aired discontent, those voices were ignored or discouraged, silenced or removed.

Yet these young voices come from leaders around the globe who are inheriting the house. They must decide how to raise their families in this place. They are the ones who still have more than half their lives in the future. Their voices will naturally be the voices of challenge and change, and we need to hear these voices more now than ever before.

Naturally, the Church is delightfully a multigenerational house, and we need all the voices. We need to hear from our leaders with the wisdom of vast experience. Those voices have much to teach us all, but we must be careful that their voices do not drown out the questions and hopes of the young.

Introduction

Renovating Holiness is a joint project by more than 100 Nazarene leaders from around the globe. We have intentionally sought as much diversity as possible in terms of ethnicity, gender, and location. We have also limited our contributors to members of Generation X (born from 1960 to 1979) and the Millennial generation (born from 1980 to 1999) in order to amplify the much neglected voices of our younger leaders. These writers are Nazarenes and joyfully so, and yet they call for change. They call for change in doctrine, in teaching, in practice, and in perspective. Mostly, they call for a renovation that enables them to raise their children and their children's children in this church they love.

This book is a call for change, but even more it is a call for open conversation about change. For too long, we have considered the doctrine of holiness off limits, our own sacred cow, impervious to all forces of cultural change.

Several of our contributors remind us that our holiness has also been unhealthily uninfluenced by the various local cultures in which it has been planted. In this globalized postmodern world, we need a vast recontextualization of holiness into a million different micro-cultures around the world. Our leaders need the freedom to embrace that messy process of incarnation without fear of retribution from above. We need to rip up the standardized carpets to discover the rich and varied hues of hardwood flooring sustaining our house around the world.

As a global denomination, we need to talk openly about what needs to change in our doctrine, practice, and structure to allow us to embody more faithfully the parts of our tradition that must never change. We need safe space—officially safe space—to dialog together about our deepest hopes, fears, and longings for our church. Our hope is that this book will serve as a catalyst for many, many safe spaces for conversation about holiness in small groups, classrooms, district assemblies, and workshops around the world. (Check out our free discussion guide available at renovatingholiness.com.)

We have a beautiful church, a beautiful and strong theological house. We are now in the process of reclaiming our best strengths, repairing our weaknesses, and expanding for greater hospitality. May God give us the strength of vision to renovate well and to build boldly into the future.

After nine years with Korea Nazarene University and KNU International English Church, Josh, Sarah, Emma, and John David have settled in Chesterton, Indiana. In addition to engaging in medieval jousting fantasies with his kids, Josh splits his time building missional communities at Duneland Community Church of the Nazarene and fighting human trafficking with Free The Girls (www.freethegirls.org). Josh is also an adjunct professor at Olivet Nazarene University. You can follow Josh on Twitter @JoshBroward and at his blog: www.humblefuture.com.

The Guilt-Ridden Sanctified

Sherri Walker

I was in my teenage years when I first became aware of the idea of a second work of grace, known in our tradition as entire sanctification. I remember being drawn to the idea of complete surrender to God, being freed from sin, and being filled with the Holy Spirit. I was at a summer camp at the age of 15 when I first consciously surrendered my life to the Lord. It was a tremendous spiritual high.

However, I did not experience any significant life-change. The focus at camp, as well as each time I went to youth group, was on turning away from a list of things and following a list of don'ts. However, I had grown up in the church. As far back as I can remember, I had tried to follow the rules and obey my parents. How could I know if I was different when the bar by which we were measured changed?

I remember that camp as a significant moment in my life, but I also remember the deep guilt I began to feel. That camp began a painful questioning period of whether or not I had truly surrendered all of myself; there seemed to be always something more I was holding onto. It was a cycle of guilt: praying to surrender, spiritual high, feeling the same, and feeling guilty that nothing had changed. I would be surrounded often by these God-sized experiences with the Spirit moving, and it would seem that nothing noticeable had really changed in me. I would still struggle with trying to control portions of my life, to control God. Then the guilt would set in. I thought I had already done this. Is it not working? Did it not take? Am I not filled with the Spirit?

In college, I was taught that sanctification was not something we did but something God offered to us. All this time, I had thought that the reason I wasn't completely surrendered and filled was that I wasn't praying enough, reading my Bible enough, or caring about other people enough. At that point, I began to wonder if God was withholding God's Spirit from me. I wondered why

5

I continued to struggle with the same sins and temptations and what I was doing wrong not to feel like I was sanctified.

As a person preparing in education for the ministry, I remember filling out paperwork where I would have to describe the date and experience of being entirely sanctified. I would reluctantly write what I thought my story was, all the while feeling guilty that I didn't have a clear "crisis moment," a dramatic re-direction, or remember a specific moment where my "heart was strangely warmed." I didn't know if what I was writing was the truth or something I had just made up. How could I know that I was filled with the Spirit? How does one know that he/she is entirely sanctified?

It wasn't until I was a youth pastor that I realized I was not alone in my anguish. I was sitting among 9,000 other teens and leaders at a Nazarene Youth Conference listening to one of our General Superintendents preach a sermon about being entirely sanctified. I remember sitting in the hotel room following that evening service with a few of the girls from my youth group who were in anguish. They had so many questions about what the preacher meant. They didn't understand why they hadn't experienced something like this. They were guilt ridden over the fact that they had not experienced any grand gesture from the Lord assuring them that they were entirely sanctified.

I understood their anguish, their wavering back and forth, feeling as if their confessions and surrender were not good enough, wanting so badly to experience entire sanctification as these adults were describing it. As I sat in that room with two of the most spiritually mature high school students I had ever known, I had an "ah-ha" moment of my own.

Perhaps there is a flaw in the way we speak of entire sanctification to our teenagers and young adults. Instead of our young people experiencing more and more freedom as they spend time learning about God and in his Word, they are experiencing more and more guilt. Have we created a community where people are more comfortable hiding their struggles, questions, and guilt?

Most descriptions and messages of entire sanctification include some sort of language about surrendering of one's self. What does it mean to a 15 year-old to surrender her whole life to Jesus? What is she surrendering? Most of the decisions she makes are directly influenced by her parents and the environment around her. Does she really have the moral development to know what it means to surrender? What happens in two years when a 17 year-old begins to make her own decisions? She will suddenly realize that there are new things to surrender and begin to question whether she had ever surrendered herself to the Lord in the first place. Surrender becomes a burden to the developing child as she tries to figure out what that even means. "Did I really surrender?" "How can I tell if I have surrendered everything?"

It seems historically we have answered these questions with a list of dos and don'ts. Children are still very concrete. They are satisfied to do or not to do things based on a fear of punishment. So we tell our children they need to pray and read their Bible more. They shouldn't "smoke, drink, cuss, or chew . . . or go with the girls or guys who do." However, the older they get, the list continues to grow longer and longer. In addition, as they begin to develop more fully, the risk of punishment is no longer enough. They want to know why they would or would not do certain things.

A list of dos and don'ts doesn't answer why they should be surrendering their life to Christ. A list of dos and don'ts doesn't even resolve in their heart that they have surrendered everything. Otherwise, the questions and yearning wouldn't remain even when the "rules" are followed.

What happens when our children begin to dig more deeply into the meaning of sanctification and life itself, only to find that we have no more to tell them? Our church's articulation of this work of grace, our narrative, teaches our children that they are trading their old bondage and slavery to sin for a new bondage of surrendering to rules, expectations, boundaries, and inevitably, guilt.

Instead of our narrative focusing on moments of surrender, could we speak of sanctification as an ongoing growth of freedom? I believe that the process of sanctification is a process of being more fully who God created us to be. It helps to think of it as a healing process. We are on an ongoing process of healing, a journey that God is taking with us, offering us grace and growth in the moments we are ready.

That journey certainly has moments of crisis, but it is a journey first. A 15 year old will not know how to live the same life of freedom as a 22 year old, nor a 22 year old as a mother of two children. Yet, in each of these stages of life, there can be an understanding of what freedom means in their context. We are on a journey of life and each day should bring us a new clarity as to what it means to be who God created us to be. There will be moments when we experience new parts of the journey, and just like a person who is healing from abuse or disease, there will need to be a patient process of healing.

It seems to me, the best thing we can do for our teenagers and young adults is to focus on the freedom found in Christ. We can offer them the chance to give over to God what troubles them, what weighs them down, what burdens them. This deliberate offering will lead to freedom, light, and joy . . . eventually. For some, this process of offering their troubles will be a long, tiresome process. We are called to journey with people, not just get them to an altar a second time. This journey will look different for everyone. However, this gives us the opportunity to trust the Spirit who is in them to guide them to make the best decisions, to choose the right path to life.

How can I tell if I am entirely sanctified?

Is everything at peace in my heart? Do I feel alive and free in Christ? Does that feeling of freedom open my eyes to see others who also need to experience freedom in Christ?

Surrender focuses on giving up self. There is not anything wrong with holiness being connected with surrender. The Apostle Paul talked about the crucified life. There is a place to die to the inward self-centeredness, and I believe that lifelong surrender leads to freedom in Christ.

However, surrender is not where the conversation should begin. Surrender does not adequately reflect all that Christ desires for his children whom are set apart, and it is a concept that is highly influenced by age-appropriate moral development. Surrender focuses on giving up self; freedom empowers us to discover our true selves, in Christ. If we change our narrative, we will see more of our teens and young adults begin to experience in their own unique way what it means to live the way God is calling them to live.

Sherri Walker serves in the Admissions Office at Northwest Nazarene University as a Senior Admissions Counselor and Director of Summer Ministry Groups. After receiving a BA in Public Communications and a Master of Arts in Religion from NNU, she has spent her life serving in higher education and church staff ministry. She has a deep desire for the Church to understand who she is, why she exists, and how to communicate those values effectively.

The Language of Holiness:
Anguishing at the Altar and Becoming a Muslim
Gabi Markusse-Overduin

"Mom, I just need to know it would be fine with you if I came home and announced that I had decided to become Muslim!"[1]

Ouch! How could I say to her that it would be fine? My thoughts race to figure out how to respond properly.

As our conversation continues, I slowly begin to realize that our 19-year-old religion major is not seriously considering leaving the faith in which she was born and raised and to which she publicly attested two years ago at her baptism. What our daughter desperately needs is the freedom to develop her own understanding of her faith. She longs to be trusted in the relationship that Jesus has with *her* and to be respected in her choice of words to describe that relationship.

But why does she have to use these foreign words to describe something that should feel so familiar to me?

Somewhere inside of me, a still small voice begins to beckon me back to a time some 35 years ago.

I see myself sitting in a pew, in a traditionally built sanctuary. It is Sunday evening. The Pastor has just finished his sermon and now he calls those who want to be sanctified to come forward and to kneel at the altar. God will sanctify and will fill the supplicant with joy and peace, is the promise given. I yearn for a magic touch that will seal my fate with God and perfect my life. And I find myself again and again anguishing at the altar, week after week. The promised showers of joy and peace never came. According to my interpretation of the words of the Pastor, that was a clear sign that the blessing had not been given.

Oh, how I longed for sanctification in those days! I loved God dearly and had a close relationship with Him. From childhood on, He would open His Word to my hungry heart, explaining its secrets to me. He was the one, I knew, who had access to my heart, and He led me to love the people I met from whom I normally would flee.

---

1. All quotations from my 19-year-old daughter, Esther Markusse, are from actual conversations and are used with her permission.

Why then would God refuse to give this "sanctification" to me? My all He had; what more did He want? Why, oh, why did God not want to give this blessing to me?

One day, desperate to find answers, I went to the office of the youth pastor, "I want to be sanctified, Pastor, and I don't know how!" He could not help; he merely noted that I was one of the most holy young people he knew. That answer did not satisfy my anguishing heart. Once again, I saw God's magic touch pass by beyond my reach.

But is this really what was happening? This is how I interpreted the words given from the pulpit by my dear Pastor. These words had touched *his* heart so many, many years before.

As I grew older, my hope of this "touch" from God called "entire sanctification" by my grandfatherly pastor, slowly faded. But my desire for growth in holiness never faded. As a senior at university, I decided to try one last time. I had since changed churches, and this pastor was not only someone who exemplified everything I understood to be holy, and wise, and loving, and intelligent, but he was also much closer to me in age.

"Pastor, can you help me? I long for sanctification, and perhaps some would say, 'oh, you already have it,' but that doesn't satisfy me. What should I do?" His answer to me was brilliant, and exactly what I needed to hear, "As long as you want more of God, keep asking Him." I don't think he was aware that he was saying something profound, but this was language I understood.

And that, I think, is the key to why it touched me as it did. I was an honest young adult, seeking after God. The language of the previous generations had communicated to me that I was still missing something that would never come to me. I continuously experienced being "ignored" or "passed by" when the blessing was passed out. But this time the words rang true in my heart and freed me from my anguish.

Looking at these words now, nearly 30 years later, they may need a bit of tweaking here and there. They do not stand on their own. What they communicated to me then is that God was working His holiness into my life slowly and surely as I grew in understanding and longing for more of Him. These words somehow allowed me to leave the "magic touch" definition of sanctification that had been communicated to me by the words of the generations before me, and they allowed me to embrace a definition of sanctification that essentially meant "more of God" in my life.

As my life, and God's relationship with me, has grown throughout the years, I have learned to keep my focus off of the "peace" and "joy" that my first pastor had thought good to promise. These have never proven to be a good measuring stick of God's work in my heart.

"More of God" in my life has come to mean that I look to Him as Creator of heaven and earth and that I, therefore, care for the environment. "More of God" in my life has come to mean that I seek for justice for victims of abuse of power—sexual, physical, emotional, and financial. "More of God" in my life has come to mean that I seek to understand how the Scriptures speak into my world today and into the world of my 19-year-old daughter. And often, I find that the Scriptures speak in different words than what I heard some 35 years ago.

As a young adult, I needed the freedom to develop my own understanding of "sanctification." I longed to be trusted in the relationship that Jesus already had with me. This pastor—of my own generation—finally gave me words, however simple, through which I could experience that freedom and trust.

"Being Muslim is really no different than being a Christian." *Oh my! What should I say now?*

"Why do you flinch when I talk about a gay person coming out of the closet?" *She sees more than I think I let on! Is she trying to tell us something?*

The answer to that last question is, of course, "Yes." She is indeed trying to tell us something. She is trying to tell us that God is working the love of Christ in her heart for all people through His Spirit; she is trying to tell us that *no one* falls outside of God's love. Is not this evidence of God's work of holiness—yes, sanctification—in her life?

As a religion major, she is preparing herself to become a high school religion teacher in a postmodern, post-Christian society. She is a child of her time. And Jesus has a relationship with her that fits her language and the needs of her culture.

God reveals himself in community, to community. No one person has all the wisdom and knowledge of God available. Our Stories are examples of this, written by many throughout many years, in many styles, speaking of many works and words of God in many situations, all pointing to the One God, and One Christ, through the One Spirit. As Paul said so many generations ago, "And I pray that you, being rooted and established in love, may have power, *together with all the saints*, to grasp how wide and long and high and deep is the love of Christ" (Eph. 3:18).

Together with all the saints. Not only those of my generation, with my choice of words. God will speak to each generation, and *together* we will begin to grasp His love. My daughter has understood the love of Christ for those of all religions and whatever sexual orientation. Why am I so afraid to trust this love? Just as I needed to find terms and ways of thinking that would help me to understand the work of God in my heart and life, she needs this freedom as well. Just as I needed to be trusted to allow God to give more of Himself to me, she needs to be trusted that she will continue to allow God to give more of Himself to her.

And meanwhile, will I—a person of another generation and other words—listen to her and allow her words to help me to grow in grasping "how wide and long and high and deep is the love of Christ"?

Gaby Markusse-Overduin, Ph.D. in Theology, is currently co-pastor of an inner city church plant in the university city of Utrecht, the Netherlands, and leads the Dutch Learning Center of the European Nazarene College.

The Credibility Gap

Arthur van Wijngaarden

In talking to my non-Christian friends, one question that keeps coming up is what makes us Christians different. This question is often out of sincere curiosity and out of a bit of suspicion about my thoughts on non-believers as well. Our Christian history of (often) not practicing what we've preached is still apparently haunting us, even in a generation that was raised by people who've already left the church behind long ago. There remains an air of cynicism about Christians and their claims and the judgmentalism that all too often comes with the claims. If you come from a tradition like ours that has holiness as a central doctrine, including the possibility to *become* holy, it seems you're opening yourself up for an extra critical evaluation. We run the risk of a serious credibility gap here. So how do we explain this holiness, the need for it, and our desire to be holy?

A credibility gap is the (experienced) distance between what people say about a situation and the reality of it. In our case (including my own life), it is the gap between professing the need and the desire for holiness and the reality in which we're not yet holy.

At the same time, consider the gap between what is expected of us by our faith—"Be perfect as your father in heaven is perfect" (Matthew 5:48)—and what is said about our own potential—"For I have the desire to do good, but I cannot carry it out" (Romans 7:18). How am I supposed to bridge *that* gap?

Still, we believe in holiness, the need for it, and the possibility to attain it here on earth. And we should—because it *is* one of the main things that sets us apart as Christians: the hope for the liberty of suffering from sin *in this life*.

In my experience, many people who consider themselves non-Christians see the world for what it is, a place that is far from perfect. And, what's more important, many see the fact that their actions contribute to this imperfectness. There are many who try to make the world a better place and realize that our egos are a big part of the problem. Maybe it is the divine spark (what we would call prevenient grace) that helps people see this, but they are fighting the same fight as we are—the fight against selfishness that makes the earth such a hard place to live in sometimes. In this sense, it might even be inappropriate to talk about

13

"us" and "them," since that creates an unnecessary distance between fellow human beings.

The Church of the Nazarene has helped me understand one big lesson about holiness: it is a thing of the heart. John Wesley, in *A Plain Account of Christian Perfection*, describes holiness in various ways. He calls it "purity of intent," "love filling the heart" to the extent that there is no more room for sin, and—I love this one—"having the mind that was in Christ."

On the other hand, the big misunderstanding about holiness, among Christians and non-Christians alike, is that holiness is about following rules. That it is a rule-perfection, like getting a score of 10 out of 10. And worse, that it is something that you can *achieve*. I shiver even as I write it. What is it that really sets us apart as Christians from non-Christians? Isn't it simply that we have woken up? We have become aware of the reality of sin in our lives, of the true state of our hearts, and—most importantly—of our own ability to change this.

The realization of our own inability to change ourselves from within is a big part of the transition to a life with Christ. He is, in this sense, our hope. We realize that without Him our hearts would forever be aimed on our own desires. We realize that we will never be able to bridge the gap between what God wants for us—healing for our sin-diseased selves—and what we are able to achieve on our own. Without Him, we would thus be left to despair about the state of the world and our lives. In fact, I believe that one of the major reasons for sin in this world lies in the despair and cynicism of people regarding the possibility for change in themselves and other people.

Another set of questions I often hear from non-Christians is this set, "If I just try to be a good person, why is that not good enough? What's the use of being a Christian? Is there really the need for God and for forgiveness and for perfection?"

Well, I don't think there is a need for the perfection that is sometimes falsely claimed by Christians and that is marked by arrogance, a perfection that thinks it is better than others, on a higher moral ground and in the position to judge. We have no need for perfection that thinks it has *achieved* something, and that if *you* try hard enough (and you should) you could reach it too. This way of looking at perfection doesn't acknowledge the fact that it is our heart that needs changing first and that any change comes truly from God.

There *is*, however, a need for a perfection that finds its source in our hearts. For if Jesus says that all sin starts in the heart (Matthew 15:19), then the better world we all desire starts there as well. All our vain efforts of changing the outside world from our own strength and judging others who don't seem to be making the same effort leads only to widening the credibility gap. So yes, there is a need for God.

In talking about the gap, I feel there is also room for some humility when it comes to our own desire for holiness. We profess the need and desire for holiness, but how bad do we really want it?

If I look at myself, I want to be holy. But maybe not as much as I say I do. If I look at the reality of my life and the mistakes I make, I realize how much selfishness is present in my actions (and thus in my heart). If I am honest, I see that even my desire for change and for love comes from God. Whenever I seek Him and am confronted with His love for me, I become aware of my need of Him. It awakens in me the desire to become part of His love, to allow this love to become the sole purpose of my life and the full extent of all my intentions. But these feelings are often short-lived. My own desires take over sooner than I care to admit.

My conclusion then is that my love *for* God and the desire to change comes from the love *of* God. My desire to be holy and be changed comes out of the experience with God's love. If left to my own devices, I want just one thing: that which satisfies my desires. So even the true desire that I have is in effect something that finds its source in God.

Just one question remains. If my desire for holiness comes from God, and if the true change of my heart comes from Him what does there remain for me to do? It might help close the gap to be humble, but is there nothing we can *do?*

Personally, I think there are two things we can do to help bridge the credibility gap that often comes with pursuing holiness. First, to remain true to Wesley's thought, we should actively fight against sin and selfishness. We know that it is God who changes us, but that is no free pass to keep on sinning freely until God does his "magic." We are asked to "use the grace we have" until that time when we are changed.

In talking about a credibility gap, we should be careful not to judge the amount of grace other people have when it comes to their sins. But it is clear that we shouldn't give in to sin. We must resist sin with all that we have, which if we allow God's grace to work, is quite a lot.

Second, we should have the courage to hope for and desire holiness, and to seek it earnestly. We must fight against the temptation to think that we will never change, that our selfishness will ultimately get the best of us, and that sin is inevitable. We should therefore keep on searching for God, so that the confrontation with His love, no matter how difficult this can be, will keep on filling us with desire, hope, and love.

To sum up, the credibility gap is comes from the confusion of what we mean by holiness, the means by which we can achieve it, our (perceived) arrogance about our own effort and desire, and the harsh reality that often contradicts all of this. Bridging the gap is not about lowering our standards of holiness or giving up on the possibility to be made holy here on earth. Neither is it about trying harder to achieve holiness. It is bridged by explaining what holiness truly is (no rule-perfection but a heart filled with God's love), by being honest ourselves, and by being humble about the true depths of our own desire and efforts. At the same time, I believe we shouldn't stop actively fighting sin in our lives with the means that God has given us. And, above all, we have to keep returning to God to allow Him to look right through all our efforts, failures, and desires, so He can change us *from the inside out.*

Arthur van Wijngaarden lives in Rotterdam and works as a project manager for the Dutch Department of Education. He studies theology in a distant learning program from EuNC, and he is a lay preacher in the Netherlands District. He has a girlfriend, and when he is not working, studying, or spending time with her, he likes to play soccer or go biking.

Entire Sanctification—A Smoldering Wick?

Caswald Jemmott

The Church of the Nazarene is an unashamed holiness denomination and has been known by that moniker throughout its existence. There is no doubt in the minds of the hierarchy of the church, in the pronouncements of the church, and in the publications of the denomination, that the Church of the Nazarene is a "holiness church." However, that does not seem to translate into the reality of many congregations, and certainly not in my neck of the woods (Barbados).

A few years ago, while teaching a "Doctrine of Holiness" class, I was confronted by a student who related how he had attended a "holiness convocation" at one of our local churches and had left thoroughly confused. According to him, no two Nazarene ministers had the same explanation of entire sanctification. Others within the class also confessed their lack of understanding of this distinctive doctrine of the Church of the Nazarene. Some of those within the class were long-standing members of the Church of the Nazarene, and many served on local and district boards and committees.

When the term "entire sanctification" is spoken within the church, a glazed look comes over the faces of many in the congregation. It is as if one has suddenly started to speak a foreign language, and many seem to "zone out." It appears that one has gone on some esoteric flight of fancy teaching, trying to explain a concept only the more mature or "spiritual" (translate as old) members can understand. If the members of our congregations do not have a clear understanding of the doctrine of entire sanctification, then how do we expect to see holiness lived in the marketplace by our members? Even more, how can we expect to give a clarion call to others to live a life of holiness?

Let's face the truth. Not many Nazarenes understand the doctrine of entire sanctification. Even fewer actually embrace it, and still less seek to live that truth in everyday life. We face the *distinct* possibility that the teaching and experience of entire sanctification may once again become simply an officially espoused belief that falls into neglect—just as it did in the Methodist Church before Phineas Bresee and others revived interest in the experience and its necessity to enable holy living.

This state of affairs leads me to ask the question as to whether the doctrine of entire sanctification is a smoldering wick. The image of something smoldering suggests a fire that once burned brightly but now only smokes. The coals in the fire are glowing. There is still heat emanating from them, but there is no raging flame. In many ways, that appears to be an apt description of the situation surrounding the doctrine of entire sanctification.

One subtle, seemingly harmless reason for our uncertain sound in the marketplace is the desire not to disturb the peace of a growing ecumenism. There is a worldwide push towards ecumenism and the call for Christian unity to enhance the appeal of the gospel as many see the divisions in the church—indicated by the plethora of denominations—as a repudiation of Jesus prayer, "May they be brought to complete unity to let the world know that you sent me" (John 17:23).

Holiness churches and denominations have come a long way in terms of their acceptance by mainstream evangelicalism and would prefer not to rock the boat or create any waves that would fracture a fragile peace. Indeed, we do not want to allow people to point constantly at the lack of unity among the followers of Christ, and so we keep silent. The problem with this silence is that we lose our voice as a strident call for holiness and holy living by members of the body of Christ. Since we prefer not to be outsiders, we compromise the call to remain true to our insistence that entire sanctification is God's will for all believers. This desire for acceptance among our Christian brethren appears to come at the cost of de-emphasizing our distinctive doctrine and a willingness to settle for a generic type of Christianity.

Furthermore, there is considerable difficulty in finding strident voices in support of the doctrine of entire sanctification among biblical scholars and theologians to articulate the teaching, especially beyond the confines of the Church of the Nazarene and Wesleyan-Arminian circles. In fact, even these few voices are muted in the whole theological conversation.

In addition, we are bombarded in the media and bookstores with Christian material that is not of the Wesleyan-Arminian persuasion. Much of this material is helpful for Christian living but also antithetical or antagonistic to our position. We now live in a technologically advanced age where the information through the internet and other media have a great influence on the minds and hearts of people, and many of our denomination are heavily influenced by televangelists and the teaching ministries of those with Calvinistic leanings. The net effect of this is that many members of the Church of the Nazarene are more familiar with these perspectives than with the doctrinal stance of their own denomination.

This introduces another reason why the doctrine of entire sanctification may be a smoldering wick. We are not teaching, preaching, and living it enough that it is "caught" by younger generations. There is an almost deafening silence in our pulpits about entire sanctification. In fact, we have nearly ceased to preach about it in the church, preferring to concentrate on the "felt needs" of persons and teaching them how to live successfully in the world. I cannot recall the last time that a church in my area has had deeper life services that concentrated on challenging believers to seek the experience of entire sanctification. How can we fail to challenge people to experience the cleansing, purifying power of the Spirit and then expect them to live victoriously over sin in their everyday experience? What is the cause of this reticence where entire sanctification is concerned? Are ministers not convinced of its truth and efficacy? Have they themselves experienced the grace of entire sanctification and the difference that it makes in their own life and ministry? Is it due to the lack of understanding on the part of our ministers?

The question of understanding raises the issue of whether we have articulated the doctrine clearly. For instance, while I was growing up, the language of eradication was a vital part of the predominant terminology used in speaking about entire sanctification. The sin nature was equated with a physical substance that could be "taken out" of a person or eradicated from their lives was prevalent. By the time I went to college, this type of terminology was replaced by relational language—the sinful nature was now described as a mindset that is hostile to God or "love locked into a false center, self."[2] The problem then became explaining the doctrine to those of the previous generation in the churches who viewed the new terminology with suspicion. Some of my contemporaries in college even had difficulties with credential boards comprised of older ministers who only knew the eradication language. New church members are understandably confused when they see two generations referring to the same experience but using distinctly different terminology.

Equating the baptism with the Spirit with entire sanctification has also been a cause of confusion and misunderstanding. The term "baptism with the Spirit" is a biblical concept, but it has largely been taken over by Pentecostals and those of the Charismatic movement. Within the holiness tradition, when we speak of "baptism with the Spirit" we usually mean that the consecrated believer is cleansed from original sin and empowered by the Holy Spirit to live victoriously, triumphing over sin and Satan. Pentecostals, similarly, use it to speak of the Holy Spirit's empowering of the believer, but with the expected evidence being the

---

2. Mildred Bangs Wynkoop, *A Theology of Love* (Kansas City, MO: Beacon Hill, 1972), 158.

ability to "speak in tongues." Therefore, in ordinary conversation, many persons equate speaking in tongues with the baptism with the Spirit so that when we Nazarenes speak of being baptized with the Spirit, we intend to speak of cleansing whereas other people believe we are referring to speaking in tongues. For the person not properly and carefully taught, there is the potential for significant misunderstanding here.

The Church of the Nazarene, along with other holiness denominations, possesses in our doctrinal statements a biblical truth so powerful that—if it were embraced, experienced, and expounded—would shake the gates of hell. We owe it to our world and especially our generation to teach, to preach, and to live the message of full salvation in such a way that it may grasp the truth and power of full salvation and be transformed to live as God's holy people in this world.

If entire sanctification is indeed "a smoldering wick," then we need to take heart that it will not be snuffed out. Isaiah states, "A bruised reed he will not break, and a smoldering wick he will not snuff out" (Isa 42:3). There is hope yet for entire sanctification to once again burn brightly in the doctrinal firmament as it did in the early years of the Church of the Nazarene and the Holiness Movement.

Caswald Jemmott is a lifelong Nazarene and has been the pastor of the Hope Road Church of the Nazarene in Barbados for the last 14 years. He holds a Bachelor of Theology degree (Canadian Nazarene College, 1992) and an M.A. in Biblical Studies (1997) from Asbury Theological Seminary in Kentucky. He has been married for the past 26 years to Janice and has two teenage daughters, Danielle and Ashley.

The Freedom of Holiness
Robbie Bender-Cansler

A friend of mine once spoke to me of the time he felt free enough to taste wine. He and his wife decided to go on a tour of a vineyard, and as the tour was ending, there was a wine tasting. He said the wine tasted horrible, but that if it were not for holiness, he would not have felt free enough to take a sip in the first place. That moment was the freedom of holiness in a small yet profound way for this individual.

For many of us who have grown up in the Wesleyan/Holiness movement, this story is provocative because Holiness has become a set of rules and regulations to be followed—not a sense of freedom to experience sips of wine while enjoying the view of God's creation.

Holiness is meant to be a source of freedom, to experience cultures, foods, art, music, and life without the burden of guilt and shame associated with sin, yet holiness has become viewed as a burden. Holiness was meant to be freedom through the Holy Spirit to live life abundantly, but we have become slaves to the rules and regulations placed upon us.

Galatians 5:1 says, "It is for freedom that Christ has set us free. Stand firm, then, and do not let yourselves be burdened again by a yoke of slavery." Paul was correcting a deep issue that the church in Galatia was facing; some leaders of the church were declaring that one must be circumcised in order to be a follower of Christ. They were insistent that these new church members follow this rule, or they would not be allowed to be a part of this group.

As 21st century readers of this text, we see the ridiculousness of it. The church in Galatia seems so wrong to hold people to this type of standard, as though the gospel message is a series of hoops one must jump through to be considered "in." But, this is exactly the same type of legalism to which we have been subjected. Legality has stepped in and stated that in order to be considered a holiness person you must not do a laundry list of extra-biblical things.

Holiness churches would look different if instead of focusing on the "do-nots" we focused on the freedom found in Christ. If holiness people became people who lived life abundantly, the world truly would have the potential to be transformed through the freedom they see in our lives.

In focusing on the "do-not's" instead of the "do's," the primary issue is our fear. As a society, we are wildly afraid of freedom. We prefer stability, consistency, and safety. This can be seen in many areas: the emergence of helicopter parents, our national defense budget, some of our reasoning for homeschooling, and our suburban privacy fences and alarm systems. Many good Christian parents will say that their sole objective as a parent is to keep their children safe. Safety has become the main priority.

Holiness, however, is not safe. It's wild and a bit unpredictable. Even though many good Christian parents say their role as a parent is to keep their child safe, I'd say that their main purpose is not to have safe kids, but holy ones.

We've reduced holiness to a set of rules because rule-based living is easier and more sanitary than the wild and messy alternative. The Galatian church sought the same thing. This large, overwhelming movement of people coming to Christ was getting out of control. In order to make it easier to see who was in and who was out, they came up with a system of requiring circumcision.

This is exactly what the holiness movement does when reducing holiness to a set of rules. It becomes about managing who is in and who is out. It becomes more about what we can write on a board report, and less about real, living, breathing people who have been shackled by one thing or another their entire lives, and long for freedom. It becomes safe, sanitary, and manageable.

Our holiness churches' relationship to urban churches illustrates our inclination toward sanitary safety instead of dangerous holiness. My husband and I are in the beginning stages of a church plant in Hammond, Indiana (between the gang-ravaged cities of Chicago and Gary). Unlike many church plants, we have been given a building. It's an old limestone, Nazarene church building with stained glass windows built in 1939. It's in the middle of a neighborhood, right off the main road through this small city of nearly eighty thousand people. Currently, this is the only Church of the Nazarene within the city limits of our city.

Out of curiosity, I researched into the history of the Church of the Nazarene in Hammond, and discovered that the first Nazarene church, in Hammond, was started in 1906. The original church was in the first wave of holiness churches in the United States. As I delved deeper into why this church no longer exists, I discovered that it moved out of the city due to "rising crime rates." In order to stay there, the church would have needed to reorient its purpose, and probably its view of holiness as well. Holiness is not about safety; it's about freedom.

With a staunch view of what not to do and whom to avoid, the church virtually ceased to exist in urban areas throughout the United States. As young adults are seeking to move to cities versus suburbs, this has posed a problem for the church. Our desire for safety and control has caused entire neighborhoods and communities to miss participating in the wild depths of freedom that come with holiness.

As a church, we now have many safe people, but we are lacking in holy people. We are bonded, not to Christ, but to our fears of avoiding anything that could be construed as worldly. The world needs people devoted to holiness and the freedom that holiness instills in their lives.

What does this type of freedom look like? What does this type of holiness look like? The ultimate expression of this freedom is love of others. It's the first in the list of the fruits of the Spirit, the expressions that show we are living a life of Holiness.

The freedom of holiness looks like a mom that has little, but who goes out of her way to share that little with the kids her children bring home. She embraces them, feeds them, and tells them about the love of Jesus, never telling them that they must look different or act different to warrant her love. Years later these kids, who now have children of their own, still come to her to say thanks and to receive hugs. This is holiness—loving without condition those who seem to go unnoticed by the world. She taught them discernment and wisdom, not by the list of rules that she gave them, but by the way in which she lived her own life. She lived in freedom and in submission to the work of the Spirit.

The freedom of holiness looks like that mother's daughter, who started to exhibit these gifts and talents for ministry and preaching. As this daughter grew and asked questions about Jesus, the Bible, and the church, the mom didn't shame or shun those questions but embraced them. The daughter learned of a God that is big enough for our questions, for our doubt, for our fears. The daughter learned of how the Holy Spirit gives us freedom to go places and embrace people that may be different or even scary, but to whom we still must go. When that daughter said, "God wants me to be a pastor," the mom was proud. Despite the hard road ahead and despite a church culture that told her she was the wrong gender, the daughter was free enough to walk with strength.

That mother embodied the freedom of Christ when chose to speak of a church without walls and a love without boundaries instead of criticizing her daughter for hanging out with the outcasts on the wrong side of town. Later, that mother's support was steadfast when that daughter said, "God is calling me to plant a church. We have no money, but we feel like we must go." The daughter followed because that is what holiness means. That's what being free is.

We are free to experience the richness and beauty of a God that loves us, who desires so much more for us than a list of what we can't do. God desires that we experience love in its depths and that we are unburdened enough to share that with others. God wants us to be free to cast off the chains of desire for money, accolades, and prestige, to experience truly what a life lived in submission to the Holy Spirit looks like.

Holiness is a life that means trading our addictions and our selfish desires for a life of joy, love, and peace, but it's more than that. Holiness is the freedom to share freedom with others.

It's a life that my mom passed on to me, not through rigid rules or legalism, but through love. I learned to love and to embrace the holy life, through love and the freedom my mother lived. Now, through holiness, I am free to love others without judgment, ridicule, rules, or boundaries. This holy life is often messy, unsanitary, and unsafe, but that sounds more like the Christ who drank with sinners, touched lepers, and died on a cross.

Robbie lives in Hammond, Indiana with her husband Mac, where they are in the early stages of a church plant called "The Mission Church of the Nazarene." As the pastor of the Mission Church, it is Robbie's desire for the new church to be of and for the neighborhood.

Optimism and Hope

Jason Robertson

One of my favorite quotes hangs in a prominent place in my office, "Sanity may be madness, but maddest of all is to see life as it is and not as it should be." These words were spoken by Miguel de Cervantes' fictional character, Don Quixote, who incessantly looks beyond the impostor reality of what is, to the *real* reality that is ever apparent to him while seemingly eluding others. This alternate reality is a figment of his imagination, which is why he is generally considered insane. However, it's this persistent visioning beyond life's circumstances, as well as the sheer refusal to define reality as merely *that which is*, that make Don Quixote one of my favorite fictional characters.

Those in the Wesleyan-Holiness tradition have persistently emphasized the robust nature of God's grace. Our tradition has taught us that God's grace, rightly understood, beckons us to see life not as it is but as it should (or could) be. This notion is captured in the familiar adage, "the radical optimism of grace." In recent days, I've encountered this phrase with greater frequency. I'm sure it's coincidental, but in light of this, I've considered the possibility that there is a renewed vigor amongst Wesleyan-Holiness folks in (re)claiming this as a hallmark of our tradition. This would be a reasonable response to the pervasive spirit of despair of our time.

There's little doubt that optimism is a part of the very fabric of the Wesleyan-Holiness tradition. It was an English Methodist, Gordon Rupp, who in 1952 coined the phrase "optimism of grace."[3] Since then, this phrase (with the later-added emphasis of "radical") has been adopted as a defining mantra of holiness theology. In addition to being a way to describe a core theological commitment, "optimism" has also been used to describe what can almost be considered a virtue of Holiness people. It has been well documented that the Holiness traditions were birthed at a time of great optimism. In his important work, *A Century of Holiness Theology*, Mark Quanstrom begins by detailing the spirit of optimism that pervaded all of American culture and how Holiness groups were caught up in that spirit. I'm sure many Holiness folks today would love to recover that

---

3. For more complete context of Rupp's usage of the phrase, see Henry H. Knight III, "Realism, Hope, and Holiness in the Wesleyan Tradition," *Wesleyan Theological Journal*, 40:1 (Spring 2005), 26.

spirit of optimism. And while I, too, would welcome back this energizing spirit, I can't quite bring myself to say that what holiness people need is to be a little more optimistic. At the risk of sounding un-Nazarene, I'll admit my unease with the language of *optimism*, and I want to identify briefly two reasons why.

First, I don't think *optimistic* is an accurate description of the prevailing spirit of Holiness people living in a post-Christian context. I don't say that with an accusatory tone; rather, I point it out as a matter of observation. I hear some who, bemoaning the secularization of American culture, speak as if our best days are behind us. The reality is that the first decade of the twenty-first century was markedly different from that of the twentieth. It's highly unlikely that the history books will one day describe ours as an optimistic age.

Secondly, and more to the point, I have always thought of *optimism* as lacking theological depth. I want to make clear that I don't summarily reject the notion of optimism. As I read the way holiness writers apply the concept, I find myself affirming much of what is said. I've observed that whenever someone writes about *optimism* they can't help but also write about *hope*. In reflecting on this, a couple questions emerge: Why do we place greater emphasis on optimism than hope? How are we to understand the difference between optimism and hope? Does the notion of hope provide a richer picture of how we might understand God's grace?

Admittedly, hope is a hijacked word that comes with its own baggage. It's a word often used on refrigerator magnets adorned with rainbows and cute little birds. I remember that, as a college student, I thought the most profound thing I had ever heard said about hope came from Andy Dufresne in *The Shawshank Redemption*, "Hope is a good thing, maybe the best of things, and no good thing ever dies." To be sure, the over-usage of *hope* in popular culture has rendered it an impoverished concept that has lost its theological weightiness. Even so, I still propose that *hope* is a more accurate rendering of the Wesleyan spirit than *optimism*.

I recently had the opportunity to share my musings on hope and optimism at a conference for pastors. The dialogue that followed reminded me of the importance of language. The Christian tradition is a reforming tradition, and this necessitates the evaluating and reevaluating of theological commitments, as well as the language employed to communicate those commitments. It was with that spirit that I was reevaluating language that had become commonplace in holiness circles. I detected some confusion about the fundamental differences between hope and optimism. There seems to be the perspective that optimism is weightier than hope for optimism carries with it a strong sense of expectation. Implicit in this view is that hope lacks an element of expectancy. This is not only a false distinction, but, more tragically, it's a complete underselling of the biblical notion of hope. This perspective assumes a secular understanding of hope, which is little more than wishful thinking. With this understanding, hope will always remain on the periphery of holiness theology, and I want to argue that it should be central to a Wesleyan eschatological vision.

Consider the place Jürgen Moltmann gives hope in Christian Theology, "In actual fact, however, eschatology means the doctrine of Christian hope . . . From first to last, and not merely in the epilogue, Christianity is eschatology, is hope, forward looking and forward moving, and therefore also revolutionizing and transforming the present."[4] Moltmann's sentiments resonate well with Wesleyan eschatology as well as stake a claim that hope is both revolutionary and transformative of the present. Expectation, then, is not an adequate way of distinguishing between optimism and hope.

I would propose the one fundamental difference between optimism and hope deals with vision. In *The Prophetic Imagination*, Walter Brueggemann suggests this and promotes hope as being something more substantive than optimism:

> Hope . . . is an absurdity too embarrassing to speak about, for it flies in the face of all those claims we have been told are facts. Hope is the refusal to accept the reading of reality which is the majority opinion . . . On the other hand, hope is subversive, for it limits the grandiose pretension of the present, daring to announce that the present to which we have all made commitments is now called into question . . . I am not talking about optimism or development of evolutionary advances but rather about promises made by one who stands distant from us and over against us but remarkably for us.[5]

To be Wesleyan is not to be blind to the present but rather to be fixated on the holistic, salvific work of God. This is at the heart of Wesleyan eschatological vision. It *is* revolutionary, and it *is* transformative of the present.

I'm not trying to push an agenda to eradicate the word *optimism* from our vocabulary. I'm not naïve enough to think that a mere substitution, "the radical *hope* of grace," helps us in any way. While reflecting on language has been the occasion for this essay, I've found myself more drawn to exploring in greater depth the implications of Wesleyan hope, understood eschatologically.

---

4. Jürgen Moltmann, *Theology of Hope: On the Ground and the Implications of a Christian Eschatology* (Minneapolis: Fortress, 1993), 16.

5. Walter Brueggemann, *The Prophetic Imagination* (Minneapolis: Fortress, 2001), 65

If I could summarize this essay in one statement, it would be this: To be Wesleyan is not just to live or reason optimistically, but rather to embrace and embody hope as a result of our eschatological visioning. This is to say nothing of what this "eschatological visioning" will yield. As Michael Lodahl once questioned, "What *are* we hoping for?"[6] Certainly, a deeper exploration of a Wesleyan eschatological vision is warranted. That said, I propose one way to move forward is to put to rest any efforts to manufacture an attitude of optimism. This can lead to a fixation on the present and results in little more than tilting at windmills. Instead, a rediscovery of the biblical notion of hope is essential. This will orient us toward the new reality that God is drawing us into, giving us a vision that radically transforms the present.

Jason Robertson is a professor of Christian ministry at Olivet Nazarene University. Prior to arriving at Olivet, Jason was a teaching pastor at Beavercreek Church of the Nazarene in Ohio. His interests include issues in faith and culture and missional ecclesiology. He loves all things outdoors especially with his wife, Jenelle, and their three boys, Zachary, Colton, and Bennett.

---

6. Michael Lodahl, "Hoping," http://didache.nazarene.org/pdfs/guattheo02-Hope-Lodahl,Michael.pdf. Accessed September 2, 2014.

Choosing the Right Words

Kim Hersey

Is it all that important that we use exactly the right words? As the oft-quoted Shakespearean saying goes, from the mouth of Romeo, "That which we call a rose by any other name would smell as sweet."[7] If the playwright's thought is accurate, then it seems also true that "entire sanctification" by any other name is still holiness. What matters is the essential nature of the rose, or holiness; what does not matter, in any absolute sense, is the wording we choose to declare the theological truth of holiness.

Although it was nearly two decades ago, I will never forget my first District Licensing interview. Slightly nervous, with sweaty palms and atypically dressy clothes, I waited my turn in the education wing of the local church being used for interviews. Finally, someone came to greet me, and guided me to the last door on the right. I walked in, sat down, and introduced myself to the interviewer. We exchanged pleasantries, and after a few basic background questions, the seasoned ministry veteran asked me to tell him what entire sanctification meant.

I launched into what I understood to be true about the combination of crisis and process in holiness. I discussed prevenient, saving, and sanctifying grace. I covered the partner concepts of cleansing and empowerment. The interviewer simply nodded his head slightly, following up each statement I presented with just one syllable, "And?"

Recognizing that theology was getting me nowhere, I turned to the Scriptures, and quoted 2 Peter 1:3-4, "His divine power has given us everything we need for a godly life through our knowledge of him who called us by his own glory and goodness. Through these he has given us his very great and precious promises, so that through them you may participate in the divine nature, having escaped the corruption in the world caused by evil desires" (NIV). I explained that I thought this was the best summarized definition of holiness that we have from biblical text because we are given everything we need for godliness and given the power to escape sin's corruption. Finally, after what seemed like an eternity and with the slightest look of disappointment on his face, the interviewer asked, "Well, would you say that sanctification means to be filled with the Spirit?"

---

7. William Shakespeare, *Romeo and Juliet*, Act II Scene II.

Fortunately, my youthful optimism and general nervousness overcame my knee-jerk response, and I refrained from speaking my mind, "Well, duh! I thought you wanted me to *explain*." I simply nodded, and we moved on to the next question.

For me, that interview illustrates the reality that no single phrase can completely capture the essence of sanctification. No single model, no particular approach, no solitary term can completely communicate the depths and nuances of the doctrine of holiness. When our focus has been on using the correct terminology, the result has been frustration and discouragement for those who are trying to "get it right." It is both necessary and wise intentionally to diversify the language we use to describe and to explain holiness.

Put another way, does it matter if I speak of "sinless perfection" or "sanctification," or can I speak holiness as love in all its fullness, love that is growing toward perfection? Words like "holiness" and "sanctification" are meaningful, and perhaps even helpful, to those who have been Nazarenes for decades. Those specific, technical words represent decades upon decades of careful theological thought and study, and the vocabulary works well in particular settings, where the language is familiar.

However, those same descriptors fail to communicate meaningfully outside a small circle of people. Phrases like "learning to love well" make a lot more sense to my friends without Christian backgrounds or theology degrees. "Growing in faith and Christlikeness" communicates the heart of our Christian journeys, to both new believers and seasoned Christians from other faith traditions, but wording like "second blessing" just doesn't work for them.

It is time we recognize and embrace the empirical evidence that language is always changing. Google, tweet, and text are all common verbs in 2014, but just twenty years ago, text was a noun; tweet was unique to a songbird; and Google had not yet come into existence. Why should our language about theological concepts be any less dynamic? The purpose of language is to communicate. Words help communicate an idea; they do not become the idea itself.

That is not to say that all words are created equal when it comes to communicating the idea of holiness. "Eradicate" has been particularly troublesome to me, and "entire sanctification" has always sounded redundant. For others, "entire" may be crucial to clarify a holiness that can happen now rather than only after human death. "Eradicate" may even serve the same purpose in certain local settings, where the primary understanding is that all people sin all the time with no hope for anything different. For some, the "prevenient grace" I treasure, in its relationship to holiness, is a limiting factor that prevents a synergistic relationship between God and humanity, by placing all the impetus on God alone.

Certainly, words emphasize some aspects of holiness over others. We may feel threatened if our particular favorite nuance about holiness seems to be left out of the terminology. However, we would be wise to take our cues from the Gospels. Luke and Matthew clearly emphasize different nuances of Jesus' teaching, and John has a different message to communicate than any of the other Gospels. As holiness people who embrace that diversity within Scripture, we ought to be able to embrace the differences in theological descriptions without condemning our less favored choices.

Even as we embrace diverse language, some sense of commonality is critical to understanding. Both the sender and the receiver of the message must have a common understanding of the idea being discussed, regardless of the wording used to communicate. If you know the plant as a "wildflower," but I know it as a "weed," then we are bound to have conflict when we weed the flowerbed. However, our conflict will be rooted in miscommunication rather in the actual characteristics of the roots, stems, and leaves. Similarly, the conflicts that arise around the terminology about holiness are often conflicts about communication more than concepts.

I believe that language is so contextual that we have no alternative but to accept and trust that communication about holiness is happening in each unique relationship, even if it sounds quite different from the way we would choose to express that truth. If the Holy Spirit brings about holiness, it seems reasonable that the same Spirit will help us communicate the truth of sanctification to another person, in the context of relationship.

Some are concerned that, without particular words, we Nazarenes lose our uniqueness and our identifying doctrines in the broader picture of Christianity. I respectfully disagree. Our uniqueness is the essence behind the words; our theology is not changing as much as our vocabulary is. The words we use to communicate that theology absolutely *must* change if we are to continue to communicate our unique contributions to the Church at large in ways that will be understood into the 21st century and beyond.

As our lives embody the reality of holiness theology, our journeys become catalysts for conversations. Those conversations with other people are located soundly within authentic relationships, in particular cultural settings. It is in those settings that our words must be carefully chosen to communicate the truth about holiness in ways that the people with whom we're conversing can understand. We must take into account their backgrounds, conceptions, misunderstandings, and more—as we share the beautiful truth about all that God wants to do in our lives and all God wants to help us become.

The bottom line is that there's a far better way to approach holiness than that of determining the list of acceptable and unacceptable terminology. As we embrace all that the Holy Spirit wants to do in our lives, we are growing in holiness. As we learn to love as God loves, we are moving toward God's perfection. As we trust God's forgiveness and cleansing, we are free from sin and escaping the corruption in the world.

To return once again to Shakespeare, I don't care what labels get used to describe the sweet scent and soft petals, or even the harsh thorns. I want both roses and holiness in my life!

Kim is a forty-something ordained elder in the Church of the Nazarene, who also teaches middle school mathematics. She loves the outdoors, frequents Disney theme parks, and treasures thoughtful conversations with friends.

If John Wesley Could Speak to Nazarenes Today About Holiness

Brent D. Peterson

What if a voice from the past were to speak to us today? Of course, like many writers who have come before, John Wesley continues to speak through his letters, sermons, journals, and various pamphlets that have been studied by his theological and ecclesial heirs. Yet the issue of hermeneutics and historical location reminds us of the arduous and perhaps impossible task to hear Wesley without also really hearing our own voice, which always contextually mediates his. Nonetheless, this essay will offer some comments as to what I believe John Wesley would say to the Church of the Nazarene today regarding the issue of holiness and specifically God's gift of entire sanctification. Of course, my personal bias saturates this conversation both concerning my perspective of John Wesley and the Church of the Nazarene.[8] As such, these comments begin with words of thanksgiving, then some words of rebuke and correction, and finally some words of exhortation and challenge.

Words of Thanksgiving

One of the first comments John Wesley would make to the Church of the Nazarene is thankfulness for its continual passion to celebrate the gift of entire sanctification. In many ways, Wesley's Methodist heirs in the United States were less passionate about both Wesley and the doctrine of entire sanctification. While the Church of the Nazarene's preaching and doctrine over entire sanctification has warped and woofed throughout its century of existence, it has been consistently a primary passion and calling of the denomination.[9] It is the affirmation that Christians can do much more than simply excel at confessing their sin. With the Apostle Paul, we affirm that God offers people not only forgiveness, but also victory and freedom over sin by the power of the Spirit.

---

8. Most of my academic career has not only considered John Wesley and the Wesleyan theological tradition, I am also a fifth-generation member of the Church of the Nazarene.

9. See Mark R Quanstrom's, *A Century of Holiness Theology: The Doctrine of Entire Sanctification in the Church of the Nazarene 1905-2004* (Kansas City, MO: Beacon Hill, 2004).

Sin Less Not Sinless

Within this passion and zeal for heart holiness, Wesley would also be pleased that the denomination has corrected its teaching and practice in regard to the possibilities of entire sanctification. Within the many influences that shaped the Church of the Nazarene, specifically the American Holiness tradition, it was taught that when one was entirely sanctified one's sinful nature was eradicated; thus, persons would cease to sin. In essence, entire sanctification was believed to create a state of sinless perfection.

Many problems resulted from such teaching. Not only did this foster a spirit of judgmentalism and legalism, but it also reinforced guilt for the sins in one's life while providing no liturgical place for sanctified Christians to confess sins. Moreover, for some it exacerbated a spiritual pride where persons who testified to entire sanctification also asserted that as such all things they did (sometimes evil) were ordained by the Spirit (or at least excused).

As John Wesley's work and theology began to have greater influence in the Church of the Nazarene and the broader Wesleyan tradition, it came to light that Wesley consistently and adamantly rejected any type of sinless perfection.[10] Yet even in rejecting a complete sinlessness, it is our hope that by the power of the Holy Spirit, Christians can be set free from the power and bondage of sin so they indeed can *sin less* often. We have improved here, and Wesley would be grateful.

Words of Rebuke
Sanctification Centered on Abstaining from the Acts of Sin

Within these places of affirmation, I do think Wesley would offer some words of rebuke. Growing up in the Church of the Nazarene, entire sanctification seemed equated to abstaining from many personal behaviors that were considered unholy. So implicitly, salvation and sanctification were defined by what behaviors Christians did not do, rather than what they did do.

I am not suggesting how persons behave is antithetical to the goal and healing of sanctification. Rather, it is dangerous when one views sanctification more in terms of not sinning, rather than in terms of love. Moreover, there is a danger that by keeping the conversation about behaviors or acts of sinning (lying, cheating, stealing) what is lost is that sin is inherently relational.

Be Ye Separate—From the Poor and Broken?

Moreover, in the Church of the Nazarene's attempt to live into the holy life, there was a concerted effort to live far from sin. A motto of the Church

10. See Wesley's A Plain Account of Christian Perfection and Sermon 40 "Christian Perfection."

of the Nazarene for many decades was "Be Ye Separate." To distance oneself from sinfulness would certainly be affirmed by Wesley. However, one of the byproducts of *be ye separate* was not simply separation from sin but also from those the Church of the Nazarene deemed as sinners.

What developed was a strong sacred/secular dualism that was not only spiritual but also geographical. For example, it was affirmed that some parts of creation are holy and present with God, while some places and people (heathen or pagan) were void of God. Ironically, the Church of the Nazarene's roots were in the urban slums of Los Angeles and other cities. The name Church of the Nazarene was chosen because it was a name of derision, a name associated with the outcasts and marginalized. This early passion for the poor, lost, and broken would have had no bigger cheerleader than John Wesley who worked tirelessly with the poor and disenfranchised of England.

Unfortunately, for a variety of reasons, this care and compassion for the lost, marginalized, and "dirty" of the world was lost along the way as the Church of the Nazarene felt called *to be separate* from sin and those dirty sinners. All too often, our people were living personal lives of "holiness" while ignoring fellow neighbors thrown into the ditch.

Wesley would be saddened and offer sharp rebuke that our calling to be entirely sanctified encouraged our flight away from the dirty, broken, and lost. However, within the last thirty to forty years many in the Church of the Nazarene have begun to recapture the imagination to live and be with those on the margins. To this end, Wesley would rejoice and call us to deeper levels of engagement into the places of darkness, pain, and brokenness.

Stewardship and Holiness

Finally, Wesley would caution and rebuke many in the Church of the Nazarene for the way in which we use our resources of time, money, and creation. Wesley is famous for affirming in his sermon, "The Use of Money," "Gain all you can, save all you can, give away all you can."[11] Wesley would encourage persons to be entrepreneurial in industry, while doing so caring for all persons associated in one's business pursuits. Yet Wesley, whose income increased greatly as his fame spread, did not increase his yearly personal spending.

One wonders what words of rebuke Wesley might offer to my personal spending habits or the spending habits of my denomination, especially in light of the poverty and hunger that exists in my neighborhood and around the globe. The

---

11. Sermon 50, in Sermons II, ed. Albert C. Outler, vol. 2 of *The Bicentennial Edition of the Works of John Wesley* (Nashville: Abingdon, 1976).

Church of the Nazarene is not immune from the addiction of materialism and consumerism. John Wesley would offer words of rebuke and call for repentance.

Exhortation and Encouragement

Finally, I wonder what words of exhortation and encouragement, specifically regarding entire sanctification, John Wesley might offer to the Church of the Nazarene. Certainly, some of the words of rebuke above would be included.

Always ground entire sanctification in the work of God centered in the redemption and reconciliation of relationships between God, others, and myself. Do not reduce sanctification to personal or private behavior. As such, see one's healing by God as sending Christians into the world, especially to the lost, poor, and dirty as the vocation of the Church as the body of Christ.

Wesley would also want us to remember that the final goal (*telos*) of God's healing of entire sanctification is not about me getting to heaven—often imagined as my hedonistic utopia. Sanctification is a part of God's redemption of all things. While God loves and cares for me, I am simply a piece of God's entire creation. Too often, our imagination of entire sanctification is getting bodiless souls safely to heaven. Wesley would encourage us to see God's plan of redemption and restoration involving all of creation.

Moreover, Wesley would call for Nazarenes to practice more intentional accountability with the renewal of the bands and societies. Holiness occurs within the community and accountability of faith.

Finally, and here my own bias comes into full light, I think Wesley would be pleased as the Church of the Nazarene has begun to reclaim a more robust celebration of the sacraments. Like many parts of Christendom, the Church of the Nazarene over the past 20 years has embodied a renewed sacramental vibrancy and practice. John Wesley's sermon "The Duty of Constant Communion" captures well Wesley's Eucharistic zeal as a celebration where God heals persons from sin, more fully renews the Church as the Body of Christ, and sends Christians into the world to be more fully the body of Christ. To this end, John Wesley would say, Amen and Amen!

Brent is an Associate Professor of Theology at Northwest Nazarene University. His teaching and research largely focuses on the Church, sacraments, and mission. He lives in Nampa with his wife Anne, and his awesome kids Noah, Alexis, and Sydney.

The Impossible Silence of Holiness:
Reflections on a Holiness Church During Apartheid in South Africa
Gabriel J. Benjiman

Examining our theological tradition and experiences helps us improve how we express God's love. We must reflect upon our hermeneutic and application of the Word with a strong rationale for being better at incarnational holiness. Holiness is about making the highest choices for the One we claim to love the most! Holiness is about being willing to be a blood witness for Christ if love so demands. Christ's Love was willing to be dismembered in order to "re-member" the body! Dying for God is not the point here. Living for God in loving ways is the point even if that means becoming a martyr.

Apartheid in Church History

In 1994, South Africa emerged out of the struggle in which mostly Black South Africans had fought against "apartheid." This was not only a struggle for human rights but also a fight for the preservation of dignity and justice by the oppressed.

Beginning in 1910, the Afrikaner government began legitimizing apartheid structures. This ensured separate and unequal development among the various race groups. Indians, Coloreds, and Black Africans were collectively classified as "Non-Whites." These non-White groups were primarily servants of the White South Africans.

Europeans (Dutch and Huguenot settlers in particular) saw themselves as superior to the non-White "barbarous" tribes. A Calvinistic perspective of predestination combined with a misreading of the judgment of Noah's sons was used to formulate a theological justification for apartheid: some ethnicities are destined for servitude. Hence, the Dutch Reformed church officially favored apartheid.

Apartheid as a construct was not so much political as it was theological. The Dutch Reformed Church (DRC) in South Africa built this dehumanizing structure of control, manipulation, and death on small theological corruptions like those noted above. Later, stronger theologies in support of apartheid emerged and were countered by African theology, Black theology, and Liberation theology.

Some parts of the South African church began to take an anti-apartheid stance by integrating Dietrich Bonhoeffer's thoughts into black theology. Bonhoeffer famously enumerated "three possible ways in which the church can act towards the state which is violent against the people"—(1) "seeing things from below," (2) the "Church as a Confessing Body," (3) "jamming a spoke in the wheel."[12]

Seeing Things from Below

Theology done by Africans was not necessarily Black theology. Desmond Tutu limited the definition of African theology so that it meant doing theology as an African who affects African culture. He used theology to highlight our South African heritage instead of the degradation suffered by South Africans under the oppressive regime of the Apartheid Government. Its main concern was "what does it really mean to be Black and Christian in the South African situation, and its theological concerns are with liberation, reconciliation, and one true humanity."[13]

Tutu like all the other African and Black theologians was asking the question that Bonhoeffer asked shortly before his execution as a martyr for the faith, "Who then is Christ for us today?" This Christological focus with its multivalency presented Christ in new and hopeful ways to the Black oppressed in the midst of apartheid.[14]

Being a free Black South African was a by-product of the willingness to be a "blood witness"—a martyr for Christ. Martyrdom for the African pastor/theologian/Christian was about finding ethnic and individual identity when attempting to answer the kind of Bonhoeffer question "What is Christianity really, and who is Christ for us today?"[15] Any other questions that face theologians in Africa will ultimately be determined by what they understand to be the nature of the person and work of Jesus Christ.[16]

While searching for the answers, Black people took to protesting the dehumanizing harsh new laws. New laws were enforced based on the belief that God had given South Africa to the White Afrikaner as He gave the Promised Land to Israel. Protest marches often ended in death and suffering. The massacre at Sharpeville prompted the World Council of Churches meeting with its member churches at Cottesloe. To many this was reminiscent of the Geneva meetings with Bonhoeffer and the German Evangelical Churches.[17]

12. Eric Metaxas *Bonhoeffer: Pastor, Martyr, Prophet, Spy* (Nashville: Thomas Nelson, 2011), 153.

13. Desmond Tutu, "Black Theology and African Christian Theology—Soulmates or Antagonists?" *African Reader in Christian Theology* John Parrat, ed (London: SPCK, 1991), 46.

14. John Parrat, "Who Then Is Christ for Us?" *African Reader in Christian Theology,* 158.

15. Ibid.

16. Ibid.

17. P.G Meiring, Bonhoeffer in South Africa: Role Model and Prophet," www.ve.org.za/index.php/VE/article/download/101/75 accessed July 25, 2014.

The outcome was not altogether pleasing because the World Council of Churches together with most of the member churches agreed that racial prejudice was unacceptable. However, the majority of the Dutch Reformed Church (DRC) rejected the conclusions of the "Cottesloe Consultations," and they withdrew from the South African Council and World Council of Churches. (Sadly, the Church of the Nazarene also rejected the anti-apartheid voice of the WCC and SACC. By doing so, the Church of the Nazarene in a post-apartheid country has lost its authority to claim that it spoke prophetically against the injustice of this unholy, unbiblical practice of apartheid.)

The leading DRC theologian, Dr. Beyers Naude, condemned the stiff-necked approach by the leaders of the DRC and its supporters. He suffered for this as a blood witness for the truth. He was excommunicated and arrested by the secret police. His family home was frequently invaded by the police.

The Church as a Confessing Church

Naude and some colleagues established the Christian Institute of South Africa (CISA). In this organization, serious thought was given to the call for a Confessing Church in South Africa as modeled by Bonhoeffer. They called on the church to confess that apartheid was a heresy, that apartheid was a sin![18]

Koopman proposes that Calvinism was so strong in influence for apartheid that it even influenced other denominations.[19] The National Party government that upheld the doctrine of apartheid stated, "Churches and societies which undermine the policy of apartheid and propagate doctrines foreign to the nation will be checked."[20] Were some Wesleyan influenced denominations afraid to stand up because of such threats?

Others of "non-holiness" persuasions like Naude called for the Church to be in a place of "Statu Confessionis," and it worked. The Belhar Confession lead to repentance and ultimately toward a change in the politically hardened landscape, by affirming that, "in no way cultural differences, differences in language or background may be the measure of other people and their commitment to Jesus Christ … Apartheid in all its different forms was an attack on Christianity because it entrenched being not reconciled as the point of departure of the church."[21]

---

18. J. W. de Gruchy, *The Church Struggle in South Africa* (Minneapolis: Fortress, 2004), 195.

19. Nico Koopman, "Reformed Theology in South Africa: Black? Liberating? Public?" *Journal Of Reformed Theology*, 1:3, 294-306.

20. Statement by the National Party of South Africa, March 29, 1948. http://www.fordham.edu/halsall/mod/1948apartheid1.html, accessed July 25, 2014.

21. Pieter Vester, "Challenges to Christian Mission from the Struggle for Human Rights in the South African Setting." http://www.byteboss.com/view.aspx?id=2919191&name=6._Pieter_Vester, accessed July 25, 2014. p. 4

Through this confession and other similar efforts, the church in South Africa was beginning to take on the willingness to be martyrs for the cause.[22] Finally, the Church in South Africa renounced apartheid through open confession.

The "Spoke in the Wheel"

Here the Church decided that it was necessary to shove a "stick in the spokes" to curb the momentum of poor state theology. The state theology at that time believed that it was necessary for the State Church to enforce the rule of God to maintain Law and order according to the Calvinistic claims that God had given the White Afrikaner the land as promised. The Kairos Document was a powerful critique of the "neutral" church theology also, functioning as pawns of the state. The SACC and Naude's CISA were the catalysts of the Kairos Document. They rejected the cruel prejudiced warped Calvinism of the State Church and opposed the "passive/non-struggle" approach of the "neutral" Churches. They called for the active struggle against the machinery of oppression.[23]

This took the form of strikes, rolling mass actions, consumer boycotts, and "stay aways." "In other words, the present crisis challenges the whole church to move beyond a mere 'ambulance ministry' to a ministry of involvement in participation."[24]

This is what Bonhoeffer meant when he spoke about "seeing things from below," "thrusting a spoke in the wheel," and maintaining a "Status Confessionis." This is what it means to be a blood witness—a witness willing to lay down one's life for the cause of holy, wholehearted love for God and His righteousness.

The Church of the Nazarene in the Struggle against Apartheid

I have constantly asked the question about the doctrine of Holiness and what that heart of Christian perfection and holy love would do for the hurting members of the Body. What do Holiness and Entire Sanctification come down to when called upon to bear "witness" for the one it claims it loves? I am forced to ask, "Why was the Church of the Nazarene 'neutral' in this war against injustice?"

The Church of the Nazarene decided to stay out of the politics of the culture within which it ministered. Why did the leaders not release the national clergy to participate actively within the SACC? Why did we willingly oppose the SACC? In popular media culture, one website under the official domain of Nelson Mandela

22. David Bosch, *Transforming Mission* (Maryknoll, NY: Orbis, 2011), 407

23. Ibid.

24. Ibid.

lists the Church of the Nazarene first among the most important evangelical churches who remained "neutral."[25]

Why were we not those who "see things from below"? Why were we not filled with courage as our hearts were filled with love to "put a spoke in the wheel"? Where was our identity as the "Confessing Church"? Bonhoeffer fought against injustice. African leaders from other doctrinal persuasions and denominations fought against injustice. If we chose to remain passive in injustice and blatant prejudice and in the death of the "innocents," can we still be righteous? Are we not complicit by our neutrality and silence?

Reflections

I personally remain under the weight of this very same barrage of questions when I do nothing about prejudices that prevail today. I remain deeply concerned for the claims I make about being "entirely sanctified" when I am not willing to become a true and willing blood witness without counting the cost even if it is measured in the currency of my own blood. Sexism, abortion, ethnocentricity, xenophobia, racism, and the list persists. These blind spots require us as the Church of the Nazarene to measure our "holiness of heart" claims against our life's actions.

Gabriel J. Benjiman serves as Lead Elder at Morningside Community Church, a multiethnic and multiracial church in Durban, South Africa. He serves as a mentor to several pastors and has his heart set on Christ's transforming mission in community. He has been involved in theological and leadership training for over 18 years, and he studied at Ambrose University, NTC South Africa, and Northwest Nazarene University. He is joyfully married to Maryann, and they enjoy the blessings that come from raising their two daughters.

---

25. Padraig O'Malley, "Churches," http://www.nelsonmandela.org/omalley/index.php/site/q/03lv02424/04lv02730/05lv0 3188/06lv03195.htm, accessed July 25, 2014.

Discovering the Values of Holiness
Grant Zweigle

My grandmother lived in a German Mennonite Brethren community in Southern Russia as a young girl. When her parents immigrated to Canada, they made their new home in a German Mennonite Brethren community in Yarrow, British Columbia. My grandmother learned some English in school, but spoke German at home and in church. Her family maintained their cultural distinctiveness in their new home, even as they adapted to a new way of life in Canada.

My mother spoke some German in home and in church, but English was her first language. Her parents brought her up in the German Mennonite way, but as a young adult, she forged her own way and more fully embraced the life and culture of Canada than her parents did.

My mother never spoke German to me. When I was two, my Canadian mom and American dad moved to the United States. I am culturally an American and an English speaker. I tried studying German in high school and college, but it didn't stick. I have always known my ancestry is German Mennonite with a Canadian flavor, but it did not seem to have much bearing in my everyday life.

Eight and a half years ago, I moved back to Canada to pastor First Church of the Nazarene in Vancouver, British Columbia, Canada. Since coming back to Canada, I have been able to spend more time with my grandmother who is now 95. When I visit my grandmother, she shares stories with me about her childhood in Southern Russia; about why and how her family came to Canada; and about the joys and struggles of making a new life in a new land.

Over the course of her lifetime, my grandmother has learned to adapt to the cultural changes taking place around her. Some of these changes were forced upon her, but some she willingly embraced. As I've listened to her stories, I've discovered that many of the values that are dear to my grandmother are dear to me as well. Some of these values transcend culture. These include hospitality, generosity, stewardship, courage, diligence, faith, hope, and love. As a dad, I now want to instill these values into my two boys. I like to take my boys to visit their great-grandmother so they can hear her stories and be inspired by the values that have shaped our family.

Our spiritual grandparents and great-grandparents in the Church of the Nazarene had to adapt to cultural changes taking place around them. Some of these changes were forced upon them, while others they willingly embraced. As the spiritual grandchildren of these holiness pioneers, we would do well to listen to their stories, and in doing so, we might discover values that we can embrace and pass on as well.

Vancouver First Church of the Nazarene is a traditional Nazarene church in the midst of a rapidly changing urban context. Many of the core members of our church are of that generation of spiritual grandparents who lived a life of holiness in the midst of changing and challenging circumstances.

Several years ago, we went through a process of Appreciative Inquiry to discover the values that undergird this historic Nazarene congregation. The process included sitting in living rooms and around dinner tables to share our stories. Through sharing our stories, we discovered a rich set of transcendent values that shape our mission in Vancouver today.

Through this process, we discovered that as a congregation we value:

- Godly hospitality
- Intercultural relationships
- Spiritual transformation
- Service to one another
- Godly wholeness
- Worship
- Vital relationships with the Triune God
- Loving our neighbors

These values were discerned from stories and experiences that crossed generational and cultural lines.

It might seem strange that a traditional Church of the Nazarene like ours did not say, "We value holiness." This is because for us, holiness is not a value in and of itself. Holiness is our way of being in the world that is expressed through specific practices that flow from all of our congregational values.

What sort of practices? We are a people who . . .

Practice Godly hospitality by making space for newcomers to Canada

- Seek out and invest in new relationships that cross cultural boundaries
- Meet in small groups for spiritual transformation
- Rearrange schedules to serve one another
- Desire to be whole, healed from the vandalism of sin

- Remain committed to public worship in a city that no longer protects time for the sacred
- Seek warm, intimate fellowship with God
- Seek creative ways to love our neighbors.

These are the practices of holiness people. These practices are derived from the values of our spiritual grandparents in Vancouver, and these have now become the values of their spiritual grandchildren and great-grandchildren as well.

We believe that these values and the practices that flow from them are what identify us as holiness people. What does this look like in everyday life? In our context, this looks like welcoming immigrants and strangers and seeking to build meaningful and supportive friendships with those who come to Canada and would benefit from a warm and encouraging welcome.

Vancouver First Church has historically been an English-speaking, white, Canadian congregation. Today two-thirds of the neighbors around our church speak a language other than English as their first language. In the 1980's, the congregation responded to this demographic change by sponsoring ethnic congregations, including a Spanish, Tigrinya, Mandarin, and Korean-speaking congregation. By making space in their building for these new immigrants, the congregation lived out their values of Godly hospitality, serving one another and loving their neighbors.

Soon it became clear that making space for other congregations to meet in the building was not enough. Because they valued intercultural relationships, the predominantly white English-speaking congregation desired to welcome and include immigrants and new Canadians into the English-speaking congregation, not just to have them worship in another part of the building.

In order to achieve this, English-as-a-Second-Language classes were started. The church made funds available to hire a part-time associate pastor to focus on intercultural ministries. Today on any given Sunday, you might find Canadians, Filipinos, Americans, Chinese, Thai, Vietnamese, Pacific Islanders, Indians, Sri Lankans, Venezuelans, Mexicans, Ghanaians, Nigerians, Kenyans, Russians, Dutch, Irish, and British people worshipping alongside one another, celebrating birthdays in the fellowship area, praying for each other, serving one another, discipling one another and going on mission together throughout the city and around the world.

At my grandmother's 90th birthday party, my Egyptian uncle, who married into the family, spoke about how he was warmly welcomed into this German Mennonite family. There was always a place at my grandmother's table for someone who was hungry, someone who needed a friend, someone different. My grandmother was not from a holiness tradition, but this is holiness in action. Jesus, the Holy One, welcomes everyone at his table. This way of holiness can be found among God's people everywhere.

When we stop, watch, and listen to our spiritual grandparents, we might discover values and practices that embody holiness in compelling and visionary ways. Having pastored many of these spiritual grandparents, I have discovered a rich and compelling set of values that make the life of holiness alive and compelling for my generation and me.

Grant pastored in Kansas City, MO, Seattle, WA, and Vancouver, BC, Canada. Grant and his wife Aisling are relocating to Manila, Philippines with their two boys in 2015. Grant is completing a Doctor of Ministry at Nazarene Theological Seminary.

Holiness as the Impetus for Social Action[26]

Rodney L. Reed

When we think about "renovating" how we have understood the doctrine of holiness, it conjures up images of renovating an old house—tearing out fixtures, redesigning rooms, replacing furniture with something more modern. However, in some cases, in the process of renovation, we make a discovery about the house. Perhaps, when the old carpet is removed, a beautiful wood floor is revealed. Or perhaps, when a wall is being demolished, a long hidden closet is discovered along with all manner of hidden artifacts from a by-gone era. Often the most valuable historic finds are preserved and re-incorporated into the design of the home.

The history of the holiness movement contains some of those "hidden treasures" that beg to be discovered and reincorporated into the "house of holiness" as succeeding generations of holiness folk continue the renovation project. Specifically, in this essay I would like to share with you how in the nineteenth century the doctrine of holiness served as an impetus for social action among many holiness advocates.

The Social Activism of the 19th Century Holiness Movement

Slavery: The single most significant social issue in the United States of the nineteenth century was the issue of slavery. Timothy Smith (in his groundbreaking Harvard research, later published as *Revivalism and Social Reform*) and Donald W. Dayton (in his *Rediscovering an Evangelical Heritage*) both underscored the key role that holiness revivalism played in ramping up opposition to slavery in the US.

In 1834, Theodore Weld led a large number of his fellow seminary students to reject a gradual approach to ending slavery. Instead, they embraced immediate abolition, and Weld went on to become a leading organizer and writer supporting the freedom of the slaves.

Asa Mahon and Charles Finney led in the founding of Oberlin College as a racially integrated and radically abolitionist school, which served as a key stop on the so-called "underground railroad" for slaves escaping the slave-holding states. They accepted the transfer of Weld and many of his fellow students from their previous seminary.

26. This essay is a distillation of research that is comprehensively presented in the author's book, Holiness Movement, 1880-1910 (Salem, Ohio: Schmul, 2003). I refer the reader there for all bibliographical details and for further reading.

The work of Orange Scott and Luther Lee helped to ensure that Northern Methodists would oppose slavery eventually. However, when that time did not come soon enough, they founded the Wesleyan Methodist Church to express the cause of immediate abolition. The same abolitionist sentiments were involved in the founding of the Free Methodist Church. One of the reasons for it being called "free" was to underscore the church's opposition to slavery.

Even the first general superintendent of the Church of the Nazarene, Phineas Bresee, while he was a young Methodist pastor in the state of Iowa created significant controversy when he draped his pulpit with the Union flag to express his opposition to slavery. All these persons and institutions were firmly convinced of the evil of slavery as an institution, and all were equally committed to the doctrine and experience of Christian holiness or sanctification.

The Poor: The nineteenth century saw the rapid industrialization and urbanization of the United States and England. This created unprecedented wealth for some and unprecedented poverty for others. Most of the established churches of that time rose in wealth with their members. They left the downtown areas and moved to the uptown avenues. This created a vacuum of churches in the urban centers, which were being flooded by migrants from the rural countryside and new immigrants from other countries. Into this vacuum stepped the holiness movement.

Early among the efforts to reach those caught up in the new blight of urban poverty was the Five Points Mission in New York City, sponsored by a group of Methodist women led by Phoebe Palmer, a prominent holiness advocate in Methodism. Elsewhere in New York City, a reformed drunkard, robber, and ex-convict by the name of Jerry McAuley started the Water Street Mission. Both of these missions helped thousands of men and women whose lives were caught in slavery to alcohol, drugs, gambling, unemployment, and degrading poverty find lives of respectability and salvation.

On the opposite coast, Phineas Bresee and others began the Church of the Nazarene in Los Angeles precisely to fill this gap. They chose the name, "Church of the Nazarene," specifically to identify the church with the lowly and despised. The Church of the Nazarene's preamble to its first statement of faith in 1895 claims, "The field of labor to which we feel especially called is in the neglected quarters of the cities and wherever else may be found waste places and souls seeking pardon and cleansing from sin. This work we aim to do through the agency of city missions, evangelistic services, house to house visitation, caring for the poor, comforting the dying."

The eastern parent group of the Church of the Nazarene was similarly oriented toward city mission work. The clearest expression of their commitment to ministry in the neglected quarters of the cities is in the following entry in the 1894 edition of the *Beulah Christian*, one of the periodicals of the eastern USA Nazarenes.

> There are two churches centrally located in the midst of sin and wickedness in a certain city. One wants to sell its property and move away; the other wants to buy, or build, and remain. The field and the prospect for doing good being the same to each, what makes this difference? We answer, Holiness. One is without it, and weak, and wants to get away from its wicked surroundings, lest it be defiled; the other is strong in God and his power and wants to be in the midst of these surroundings that it may put an end to sin and extend the kingdom of the Master.

All four of the main parent bodies which came together to form the Church of the Nazarene had strong city mission work in the major urban centers of the United States at the turn of the century. Elsewhere in the Holiness Movement at that time Seth Rees, Martin Wells Knapp, William Lee, and many others were doing the same thing: establishing city missions and storefront churches in the slum areas of the new urban centers, and reaching out to the poor and destitute in the name of Christ.

But the best and clearest example of this is found in the Salvation Army that, even up to the present, is an active member of the Wesleyan Holiness fraternity of churches. From the very beginning, William and Catherine Booth made urban city mission work the calling card of the Salvation Army. We cannot begin here to document all the social work of the Salvation Army around the world.

These were not primarily wealthy churches in the suburbs patronizingly doing "hit and run" type ministry in the urban centers. These were holiness churches being established in, among, by, and for the urban poor.

Human Trafficking and Prostitution: We hear a lot about human trafficking in the early part of the twenty-first century. Yet our holiness foremothers and forefathers were already deeply involved in addressing this issue over 100 years ago in what was then called the "white slave trade."

Lydia Finney, the wife of Charles Finney, led in the organization of the Female Moral Reform Society in 1834, the mission of which was to redeem "fallen women" (prostitutes). By 1840 over 500 local chapters had been organized across the US. Charles Crittenton and Emma Whittemore both organized national chains of homes for unwed mothers and prostitutes. Crittenton made such a noted contribution to society that U.S. President William Taft attended his funeral.

All of the parent bodies of the Church of the Nazarene were heavily vested in this kind of "rescue work" among fallen women. When these parent bodies met to seal their union in Pilot Point, Texas in 1908, they were actually meeting on the grounds of one of their rescue homes for fallen women. When the united church established its denominational periodical, the *Herald of Holiness*, the first Easter issue (1913) featured the church's ministry to prostitutes.

The Salvation Army led the way here as well, sponsoring many rescue homes for trafficked women. Salvation Army rescue work gained significant notoriety in 1885 when *The Pall Mall Gazette* ran a series of front-page articles exposing the extent and the evil of prostitution in London. More specifically, it focused on the plight of minors and the crimes committed against them, which included their entrapment or purchase, physician-certification as virgins, sale, movement across international borders, and their physical violation.[27] A Salvation Army officer actually went "under cover" as a brothel procurement agent, traveled to another country, purchased such a child and brought the child back to England as proof of this human trafficking. As a result of this exposé, there was an intense uproar over how this could be happening in England (supposedly the most advanced and Christian nation in the world), and as new legislation was passed protecting against human trafficking and raising the age of legal consent to sex.

Holiness advocates repeatedly claimed that procurement of women (even young girls) for the brothels of the rapidly growing cities was a business and called for government action. Furthermore, the holiness folk were sharply critical of the "double standard" in which men guilty of sexual sins were often forgiven under the rubric of "boys will be boys," while women guilty of the same thing (often under pressure from the men) were ostracized by society. These holiness folk called for a change in society's attitude toward the prostitute and fallen woman. Instead of condemning her and pushing her further down, society and the Church should be extending a hand of love and compassion.

The Role of the Doctrine of Holiness

The list of social causes to which the holiness folk of the nineteenth century gave themselves could go on and on. Women's rights, children's welfare, prohibition, prison reform, and education were all on their compassionate radar. In all of these reform issues, holiness advocates were in the vanguard.

---

27. "The Maiden Tribute of Babylon," *The Pall Mall Gazette* (July 6-10, 1885).

What was it about this doctrine and experience that served as a catalyst to their social activism? Let me suggest six ways their understanding of holiness contributed to their social activism.

1. Holiness meant *separation* from sin and worldliness.
2. It implied *total consecration* to God and His will.
3. It fostered a *radical love* for others even those on the lowest rung of society's ladder.
4. It demanded a determined *pursuit of perfection* of intention and action.
5. It brought about an *empowerment for service* and a belief that all things are possible with God.
6. And just as important, these holiness folk were convinced that this life of holiness with all its facets was not only applicable to the individual believer but was relevant to society as a whole. They were seeking for nothing short of the *sanctification of society.*

From our vantage point, perhaps they were naïve at times in their optimism about what it would take to eradicate sin and wickedness from society. However, we should not underestimate the good they accomplished, as they were motivated by their cardinal doctrine.

Conclusion

Let the renovation of the "house of holiness" continue. But as we scrape off some of the layers of our history and practices that may no longer be useful (e.g., legalism and claiming too much for the experience of entire sanctification), let us not miss seeing some of the original beauty of the house. Let us work together to preserve and to restore the social activism that never should have been forgotten in the first place.

Rodney Reed serves as the Deputy Vice Chancellor of Academic Affairs at Africa Nazarene University (ANU) in Nairobi, Kenya. He earned a Ph.D. in Theological Ethics and has written on the ethics of the Holiness Movement as well as African Christian theology and ethics.

The Globalization of Holiness?

Deirdre Brower Latz

I had a startling realization recently as I facilitated a Master's class in Christian Holiness. We were wrestling with the issue of holiness and context. We were talking about the implications of the doctrine of Christian holiness for the churches we lead and the people we are. We shared about what it means to be or be-in-the-process-of-becoming "holy," and then we went beyond that to discuss what it means for holiness people to engage with the world we inhabit. We talked about how what I do in Manchester may (or may not?) effect the people of the Church of the Nazarene in South Africa (or anywhere else for that matter—it just so happened that this class was actually in South Africa). We discussed how decisions I make as part of the body of Christ have a global butterfly effect. We talked about how the decisions of them, their congregations, and their churches also have a global butterfly effect.

My realization was this: If holiness is a legitimate Christian doctrine then it needs to be globally *true*. If it is *true*, it will need to be locally and particularly *understood*. If it is *understood*, or, more properly, *embraced*, then it will *transform* (shape, direct, re-form) people and communities in the **particular,** in the **local**, in the **now**, and in a way that is corresponding to God and responding to the real manifestations of the anti-holy. And such a locally shaped response will be **recognizably holy** to local people. That is, people within the community of faith and those observers of such a community will be able to see, smell, taste, hear, touch, and sense the presence of a holiness person.

That seems a glib statement, except that I happen to believe it is true. In the broadest sense, a holiness person should be identifiable as someone who reminds others of the source of all holiness: Jesus.

Now, so far, I imagine that nothing I have said is remotely controversial. As humans, we live in a world where we adjudicate between truth by the evidence of our own eyes, experiences, and realities (as well as things that seem truly true, and we believe to be true, and so on). And, in fact, as a group thinking corporately about holiness we realized that we shared intuitive understandings of

51

holy-people: they have integrity; they reflect love in all their actions and speech; they are gracious to others; they are hope-bearing.

Corporately though, even globally, what does it mean to be holy? How is our theology of holiness formed? So we went on to talk about holiness as a corporate reality. What does it mean to bear responsibility for one another? Does holiness look the same in Longsight, Manchester, UK (an urban deprived area, high youth unemployment, low literacy, multicultural, quite segregated community) and Soweto, South Africa (an urban deprived area, high youth unemployment, low literacy, multicultural, quite segregated community)?

Or, to use a better example of the way this becomes a possible challenge for us, does holiness look the same in those places and rural Africa or Appalachia, where the local expression of life is subsistence, with large families? Does holiness look different someplace where polygamy is common, or in a place where child brides are the norm?

Does holiness shape itself differently within the varied contexts that we encounter? And to what extent is holiness uniform (Is that even what it means to be global?) in its practices and to what extent is it possible for holiness to be truly locally formed, so that in *concept* we are global but in *practice* we are particular (or, in the oldest holiness language, peculiar)?

It may be, of course, that the particular and universal/global define one another. It may be that they engage in constant dialogue, and one illumines and sharpens the other.

I think that some of the arguments are relatively straightforward. However, as the Church of the Nazarene has intentionally embraced the "global" (e.g. our Global Ministry Center) and the "international," some of the tensions or questions of the juxtaposition of global and holy become quite striking. In what nature are we global? Our existence is global, but what kind of an existence is it?

Are we a *franchise model* where each local setting is merely an **extension** of the center but is still recognizably part of the franchise? Sure, we have Halal burgers here, or Aussie burgers there, but you can still recognize the "golden arches."

Or is it a *diaspora* model, spread around the world and in each setting reflecting the local community it is birthed in, precisely because it assimilates and engages and connects to that community but retains some sense of the *home* from which it has dispersed?

Or perhaps the existence is that of the global/universal that overshadows the particular and sees the local as predominantly something to be redeemed? The local thus becoming indistinguishable from the global but separated from its own soil and local community.

These questions (and others) form and shape us: mostly (I think) liturgically in our **practice** reflecting (or not) the universal, global, center or the local. An example of this is a recent statement by a leader that they were delighted that they could immediately recognize the church in *X* place as Nazarene. They sang the same songs transliterated from English, to the same tunes, were doing the same Bible study, and so was clearly Nazarene. I (and others) wondered if that was as good as it sounded. I'm afraid it seemed as if what he was saying was, "It's *like us*; therefore, it's one of us."

But that very unwillingness to allow a different nation to be *like us* but *other* is a problem. We mostly agree that holiness should be *detached* from prescriptive legalism (although we recognize that is often an easy way of working out an ersatz version of it, and often our inherited way). We generally agree that holiness should be *attached* to new life in Christ (in other words, not optional, but intrinsically part of what it means to be a Christian, a new creation becoming who we are called to be). We mostly agree that holiness is a distinctive part of our church, and, in fact, it is a gift of the Holy Spirit to help us become more like the One we follow. We also agree that holiness is not to be abusive, oppressive, culturally dominant, or inhospitable.

We tend to agree with the easy bits of holiness, or the holiness for the Other. For example, polygamy seems clear-cut in my framework of reference. It doesn't exist here in the UK now, either culturally or legally, and so holiness will never co-exist with polygamy here. However, in another setting that is a living question. Therefore, we are much less able to be dogmatic about pastoral holiness.

My primary argument is that within the world we live, increasingly framed by globalized realities, to renovate holiness will mean a great deal of wrestling with some core issues. And this matters because what we centrally *say* about holiness and its concomitant practices truly does have bearing upon the local expression of holiness. We risk either holiness becoming overly individualized or overly disparate. We risk holiness becoming franchised and never truly embedded in a cultural expression of faith, and on the other hand, we risk holiness becoming overly syncretized—seamlessly adapting to its new terrain but allowing no distinction from it. We face a massive challenge in contextualizing holiness effectively.

Because I am a Wesleyan, I find myself groping for a middle way. What might it mean to be part of a church that celebrates the vibrant and dynamic concept of holiness, shares an understanding of key elements of solidarity, **but** allows people to work those elements out locally and in the particular? What might it mean to agree to a liturgically shaping practice that says our holiness will always be expressed in the Eucharist, or in male **and** female leadership, or in anti-oppressive practice, or in caring for poor people in our midst, or based on Scripture, tradition, reason, and experience? What might it mean to allow some freedom within the boundaries of an agreed creedal stance that we share with the church universal–global? What might it mean to have so much confidence in the Holy Spirit, that the dynamic of that same Spirit is understood to be at work in an infinite variety of local ways for the sake of Christ being known globally and through the Church in all generations which will bring glory to God the Father?

You can see that my essay is suggesting that this task is still primarily unfinished in the Church of the Nazarene. We have accepted that we are a holiness denomination and that we are a Wesleyan Holiness denomination, and we have embraced that as an intracultural, intercultural, and global mission reality. But to this point, it seems we have opted for a centralized franchise model of global holiness. I think that is not sufficient for the future.

Please understand me. I am not advocating an abandonment of holiness—to the contrary! I am advocating a rooted, deepened understanding of holiness that is intimately connected to the shape of the place it is found. Our holiness must be identifiable, rich, honed, practice transforming, and thus witnessing to all it encounters that *this* is what a holiness people of God are like. Our holiness must instill in people everywhere a sense that this too is possible for them—for it **belongs** to them.

Deirdre is based in Manchester (United Kingdom), where she is Principal of Nazarene Theological College and part of the Longsight Community Church of the Nazarene. Her areas of interest are related to the topics of justice, holiness, and theological reflection for the sake of the church's witness of God's love to the world.

The Tension of Globalized Claims in a Contextualized World

Padraic Ingle

As the world is shrinking, there is a growing recognition that a person can no longer be content with only one expression of a view or an experience, but must come to grips with many. Take for example the languages of our human race, where in one sense there are over 7,000 different ways to say "Hello": *As-salam alaykom, guten tag, nia hao,* etc. All of these are traditional welcomes, yet when translated they each mean something very different than simply "Hello." *As-salam alykom* is Arabic for "Peace be with you," which implies much more than "Hi." Language is different than belief, but both are intimately connected, and this example highlights that what we view as commonly held assumptions may not always be such.

Within our current cultural dynamic, the world is no longer a big place. We now find ourselves interacting with people of very different, yet valid, perspectives. For instance, I regularly have interactions with an agnostic professor of Physics from Britain, an Islamic doctor from Jordan, and a Roman Catholic from Mexico. To assume that they should submit to my personal beliefs would completely invalidate their unique perspectives. There is no longer a single narrative that fully captures the complexity of the human race; there are many.

This idea is commonly referred to as contextualism, which emphasizes the *context* in which an action, belief, or expression occurs, and argues that these can only be understood relative to that context. Globalization has brought this concept to the forefront of religious communication. One must now deal with the realization that to communicate certain perceived truths as absolute is lacking by nature.

Allow me to take this idea of contextualization one step further. One of the greatest and most popular beliefs of early modernity is that all truth can be known through reason and the scientific method. At this point in Western Culture, religion was contextualized from a practice of theology into a practice of philosophy.[28]

---

28. See John Caputo, *Philosophy and Theology* (Nashville: Abingdon, 2006).

However, as the thoughts and practices of modernity continued to develop, the confessional communities of the major religion in the West (The Church) no longer held authority to make reasonable truth claims in the social, economic, or political spheres. Leslie Newbigin points out that in modernity truth was no longer determined by the church-state and that knowledge had been divided into two spheres: public knowledge (provable by science or reason) and private knowledge (experiential and unprovable by science or reason).[29] Throughout modernity, the Church adapted to this split by creating dichotomies between Christian rationalism and personal, privatized experiences. Everything we have learned about the Christian faith and how to propagate it has been built on this assumption of the split between public and private knowledge. Our Western Christian style of evangelism has been thoroughly contextualized into a kind of salesmanship approach to religious experience that is assumed by a private knowledge view of faith.

This Western understanding of the split between reason and spirituality has caused an even greater tension with the globalization of our world. In the words of Robert Weber, "Reason has a place in story. It is Christian rationalism that has failed, not intelligent discourse."[30] Herein lies the tension: In this new global and contextualized culture, one cannot simply expect others to submit to their unique, rationalized systems of truths. Instead of living within the tension and seeking a more holistic response, many have accepted a type of binary thought where one has to hold to either (a) extreme and exclusive claims based upon limited authority held within texts, or (b) an individualized spirituality formed by limited acts and experiences.

Even so, this modernist situation is nothing new; by almost all accounts, in both ancient and recent periods, religion is culturally embedded. Every expression of religion is in part an expression of culture, and no culture transcends its location.

In its earliest foundations, Christianity was faced with making exclusive claims based upon spiritual experiences and interpretations of texts within a religious pluralistic context. The two brief accounts that come to mind are Peter's vision in Acts 10 and Paul's speech in Athens found in Acts 17. In both accounts, neither Peter nor Paul shied away from the exclusive claims found in confessing Jesus of Nazareth as the Christ. Yet they also did not combat the pluralistic culture in which they were living, but instead they embraced it in such a way that their confessions and the confessions of culture were both richly and fully transformed.

29. Leslie Newbigin, *The Gospel in a Pluralistic Society* (Grand Rapids: Eerdmans, 1994).

30. Robert Webber, *The Divine Discourse: Recovering the Passionate Spiritual Life* (Grand Rapids: Baker Books, 2006), 17.

Likewise, this current spiritual buffet is perfect for us Wesley folk. As Rob Staples often states, Wesley's approach to the Bible was soteriological rather than epistemological. Wesley saw the purpose of the Bible as unfolding the way of salvation rather than answering questions of history or science or philosophical questions about the structure and meaning of knowledge.

Wesley's view of grace was so optimistic that he claimed everyone was experiencing the *way of salvation* to some degree. Herein lies the uniqueness of being Nazarene: our confession that holiness is a thread running all the way through a believer's and a community's path of salvation. Nazarenes confess that holiness is socially and personally transforming. If one is seeking to love God, then one must also be seeking to love others and in so doing will experience a transformation that can only be described as holy. This holy love can only occur in the presence of others, and it can only be sustained by a community that confesses this reality.

In one of his final lectures, Jaroslav Pelikan stated, "The locus of creed and confession is the believing community, and therefore an essential component of the need for creed is the need to be situated within that community."[31] Karl Rahner makes the argument: Given that human beings are not pure individual spirits, but embodied spirits-in-the-world with a social nature, all their relationships are mediated through the structures present in their society at any historical moment.[32] The same holds true for relationship with God. It is quite unthinkable that salvation could be achieved as a private, interior reality outside of the religious bodies in the environment in which people live. Yet this is what we have done by failing to adequately address the complexities of our global surroundings.

Growing up as a member of the Church of the Nazarene in a progressive western city was always fun. I found myself faced with the tension of making specific truth claims in a globalized and contextualized world. Caught between two groups of people, the "non-denoms" and the "none," I experienced in real time the dilemmas of being a confessing person in an atmosphere of pluralism.

The "non-denoms" were followers of Jesus who only participated in churches with "Community," "Bible," or "Fellowship" in their name. I had to convince these friends that being a member of the Church of the Nazarene did not mean that I was a part of a cult, but a denomination that saw itself as part of the larger ecumenical church. Of course, using words like "ecumenical" as an 8th grader

---

31. Valerie R. Hotchkiss, *Orthodoxy And Western Culture: A Collection of Essays Honoring Jaroslav Pelikan on His Eightieth Birthday* (St Vladimirs Seminary Press, 2006).

32. Karl Rahner, *Spirit in the World* (New York: Bloomsbury Academics, 1994).

always got me strange looks. Then, I had to explain we were just one tradition continuing in the long line of the Tradition.

On the other side, I needed to convince my non-Christian friends that I was not judging them—just trying to figure out what they believed and how it compared to what I believed. I did not want to come across as superior to them, nor was I really convinced that I needed to convert them. I was simply excited to explore spirituality with them and desired for them to reciprocate the feelings.

Every once in a while, I was able to convince both parties to come to a Nazarene Bible study or small group with me. Without fail, someone would bring up the doctrine of holiness, and I would revert to square one with all my friends.

This cycle left me questioning my convictions, as I found myself living within the tension of competing worldviews and beliefs. In my Church of the Nazarene community we could discuss the nature of holy living and the temptation of sin, but in my non-church communities those conversations seemed irrelevant. Yet they were just as concerned as my Christian friends with experiencing life to the fullest and we could regularly dialogue about how that looked in our daily interactions.

Now, I am a pastor in the Church of the Nazarene. There are those of us young Nazarene leaders who cannot speak the word "evangelism" without choking. When asked if we hold to the denomination's view of sanctification, we utter a drawn-out "yes" with a quick definition of what we mean by sanctification.

This does not mean that we are not part of the denomination, for if I could not confess to the articles of faith, I would not have pursued my ordination. It means that I and many of my peers recognize the complexities of our current situation.

I am grateful for the heritage of the Church of the Nazarene. It is rich in love and action and without it I would not be the person I am today. I am convinced that the Church of the Nazarene—in the spirit of John Wesley—is positioned to offer a *Via Media (middle way)* amidst the tension of our globalized, pluralistic world.

I am not fully convinced that we need to renovate our understanding of holiness but more our understanding of the complexities and nuances of being a confessional people in the midst of a global culture. As culture changes so must our confession of holiness change. Instead of looking for the many ways we are different, we must look for the many more ways our confessions testify to similar experiences within the differing communities of our world.

As members of the Church of the Nazarene we follow a tradition that seeks authentic transformation through a loving relationship, and this relationship we call holy. Why should we limit this holy relationship to that which we can perceive and grasp and understand? Instead, let us welcome others into our communities, trusting that what we confess points to a reality that is so transforming that people cannot help but be changed by it.

A graduate from Southern Nazarene University and Nazarene Theological Seminary, Padraic has been pastoring for 10 years in Oklahoma, Ohio, and Colorado. His hope is to communicate effectively the transformative love of God to people who have lost interest in the voice of the institutional church.

A View from the Dutch Pews

Ank Verhoeven—van der Vaart

Personally, I feel torn. I love theology; I really do. I love to talk about it; I love to think about it; I love to study it. But I so hate how it can divide people.

I just read a discussion on Facebook, of all places, about creation versus evolution. There are arguments back and forth, but all seem to be missing the point of the relationship between God and man. In a loving relationship people are never testing the words of their significant other to be scientifically true, are they? It just matters if everything that is significant for the relationship is true, and more importantly, trustworthy. Why should God's Word be treated so differently?

In the present discussion concerning entire sanctification, it is no different. There are arguments against arguments, dividing people more than unifying them. In my opinion, that should never be the purpose of the discussion. Is the Church of the Nazarene not the place where tolerance for differences in interpretation should be most expected and even valued? I cannot accept the fact that a theological difference could lead to division in our denomination. That is why I wanted to participate in the project in the formation of this book.

I put myself to the task of discovering how the people of my own congregation perceive the concept of sanctification, hoping to find points that would bind us, instead of divide us.

The Dutch are Calvinistic from origin. A couple of years ago, there was an internet test issued on how much people score on a Calvinistic attitude towards life, and even atheists (and Nazarenes) scored well above 60%. Calvinism among the Dutch is often characterized by remarks as, "If you're born for a dime, you will never become a quarter," or "If your head sticks out above the wheat on the field, don't be surprised if you lose it in the mowing." All of these sayings are trying to make sure that you remain a very humble person. Success is in no way applauded as it is in the United States. The possibility of being holy or perfect, even in the meaning of John Wesley's "Christian Perfection" is, therefore, hard for us Dutch to wrap our brains around.

Although all of the members of my Dutch congregation (Vlaardingen Church of the Nazarene with average weekend attendance of 1,400), when they said yes to joining our church, confirmed their belief in sanctification and their longing for Christlikeness, hardly anyone I spoke with really even understood the concept of (entire) sanctification as it is presented in the Church's Manual or theology. Hardly ever is it explicitly discussed in our church, or in the small groups. Consequently, I received a large variety of answers to questions on the topic. After being presented with the concept in a compact, coherent way, most church members more or less agreed on the following points though.

Most agree that a life of faith begins with the moment of justification, perceived as the will to surrender life to God, answered by God with the forgiveness of sins, and adoption into His family. Old ways should be left behind, and a life with the Lord should be undertaken. Then follows the "growing in grace." With the help of the Holy Spirit, we need to put our "flesh" to death, and let our "new creation" take over our choices more and more. This is perceived as hard work. The end of this process would be Christlikeness. Being entirely sanctified is perceived as a synonym of being Christlike.

A complication in thinking about the process of sanctification is that we see similar growth in people who are not Christians. We can explain that somewhat through the concept of prevenient grace, but that does not completely take away the confusion it causes with the average church member.

Another point of confusion is the fact that entire sanctification seems to be the end point of this "growing in grace," while at the same time it is a gift from God, which should not be seen as a result, much less a "reward" for all our own hard work. Although all members with whom I spoke realize that it is only by God's Spirit that we are able to make better choices, it still feels like we are the ones doing the work to make that possible. According to the stories about sanctification within our denomination, this gift of grace is however given for naught to some people at the moment of justification, at least seemingly without all the hard work of putting the "flesh" to death. This is perceived as quite unfair in relation to the hard work.

In discussing the topic, most people gave up their attempt at understanding the concept at this point. Even though at the beginning of the discussion most were very adamant in stating that they do believe in sanctification, here they conclude that they do not quite understand the whole thought process around it. They simply try to be good people and to live Christian lives, and if God decides to sanctify them one day, as in making them "Christlike," that would be more than welcome.

Interestingly, these difficulties towards sanctification and Christian perfection are no different now than in the days of John Wesley. Reading *A Plain Account of*

Christian Perfection, I find the same hurdles, addressed by Wesley. For example, we (Christians) do not know of any people who are completely without sin. Wesley also addresses the argument of unfairness (If it is a gift from God, regardless of the good works of the person, why is it not given to everyone?), and of Biblical reference (Nobody but Jesus is perfect, not even in the Bible.).

Apparently, sanctification and Christian perfection (as in Christlikeness) are not easily understood, nor easily believed in, if not experienced first or even second hand. The possibility of experiencing this "phenomenon" unfortunately only seems to be present during times of revival. This also goes on within the Church of the Nazarene. Having started from a revival movement, in which people—so we are told—experienced and witnessed entire sanctification, we are now at a point that most members have never met anybody they might even suspect to be entirely sanctified.

Personally, I feel we misunderstand the concept all together. The terms are being used inconsistently and therefore lead to much confusion. It is my belief that Scripture teaches us that by believing in Christ, we are in one instant entirely sanctified. From that moment forward, our hearts are focused on Christ, longing to follow Him, and to become like Him. Our flesh might very well still draw us to our sins, but our hearts are now willing to make the right choices. The Holy Spirit is the sanctifying gift of grace to support us in that process. Being sanctified in this sense is a "position," or an attitude towards life. This is how Paul addresses the listeners of his letters as "holy people." This in no way means their outward lives are completely sanctified, as in perfect in every way, sinless, and in full union with Christ. Why else would he urge the "holy people of Philippi" (1:1) to behave as God would want them in the second chapter?

I discussed all of this at length with our own minister, and within some of the small groups of our church. We concluded that we choose to believe in the possibility of entire sanctification as described in our Manual, but that we accept that the outward fulfillment, for reasons beyond our knowledge and understanding, (almost?) only seems to happen in times of revival. At other times an extensive period of "growing in grace," as a joint enterprise of God and the believer, following the moment of justification, seems to be the common path of Christians. This growing in grace is most definitely a work of God, not something we could do on our own. (In this, the confusion about the non-believers remains.)

Biblically, we apparently are sanctified and holy, simply because we believe, as Paul addresses all followers of Christ as holy in his letters. We do not believe Paul meant to say all of those people were sanctified as meant by Wesley—not even "perfected in love." We believe this word was used to acknowledge those who chose to follow Christ as "set apart" (another definition of holy) from others, in this case for the purpose of spreading the Word and living the Gospel. We could also agree with stating that this is another way of saying that our "spirits" are already sanctified by God, so that we can spread the Word and live the Gospel, but at the same time, the outer, practical consequences of this inner sanctification work out gradually over time.

Although God might show us, at various times, and through various persons throughout history what an entirely sanctified person is like—maybe to remind us of what our full redemption will look like—we accept that we live in the "already not yet" period in history. Nothing in Scripture suggests that the fulfillment is already complete, not of the world, nor of our own Christlikeness.

We argue that the name the first Christians chose for themselves, "followers of the Way," suggests two things. Firstly, "followers" suggests not having reached a destination (yet). Secondly, the "Way" (as Jesus calls Himself) also does not suggest a destination, but a dynamic future. He did not call Himself the "endpoint" in this sense.

Also, John 1:12 states that by believing God has given us the possibility of becoming children of God. He does not say we already are! The flesh in which we now live in this world, might very well never allow us to be completely Christlike. It is up to us to set our "flesh," our egos aside as much as possible so the fruit of the Spirit can grow to fullness. We do believe that our attempt and desire to do so is in itself pleasing to the One who loves us (not whether we are able and successful at it).

We have trouble accepting the title of holy for ourselves, even after discussing what this could entail according to Scripture. This might be due to our Calvinistic upbringing. As members of this congregation of the Church of the Nazarene, we therefore are committed to be followers of Christ, followers of the Way. We have not arrived at our destination, if this is ever completely possible in this life (besides a few exceptions). We do our best to make room for the light of Christ to shine through our lives and into the lives of others. In that process, we hope to become more like Him, by His grace alone.

Ank lives in the Netherlands with her husband and two young daughters. She serves as a pastor in the Protestant Church of the Netherlands, where her focus is on local missionary activities. Her dream is leading a center where people engage in new and contemporary ways of building a relationship with Jesus, and growing in faith.

African Holiness:

Translating Holiness into Authentically African Language and Living

Gift Mtukwa

Holiness drew me to Christianity. At the time I found the Lord, I did not have the terminology to articulate this desire. I grew up around people who professed Christianity. As a result, I went to church sometimes, especially for important events in the Christian calendar. There was not much difference between Christians and non-Christians in my neighborhood, except that "Christians" went to church on Sunday and "non-Christians" went to the beer hall to drink.

At the time, I did not know that Christianity could actually make a difference between Christians and non-Christians. My resistance to accept the Christian tag was compounded by a self-righteous attitude. I was a "good" person; I considered my life better than that of most people in my neighborhood. Most Christians did not have strong moral values; in other words, they did not have high regard for holiness. Some of them participated in traditional ceremonies that invoked the ancestral spirits. Some even visited witch doctors, and some were suspected to be wizards. For these and other reasons, I did not want to be a Christian.

After high school, though, I moved to Harare (the capital of Zimbabwe) where I lived close to members of the Church of the Nazarene. These people were known in our neighborhood as Christians, and they walked the talk—meaning they lived holy lives. When they invited me for a home bible study, I did not hesitate to join them. I wanted to be like them, or at least a little bit like them. The following Sunday, I followed them to a local Nazarene church. This journey finally took me to Africa Nazarene University to learn more about Christian holiness. I became a Christian because of this emphasis on holiness, and I am grateful to those who preached, taught and lived holy lives for me and others to emulate.

Holiness Terminology in Africa

Holiness vocabulary does not translate very well in most African languages. For example, in Swahili the word *utakatifu* is one sided in the sense that holiness is understood only as separation from sin. The positive side of holiness is missing in this understanding of holiness. In their article, "The Idea of 'the Holy' in

Swahili," P. J. L. Frankl and Yahya Ali Omar reveal that Christian missionaries assembled the word utakatifu, since it did not exist prior to Christian missionary activity in East Africa. Frankl and Omar describe the process. "A missionary took the stem of the intransitive verb –*Akaka* 'be thoroughly clean' and formed it into an adjective by suffixing –*Fu*, giving *takatifu* 'holy,' and then changed it into an abstract noun by means of the prefix *u*- giving *utakatifu* 'holiness,' or into a concrete noun with the prefix *m*-, giving *mtakatifu* 'holy person, a saint'."[33]

Similar difficulties exist in several other African languages. Africans have to be intentional in teaching holiness since this is a concept that does not translate directly from the Bible into the African religious milieu. Phillip H. Troutman asserts that African traditional religions have their own concepts of "the holy numinous," and we must seek to articulate a differentiated Christian doctrine of holiness.[34] However, our articulation of holiness must begin where the people are and, then, take them forward using their own concepts of the holy.

Holiness in the African Perspective

The question we ought to ask is whether holiness ought to look the same in every culture. Should holiness look the same way around the world? The substance of holiness remains the same in any part of the world. The negative side of holiness is that God cleanses sinful hearts, and on the positive side, God fills our hearts with love. Holiness is about being set free from the tyranny of sin and receiving the impetus to live a life of love. These are the non-negotiables of Christian holiness. Without this happening, we cannot talk about being holy.

However, what holiness looks like in the African setting is not how it might look in North America or Europe. This is specifically so because sin takes different faces in different cultures. Love is no exception either. Even though the substance of love does not change from culture to culture, how love is expressed is very much culturally conditioned. The variables that constitute what it means to be holy are influenced by the surrounding culture. Therefore, it is worth pursuing the question, *What ought to be the shape of Christian holiness in Africa?*

At the center of the African worldview is the idea of community. Africans are known to be those who live by the maxim, "I am because we are, and, since we are, therefore I am."[35] Africans cannot talk about themselves without reference to others. The holiness message needs to be related to this worldview. Even though

33. P. J. L. Frankl and Yahya Ali Omar, "The idea of the 'The Holy' in Swahili," *Journal of Religion in Africa*, 29: 1 (Feb., 1999), 109-114.

34. Phillip H. Troutman, "Towards an African Theology of Christian Holiness: 'A Journey from Israel to Africa'" in *Africa Speaks: An Anthology of the Africa Nazarene Theology Conference*, Linda Braaten, ed (Florida SA: Africa Nazarene Publications, 2003), 107-111.

35. John Mbiti, African Religions and Philosophies (New York: Doubleday and Company, 1970), 141 .

the holiness message will affirm being communal, it needs to go beyond the cultural and help Africans expand their community to encompass the other, those from other communities who are often treated as if they are less than human.[36] In this respect, the Christian message of holiness speaks to the issue of tribalism that is rampant in Africa today.

Furthermore, the African community consists of the living, the unborn, and the living dead. John Mbiti prefers the term *living dead* to talk about African ancestors.[37] This broad communal aspect of the African worldview has been used to talk about the community of the Godhead, our understanding of the church—African ecclesiology and the idea of *sanctorum communion*—communion of saints.[38] Rodney Reed and I have argued against applying the term ancestor to Christ due to its potential to exacerbate negative ethnicity.[39]

Some African theologians like Harry Sawyer and E. Fashole Luke champion the idea of communion of saints that include the African ancestors in this communion. In Luke's own words, the communion of saints implies "fellowship with holy people of all ages and the whole company of heaven." [40] This is another area where the African church needs to protect her holiness. The ancestral cult actually includes more than fellowship but also worship of one's ancestors and interaction with evil spirits that at times possess the participants. A respect for one's elders (and ancestors) can be encouraged and praying to one's ancestors ought to be discouraged.[41]

Another major issue concerns the place of the individual in the African setting. Some critics of the African communal worldview have noted that too much emphasis on the community does not allow space for the individual to breathe. However, it is worth noting that the individual is not forgotten as such, but he/she has obligations just as the community has its own obligations to fulfill. The African perspective can help to uphold both the personal and the communal aspects of holiness. An unhealthy emphasis on one or the other robs the church an important part of herself. At times, holiness folks have focused on personal holiness at the expense of communal holiness. The African community dealt with those who transgressed or those who did not honor their obligations as a way of

36. Gift Mtukwa, "God is his Place: Paul's Teaching of Active Non-Violent Resistance to Evil in Romans 12:17—21" (MA Diss., University of Manchester, 2014), 15-46.

37. John Mbiti, *African Religions and Philosophy*, 2ⁿᵈ Edition (Oxford: Heinemann Educational Publishers, 1989) 81-82.

38. John Parratt, *Reinventing Christianity: African Theology Today* (Trenton: Africa World Press, 1995), 93.

39. Rodney Reed and Gift Mtukwa, "Christ our Ancestor: Visions of Christology and Dangers of Contextualization," *Wesleyan Theological Journal*, 45:1 (Spring, 2010), 144-63

40. Parratt, 97.

41. Gift Mtukwa, "Ancestral Cult and the Church in Africa," *The Africa Journal of Wesleyan Theology*, 1:1 (2014), 7-24.

protecting the holiness of the community. Yet, the church ought not to concern itself only with individual holiness and forget the communal implications as well.

Finally, sin is relevant when talking about holiness in the African perspective. John Wesley defined sin in a letter in 1772, "Nothing is sin particularly speaking, but a voluntary transgression of the known law of God. Therefore, every voluntary breach of the law of love is sin; and nothing else, if we speak properly."[42] In the African understanding, sin is what one does against one's neighbor, meaning sin is defined socially rather than theologically or religiously.[43] Tokunboh Adeyemo writes concerning the concept of sin in Africa, "It recognizes sin as an evil, upsetting the equilibrium of society or of personal relationships."[44] However, even in the African worldview, we need to clarify that sin is broader than just what one does against the neighbor but also what one does against God, as well. We need to be reminded by David that, "It is against you, and you alone have I sinned" (Psalm 51:4).

Conclusion

Holiness is an important biblical teaching. God is holy and he requires a holy people. African Christians and theologians need to understand holiness and the African worldview and find the points of contact between the biblical text and African religions and philosophy. We need to continue asking what it means to be holy people of God in the African setting. The Holiness message needs to have an impact on African realities like wife inheritance, polygamy, AIDS, tribalism, and countless other African issues. We must continue the difficult but important work of being thoroughly both holiness and African.

Gift was born and raised in Harare, Zimbabwe and currently lives in Nairobi, Kenya. He teaches Bible and theology in the Religion Department of Africa Nazarene University and is the pastor of the University Church of the Nazarene. He holds a bachelor and a Master of Arts in Religion from Africa Nazarene University and is currently pursuing a Master of Arts in Theology at Nazarene Theological College in Manchester.

---

42. *The Works of the Rev. John Wesley*, comp. John Emory 8 vol.s, 3rd. ed (New York: The Methodist Concern 1831), 56.

43. Gailyn van Rheenen, *Communicating Christ in Animistic Contexts* (Pasadena: William Carey Library, 1991), 275-304.

44. Tokunboh Adeyemo, *Salvation in African* Tradition (Nairobi: Evangel Publishing House, 1997), 50.

Holiness and the Scourge of Corruption

Filimao M. Chambo

Corruption continues to be one of the major setbacks for alleviation of poverty in Africa and other parts of the world. Most analysts agree corruption affects the proper functioning of socio-economic and political systems of many nations and has ramifications that weaken the legal system as well as proper governance. Unfortunately, attempts to eradicate corruption are costly, and there seem to be few success stories of reducing systemic corruption.

The prevalence of corruption is a sign of sin's pervasiveness in the world. This immoral behavior is a symptom of a self-centered lifestyle, characterized by greed, dishonesty, tyranny, and absence of moral will for the common good and welfare of others. The prevalence of corruption in Africa[45] is intriguing considering that this behavior is contrary to the symbolic moral systems, which are characterized by a communal way of life, and a system that fosters mutual support, integrity, and respect.[46]

This perversity is even more intriguing when we take into account the fact that, in the 21st Century, Africa is quickly becoming the most Christian continent. Thus, with such a great number of those who profess to be Christians, it seems appropriate to expect the Christian Church to have a role to play in the struggle against the scourge of corruption. Christians should not conform to the patterns of the world (Rom. 12:2); instead, they should be the salt and the light of the world (Matt. 5:13-16). The praxis of the Church should be shaped by the ethical principles of the Kingdom of God.

The opportunity to travel across the continent has afforded me an opportunity to converse with and to listen to various perspectives on this subject. Unfortunately, what I have learned and observed leads me to deduce that many people, both Christians and non-Christians, seem to see corruption as a justifiable way of life.[47]

---

45. Africa is not the only continent faced with the challenge of corruption, but for the purpose of this paper, my focus will be Africa.

46. The principles of communal life in Africa require that one should put other people's needs, freedom, and welfare above personal, selfish ambitions. Thus, the vision for eradication of poverty has become something that looks impressive on paper but its implementation is blurred by desire for personal accumulation of wealth.

47. It is important to note that not all those who are involved in corruption do so voluntarily. There are those who engage in corruption activities because of being blackmailed and/or threatened; failure to comply with the rest of the team in participating in corrupt activities can result in loss of job and sometimes even death threats. It is further complicated when taking into account that the judiciary system in most cases is extremely inefficient. One Christian told me that it was harder for him to take a stand because he was afraid that this could result in harm to his family.

While there is a desire for an alternative way of life that is characterized by integrity, transparency, good governance, common good, and moral will for community development, there also seems to be a strong belief that because systemic evil has gone too far, it is unthinkable that change of behavior could possibly occur. In this context, transformation of lives and society is perceived as an ideal that is not achievable.

This raises the question of how successful the church has been in contextualizing the holiness message to make it fitting to the context where social evil is on the rise. Walter Motaung, argues, "even though the Church of the Nazarene in Africa was coming into contact with serious structural and social challenges which beset the people we are trying to win for Christ, the Church failed to understand sin in socio-economic and political terms."[48] Instead, the Church chose "to supply bandages for wounds inflicted by unjust socio-political structures, rather than confront, challenge, change and remove them."[49] The Church lacked the capacity to understand, to acknowledge, and to talk about socio-economic sins. Thus, the message of holiness was not presented in a holistic way.

This selective approach to biblical truth needs to be addressed. It is vital for the Church to rediscover and then to proclaim the transformative Scriptural message of heart holiness that effects change in all spheres of life, not just the inward and private. Evil does not and cannot have the final word. Radical transformation of people's behavior and change of life is possible through the salvation work of Jesus Christ. In Christ, there is newness of life and behavior of the whole person, not only of the soul as perceived by many. It is holistic. Hence, we see the need to reinterpret the Gospel to challenge the disciples of Jesus Christ to be agents of change in their nations. We are God's instruments being formed into God's holy people who are, both individually and communally, living a life that is more fully conformed to the Word of God. Jesus seeks to save the whole person and that affects all relationships at all levels. Therefore, the church must not be silent or ashamed to address social injustices.

It is important to note that our forefather's theology was influenced by socio-cultural needs of their context. When the Church of the Nazarene began, Dr. Phineas Bresee stated that the new thing that the Church of the Nazarene was adding to its movement was a determination to preach the gospel to those in need and to give the poor a church where they could feel at home. This was not replacing the preaching of the message of salvation and holiness, but it was

---

48. Walter Motaug, "The Great Commission: A Socio-Ethical Comment," in *Africa Speaks: An Anthology of the Africa Nazarene Theology Conference* L. Braaten, ed. (Florida: Africa Nazarene Press, 2003), 228-229.

49. Ibid.

adding a new emphasis that the disciples of Jesus pay special attention to loving and serving those in need. That is, the poor not only are part of the Church and should make it their home, but they should also be cared for. The reading of the Biblical text was done through the lens of this commitment, to address the needs of the people in their time. As a result, they devoted themselves to investigate the Word of God anew with the hope to find new meaning for their time.

Although I recognize that the task of being a prophetic voice is a difficult one and that it can pose danger to one's life in the face of the scourge of corruption, I take courage in the assurance afforded by Jesus in Matt. 28:20 who promises never to leave us alone. Therefore, the Church should not be silent in the face of social injustice and its destructive powers. Like the apostles, a community of disciples of Jesus will affirm that it is better to obey God rather than people (Acts 4:19-20 and 5:29).

The Church is empowered by God to reshape the community's life in response to the Gospel of Jesus Christ. As Hays comments on the book of Acts, "If any authority tries to hinder this mission, the Church can only stand and testify against that authority. As the stories . . . indicated, God will often intervene miraculously to vindicate the Church's resistance—for instance, by sending angels to let the apostles out of prison (5:19-21)."[50] God's grace and power can work through His Church, much more than we can imagine (Eph. 3:20). I believe that in him there is hope for Africa.

The Church should be the force that helps people turn from sin and its power to God (Acts 26:18). Our task, according to Hays, is "re-socializing them into a community that lives by very different norms—the norms defined by Jesus' life and teachings. Such movement—when lived with integrity—inevitably has an explosive effect in the surrounding culture. That is Luke's vision for the transformative power of the Church: it turns the world upside down not through armed revolution but through the formation of the Church as a counter-culture, an alternative witness-bearing community."[51]

Our goal as Christians must not be to turn the world upside down through armed revolution, but through the power of the Word of God. Moved by the Spirit of God to proclaim the truth, we challenge what is wrong, rebuke where needed, and rebuild the nation. This task will sometimes come at a high cost. There are testimonies of people who have been ostracized and persecuted by others because of their Christian stance on the fight against corruption and other

---

50. Richard B. Hays, *Moral Vision of the New Testament: Community, Cross, New Creation* (San Francisco: Harper, 1996), 128.

51. Ibid.

systematic evils. I have come to respect and appreciate their resilience and faith in the Lord in the midst of suffering, for doing what is right.

As expressed in Luke 3:10-14, the people of God, filled with optimism for the transformation of their world, will model integrity and honesty in their communities. They will not abuse their positions of authority to take more than what they ought. Change of behavior, which results from the redemptive work of the Lord Jesus, leads to realization and appreciation of the dignity of all people as equal and deserving to be treated justly in Jesus. Instead of seeing potential candidates to pay bribes or to be extorted, Christian public officers see God's children with whom God may want us to join hands together to work for the economy of the country and even possibly sharing with one another material possessions to alleviate poverty. With authentic holiness, selfish interest is replaced by a desire to belong to God's community. When a radical transformation takes place, people begin to depend on God and trust Him with every single detail of their lives and needs (Mat. 6:19-34).

Filimao Chambo is Regional Director of the Africa Region Church of the Nazarene, with the primary responsibility of overseeing the church planting and development efforts of the Church of the Nazarene in the continent of Africa. Filimao has more than 20 years of ministry experience in Church Ministry and education. Filimao is married to Samantha, and they have two children: Tsakani Gabriella and Emanuel.

Holiness: The Missing Link
to the Evangelization of Africa

Samson Rodrick Kalitera

In recent times, the continent of Africa has experienced the merging of many outstanding evangelistic efforts from African churches and missionary partners from across the globe. As a result, Christianity has experienced astonishing numerical growth during the past 100 years, becoming the most popular religion on the continent.[52]

However, for many in Africa today, evangelism is neither necessary nor welcomed. Many see evangelism simply as a crass tool for obtaining power and money. Sometimes, it is practiced because of pride and selfishness (in order to have a large congregation). At other times, attempts at evangelism happen because of fretfulness and fear, more especially when a congregation is facing a numerical decrease of membership.

Unfortunately, many people in Africa have understood "mission" mainly as "foreign mission" (from "white" to "black"), not something to be practiced by all members of the Body of Christ but rather by those who are "materially" well off. To others, it is the work of the skilled "evangelists" but not of the entire Church. For some other Christians, evangelism is a "one day event" every year that is fixed in their calendars.

For non-Christians, evangelism is perceived both as a practice to be feared and as a barrier to mutual respect and cooperation. Still to others, evangelism represents the colonization of black people, fraudulent televangelist preachers, crusades, and forced conversions.

All of this confusion makes one ask, "What does evangelism really mean?"

In a military context, the term "to evangelize" meant, "to bring good news of the results of a military engagement."[53] However, for Israelites, the "good news" is that God has redeemed and rescued the nation from the hands of the enemies. The prophet Isaiah proclaims the triumph of God's final salvation (40:9-11; 52:10; 60:6; and 61:1). Isaiah also talks about the return of Israel from exile: "How beautiful on the mountains are the feet of those who bring good news,

---

52. P Johnstone & J. Mandryk, *Operation World 21st Century Edition* (Cumbria UK: Paternoster Lifestyle, 2001), 21.

53. Alex Varughese, ed., *Discovering the New Testament* (Kansas City: Beacon Hill, 2005), 82.

who proclaim peace, who bring good tidings, who proclaim salvation, who say to Zion, 'Your God reigns!'" (52:7).

The term *euangelion*, translated in English as "gospel," was adopted by the early Christians and carries a similar trajectory of meaning as in the Old Testament. For Christians, the good news is that Christ has triumphed, that salvation is accomplished, and that Jesus is the fulfillment of God's promises to Israel. Through this message, outsiders become insiders, and transformation comes to the lives and the societies of those who hear and believe. This message is *the gospel*, and its proclamation is what we call *evangelism*.

Walter Brueggemann defines evangelism as "an invitation and summons to 'switch stories,' and therefore to change our lives."[54] The story of God makes us participants or pilgrims who seek and live into the story and are not just mere "tourists" in our Christian journey. Indeed, our lives are formed by this story. Its beginning becomes our beginning; its journey is our journey. Its end also becomes our end or goal. We become Christians not only by hearing this story but also by living in it and living out the story.

So then, how does holiness factor into evangelism? Stone explains, "Holiness is never a way out of the world but ever and always a way into the world. It is for the world that the church is called to be both in the world and visibly different from the world."[55]

Lyons argues that one of the purposes of holiness "is that our lives might be a witness for God before the world" and that "the purpose of the transforming work of God called sanctification is worship and witness, not primarily in the sense of talking, but more importantly in the sense of walking."[56] If the lives of the redeemed—whom Paul calls the "saints" in his letters—do not reflect Christ's love, or if their lives look just like the lives of those who have not been washed by the blood of Christ, then on what grounds can we possibly tell the "unsaved" that they need to change? The Gospel demands that all disciples of Christ should be living out the change that God has brought into their lives.

This is why Richard Heitzenrater can afford to say, "When holiness is your goal, you do evangelism differently."[57] This is emphasized by the Apostle Matthew when he says, "You are the light of the world—like a city on a hilltop that cannot be hidden. No one lights a lamp and then puts it under a basket. Instead, a lamp

---

54. Walter Brueggemann, *Biblical Perspectives on* Evangelism (Nashville: Abingdon, 1993), 11.

55. Bryan Stone, *Evangelism after Christendom: The Theology and Practice of Christian Witness* (Grand Rapids, MI: Brazos, 2007), 191.

56. George Lyons, *Holiness in Everyday Life* (Kansas City, MO: Beacon Hill, 1991), 13.

57. This is a comment that Heitzenrater makes on the evangelism of John Wesley and the beginnings of the Methodist movement; cited in Stone, 259.

is placed on a stand, where it gives light to everyone in the house. In the same way, let your good deeds shine out for all to see, so that everyone will praise your heavenly Father" (Matthew 5: 14-16).

According to Joe Jones, evangelism includes "all those ways in which the church conveys to the world the good news of Jesus Christ and invites the world to respond to this news with renewal of life and new hope. Evangelism is practiced when the church intends its witness to the reality of God in Christ to be received in faith and in the adoption of a new way of life."[58] Certainly, evangelism ought to be seen as a set of practices that includes verbal acts of communication as well as those acts that are nonverbal. It should not be thought as an event or a hobby but as a lifestyle. In the same vein of thought, Jonathan Falwell talks about the practice of evangelism as a combination of "Go and tell" and "Come and see" approaches.[59] Even though many Christian theologians define evangelism only based on verbal communication, one can agree with Falwell that it is impractical to restrict the work of evangelism to proclamation without also inviting the people to "come and see."

Indeed, the practice of evangelism is an invitation to be part of the body of witness and to be formed by it. To be part of such a community means to put an end to the selfish lives that we used to live. Stone argues that only true disciples of Jesus who "have been made into the temple of God in which the Spirit dwells, built upon the church's only secure foundation, Jesus Christ," can do evangelism.[60] This Spirit of God dwells in a life of a believer and gives a variety of gifts and offices to every believer whether one is a member of clergy or laity.

To be a part of God's family is to follow Jesus and to seek His kingdom above anything else, to become like Christ, to grow in His character, and to become lively participants in His mission on earth. If the Church tends to be less than the temple of the Holy Spirit, then its teaching and practices lose their meaning and power as testimony to God's Trinitarian movement into the world. This demands that every individual who makes up the body of Christ must allow this divine movement of God to take root in his or her heart.

The church in Africa today has come up with new and creative ways of spreading the gospel to all those who have not yet accepted Christ as Lord and Savior. These tools are more indigenous, relevant, and user-friendly. Many evangelists employ whatever creative means that can work in order to achieve that end or fruitful results.

---

58. Joe Jones, *A Grammar of Christian Faith* (New York: Rowman and Littlefield, 2002) Vol. 2, 628.

59. Jonathan Falwell, *InnovateChurch* (Nashville: B&H Publishing, 2008), 42.

60. Stone, 12.

Successful evangelism to most Christians in Africa is the one that is marked by numerical measures of success. Those who do well by converting more people to fill the church pews are rewarded. Those who do not show results are regarded as people without the Spirit of God, and eventually they end up facing the consequences of not bringing new converts into the church. The practice of evangelism, in this sense, tends to be evaluated or measured by numerical success. In other words, numerical results become the "end" of evangelism instead of "witnessing."

On the contrary, Bresee advises, "Don't count them. Weigh them. Not quantity, but quality."[61] Certainly, this problem can be dealt with by making the practice of evangelism inseparable from holiness.

For John Wesley, "true Christianity" is to have Christ's attitude and to be renewed in his image, to walk just as Jesus walked, and to evangelize just as Jesus did. Wesley, just like Luther and others before him, preached the message of justification by faith and the necessity of new birth. However, for Wesley, the goal of salvation that Christ offers is far more than justification; it includes sanctification: a renewal into the image of Christ, hence, becoming more like Christ. And this Christlikeness will shape and fuel our evangelism.

Samson Kalitera is a lecturer and assistant chaplain at Africa Nazarene University, Kenya, where he is also a Doctor of Ministry student. He is married to Betty Wisiki with one child, "Atikonda," which means, "God loves us."

---

61. As quoted in Stone, 257.

Wesleyan Sanctification
Encountering Buddhist Enlightenment:
Exploring Evangelistic Dialogue with Korean Buddhists
Musung Jung

I. The Korean Context

The two most dominant religions in Korea are Christianity and Buddhism. According to the 2012 survey, 22.5% of the Korean population identified themselves as Christians whereas 22.1% confirmed themselves as Buddhists.[62] This situation puts the Korean Church into an evangelistic challenge regarding how effectively to reach out to Buddhists.

The fact of the matter is that the Korean church at large has engaged in aggressive evangelism to Buddhists with little concern or respect for their religious reality. As a result, their antipathy to Christianity has increased, and their receptivity to the gospel has decreased.

To break out of this vicious cycle, the Korean church needs a paradigm shift a triumphant evangelism to a dialogical one. As Daryl Balia and Kirsteen Kim rightly state: "Witness does not preclude dialogue but invites it, and dialogue does not preclude witness but extends and deepens it."[63] Such evangelistic dialogue with Buddhists requires that the Korean Church discover some meaningful points of contact between the two religious traditions. In this regard, the Korean denominations rooted in Wesleyanism can play an important role by exploring and presenting the correlation between Wesleyan sanctification and Dono-Jeomsu (a particular understanding of enlightenment within the Korean traditions of Buddhism).

II. Buddhist Dono-Jeomsu (Enlightenment)

Dono-Jeomsu was first proposed by the Buddhist monk Jinul (知訥, 1158–1210), the forerunner of Korean Zen Buddhism, as well as the founder of the

---

62. *An Analytic Report on Korean Christianity: The 2013 Report on Korean Religious Life and Attitude* [한국기독교 분석리포트: 2013 한국인의 종교생활과 의식조사 보고서], ed. Korean Association of Christian Pastors (Seoul: URD, 2013). The Korean Christian population is classified into 22.5% Protestants and 10.1% Catholics. In this article Korean Christianity, Korean Christians and the Korean church point to the Protestant circle. The Catholic side has traditionally taken the pluralistic position as well as the dialogical attitude in Korea's multi-religious milieus, which has enabled it to develop an amicable relationship with the Buddhist group.

63. Daryl Balia and Kirsteen Kim, eds. *Edinburgh 2010—Witnessing to Christ Today* (Oxford, UK: Regnum, 2010), 48.

Jogye Order (曹溪宗), the largest Buddhist denomination in Korea today. Dono (頓悟) signifies "sudden enlightenment," and Jeomsu (漸修) denotes "gradual cultivation." Combined together, Dono-Jeomsu involves the unified idea of "sudden enlightenment followed and supported by gradual cultivation" in search of the purest and highest state of one's mind, namely nirvana (涅槃).

According to Jinul, any human being is a prospective buddha with the indwelling buddhahood. ("Buddha" literally means "the enlightened one.") He explained, "Everyone is originally a Buddha . . . [and] possesses the impeccable self-nature . . . The sublime essence of nirvana is complete in everyone. There is no need to search elsewhere; since time immemorial, it has been innate in everyone."[64]

The problem is that one's deluded ignorance and this-worldly attachment cloud and blind oneself to this noble truth. Furthermore, one's mind (with such benightedness and preoccupation) fails to operate fully awake and keenly alert in accordance with one's original buddha nature.

Jinul, thus, claimed that the first and foremost task for humans is to be ontologically enlightened into the supreme truth that a buddha is existentially within oneself. This enlightenment in one's whole being can occur instantaneously in the explorative process of the twofold practices of both meditation about the Buddha-Mind and the scriptural studies about the Buddha-Word.[65]

Jinul, though, held that this cultivation prior to the sudden initial awakening is a far cry from being the full reality. In the wake of sudden enlightenment in a critical moment, the real practices of cultivation begin. These ought to be constantly done all through one's life for the purpose of the complete elimination of all false thoughts and habitual residues lingering in one's mind and behavior. This gradual cultivation can eventually sublimate initial enlightenment into ultimate enlightenment, the perfect pure state of one's mind, in which one's inherent buddhahood is not only fully activated inwardly but also wholly manifested outwardly. Because of this sudden-enlightenment-gradual-cultivation life, one becomes the embodiment of the Buddha-Mind and Buddha-Word, thereby challenging and inspiring other sentient beings to reach the same stage of nirvana in the here and now.

III. Points of Contact

Inter-religious dialogue starts with the positive appreciation of God's grace and imprint on one's counterpart. This perspective is in line with the Wesleyan

---

64. Robert Buswell, *Tracing Back the Radiance: Chinul's Korean Way of Zen* (Hawaii: University of Hawai'i Press, 1991), 120.

65. Geonkee Kang, *A Study on Jinul* [지눌연구] (Seoul: The Buddha World, 2001), 41.

tradition postulating that other faiths are under the infinite orbit of God's prevenient grace.[66] Rendering Buddhist Dono-Jeomsu a dialogical partner with Wesleyan sanctification is, therefore, natural and commendable in the Wesleyan tradition.

When it comes to their conjunctive comparison, there are two approaches available: (1) the conversion-and-sanctification approach and (2) the entire sanctification approach. Both approaches recognize human potentiality and attainability of the highest religious level but in different dual structures.

In the first approach Dono and Jeomsu correspond to the conversion experience (or the initial sanctification moment) and the succeeding sanctification movement, respectively.[67] The instantaneous awakening into one's buddha-like existence is never the final destination of Buddhist growth; rather, it must be followed by the gradual cultivation of one's mind until the consummate point of nirvana. Likewise, the conversion experience of the regenerative adoption as God's child should be accompanied by the sanctification process of the continual evolvement into the whole measure of the "fullness of Christ" (Ephesians 4:13).

On the other hand, the second approach likens Dono and Jeomsu to the entire sanctification state and the ensuing gradual progression. One's steady progress to the sublime essence of nirvana via both meditation and the scriptural studies goes even after one's sudden enlightenment. Similarly, entire sanctification is not the end of the road in one's Christian journey but the beginning of one's "gradual progression in sanctification . . . extended beyond the boundaries of this life," namely glorification.[68]

In spite of the aforementioned commonality, Wesleyan sanctification is fundamentally different from Buddhist Dono-Jeomsu. The former is essentially theocentric, and the latter is primarily anthropocentric. As is generally known, Wesleyan sanctification is divinely initiated and driven. Both initial sanctification (i.e. conversion) and entire sanctification are definitely the gift of God in the divine mechanism of justifying grace and sanctifying grace.[69] The Spirit of God from above is the driving force behind one's holiness of heart and life.

---

66. The Wesleyan tradition confirms God's preceding grace not only operative in God's creation but also conducive to God's salvation. Notably, Richard Watson, who is considered as the first Methodist systematic theologian, stated "by virtue of universal prevenient grace the heathens are supplied with the means of salvation." Richard Watson, *Theological Institutes* (New York, NY: Lane & Scott, 1851), 2:447.

67. This approach was originally suggested by Sunil Kim in "Conversion in a Korean Context," *Global Dictionary of Theology*, eds. William Dyrness and Veli-Matti Kärkkäinen (Downers Grove, IL: IVP, 2008), 201-202.

68. Melvin Dieter, "The Wesleyan Perspective," *Five Views on Sanctification*, Anthony Hoekema, Stanley Horton, Robertson McQuilkin and John Walvoord (Grand Rapids, MI: Zondervan, 1987), 13.

69. Theodore Runyon, *Exploring the Range of Theology* (Eugene, OR: Wipf & Stock, 2012), 214.

On the contrary, Buddhist Dono-Jeomsu is humanly initiated and driven. Both sudden enlightenment and gradual cultivation are contingent decisively upon one's dual practices of meditation and the scriptural studies.[70] The buddhahood from within is the prime mover behind one's pureness of mind and behavior. This fundamental differentiation results from, and simultaneously leads to, Christianity as a religion of grace[71] in stark contrast with Buddhism as a religion of works.

IV. Toward Evangelistic Dialogue

The effective evangelism to Buddhist believers is a formidable challenge but not impossible. When the Korean Church undertakes evangelistic dialogue, the Christian-Buddhist relation can be improved to the result of creating openness to the gospel. This method is actually how both Jesus and Paul engaged those with other living faiths (cf. John 4; Acts 17:16-34).[72]

Accordingly, comparative studies between Wesleyan sanctification and Buddhist Dono-Jeomsu are worthwhile and biblically faithful.[73] The current research is just a preliminary attempt, which reveals that their consonance converges in the dual structures of crisis /consummate moment, and follow-up process in religious experience and their dissonance diverges in divine enablement from above versus human achievement from within. With these points of contact (and others), Korean Wesleyan/Nazarene churches can enter into evangelistic dialogue in order to fulfill the Great Commission of making disciples of the Korean Buddhist people group.

Musung Jung is Assistant Professor in the Department of Christian Studies at Korea Nazarene University. He studied at Yonsei University, Northwest Nazarene University, Korea Nazarene University (B.Th.), Emory University (M.Div.) and Asbury Theological Seminary (Ph.D. in Intercultural Studies).

---

70. In Buddhist Dono-Jemosu dual practices can be divided into two: 1) preliminary dual practices before sudden enlightenment and 2) authentic dual practices after sudden enlightenment.

71. Wesley made it clear that justification and sanctification alike are not so much the product of human endeavors as the outcome of God's redemptive grace synergized by faith alone, "Exactly as we are justified by faith, so are we sanctified by faith. Faith is the condition, and the only condition, of sanctification, exactly as it is of justification. It is the condition: None is sanctified but he that believes; without faith no man is sanctified. And it is the only condition: This alone is sufficient for sanctification. Every one that believes is sanctified, whatever else he has or has not. In other words, no man is sanctified until he believes: Every man when he believes is sanctified "The Scriptural Way of Salvation." *John Wesley*, *"The Scripture Way of Salvation," Sermons on Several Occasions* (London, UK: T. Tegg, 1829), 213-222.

72. Jesus and Paul carried out evangelism in dialogue with a Samaritan woman and some Greek residents at Athens, respectively.

73. In comparative studies between Christianity and other religions, the gospel should take the integrating center or "possessio" role. Central to Bavinck's missiology is the term, possessio, by which he means, "adopting, taking over, taking possession of." Johan Bavinck, Inleiding in de Zendingswetenschap (Kampen: Kok, 1954), 181. Quoted from Anton Wessels, "Biblical Presuppositions For and Against Syncretism," *Dialogue and Syncretism: An Interdisciplinary Approach*, eds. Jerald Gort et al (Grand Rapids, MI: Eerdmans, 1989), 62.

Holiness: The Most Hipster Doctrine

Emily JoAnn Haynes

The Walls Are Moving

Our communion wafers are not organic.

I know some members of the Church of the Nazarene who do not seem to care.

I have grown up hearing in the Church of the Nazarene how our beliefs about holiness make us distinctive, set apart. We have this strong doctrine which helps us know who we are, how God works, and from where we have come.

However, when it comes to putting that into practice, my contemporaries who crave authenticity, significance and connection, have found our distinctive doctrine to be shallow and convoluted. It doesn't matter what you say if you can't back it up with what you do. They crave a holiness orthopraxy that is as strong as our orthodoxy.

I must admit that I do too.

The walls are moving for we who are members of the Church of the Nazarene. The picture is no longer static. We have been made to open ourselves up to a different contextual story. We sit as the big picture moves by us. We experience joy and sadness, anxiety and comedy. At the end, we are still sitting in the same seat, but everything has changed.

Things used to happen one way. Now, the very same things done in the very same way have very different social connotations. Where we used to be addressing the social problems of our day, now we have lost track of where we are and what the problems really are.

On some level, we are aware of our need for change. Incrementally we have transitioned. After rightly losing our "no" to jewelry, movies, make-up, and dancing, we should wonder what we should say "no" to now. What should we say "yes" to? When we are not all plain-faced and rhythmless, how are we then to be set apart?

Our contextual walls are changing, but they are not the only ones. Church walls are moving too.

This makes some of us very nervous.

I used to hear testimonies within four drab, whitish, holy walls that sounded like this, "I want to praise God because I was saved and sanctified 40 years ago, and I haven't sinned since then."

Now, I tend to spend more time within dimly lit, exposed brick walls of old buildings. The testimonies I hear here are different. "I know I can't do what all I want to do perfectly. It makes me feel guilty that I can't do it, because I know it matters to God and to the world."

Both are the Church of the Nazarene.

So what now? How do we wrestle with, smooth over, rectify and explain our differences? Where are we as a church if our practice is lost, if our words are different, and if our practical identity is lacking?

How is God calling us here and now to follow him so radically, to surrender to him so fully, that we live out our doctrine of holiness? How do we come to a place where our orthopraxy is once again as strong as our orthodoxy when it comes to holiness?

Omni-Holiness

My husband and I co-pastor a church that we started five years ago.

Apparently, we are hipsters, though I am sure we were just trying to be members of the Church of the Nazarene when they started calling us that. Wikipedia has a definition of hipster that includes associations like, "non-mainstream fashion sensibility," "organic and artisanal foods," and "Bohemians who reside in gentrifying neighborhoods."[74] These are fancy code words for: we shop at thrift stores, grow our own food and intentionally live in communities alongside the poor. It's not glamorous, and sometimes it's not pretty, but apparently, it is trendy right now.

We have a deep-seated belief that carries us forward: we believe that God cares about every part of our lives.

As this foundation of belief works its way through me, I realize the irony of being dedicated, baptized and ordained in the Church of the Nazarene. The beautiful and distinctive doctrine of holiness became language I would eventually use to describe the holistic work of God I was experiencing in my community and life. Somewhat naively, I started to associate this as the normal outworking of entire sanctification, the Spirit moving me to action.

Imagine my surprise to find that this was not the normative way of talking about the practical application of entire sanctification. In fact, in the presence of

---

74. "Hipster (Contemporary Subculture)," http://en.wikipedia.org/wiki/Hipster_(contemporary_subculture), Wikipedia, accessed 6-15-14.

experienced Nazarene pastors, you would think that I was an alien from another world talking about entire sanctification this way.

Pastors can get on board with serving the poor and eating with neighbors, but when you start talking about marches against Monsanto and using cloth diapers, they get a little disoriented.

We are not accustomed to the scope of God's work in our lives affecting our diaper choices.

I am suggesting that it should.

Approximately 27.4 billion disposable diapers are consumed every year in the United States and it is estimated that it takes between 250 and 500 years for a disposable diaper to decompose in a landfill[75].

The world is dying, and we are killing it. People are dying across the world because we don't help them. Whole species are dying, and we didn't even know they existed.

It seems trite to point out that God cares about what we do, say and think.

It seems whimsical to mention Jesus' quote about the hairs on our heads being numbered.

Do we not already know as a settled fact that God wants to redeem every part of our lives?

God cares about everything; this is what we are talking about when we talk about holiness. In other words, everything we do matters to God. He cares about the choices we make because he cares about everything that our choices impact. The world's sustainability . . . the people to come . . . our families . . . His soil . . . our bodies . . . our neighbors . . . the poor . . .

He has a vested interest in things turning out well. His kingdom is coming, and it is one of wholeness, goodness, health, beauty, peace, love and God. What we do here and now can bring His Kingdom a little closer or it can push it a little further away.

This is where I get hipster (Nazarene?) on you.

So that means everything matters:

- How our food is grown matters.
- If workers are paid a fair wage matters.
- Saving endangered species matters.
- It matters if we fill up landfills with billions of baby diapers.
- How you spend your money matters.
- What you do with your body matters.

---

75. Real Diaper Association, "Diaper Facts," http://www.realdiaperassociation.org/diaperfacts.php, accessed 6-15-14.

- It matters if you use a sword (aka gun) or a plowshare.
- The example you set for others matters.
- What bank you call your own matters.
- How you treat your neighbors matters.
- What you do with your time matters.
- Freeing slaves and rehabilitating prisoners matters.

I dare you to name something that doesn't matter to God.

Christians have lived for long enough thinking evil thoughts like, "That is not God's work," "This world is only temporary, we don't need to save it," and "What I do won't make a difference."

These are not things Jesus would have said.

If we, in the Church of the Nazarene, could finally start to believe that holiness is really about living a life of wholeness, then we would change the world with God. If our "distinctive doctrine" started to be translated as insistence that God cares about every part of our lives, then we would start to look very different from everyone else. We might shop in thrift stores to be able to afford to give clothes to those who need them. We might start to grow our own food as a way to connect to the soil and educate our neighbors about how they can free themselves from a corrupt system. We might create alternative societies where people have common possessions and pay off each other's debts. A life of wholeness will allow us to conceive an idea, draw out some blueprints and find out where the walls are going to be built again for the right practice of our orthodoxy.

A life of holiness will allow us to do weird things that no one can explain, but everyone wants to be a part of.

So, then I implore you Nazarenes: stand up for wholeness! We have a calling here to live a life, empowered by the Spirit of God to be a unique and refreshing voice to our world.

If, in the deconstruction of our old orthopraxy, we would be renewed in the light of what God is doing here and now and join with Him, we could literally change the world. If the 2,263,249 (and counting) Nazarenes in the world could agree that everything matters and work together to make a difference, the Kingdom might just start to roll in.

Our lines may not always be drawn in the same place, but if we allow God to choose where he wants to build the walls for his church, if we are humble enough to be led into all truth, miracles might happen. God might actually choose to use us once again to be a distinctive voice—calling the world to the most authentic, holistic and loving God there is.

Emily has been a pastor, along with her husband Caleb, in Nashville, Tennessee for the past five years. Her other occupation is in the non-profit sector where she works in marketing and fund development. Her daughter, Story DeAnn, was born in May of 2013. She defines herself as a wife, mother, witness, advocate and adventurer who loves good coffee, authentic conversations, creativity and community.

A Theology of Hope:

How Holiness Doctrine Will Reach Millennials

Grant T. Miller

Take a quick scan of any contemporary religion journal or religious news service, and you'll quickly recognize that there is a struggle taking place for the identity of evangelical Christianity. Visit any number of online forums and you'll find Christians arguing about Holy Scripture, science and origins, egalitarian vs. complementarian models of marriage, human sexuality, and any number of other issues.

In response to these confounding debates, we've seen a string of reports that show members of the Millennial generation are leaving the church and doing so very quickly.[76] The reasons for this departure are broad and varied. However, despite decreasing attendance at church, spirituality and optimism remain important characteristics of this generation. Many Millennials give this self-description of their religious engagement, "I'm not really religious; I'm just about following Jesus." I recently heard this statement from a new friend that had moved into the area when talking about trying out local churches.

There are likely a number of explanations for this trend. Perhaps it is simply a hallmark of every twenty-something to move away from the church for a time (although some in the field would claim that Millennials present a unique case due to the digital era in which they came of age). Perhaps by creatively addressing more contemporary issues, the Church can create a more desirable atmosphere. However, I hesitate to affirm any explanation that would simplify the issue, and if I might be so bold as both a Millennial and a committed church member, I'd like to propose that this departure of young people has less to do with any one controversial issue or teaching and more to do with a scarcity of hope being conveyed in our churches.

It's a well-documented and heavily discussed point that one of the trickiest edges that we walk as a Wesleyan-holiness denomination is that of legalism. Drinking, smoking, dancing, and other behaviors that we've historically avoided

---

76. There a number of resources available with consistently similar data, but two excellent places to start are David Kinnaman's book, *You Lost Me* (Grand Rapids, MI: Baker, 2013) and Pew Research Center: http://www.pewresearch.org/fact-tank/2014/03/07/6-new-findings-about-millennials/.

out of a desire for purity can easily become a list of do's and do not's, and as yet another generation comes of age, we look at the list and ask, "Why?" The answer we get—or more often, the lack of an answer—can suck the hope out of a generation.

The answer to that question of "Why?" *must not* be missed as an opportunity to tell the story of holiness. If we fail to communicate the history and power of our theology, then we have no ground to bemoan the exodus of any persons from our churches. Without the accompaniment of the compelling truth of God's call to a sanctified and holy life, our lists of sins to avoid have simply the form of godliness while lacking power, and when a generation that is identified by a profound sense of hope and optimism is presented with such a clear dichotomy, it makes sense that they would show themselves to the door. This is what's happening right now in much of the evangelical world.

When I came to the point of asking "Why?," I was lucky to have mentors who told me the story of our church and helped me to understand a call to holiness living. I was given resources and opportunities to discuss and learn about sanctification and Christian perfection, and as I began to grow in understanding, I felt that Millennial piece of me—that part so closely tied to my generation's characteristic connection with optimism, ambition, and love for community[77]— had found the theology it needed to thrive.

However, I know many peers who were not so fortunate, and as a result find themselves with a wishy-washy spirituality. And herein lies a unique and powerful opportunity for those looking to the future of our church and how a renovated approach to holiness can be key for the proclamation of the Gospel. There is a hole in the theology of our young people that has been rent by arguments and hypocrisy across and within Western denominations. This hole has caused millions of young people inside and outside the church to develop a deep desire for spirituality, but also to have little hope in the church to help provide growth in that area.

The hidden power and point of connection with this generation that the Church of the Nazarene and other Wesleyan-holiness denominations possess is that our identity is rooted on perhaps the most optimistic theology of Christian living available. We have hope because we believe in the value and character of humanity through the immutable impression of the *imago Dei*. We believe in a compassionate and seeking God that stretches forth hands filled with prevenient grace to which all can respond. We believe in a gracious and merciful God who

---

77. For a deep look at some of the characteristics of the Millennial generation, see Tim Elmore's *Generation iY* (Poet Gardener: 2010).

in the fullness of justice takes into account the light that has been received by members of creation. We believe that by following Jesus Christ we can become whole again through his love and mercy.

It's true that these concepts are not inherently simple. Theologians within our tradition have addressed and readdressed these concepts over the years. There is also often an uphill battle to be fought in the discussion of Christian perfection, as many bring the baggage of a Platonic sense of formulaic perfection (made more difficult by our Latin root of *perfectum*), instead of the Aristotelian model of *telos*, which invites us to be made perfect by simply living into our calling and identity as human beings made to glorify and be in relationship with God.[78] But within conversations about and clarification of the doctrine of holiness, young people can connect to a rejuvenated hope in the Gospel of Jesus Christ.

I have seen this kind of rejuvenating effect take place first hand. I have laughed with delight as my friend, who grew up in the Church of the Nazarene, talked about his mind being "literally blown" by the revelation that Christian perfection was all about dynamic transformation and not a static state. I have prayed with members of a small group who were finally grasping what it meant to live and to take pride in a purposefully sanctified life. I have wept with my wife as we have been confronted with the reality of having no excuse for moral failure if we really believe in Christian perfection. The old excuse of our shortcomings -being "simply human"—is incongruous with a life that is empowered by the model of Jesus Christ.

Through these moments, I have experienced a unity with my peers that is inherent to the profound hope that is offered within holiness doctrine. Although only the sanctifying love of Christ can be credited with the transformation of the human heart, a robust doctrine of holiness can be incredibly powerful in repairing the theological hole that currently sits in the center of Millennial theology. It is a hope for dynamic and active growth every day while also looking to a deeper future experience. John A. Knight, speaking to this tension 40 years ago in *The Holiness Pilgrimage*, states it elegantly, "Every step taken on the journey of holiness permits one to enjoy increasing, but real, degrees of wholeness and balance. Holiness, therefore, is both a possible present reality and an anticipated future hope—and it is these things simultaneously."[79]

This simultaneous hope of perfection today and greater perfection in the future has given many trouble in their understanding of holiness living, but I have

78. For the explanation of this concept I owe personal thanks to Dr. Brent Peterson and Dr. Diane Leclerc, especially Dr. Leclerc's book *Discovering Christian Holiness* (Kansas City, MO: Beacon Hill, 2013).

79. John A. Knight, *The Holiness Pilgrimage: Developing a Life-Style that Reflects Christ* (Kansas City, MO: Beacon Hill, 1973), 55.

found a wonderful illustration by Reuben Welch (relayed by Diane Leclerc) to be beautifully enlightening. "His daughter began piano lessons early in her life. She would practice and practice a piece until it was played, for all intents and purposes, *perfectly*. But as she got better, her ability to play harder and harder pieces grew. When she was older, she was able to sit down and play an extremely hard piece *perfectly*. In both instances, she was able to play perfectly. But obviously there was growth in her ability to do more."[80]

I'll continue this analogy in conclusion. The beauty of holiness doctrine is that it is fundamentally all about putting fingers to keys, feet to pedals, and beginning to discover what it means to play well. This, I believe, is what those outside the church, especially Millennials, are looking for. As Nazarenes full of holy hope, we are in an ideal place to offer them that opportunity.

Grant Miller is a native of the Pacific Northwest and an alumnus of Northwest Nazarene University. He and his wife Jen currently live in Nampa, ID, where Grant works with students as the Director of Community Life at NNU.

---

80. Diane Leclerc, *Discovering Christian Holiness: The Heart of Wesleyan-Holiness Theology* (Kansas City, MO: Beacon Hill, 2010), 219.

Holiness and Community Outreach:
Emphasis on Youth Ministry
by Kerese Harrinandan

It was a bright sunny, Sunday morning, and I was off to church. As far as I knew, it was going to be another typical Sunday, but nothing could prepare me for what was going to happen that morning.

After I lead our church in worship in song for a few minutes, the electricity went out. In Guyana, we call that a "blackout." Blackouts are quite common to our culture here, so there was no reason to believe that there was anything unusual about this one. But then someone told me about the fire that was blazing just a few corners away from our church. I was stunned because if there was a fire, I should have known. After all, I lived on the next street. I tried to go back to song leading, but I just couldn't focus. We stopped and prayed for the family. When I opened my eyes I realized that my prayers didn't make the smoke disappear, and my heart was suddenly burdened. Singing songs of praise and thanksgiving was the last thing on my mind at that point. So we paused "having church" and went to be with our neighbors in their time of distress.

What happened next will stay with me for a very long time. Here we were, perhaps feeling good about ourselves for doing the "God thing." I imagine we all felt a rush of mixed emotions as we walked down that road—sadness, empathy, curiosity, hurt, confusion, worry, pride, and the list goes on.

But the sad thing was when we got to the scene, people didn't know who we were. One woman asked me if I was with the media. I was stunned by her question because I grew up in that community. I had been living there for over 17 years, yet I still had to identify myself by saying, "Hi, I'm from the Church." This was the first time in a long time since I had said something like that to anyone in the community. And then it dawned on me that we had become so comfortable with the idea of becoming holy among ourselves that we had forgotten that holiness is no good—and possibly hasn't been realized—if it's only shared among believers.

I've been involved in youth work for over a decade now, and there are a few things that I'd like to share from my experience as a youth leader. It is my hope that these observations might help us to understand why more and more young people are becoming frustrated with "holiness talk" in the church and are choosing either to leave or to give more of their time to social organizations.

Why Is this Important Now?

A few years ago, I saw a video in one of our District Conventions that brought tears to my eyes and which always comes to mind when I think about why I do youth ministry. It was titled, "You're Losing Us."[81] In the video, two young people said, "We want and need opportunities to minister to others in ways consistent with our ages, development, abilities and spiritual gifts." At the end of this video, a very salient question was asked, "In 10 years, will you have made a difference?"

Children and youth are not the future; they are the "now." What we do or fail to do today to disciple them so that they become the mature Christians who integrate their faith in their daily living has already begun to determine the quality of the future both they and we will have. It is because of the *now*— when our church budgets place greater emphasis on the color of the walls than on the spiritual and psychosocial well-being of our youth—that we are seeing the spiritual, social, and even political breakdown that we experience today.

Enough Talk

When I was in college, I learned about three principles that formed my philosophy of youth ministry. In his book, *The Secrets of the Simple Youth Ministry*, Carl Blunt pointed to 3 fundamentals which must be addressed in dealing with youth: identity (Who am I?), intimacy (Do I know Jesus?), and integration (How am I applying my faith to my daily living?).[82]

The youth in our churches do not want another smart tactic of evangelism or discipleship. What they want is to see the church being the hands and feet of Jesus in the community. They want to see the same Gospel that the Apostle Paul taught and lived being realized largely in and through our churches. Our youth want to experience the kind of Gospel that will turn entire communities "upside down" (Acts 17:6). They want to see the kind of holiness that doesn't allow an entire church to sit in oblivion as the world marches on in social anarchy, bold injustice and political foolishness. The youth want to see and be a part of change.

Our youth are tired of the talk about what this world should look like, while we just sit and pray, because they are convinced that we can do so much more than that. They are ready to take risks.

Take Paul Lopez, for example. Paul is a young Belizean student of the Caribbean Nazarene College. One day he was trying on a pair of new shoes, and

---

81. Nazarene Media Library, "You're Losing Us," Oct. 21, 2011, http://medialibrary.nazarene.org/media/youre-losing-us.

82. Carl A. Blunt, *The Secrets of Simple Youth* Ministry (Enumclaw, WA: WinePress, 2001).

it suddenly dawned on him that there are so many people who didn't have that luxury. Today, Paul has started a movement called "Soul for Soles." Along with a few others from CNC, Paul works hard to find donors so that that they can walk the streets of Port of Spain, Trinidad to give new pairs of shoes to homeless people and to share the Gospel with them.

This is what we need to teach our youth—that they can take initiative. But we also need to support them. It seems that talking about what "Holiness Unto the Lord" is simply not enough. Our youth want to see the love that holiness allows us to experience integrated in the way we respond to community needs, national crises and global demands. If we just keep talking, our youth will keep walking. It's just that simple.

Our Response

A few weeks after that fire in our community, our pastor decided to preach from the back of the church with the benches toward the road one Sunday morning. That day, we were all reminded that our church exists *for* the community. We were urged not to turn our backs on the people we are supposed to help, and as much as possible, to remember their need for a Savior.

Am I saying that all of our churches are failing to reach out to communities? No. I see the Church of the Nazarene being the missional church that we proclaim every day. We are going to places where God's voice has not been heard and where His message has not been proclaimed.

What I am humbly suggesting, however, is that if we do not integrate this missional focus in our local churches so that community outreach becomes a way of life, then we are missing the point of holiness, and we will lose our youth. I am saying that if discipleship—teaching people how to live like Jesus lived—is not as central to our holiness conversations as it should be, then we are never going to achieve our common goal of being holy as He is holy (1 Peter 1:16). If we don't take action in our communities together, it doesn't matter how much we recite that we are "a holy people, a Christian people, a missional people."

Kerese is a graduate of the Caribbean Nazarene College (Trinidad). She has a passion for children and youth and serves in Guyana as Minister of Youth and Music at the North Ruimveldt Church of the Nazarene. From 2012-2014 Kerese served as District NYI President and was elected in 2013 to serve the Mesoamerica Region as Caribbean Field Youth Coordinator.

Some Call It Love

James Travis Young

A Rejected Call

"Holiness isn't important to me," my friend said. He is a Millennial pastor in the Church of the Nazarene, serving the Lord with all his heart. "It has nothing to do with the problems we face," he continued. "Holiness never helped anyone, and I don't see how it is relevant in my ministry at all."

Church, *we have a problem.*

I wish I could say I was stunned by what my friend expressed, but I wasn't. I have had too many conversations with too many people my age who have come to the same conclusion for different reasons.

Some would say that the historical holiness movement was merely a massive doctrinal fad, "a practice or interest followed for a time with exaggerated zeal."[83] As the holiness movement emerged from 19th century Methodism and the tradition of John Wesley, it became a calling to a great many. It was "our watchword and song," our very identity. Even today, the primary objective of the Church of the Nazarene is to "advance God's kingdom by the preservation and propagation of Christian holiness."[84]

Nevertheless, in recent decades others have argued that "the holiness movement is dead," that in our churches, our forebears stopped doing things the way they were done originally and took alternative approaches that, apparently, "killed" the holiness movement.[85] While that remains scripturally preposterous, it is quite obvious our culture is responding differently to holiness teaching than previous generations.

This phenomenon has led to the spurious claim that holiness is simply irrelevant by today's cultural standards. In the same way, people of all ages confuse relevance with popularity. A couple of decades ago my generation wore super baggy stone-washed jeans, but today the same guys walk around with stiff robotic movements and pained expressions in their dark skinny jeans. Just because holiness isn't in style, that doesn't make it irrelevant.

---

83. "Fad," Merriam-Webster Online Dictionary, http://www.merriam-webster.com/dictionary/fad, accessed Aug. 1, 2014.

84. *Manual, 2013-2017,* (Kansas City: Nazarene Publishing House, 2013), 5.

85. Kieth Drury, "The Holiness Movement Is Dead: A Retrospective," 2004, http://www.drurywriting.com/keith/dead.footnoted.htm, accessed Aug. 1, 2014.

Possibly most alarming is the current attitude of our generation and culture that holiness is a myth, a fairy tale, folklore passed down from generation to generation. Honestly, holiness has been taught and preached very much like a doctrinal tall tale. Pentecost was a pulp narrative starring heroes of the New Testament like Peter. Confusing sermons attempted to harmonize crisis experience with prolonged process by using vocabulary such as "consecration," "sanctification," and "eradication" instead of scripture. When scripture was taught, it was to supply vague warnings, like "without holiness no one will see the Lord," which reinforced Sunday School lessons which asserted that only sanctified believers will go to heaven because they never commit any sins.

Is it any wonder why today many believe holiness to be confusing and boring at best, and at worst an out-and-out lie?

To make matters worse, the only exposure many of today's generation have had to holiness teaching was perpetrated by people who did not live holy lives. Or perhaps too many of us have observed conflict and scandal within "holiness churches" year in and year out. Study after study demonstrates that today's generation will not be boxed in by divisive and fighting churches[86] proclaiming antiquated religious doctrine[87] any more than we will endorse labels of any kind.[88] In a world where entire populations are starving, Christians are martyred daily, and wars are fought by children and terrorists, many Millennials believe the holiness of recent decades is hypocritical and does little to advance the cause of Christ.

This generation is my generation, and we are determined to escape the past and to make our own future. Therefore, the response of our culture to the tarnished holiness presented in our formative years is very much like what most of us would choose to do if we saw an unwanted number calling us on the phone. If we are actually called unto the holiness of recent decades, our generation has rejected that call.

The problem isn't that holiness is unpopular, irrelevant, or dead. My generation believes holiness is a *myth* because, frankly, we were told lies about holiness and were told about holiness by liars. It is quite apt that we have been described by Barna

---

86. Thom Rainer, "The Millennials Are Rejecting Fighting Churches and Christians," Oct. 21, 2013, http://thomrainer. com/2013/10/21/the-millennials-are-rejecting-fighting-churches-and-christians/, accessed Aug. 1, 2014.

87. Robert P. Jones, Daniel Cox, and Thomas Banchoff, "A Generation in Transition: Religion, Values, and Politics among College-Age Millennials, Findings from the 2012 Millennial Values Survey," Berkley Center for Religion, Peace, and World Affairs at Georgetown University, 2013, http://repository.berkleycenter.georgetown.edu/120419BC-PRRIMillennialValuesSurveyReport.pdf, accessed Aug. 1, 2014.

88. Nona Willis Aronowitz, "Millennials reject 'lazy, entitled' label: 'Who are they talking about?'" Today News. May 16, 2013. http://www.today.com/news/millennials-reject-lazy-entitled-label-who-are-they-talking-about-1C9948170, accessed Aug. 1, 2014.

group as a "spiritually homeless" generation.[89] I have seen my friends wander a lost highway seeking after what can only be called holiness, but not finding it with Oprah or any other guru. We have spent years approaching spirituality as "consumers," searching for the right movement to satisfy the impulses leading us to seek after righteousness.[90]

But maybe our impulsiveness is one of the keys that can unlock true holiness in any generation.

A Divine Impulse

Impulsiveness is a hallmark characteristic of today's generation.[91] We tend to get what we want. We are prone to impulse buying more than any other generation. Unfortunately, Satan is very aware of our impulsiveness, and exploits our impulsive tendencies to provoke temptation. When we believe Satan's lies, we impulsively act in ways that only serve a selfish sinful nature.

Now, if God desires us "to be holy as He is holy," then why would He allow (much less *create*) an impulsive nature in us?

First, it is evident that God Himself has impulses. For example, while we were still sinners, God demonstrated His love by *impulsively* giving His only Son to die for us (John 3:16, Rom. 5:8). Secondly, note how God's impulse to love also causes Him to *act*, and not just act any old way, but to act rashly, extravagantly, compassionately, and sacrificially! God committed the *ultimate* impulse buy: *He gave His only Son to die for us!*

Could it be that we are impulsive because we are made in His image?

I believe God created us by design with an impulsive nature so that we would have the impulse to love God, love others, and to live a holy life acting upon divine love. I believe God will use this generation, my generation, to deliver His holiness to a world that has never needed it more desperately.

My generation is uniquely equipped to respond to this divine impulse to love. Studies show that relationships matter to us more than anything else, and therefore, we excel at commitment.[92] When we fully commit ourselves in life and relationship to God, we are seeking His holiness, His very Spirit, to provide us with the impulse to love.

---

89. David Kinnaman, "Three Spiritual Journeys of Millennials," Barna Group, May 9, 2013, https://www.barna.org/barna-update/millennials/612-three-spiritual-journeys-of-millennials#.U55b_cTpdO4, accessed Aug. 1, 2014.

90. Naomi Schaefer Riley, "Bringing Millennials Back to Church," *New York Post*, April 27, 2014, http://nypost.com/2014/04/27/bringing-millennials-back-to-church/, accessed Aug. 1, 2014.

91. Brad Tuttle, "Millennials Are Biggest Suckers for Selfish Impulse Buys," *Time*, April 27, 2012, http://business.time.com/2012/04/27/millennials-are-biggest-suckers-for-selfish-impulse-buys/, accessed Aug 1, 2014.

92. "5 Reasons Millennials Stay Connected to Church," Barna Group, Sep. 17, 2013, https://www.barna.org/barna-update/millennials/635-5-reasons-millennials-stay-connected-to-church#.VEWTGCge3dp, accessed Aug. 1, 2014.

A Divine Relationship

Because the relationship between husband and wife is ultimately intended to reflect the relationship between Christ and the Church, I have gained a much fuller understanding of this relational process in the time I have been married. Marriage is the only relationship in which two individuals having completely different natures become one flesh. Because that is God's intention for us, when we join our life to His in total commitment, His response is to take us as His bride and give us all that is His, including His holy impulse to love.

When my wife and I married, we committed ourselves to each other, forsaking all others. My impulse to have a life apart from her ended—it died—because that is the only way we could truly be committed to one another. It was a commitment that had not yet been put to the ultimate test, but the very commitment itself demonstrated our willingness to belong to and love one another.

As time has continued, our love for one another has deepened even more than either of us thought was possible, and we have faced the storms of life joined in love together and emerged unmoved. Nothing has been able to separate our love for one another because we are joined together. I expect that, as we mature in our life and relationship together, our love will continue to strengthen and grow beyond our wildest imaginings.

Why would that be any less true of our relationship with God?

It is holy and pleasing to God when we sacrificially offer ourselves as His instruments (Romans 6:13, 12:1-2). When we commit ourselves to the Lord as His bride, we begin a new chapter in our relationship with Jesus, and our relationship continues to mature and grow throughout storms of life, granted we remain committed. The deeper love and commitment we have in Christ, the stronger our impulse to love. And we love the ones He loves because His impulse is in us, is a part of us.

What my generation has not yet figured out is that we already are a generation of holy people. We may not call it *sanctification* or *holiness*, but we do call it *love*. Instead of speaking in platitudes about *consecration* and *crisis experience*, we call it *commitment* and *relationship*.

My Millennial generation pastor friend, whom I quoted at the beginning of this essay, revealed a problem in the church that God has already solved. Although my friend does not believe that "holiness" is relevant or important, he is nevertheless a holy person who encourages holiness in others. Only a holy impulse to love coupled with a sacred relationship with God could have inspired him to say these words: "God's love has brought me joy. I want to encourage you to pursue God without hesitation and to be a contradiction to the sinful nature that separates us from maturity."

May future generations accept this simple holy call to love and be committed to the Lord.

James Travis Young serves as pastor of Marshall, Texas, First Church of the Nazarene. A native of East Texas, Travis was called to be a missionary at age four, and God has ignited within him a missional passion to plant churches by discipling marginalized individuals. He and his wife Mandie have two daughters and, according to God's will, are seeking cross-cultural ministry opportunities domestically and globally.

The Message of Holiness and the Holistic Mission of the Church:

Building Trans-generational Bridges

Mónica Mastronardi–Fernández

The new century has brought great challenges for the church. The world and the context of ministry are rapidly changing as are also the people to whom we minister.

There is a chasm between new generations and those influenced by modernity (the perspective of the vast majority of us Christian leaders). Many of us now face the frustration that results from our own incompetence to attract, to disciple and to engage new generations in God's mission.

However, the good news is that—for the first time in history—four generations are alive at the same time. Today we have the opportunity to make disciples in ways that includes the third and fourth generations.

We need to find new and more effective methods and strategies. For this purpose we will dialogue, from our Wesleyan theological biblical framework, with two related sciences that are seeking to innovate their methods of training and recruitment of young human resources. We will refer to the new competency-based approach to education and the management of human resources for recruiting new talents in companies.

The 15/24 Window

Young people between 15 and 24 represent 18 percent of the world population.[93] But this window of opportunity is not eternal. Due to our aging demographics, by 2050 this group will decrease to 13.5 percent.[94]

Children and young people are the most vulnerable population in Latin America. Many are mistreated, abused, marginalized, abandoned, manipulated, and enslaved. Our cities have become death camps for children and youth.[95]

---

93. In "Youth and Millennium Development Goals," United Nations Department of Economic and Social Affairs (DESA). http://undesadspd.org/Youth/OurWork/YouthandtheMDGs.aspx. Accessed August 25, 2014.

94. Walter Campos Moraga, "Cosas Que no Duele Saber Sobre los Jóvenes." Video on www.teletica.com, August 12, 2014.

95. J. Yunes and T. Zubarew, "Mortalidad por Causas Violentas en Adolescentes y Jóvenes. Un Desafío para la Región de las Américas," Revista Brasileira de Epidemiología, Oficina Panamericana de la Salud, Vol. 1, 1999. http://www.scielo.br/scielo.php?pid=S1415-790X1999000200002&script=sci_arttext. Accessed August 25, 2014.

Today churches face an accelerated desertion by their youth. Various studies estimate that between 43 to 59 percent of fifteen-year-olds leave the church. In his book *The Bridger Generation*, Thom Rainer states that only 4 percent of the "Bridges" (linkers), the Generation "Y," are or will be evangelicals[96].

The Needs of the Millennials

What attracts Millennials—the young people belonging to generation "Y"? The agencies that recruit young talent have discovered that new generations are more demanding when they are asked to commit their loyalty.

1. *Millennials are optimistic about the future.* Millennials want to contribute to changing the world; they are more optimistic about the future than their parents. They want to create, to innovate, and to propose solutions.[97]

2. *They look for attractive, challenging, and innovative projects.* Today's young people are drawn to projects providing unique experiences.[98] They ask themselves, "How can I participate? How can I contribute?"

3. *They seek opportunities for personal development.* Generation Y highly values ongoing professional training as well as opportunities to experience other cultures.[99] They like constant challenges because they get bored quickly.[100]

4. *They expect a cooperative culture.* Young people prefer to work in companies that promote values and cultivate two-way communication, where people are not discriminated by age, experience, gender, and other factors. They prefer to work in businesses that encourage informality,[101] creativity, experimentation, and collaboration. They want organizations where

---

96. Cited in: Chris Jackson. Alejados de Dios. http://vidacristiana.com/articulos-de revista/cubrir-historias/12283-alejados-de-dios. Accessed September 26, 2104.

97. Opinion of Hector Gutierrez, President of the Deloitte Foundation Peru, cited in Karina Montoya, "Deloitte: El Talento Más Joven de Hoy Busca una Empresa Socialmente Responsable." Dec. 2, 2013, In Gestión: El Diario de Economía y Negocios de Perú. de: http://gestion.pe/empleo-management/deloitte-talento-mas-joven-hoy-busca-empresa-socialmente-responsable-2082489. Accessed June 12, 2014.

98. Tania Moscoso (Junio 24, 2014). "El Talento Joven ya no Busca Trabajo; Busca Experiencias." In AEDIPE (Asociación Española de Dirección y Desarrollo de Personas). www.aedipecentro.org. Accessed June 9, 2014.

99. Ibid.

100. Cinthia Membreño (2014). "¿Cómo Captar el Talento Joven? Estudio de ManPower: Empresas Nicas Deben Cambiar su Paradigma Laboral." En Confidencial-Economía June 17, 2014. http://www.confidencial.com.ni/articulo/17947/iquest-como-captar-el-talento-jovenn. Accessed July 9, 2014.

101. Ibid.

innovative ideas are valued, where each person is placed in an appropriate role according to their skills and experience.[102]

5. *They are attracted by mentoring and coaching programs.* "Having a mentor as a companion from the time they entry the company is a differential factor much appreciated by new generations. Also the support received from a *coach*, who brings out the best that a person has (which often was not so visible to the person involved) is another crucial factor which helps young talents to identify with their company."[103]

Refreshing the Wesleyan Model of Disciple-making in the 21st Century

Can we respond to these needs and expectations of the new generations while remaining true to our biblical theological tradition and to our values and mission and vision as Nazarenes? The answer is a resounding "Yes," but it's time to return to truly Wesleyan principles of making disciples.

Latin American educational institutions are implementing a new form of education based on skill development. The centerpiece of this education focuses on two aspects: the "results" (the efficient performance of the student in a function) and the "follow up" (continuing education).

These areas remind us that we need to rebuild four bridges to disciple new generations in God's mission. We have valuable resources in our own theological tradition that we need to recover and implement in creative ways with the guidance of the Holy Spirit.

1. Learning to Learn:[104]

The objectives of our curriculum should focus on the skills that the disciple needs to develop. The primary role of teachers is to train children and young people to be responsible for contributing to their spiritual growth. As Wesleyans. we believe that growth is the fruit of grace, but also of obedience. The life of holiness is not static but dynamic, and it results in permanent growth in Christlikeness.

This approach puts more emphasis on the mastery of the tools of knowledge rather than knowledge itself. We need to train Christians who are more dependent

102. Suma 3 Consultores, "6 Estrategias de las Empresas para Reclutar y Retener Talento," 2013. http://suma3consultores.com.ar/6-estrategias-de-grandes-empresas-para-reclutar-y-retener-talento/. Accessed July 15, 2014.

103. Moscoso, "El Talento."

104. Ruth Diaz Bello, "Competencias Educativas. Definición Tipos y Componentes," 2013, http://www.authorstream.com/Presentation/MarielaVilar-1926353-competencias-educativas/. Accessed July 12, 2014. Elisabetta Pagliarulo, "La Educación por Competencias. Un Desafío para la Inserción Social Equitativa," Lecture presented in the Congreso Iberiamericano de Educación, September 13-15, 2010, Buenos Aires, Argentina. phttp://www.chubut.edu.ar/descargas/secundaria/congreso/COMPETENCIASBASICAS/RLE3185_Pagliarulo.pdf, Accessed July 9, 2014.

on the Holy Spirit through strengthening our teaching personal and communal spiritual disciplines, and this will naturally create opportunities for creative and innovative theological dialogue. We need to develop a practical theology of dependence on the Holy Spirit. How does the Holy Spirit teach me how to be more like Christ? What tools can I use in my context to facilitate my growth as a child of God?

2. Learning to Do:

The focus is to form disciples holistically to be fit to work in multiple environments and life situations. The life of purity (holiness) should not just end in satisfying our own spiritual need; rather, it should enable us to be intentional instruments for the extension of the kingdom of God.

In the past the Christian churches have been more reactionary, protecting our communities of faith against being infected by the sin of society (the world). But we need to reclaim our role as salt and light, healing communities, institutions, and governments, transforming them holistically with the light of the gospel.

We need to recover an optimistic vision of grace to accompany activist young people. In our tradition, we understand that the practice of Christian love is essential to our continued faith. Therefore, we should open more spaces for young people to participate in the ministries and ministerial leadership of the church, providing training in ministry skills and appropriate mentoring. Children and young people should be involved in mission according to their gifts, calling, and passion as soon as possible in their Christian life.

As Wesleyans we should not be afraid to try new strategies nor to dispose of old strategies that are no longer working. For this, we need the contributions of new generations to develop creative ways to serve communities and to make disciples.

3. Learning to Live Together:

The hallmark of the Wesleyan movement was the dynamic of mutual care in classes and bands. One of our challenges is to develop that environment of intimate fellowship in the faith community, a community where we are accountable to each other, where we strengthen each other to serve the world, and where the life of holiness is learned through living models.

As a multicultural church, we need to define, to teach, and to practice specific values for life in our society. How would a holy person make a difference in society? How are holy relationships different? This exercise of hermeneutics must become a cooperative process, a joint construction of knowledge based on a fair and honest exchange of Nazarenes from different cultures and generations.

4. Learning to Be:

We need to define our personal values as Nazarenes, values that are visible in the way we think, speak, and act in all areas of life. This involves self-discovery through the eyes of God (self-knowledge) projected in the Church and society from that authentic regenerated self of holiness in the image of Christ.

We can only transfer values by example. Here we see the importance of the role of the mentor, spiritual guide, or elder brother, typical of our Wesleyan tradition. We urgently need to be transformed into a discipling community, where each one takes on the responsibility to guide another one in the Christian life and service.

Conclusion

New generations present the challenge to the church of developing spiritual leadership, effective strategies, and relevant methodology. We need to return to the radical discipleship of Jesus and to rediscover the precious values of our own Christian formation in the Wesleyan tradition. Trusting the talent of youth in mission has been constant in the history of salvation and in our tradition. Only thus will we become a relevant church for the new generations. Only then will we continue to be an instrument of God's holy love transforming this world.

Monica Mastronardi Fernandez serves as the Vice President of Institutional Development for the Nazarene Seminary of the Americas (SENDAS) in Costa Rica and the General Editor of the School of Leadership Program for the Mesoamerica Region. In addition, she teaches courses in discipleship, leadership, and church development at all levels of theological education. Monica has various publications, including the well-known Bas c Discipleship Lessons, *which has been translated into more than twenty languages and dialects.*

Holiness in Postmodern Times:
Revaluing the Wesleyan DNA for More Effective Ministry Today
Rubén Eduardo Fernández

The world has gone through some drastic changes. Through technology, we learn in seconds what has happened on the other side of the planet. People access music, books, films, and different versions of the Bible on their phones. It is no longer necessary to have an office since everything can be done with a laptop. People are changing the way they think, how they see the world, what they value, and how they make decisions. Spirituality is back, and emotions take center stage. It seems that logic and systematic thinking are fast becoming extinct. Values are relative; to feel good becomes the most important criterion. For many, abstract truth does not exist; only personal truths count. Institutionalized religion is rejected.

How is the Church of the Nazarene dealing with these changes? Many Wesleyan congregations feel powerless. They preach to a public, who no longer exists, ghosts of people who went to church thirty or forty years ago. They are blind to the fact that their congregation changed with the world. The children who come to Sunday School disappear when they become adolescents. The youth want their own meeting on Saturdays, but prefer the other church nearby where the music is good. Pastors, who insist that to go forward is to go back to the old ways of modernity, are ironically, "Saved, Sanctified, and Petrified."

Research shows that about 80 percent of people living in Mexico profess a strong postmodern popular religiosity. However, a survey carried out in a Mexican Nazarene district found that 56 percent of the pastors cannot define the postmodern movement or identify its features; 20 percent even have the wrong concept. In this state of profound ignorance of the reality of the people they serve, it is not surprising that pastors have found no effective means to disciple believers and to minister to the community.

Would making a few cosmetic changes—such as changes to music, fellowship, preaching, or service to the community—really make a difference? At least we would look more like the popular nondenominational churches and keep some more members and attract some new people. Wouldn't it be better to search our

Wesleyan roots for our own models that could renew our passion and ways of doing church?

Packer wrote, "The recovery of the old truth that has been a means of blessing in the past can become again, in God's hands, an instrument of blessing to the present . . ."[105] Holiness churches have a message and a legacy and, above all, an experience to share. We need to go back to Wesley's strongly Christ-centered gospel, anchored in the spiritual realm but with feet firmly placed on the ground.

John Wesley, a Man of Change in an Era of Change

Wesley's Britain was full of extreme poverty, alcoholics, destroyed homes, child abuse, lurid theatrical productions, ineffectual churches, greed in the commercial markets, and rise of the new industrialized poor, as well as corruption in politics. McKenna summarizes, "Only a miracle could save England from a bloody revolution."[106] The miracle came through a movement of the Spirit that changed the destiny of a nation ruined by immorality and vices.

The Evangelical revival arose out of a new experience of the grace of God and Jesus in the power of the Holy Spirit. Without losing its genuine enthusiasm, it excluded excesses. Wesley and those who followed him were involved in bringing about profound social changes. Wesley knew how to combine order with democracy, freedom with discipline.

In explaining the Core Values of the Church of the Nazarene, our General Superintendents said, "We are positioned to make a major contribution to our post-modern world . . . We believe that human nature, and ultimately society, can be radically and permanently changed by the grace of God. We have an irrepressible confidence in this message of hope, which flows from the heart of our holy God."[107]

How Can We Recapture the Wesleyan DNA to Minister Efficiently Today?

I would like to make some suggestions about how we can rediscover practical elements of the Wesleyan movement that can be transferred to our current situation.

A Return to Integrity

Our forefathers in the faith had a passion for the Holy Spirit and his work. But today we no longer preach holiness, or we preach it badly. We are so general,

---

105. .Packer J. I., *El renacer de la santidad* (Miami: Caribe, 1995), 11-12.

106. McKenna, David, Wesleyanos en el Siglo XXI: La Proclamación del Evangelio con Pasión y Propósito (Kansas City: Casa Nazarena, 2000), 12.

107. General Superintendents, "Core Values: We Are a Missional People," http://nazarene.org/ministries/administration/centennial/core/missional/display.html, accessed June 1, 2014.

so ambiguous. But what is worse, many have ceased to live holy lives. We have allowed ourselves to become used to the culture around us, ceasing to be salt and light. The neon lights of the world dazzle us, and their corruption contaminates us.

We retain the discourse of holiness maintaining an outward "image of piety." Often, we are more concerned with the "image we give" than the fruit of the Spirit. Jesus said, "You will know them by what they do" (Matthew 7:16, NIV).

The postmodern generation is looking for models, principled leaders who are authentic people. We must be their models of integrity.

A Return to Personal and Communal Discipleship

Wesley's discipleship was based on the experience of the fullness of the Holy Spirit and the cultivation of the spiritual disciplines in the lives of the Methodists. Wesley implemented his discipleship system with societies, bands, and classes of varied sizes—each with different functions according to needs. People gathered to worship, to study the Word, to confess their sins, and to be ministered to.

Post-moderns need to be in groups. They discover truth more effectively in highly interactive group settings where there are real relationships, where they can learn in acts of shared discovery.

A Return to Social Holiness

For Wesley, discipleship implied training and mobilizing the members to action. Wesley affirmed that there was no holiness that was not social holiness. His movement influenced great social movements, such as education for all and the abolition of slavery.

The postmodern believer finds meaning for living in serving. Indignant about injustices, he wants to reclaim the rights of the marginalized. We must recover these concepts for a more biblical and Wesleyan ministry today. The General Superintendents expressed our need to be compassionate, "We are committed to inviting people to faith, to caring for those in need, to standing against injustice and with the oppressed, to working to protect and preserve the resources of God's creation, and to including in our fellowship all who will call upon the name of the Lord."[108]

A Return to the Supernatural in the Gospel

Have we stopped believing in God? Divine healing is one of our Articles of Faith, but we rarely pray for the sick as they did in the past. We run away from

---

108. Ibid.

the "powers of evil" instead of confronting them and liberating people. We need to re-experience more power of prayer and trust that God will do great things.

A Return to Healthy and Contextual Worship

Should our worship be based on hymns from the past or clappy choruses? Just because a tune is catchy doesn't necessarily make it a good avenue for worship. Equally, the age of a song has little bearing on its theological merit. Some songs are extremely anthropocentric, where God gets no credit.

We need to recover our "Mission in Worship" as expressed by the General Superintendents, "It is in the preaching of the Word, the celebration of the sacraments, the public reading of the Scripture, the singing of hymns and choruses, corporate prayer, and the presenting of our tithes and offerings that we know most clearly what it means to be the people of God."[109] Our worship must be solidly directed toward God to shape us as the people of God.

A Return to Evangelical Ecumenism

Speaking of our first core value, "We Are a Christian People," the General Superintendents stated, "We embrace John Wesley's concept of the universal spirit, by which we have fellowship with all those who affirm the vital center of Scripture, and we extend toleration to those who disagree with us on matters not essential to salvation."[110]

Often, we Nazarenes isolate ourselves from other denominations believing that the holiness message belongs just to us and that our understanding of it is the only one. Eunice Bryant says that Wesley had "the ability to synthesize the best elements of several theological traditions." Especially in the doctrine of Christian perfection, he made "an original synthesis of the Protestant ethic of grace with the Catholic ethic of holiness."[111] He also maintained dialogue with other traditions—such as the Moravians—in order to understand the faith better.[112]

In summary, let's ask God to help us to inject these six elements of our DNA back into our church life so we can become a people ready to reach our postmodern world.

109. Ibid.

110. General Superintendents, "Core Values: We Are a Missional People," http://nazarene.org/ministries/administration/centennial/core/christian/display.html, accessed June 1, 2014.

111. Eunice Bryant, "Theology in Action: The Theology of John Wesley," D. Min. thesis. Nazarene Theogical Seminary, 1982, 359.

112. William Greathouse, *Desde los Apóstoles Hasta Wesley: Un Resumen de la Perfección Cristiana* (Kansas City: Casa Nazarena, 1978), 124

Ruben E. Fernandez is the Regional Education and Clergy Development Coordinator for the Mesoamerica Region, in addition to being the President of the Nazarene Seminary of the Americas (SENDAS) in San Jose, Costa Rica. Ruben has served as pastor, educator, district superintendent, and field strategy coordinator for the Church of the Nazarene. He has authored two books on pastoral administration and leadership.

A Contagious Holiness:

Jesus, Dexter, and Walter White at the Super Bowl

by JR. Forasteros

"Don't get me wrong—I *love* the show. My wife and I watch it all the time. But aren't you going to get in trouble for blogging about it?"

It was early Sunday morning, and my friend Tim, who coordinates my pastoral prayer team, had met me for prayer, as was our pre-worship ritual. We always take a few minutes to catch up, and this Lord's Day our conversation had turned to *Dexter* Season 6. *Dexter* is a TV show that ran on the Showtime network for 8 seasons, a show whose titular character and protagonist was a serial killer.

I had decided to do a weekly episode recap of the sixth season on my blog, and Tim was worried I'd get in trouble. After all, Nazarene pastors aren't supposed to watch TV shows with serial-killer protagonists, much less publicly admit they watch said shows on a *blog*. Right?

Tim's discomfort was rooted not in moral outrage; he and his wife loved the show as much as we did. He was uncertain because he expected that the institution of the Church of the Nazarene would reject watching *Dexter* and that I, as a representative of that institution, was endangering my job and pastoral authority by watching it.

Tim's fear might have been a bit exaggerated, but it's not unfounded. The Church of the Nazarene has a long history of disengagement from popular culture. As an outworking of our commitment to a personal lifestyle of holiness, we have long challenged our members to abstain from things of the world deemed unholy. At one time that was the circus and movie theaters. But even as we've moved to more nuanced, moderate positions on those godless dens of iniquity, the same assumption still looms large: popular culture is toxic to our spiritual health.

But while the Church is sitting on the sidelines—or possibly even skipping the tailgate in the parking lot—the larger culture is still playing the game. At the 2014 Super Bowl, Bruno Mars crooned to an audience of millions that he "Never had much faith in love or miracles . . . I'm born again every time you spend the night. 'Cause your sex takes me to paradise . . . 'Cause you make me feel like I've been locked out of heaven for too long."[113]

Game of Thrones, Breaking Bad and *The Walking Dead* dominate cable television in North America, and none of them is shy to offer profound theological reflections. *Game of Thrones* suggests the world is a cold place full of distant, ineffective gods. It's a world where good is for suckers and where only the evil (or at least selfish) get ahead. *Breaking Bad* laments that even a kind, good father can become a monster, illustrating the problem of Original Sin far more effectively than any sermon in recent memory. And *The Walking Dead* constantly muses on the nature of God, salvation, damnation, and resurrection. (Once, in an abandoned Baptist church featuring a very Catholic crucifix. How's that for spiritual confusion?)

And don't forget *Dexter*: the reason I chose to blog through each episode of Season 6 is that season asked the question, "Can God save a serial killer?" Dexter has probably never heard the term Prevenient Grace, but he was still musing on it.

With these and countless further examples of spiritual conversations our popular culture is having right now, the Church cannot afford to maintain her position of separation and disengagement. While our culture has become less institutionally Christian, it has not become any less spiritual. In the wake of Christendom, people are asking more (and better) questions than ever. If we choose to remain distant and uninterested, we're surrendering the opportunity we have to be the image of God to those who are desperately seeking a glimpse of something holy.

Fortunately, we find a vision for cultural engagement in Jesus himself. Jesus reinterpreted the Levitical view of Holiness-as-separation to one of Holiness-as-engagement. He is a model for offering a distinctive, holy perspective in the conversations our culture is having.

We can understand the Holiness Code of Leviticus essentially as wholeness-through-separation. For Ancient Israel, an individual's body was symbolically equivalent to one's house, to the nation, and to the world itself. All these symbols were wrapped up in the Temple, the cultural and political center of Israel. The purity codes in the *Torah* regulated everything from individual bodily functions (especially those sexual or health-related) to worship practices.

The logic beneath all these commands is wholeness—anybody (or institution) that deviates from the normative whole is unclean. It belongs outside the community. It must be brought back into wholeness (through cultic sacrifice) to be welcomed back in.

---

113. Bruno Mars, "Locked Out of Heaven," 2014.

Leviticus refers to wholeness and fragmentation by the familiar terms "clean" and "unclean" respectively. Something unclean threatens the integrity of the Self, the House, the Nation and even the World. The Temple—as the place that restores and maintains cleanliness—becomes primarily about protecting God's people by ensuring they remain clean/whole/holy. Unclean things make clean things unclean.[114]

Those who are unclean—a person with a physical deformity, an immigrant, a sinner—threaten the health and wholeness (and Holiness) of everyone else. They must be removed or avoided, so they don't taint the larger community. In this interpretation, Holiness is a fragile thing that must be protected. The Holiness of the community of God is constantly threatened by contamination from the outside, unclean world. The People of God must be diligent to root out uncleanness and to keep themselves separate from the larger world.

The parallels to contemporary Holiness communities are striking. In the Church of the Nazarene, many of our historic "special rules" (now called the Code of Christian Conduct) revolve not around embodying fruit of the Spirit, but abstaining—from drinking, dancing, the circus, etc. We imagine our church buildings to be latter-day temples, protecting the People of God when we retreat from the unclean world. Those who are unclean sinners are kept outside the Church, at arm's length.

An observer of our Holiness churches is likely to conclude that Holiness is a precious, precarious quality that must be protected and preserved from contamination. But is Holiness really so fragile?

Jesus' own example indicates the answer is "No." Jesus' life challenges our assumptions about Temples, our bodies, and the very nature of Holiness.

According to the New Testament, Jesus is Himself a locus of Holiness. John presents Jesus as nothing less than the new Temple of God. In John 1, describing Jesus as the eternal, uncreated Word of God, John tells us that "the Word became flesh and *lived* among us" (John 1:14, emphasis mine). The Greek word John uses, *skenoo*, literally means "to pitch a tent," and it's the same word the Septuagint (Greek Old Testament) uses to refer to the Tabernacle. John tells us, then, that Jesus—the eternal, uncreated Word of God—became a tabernacle among us. Jesus is a walking, breathing Temple, a locus of holiness.

Jesus himself confirms this when he predicts the Temple's destruction in chapter 2. In a surprisingly friendly round of questioning by Jerusalem's religious elite in the wake of his temple cleansing, Jesus says, "Destroy this Temple, and

---

114. For an excellent analysis of the categories of Clean and Unclean in Leviticus, see Mary Douglas' landmark essay "The Forbidden Animals of Leviticus."

in three days I will raise it up." In response to his questioners' ensuing confusion, John tells us Jesus "was speaking of *the temple of his body*" (John 2:18, 21, emphasis mine).

If Jesus' body is the Temple of God, then Jesus is the very embodiment of God's holiness on Earth. And what do we see Jesus doing in the Gospels? Frankly, all sorts of things a holy person ought not be doing. Jesus touched dead bodies, persons with communicable diseases, menstruating women, and more.[115]

But what we see repeatedly in the Gospels is that Jesus is not contaminated by his contact with the unclean. His holiness is never in danger. It's not a fragile quality Jesus must protect and preserve. Rather, Jesus is lavish with his love. Not only is he happy to party with tax collectors and sinners, he heals the sick. He welcomes the outsiders. He raises the dead.

Jesus' holiness is the dangerous quality. Jesus' holiness is what is contagious. In the face of his bodily presence, *sin* is what's in trouble. In the presence of Jesus, the sick are healed. Demons abandon those they had possessed. The broken are made whole. The sinners are transformed into saints. The dead are raised to life.

Jesus commands his followers to embody this same dangerous holiness. Consider that famous parable we call the "Good Samaritan." Before the hero of the story arrives, two religious leaders come upon the beaten man and cross to the other side of the road. This is the point where many contemporary Christians shake their heads in disgust at these religious persons, but we have no prohibition against touching dead bodies.

A generous reading of the story imagines these two men as conscientious, holy men. The *Torah* strictly prohibits touching dead bodies; they make one unclean, contaminating the person of God. Their crossing of the road is a move to "avoid even the appearance of evil," to keep themselves clean and uncontaminated by the world.

And yet these devout men are not the heroes of Jesus' story. For Jesus, a Holiness that does not risk, that does not embrace the dying, the unclean, the sinners is not Holiness at all because it is nothing like the God who abandoned Heaven to embrace the world, that the world through his embrace might be rescued, might in fact be made Holy.

Though Jesus has ascended to the throne of Heaven, his body remains present in the world. As Paul teaches, the Church is in fact Jesus' body, and is still God's temple.[116] Our posture toward the larger culture ought to be one of engagement

115. See, for instance, Mark 5:35-42; Matthew 8:1-3; Mark 5:25-29.

116. Consider Paul's words in 1 Corinthians 6, "Don't you know that your body is the Temple of the Holy Spirit?" In the Greek, the second person pronoun is plural, but the object, "body," is singular. Paul is referring not to our individual bodies, but to the corporate body of the Church. We are the Temple of God, just as Jesus is.

and love, not separation and condemnation. We need not affirm that popular culture is good, that God is not present there, that the world will contaminate us if we do not remain separate. In the face of sin and evil, the Church is dangerous. When we embrace the world as Jesus embraced the world (and us), we are the contagious element.

Let us take our contagious, life-saving love into the world around us. Let us find the light of Jesus in every place. Let us enter these conversations—not as conquistadors bringing God to a godless place—but as pilgrims anxious to find God in the unlikeliest of places.

JR. Forasteros is the teaching pastor at Catalyst Community Church in Dallas, TX. He loves searching for how God is working in the world outside the Church and helping the Church to follow God into those places. He also loves karaoke and Batman. JR. and his wife Amanda love setting off on new adventures, finding the best out-of-the-way restaurants in town, and catching a good movie whenever they can.

Living Holiness in Latin America
Fernando Almeida

The title of this book challenges us to re-think our doctrine of holiness, thinking of our current times and context. Along these lines, and based on my experience of living in Latin-American contexts for the past nine years, I would like to propose some practical aspects that require consideration while ministering in these countries as a holiness church.

Brief Overview of Latin-American Context

I would like to give, in broad strokes, a brief overview of three cultural tenets that affect the way people in Latin American live out their relationship with God.

The first element to take into consideration is that the people in Latin America are very emotionally expressive. In a study on cultures of moderation and expression, José A. Soto, Roberto W. Levenson, and Rachel Ebling, assert the centrality of emotions in Latin cultures and continue their research with a comparison between Chinese and Mexican culture. What they found about the Mexican culture could be said about any other Latin-American culture:

> Relationships in Mexican culture are characterized by high levels of affection. In Mexican culture, affect is more openly accepted and more highly valued than in Anglo culture ... 'It is through ... an ability to experience in response to environment, emotional feelings, and to express these to one another and share them that one experiences the greatest rewards and satisfactions in life.'"[117]

This has significant implications as one considers ministering in this context, which we will further explore below.

Another element to bear into account is the background of oppression and exploitation in which Latin American countries were brought into existence. They came into existence because of the expansion enterprises of both Spain

---

117. J.A. Soto, Robert W. Levenson, and Rachel Ebling, "Cultures of Moderation and Expression: Emotional Experience, Behavior, and Physiology in Chinese Americans and Mexican Americans," *Emotion*, 5(2), 2005, 155. http://ist-socrates. berkeley.edu/~ucbpl/docs/84-Cultures%20of%20Moderation05.pdf.

and Portugal. The indigenous native peoples of these discovered countries were subdued through force, and they were exploited as slaves for many years.

Nicole Gregory describes some of the consequences that have remained prevalent in this context, "Inequality of wealth and disparity of power and influence are Latin American's greatest curses and are at the root of many of the developmental, social, criminal, and political problems that continue to plague the region."[118] This type of background and related current consequences affect the way nations are governed and thus how a holiness church needs to be an active voice promoting social justice, while being careful not to create its own structure of oppression.

The last element I would like to highlight is the element of corruption. The 2013 Global Corruption Barometer reported a few interesting statistics for some Latin American Countries, "Bolivia and Mexico topped the list for Latin American countries, with 36 percent and 33 percent of respondents respectively, reporting having paid a bribe. Venezuela, Peru, Paraguay and Colombia also had notable levels of bribery, with between 20 and nearly 30 percent of respondents having paid a bribe." [119] This type of report reveals the urgency that holiness not only can be thought of as a doctrine or an ideal. We Christians must live holiness in our daily lives if we are to make a real difference in the world.

Living Holiness in Latin America

In a Latin American context, we must express the doctrine of holiness in very practical ways. What follows are three elements necessary for any holiness practice in this culture.

Holiness must be felt.

In this emotional expressive and strongly relationship-oriented context, holiness is an experience that must be felt. It's not as much a doctrine to be understood as it is an experience to be lived.

This has a strong bearing on liturgy in holiness churches within this context. Worship is very lively, very informal, characterized by passionate preaching, and hardly a service goes by without an altar call—whether it is for salvation, sanctification, or to present a personal need before God. There is a strong sense that people want to feel God at work in their lives, which is quite a different approach

118. Nicole Gregory, "Inequality in Latin America," *Study Mode*, November 2013, http://www.studymode.com/essays/Inequality-In-Latin-America-44073841.html, Accessed June 6, 2014.

119. Marguerite Cawley, "Survey Highlights Latin America Police Corruption," *In Sight Crime*, July 9, 2013. http://www.insightcrime.org/news-briefs/survey-highlights-latin-america-police-corruption. Accessed June 6, 2014.

from some other parts of the world heavily influenced by the Enlightenment's emphasis on quiet reason.

In his sermon "The Nature of Enthusiasm," as well as in his sermon "The Way To The Kingdom," Wesley advocated for a religion of the heart, explaining that orthodoxy is not enough. Christians need to experience *orthokardia*, meaning, having the right heart:

> A man may be orthodox in every point; he may not only espouse right opinions, but zealously defend them against all opposers; he may think justly concerning the incarnation of our Lord, concerning the ever-blessed Trinity, and every other doctrine contained in the oracles of God; ... and yet it is possible he may have no religion at all, no more than a Jew, Turk, or pagan. He may be almost as orthodox —as the devil, ... and may, [sic] all the while be as great a stranger as he to the religion of the heart.[120]

Although in these two sermons Wesley argued for a "religion of the heart," that does not mean that he neglected the content in favor of emotions. Rather, he kept a balance between the two in order to guard against what he called "enthusiasm," which is probably the danger that Latin Americans leaders need to avoid as they lead their congregations. People need to realize that they realize that they must grow in depth as they understand more about God and bring their faith into their daily life.

Holiness must transform our day-to-day living

The dangers of shallow Christian living are present in Latin America as a whole. In my personal experience, we have many Christians struggling with simple issues of integrity in a corrupt society. One such issue is tax evasion. We repeatedly hear the phrase, "but everybody does it," from Christians as a justification for evading taxes.

This personal experience is amplified as we consider the statistics of countries where evangelicals made it into the political circles. Even these countries have a poor score in corruption rates. For example, in Guatemala some say more than 50 percent of the population is evangelical Protestant, yet it's one of the countries that scores worst in corruption, kidnapping, and extortion. In light of this, one needs to ask, how are we as Christians making a difference?

---

120. John Wesley, "Sermon 7: The Way to the Kingdom," *Sermons, on Several Occasions* (Oak Harbor: Logos, 1999).

Jesus called us to be salt and light in this world (Mat. 5:13-16), and as a holiness church in Latin America, we should recover the understanding that the message of heart transformation—although it is an inward experience—needs to be worked out externally in behaviors and attitudes that reflect this inner personal transformation.

Holiness must address social justice issues.

Latin America is the birthplace of Liberation Theology. One of the leading theologians from this theological perspective asks, "How are we to talk about a God who is revealed as love in a situation characterized by poverty and oppression? . . . How are we to acknowledge that God makes us a free gift of love and justice when we have before us the suffering of the innocent?"[121]

Our holiness message should also have something to say in light of the inequalities, social injustices, and oppressive environment. As a church, we should have a message of hope and deliverance for our people. One of things we see in the life of the Wesleys is that they did not only preach a doctrine or an ideal, but they spoke to the social issues that were oppressing people in their time.

Conclusion

In summary, as one rethinks holiness in a Latin American context, we come to three conclusions.

1. Holiness needs to allow for emotional expression without falling into the shallowness of emotionalism

2. Holiness needs to be fleshed out in daily living. "Called Unto Holiness" must be more than a catch phrase or a beautiful ideal that one needs to strive for, but never really achieves. Holiness must be lived out in day-to-day decisions and behaviors.

3. Holiness needs to address social justice issues. Holiness is transformational, and it needs to be brought into our social systems so that our churches are relevant in their contexts.

Fernando Almeida is a global missionary with the church of the Nazarene, originally from Portugal, who served for nine years in South America. Presently, he serves on Faculty at European Nazarene College in the areas of Theology, History, and Identity. He is married to Liliana, and they have two children: André and Nicole.

---

121. Gustavo Gutiérrez, *On Job: God-Talk and the Suffering of the Innocent* (New York: Orbis, 1987), xiv.

Holiness and Racial Harmony:
Three Issues to Consider
Montague R. Williams

On August 9, 2014 a Caucasian police officer in Ferguson, Missouri shot and killed an unarmed African American man in his late teens. Protests and demonstrations began shortly after and lasted for months, calling United States' citizens and leaders to revisit issues of race and racism as major topics of public discourse.

Even before this event and other recent similar events, the Church of the Nazarene's *Manual* has been urging Nazarene congregations "to continue and strengthen programs of education to promote racial understanding and harmony."[122] This charge is clearly important and helpful. However, I wonder if it is clear that "racial understanding and harmony" is part of the wider call to holiness.

Our doctrine of holiness has great potential for challenging racial division and promoting racial harmony. But there are a few areas in our articulation and practice of holiness that need to be addressed first. In this brief essay, I suggest we (1) give clearer explanation of our understanding the Kingdom of God, (2) be explicit about the communal nature of holiness, and (3) allow holiness theology and practice to shape our interaction with public policies.

Refining Our Focus on the Kingdom

We often speak about the Kingdom of God as our ultimate hope, and we follow Jesus in praying for God's will to flourish "on earth as it is in heaven" (Matthew 5:10, NRSV). Theologically, this prayer suggests that our lives can and ought to point to whatever the Kingdom looks like. The challenge we face in the Church of the Nazarene is that our understanding of the Kingdom of God remains ambiguous. We have several statements that identify our theology and practice as being grounded in advancing the Kingdom,[123] bearing witness to the

---

122. *Manual of the Church of the Nazarene 2009-2013* (Kansas City, MO: Nazarene Publishing House, 2009), 374.

123. Manual, 5-5, 28, 197, 248, 251, 264, 272.

Kingdom,[124] and participating in the Kingdom.[125] But we have no statement that clarifies what the Kingdom is, what it looks like, or what it means to participate in it.

Interestingly, it is a particular vision of the Kingdom of God that shaped the ethics of racial reconciliation practiced and articulated by Martin Luther King, Jr. and the participants in his faith-based nonprofit organization called the Southern Christian Leadership Conference. Leaning on the Johannine eschatological vision of the "great multitude . . . from every nation, all tribes, peoples, and languages" (Revelation 7:9), King spoke of the Kingdom of God as "the Beloved Community" and emphasized the importance of people from "all races, cultures, nations, and classes," working together to form "microcosms" of the Kingdom.[126] These microcosms would serve as testimonies that let the watching world have a glimpse of what is to come when the Kingdom is realized in its fullness.

This concept of microcosms of Kingdom has striking resemblance to a portion of the charge District Superintendents give to newly organized congregations in the Church of the Nazarene, which identifies the local congregation as "a community of faith that lives as an authentic expression of the kingdom of God in the world."[127] This sounds like such a hopeful way of describing the life and mission of a local congregation. If the Kingdom we are seeking embodies racial harmony, then our theology and practice must include clear connections to racial harmony. But once again, we do not know if this "authentic expression" has anything to do with racial harmony, because we do not clearly articulate what is meant by Kingdom of God. To be clear, my concern is that our lack of articulation regarding the nature of the community to which we are called results in a theology of holiness that renders "racial understanding and harmony" a side issue. We need to clarify our understanding of the Kingdom of God.

Embracing Holiness in Community

We also need to clarify and embrace the communal nature of holiness. Racial harmony is not an individual endeavor. It is about people of different races earnestly listening to and honoring the stories of struggle and confusion that

---

124. Ibid., 35, 48.

125. Ibid., 262, 274-275, 377.

126. Martin Luther King, Jr., "Where Do We Go From Here? Chaos or Community," in *A Testament of Hope: The Essential Writings and Speeches of Martin Luther King Jr.* (San Francisco: HarperCollins Publisher, 1986), 632; Walter Fluker, *They Looked for a City: A Comparative Analysis of the Ideal of Community in the Thought of Howard Thurman and Martin Luther King, Jr.* (Lanham: University Press of America, 1989), 110, 237.

127. *Manual*, 264.

come with living in a racialized context.[128] It's about people advocating for each other. It's about people helping each other recognize the role of race in society and intentionally sharing life in a manner that subverts the power of race and displays the power of the Gospel.

How can growth in these ways ever be accounted for if our understanding of holiness is solely about whether I'm personally growing or if you are personally growing? There needs to be a way of articulating holiness theology that begs the question of how *we* are growing in holiness *as a we*.

When Wesley wrote the oft-quoted lines, "The gospel of Christ knows of no religion but social; no holiness but social holiness,"[129] he was pointing to the understanding that it is impossible for one to be shaped in the way of holiness apart from a community being shaped in the way of holiness.[130] It is out of this understanding that we have accountability groups and even find meaning for offering public altar calls.

However, if we are not careful, we run the risk of going about this in a way that renders *my* faith community as merely a means to the end of *me* becoming holy. In other words, an over-emphasis on individual growth in holiness can lead one to think *my* multiracial congregation is merely a means to the end of *me* sensing that I am not racially prejudiced. Such a perspective makes use of other people or consumes other people for one's own purpose rather than becoming a part of a people as the body of Christ.

Students in Church of the Nazarene theology and Bible courses often learn reasons why they ought to be thinking of holiness as more of a communal endeavor rather than merely an individual endeavor. However, we have had great difficulty in imagining what that looks like in the life of the church. Well, I think it would look like a community continually growing racial harmony; a community becoming more and more like what is described above; a community that more and more reflects the Kingdom. We need to be more explicit about the communal nature of holiness in our local churches and not let the call to social holiness get lost in the walls of academia.

Reclaiming Holiness in the Public Square

Race in the United States has always been a legal matter. To be clear, race is not a natural way of understanding oneself but the result of categories that

128. To be clear, calling a context "racialized" is different than calling it "racist" or "racial." A racialized context is one that has been affected by a history of race classification. It suggests that this history continues to affect structures as well as the way people relate to one another. See the third sub-section of this article for further discussion.

129. John Wesley, Hymns and Sacred Poems (1739), in *The Works of John Wesley*, ed. Thomas Jackson, 14 vols., CD-ROM edition (Franklin, TN: Providence, 1994), 14:319.

130. See Kevin Watson, *Pursuing Social Holiness: The Band Meeting in Wesley's Thought and Popular Methodist Practice* (Oxford: Oxford University Press, 2014).

were created to establish economic ways of relating. This is why race is classified differently depending on the country.

In the United States, race was initially implemented as a way to justify slavery. Over time, race became a way of intentionally perpetuating the idea that some are inherently worthy of full citizenship and some are not.[131]

Today the role of race in the United States is confusing. Since the Civil Rights era, race categories have been used to address issues regarding race. So while it is acknowledged that the very creation of race classification is problematic, the categories are now needed to understand the history and the current social and economic happenings in the U.S. The confusion of what to do with this has led to public policy debates about race that fall into the ideological categories of conservative and liberal, which are portrayed respectively as personal responsibility versus social responsibility.

If we read the section of the Church of the Nazarene's *Manual* entitled "The Covenant of Christian Conduct," we find that the practices of holiness cannot easily fall into the framework of either one of these political categories. In fact, the participants in the holiness movement and the early years of the Church of the Nazarene sought out subversive practices that were much more dynamic than what a singular political party could contain. For example, the commitment to abstain from alcohol was not just so one maintains one's own personal responsibility. It was also to boycott an industry that sought to capitalize on the sufferings and vulnerabilities of the poor.[132] Even today, "The Church of the Nazarene believes this new and holy way of life involves practices to be avoided and redemptive acts of love to be accomplished *for the souls, minds, and bodies of our neighbors.*"[133] The commitment to personal growth and responsibility is not to be separated from social concern and responsibility. In a context that is politically divided between two ideologies of right and left, the praxis of holiness can offer a third way of engaging the public square.

Even beyond voting in national politics, this calls us to be diligently aware of what is happening with local laws, policing, business practices, healthcare, and schools. It is in these situations that we find the causes of injustice and hurt which lead to racial disunity. If we can resist society's grip that calls us to align with either left or right, we can begin hearing each other's stories and addressing issues in a way that reflects our citizenship in the Kingdom.

131. Michael Emerson and Christian Smith, *Divided by Faith: Evangelical Religion and the Problem of Race in America* (Oxford: Oxford University Press, 2001), 11.

132. Rodney Reed, *Holy with Integrity: The Unity of Personal & Social Ethics in the Holiness Movement, 1880-1910* (Salem, OH: Schmul, 2003), 108-17.

133. Manual, 46. Italics are mine.

Conclusion

I have the honor of teaching at one of the most racially and culturally diverse Christian colleges in the United States. Most students arrive to our campus from a congregation that is made up primarily of one racial group and graduate four years later with a whole new perspective on what Christian community can be. Conversations regarding issues of race and racism can happen among peers and friends of different racial backgrounds, and responses to such issues can be discerned together. However, the majority of evangelical congregations in the United States remain divided along racial lines, making little to no space for Christians of different races to see and hear each other well.

My concern for the Church is that this continual division among congregations will turn away young adults who have experienced inter-racial and inter-cultural community. For the sake of being theologically faithful and for the sake of our young people, we need to cultivate Christian congregations of racial reconciliation and harmony.

Holiness theology has the groundwork for doing this. But we need to be clearer with our understanding of the Kingdom and the communal nature of holiness, and we have to embrace the fact that holiness does not fit into the political boxes. Let us not conform to the patterns of this world, and may God continue to transform us so that we may discern what is the will of God—what is good and acceptable and perfect (Romans 12:2).

Montague Williams serves as Assistant Professor of Religion and Philosophy at Eastern Nazarene College. He is completing a Ph.D. at Boston University focusing on the fields of practical theology and theological ethics. Montague and his wife, Jennie, live in Quincy, MA.

Holiness and the African Renaissance

Samantha Chambo

I sat in confusion in an ethnic hair salon in the Western Suburbs of Johannesburg. I was listening to a conversation between two black South Africans who were discussing the corruption in the government. What confused me most was when the women said emphatically, "That is why you must never give a black man power; you are asking for trouble." I wanted to ask her if she was aware of the color of her own skin and why she had such a low opinion of her own people.

There seems to be a mind-set amongst some Africans that they, as Africans, are inferior to those of European decent, and they find proof for this "fact" in the obvious failure of African states. This negative mind-set is a result of various factors such as colonialism, slavery, apartheid, and the dehumanizing effects of poverty.

The call of the African Renaissance is a call to return to valuing all that is beautiful and good about Africa and her people and in so doing to change the face of the continent. I believe that the message of heart holiness has a cardinal role to play in this needed rebirth in Africa because it will transform Africans into an authentic holy community as intended by God.

According to Jose Cossa, "African renaissance refers to the rebirth of Africa marked by a return to aspects of Africa's indigenous civilization, i.e., prominence of African languages, thought patterns, traditions, art and industry."[134] However, it also entails so much more.

Former South African President Thabo Mbeki, an ardent spokesperson for an African Renaissance, highlights many other important aspects of this rebirth sweeping the continent. It involves condemning the current patterns of greed and marginalization of the poor and oppressed in favor of a more traditional value system, the system of Ubuntu. According to Reuel Khoza, "Ubuntu means 'humanness' or 'being human' and encompasses values such as the universal brotherhood for Africans (and, by extension, the whole of humankind)."[135] John Mbiti refer to this as a sense of kinship that includes not only immediate and

---

134. José Augusto Cossa, "African Renaissance and Religion: The Birth of an African Renaissance Theology," Sept. 3, 2001, http://dx.doi.org/10.2139/ssrn.282194, accessed June 22, 2014.

135. Reuel J Khoza, *Attuned Leadership, African Humanism as Compass* (Johannesburg: Penguin, 2011), xxxvii.

extended family, but people from the same tribe, animals, plants, and objects. He calls this kinship "one of the strongest forces in traditional African life."[136] Gwiyani Muzorewa also affirms, "African humanity is primarily defined by a sense of belonging, serving one's own folk, and kinship. For the African, it is not enough to be a human being; unless one shares a sense of community, one can easily turn out to be an enemy."[137]

The African Renaissance is a call to return to culture of academics that is such a proud aspect of our Northern African history. It is a call to value the art and culture and diversity that makes Africa so special. Mbeki argues:

> The beginning of our rebirth as a continent must be our own rediscovery of our soul, captured and made permanently available in the great work of creativity represented by the pyramids and sphinxes of Egypt, the stone buildings of Axum and the ruins of Carthage and Zimbabwe, the rock painting of the San, the Benin bronzes and the African masks, the carving of the Makonde and the stone sculptures of the Shona.[138]

President Mbeki also emphasizes that we will never be able to change the fate of Africa without this "journey of self-discovery and the restoration of our own self-esteem."[139] He calls Africans to rebel against the status quo and to rise up to a "rediscovered or reinforced cultural identity."[140]

Most aspects of African traditional beliefs and culture were labeled as idolatrous during the early years of the Church of the Nazarene in Africa, and congregants were encouraged to cut all ties to it and were punished if they did not. Bongani France Dlamini reports, "It was sin . . . to wear traditional attire or to attend a traditional wedding, and many other unbiblical laws were found."[141] As a result of this radical disconnect with their culture, some people in Africa felt compelled to live in a syncretistic way. Most members of the Church of the Nazarene, however, did choose to disconnect themselves from their culture and tradition in order to

---

136. John Mbiti, *African Religions and Philosophy* (New York: Anchor, 1970), 49.

137. Gwiyani Muzorewa, *The Origins and Development of African Theology* (New York: Orbis, 1985), 17.

138. Thabo Mbeki, "The African Renaissance Statement of Deputy President Thabo Mbeki," Issued by South Africa Office of the Executive Deputy President, Aug. 13, 1998, www.unisa.ac.za/contents/colleges/docs/1998/tm1998/tm980813.pdf, accessed June 22, 2014.

139. Mbeki, 3

140. Mbeki, 3

141. Bongani France Dlamini, "An Analysis of the Differing Views of Sanctification (Crisis or Process) in Swaziland Church of the Nazarene," (MA diss., Africa Nazarene University, 2010), 27.

follow the doctrine of Christian holiness as taught by early missionaries. This devaluing of African heritage was unfortunate in the light of the rich spiritual background already present in African life by God's prevenient grace. According to Desmond Tutu, this existing African spiritual paradigm "should have formed the vehicle for conveying the gospel verities to Africa."[142]

Mildred Wynkoop says, "Everything we find in the Bible suggests that God is trying to liberate us from sin and failure and false ideals and low ceilings and smallness and individualism. God wants us, in this life, to live fully, creatively. Being good is not simply *not doing things*, but living out the dynamic of God's purpose for men."[143] She explains that God does not want us to smother our natural responses, but he wants to give us a pure heart that is a result of God cleansing the heart of double motives. God does not want to curb our personal development, but he wants to mobilize our whole personality. According to Wynkoop, *"Purity is not an end in itself.* Purity permits the personality to live in full expression of love to God and man."[144]

I believe that the message of holiness will truly serve as a transforming power in Africa when we start to celebrate all that is good in Africa and bring it under the sanctifying power of the Holy Spirit.

When God said, "Let us make humankind in our image, according to our likeness, and let them have dominion" (Genesis 1:26), a seed filled with an explosion of color, light and diversity was planted. It was from these two human beings that God would create the wondrous spectrum of the human race, all of the nations that would reflect the various aspects of his beauty and glory in diverse ways.

This divine image is reflected in the traditional African sense of community, in their spiritual approach to all life, and in their respect for nature. It is reflected in the creativity and innovation of is people.

However, it is also a fallen image, and this is reflected in sometimes-inhumane cultural practices and in the poverty and marginalization of its people. It is reflected in the corrupt governments that strive to enrich themselves at great cost to the masses and in the social behaviors that led to the HIV/AIDs pandemic on the continent.

---

142. Desmond Tutu, "Whither African Theology?" in *Christianity in Independent Africa* Edward Fashole-Luke et al., eds. (London: Rex Collings, 1978), 366.

143. Mildred Bangs Wynkoop, *A Theology of Love: The Dynamic of Wesleyanism* (Kansas City, MO: Beacon Hill 1972), Kindle addition: Ch. 16, location 6605.

144. Wynkoop, Ch. 16, location 6622.

Yet God's image is being restored as millions of Africans are coming to the realization that they can follow Christ as Africans and are taking up the responsibility to make Christ-like disciples of the nations.

Just as community is the heart of traditional African life, so holy community should become the heart of the church in Africa. This new holy community can then be seen as the fulfillment, the reinterpretation, and the redemption of existing community in Africa. The challenge for believers is to transform their existing community into this holy community instead of an imperative to disconnect from it. As Kwame Bediako explains, "The Church as the community of the redeemed especially in its sacramental life, supersedes the 'old' kinship group, not by way of obliteration, but rather, by way of fulfillment."[145]

One of my favorite Christmas memories happened in the local Church of Matola Cidade in Mozambique. The congregation made a decision to have their Christmas at church and in so doing ensure that everyone had a good meal for Christmas. The church board bought a cow to slaughter for this occasion and congregation members carried fresh produce from their farms to make sure everyone had something to eat. I stood in awe as I watched grandparents, young couples, youth, and children all celebrating the birth of their Savior. There was drumming, dancing, colorful material, and a bounty of laugher and noise. It was an authentic African Christian celebration. It was holy Ubuntu.

Samantha Chambo, MA, teaches holiness theology and pastoral counseling at Nazarene Theological College in South Africa. She serves as the Africa Regional Coordinator of Africa Nazarene Women Clergy. Samantha is married to Filimao Chambo and has two children: Tsakani (age fourteen) and Emanuel (age eleven).

---

145. Kwame Bediako, *Theology and Identity: The Impact of Culture upon Christian Thought in the First Century and in Modern Africa* (Cumbria: Paternoster, 1999), 309.

Holiness Amid Alienation and Poverty in the Life of Haitians

Sadrack Nelson

The doctrine of holiness always evokes interest and controversy in the Haitian context. I still remember as a freshman at the Seminaire Theologique Nazareen D'Haiti witnessing my friends in their sophomore year wrestling with the concept of entire sanctification. To some of them, holiness was not simply an unreachable ideal, but also an irrelevant and self-contradictory notion.

When I started taking the holiness class myself, the experience was different. I had prior exposure to the doctrine before attending seminary and was more open to the possibility and experience of holiness. Upon my graduation, I was eager to teach holiness, and I participated in many efforts to create curriculum for Sunday school and to lead Bible studies on the doctrine in my local church. Years later, I myself had the privilege to teach the holiness class at our seminary.

I did my best to encourage my students to develop a clear understanding of the doctrine and to commit their lives to holy living. I understood very early that teaching holiness involves more than the ability to articulate the nuances of the doctrine; it requires willingness to be honest with my students about where I am on my own journey. My task is not only to lecture on the doctrine, but also to model holiness through vulnerability and transparency in my own life. However, as I look back on it all, I have come to the realization that the most difficult challenge to the teaching of holiness in Haiti does not lie in people's reluctance to embrace the idea, but in the condition of alienation for the Haitian people and in the situation of poverty that alienation causes.

I was trying to reproduce the teaching of the doctrine in the same way I was taught of it, without paying enough attention to the social reality or material condition of the Haitian people and the way it affects our ability to understand and experience holiness. Most of the time when we teach holiness in Haiti, we place primary focus on the personal, spiritual, and internal aspect of the doctrine—at the expense of its social dimensions and implications.

Holiness is essentially portrayed as an individualistic spiritual experience that ultimately results in social apathy and conformism. Even though we concede that holiness includes both love for God and the neighbor and involves the inward and the outward, the personal and the social, as well as the spiritual and the physical—we don't really understand significance for the Haitian context.

Therefore, I ask now, what are the implications of holiness for our context in Haiti? How are Haitians to understand total dedication to God? What does renewal and restoration into the image of God look like in the Haitian context? Can holiness be defined without any reference to the particular social reality or material existence of the people to whom it is intended?

To move forward with these questions, it is important to understand the true nature of the deep alienation and resulting poverty that affects the lives of Haitians. Haiti, as we know it today, is a product of an international system that relies on patterns of dominance and dependency for its success.[146]

As the cyclical history of Haiti convincingly demonstrates, the debilitating condition of the Haitian nation-state is symptomatic of an international system that is defined by economic exploitation and political domination, and which creates violence and inequality in the life of Haitians. From its very creation to the most recent developments in the Haitian drama, Haiti has always been shaped by political and economic interests other than that of its own people.[147] It has always been denied the right to existence as a free and self-determined country. This is not only evidenced by its role as a market for goods and source of cheap labor force in the world economy, but also by the predominance of international stakeholders in the affairs of the country.[148]

However, dominant narratives about Haiti tell a much different story and portray the country as a failed, backward nation whose desperate and hopeless situation is explained most effectively by its own internal reality.[149] The situation of poverty in Haiti is attributed to political instability, corruption in the government, and most notably Haitian culture itself, which is understood, with direct correlation to the practice of Vodou.[150] In this narrative, the root cause of chronic crisis in the nation of Haiti is internal, cultural, and spiritual.

The tendency to blame Vodou or Haitian culture masks the long and ongoing process of marginalization, disempowerment, and dehumanization in the life of Haitians. It colludes with an enduring tradition of the Christian presence and ministry in Haiti, which has considered Vodou as inherently evil and anti-Christian and helped to perpetuate the condition of alienation of the people

---

146. Paul Farmer, *The Uses of Haiti* (Monroe: Common Courage Press, 1994), 58.

147. Ibid, 76-78, 230.

148. Ibid, 76, 255-256.

149. Ibid, 53, 55-56.

150. Ibid, 53, 338.

by denying, delegitimizing, and demonizing the foundational narrative, which shapes the identity of the Haitian people. Haitian believers are required to adopt the value system and cultural identity of the missionaries, and the Haitians lose the ability to integrate their faith into the reality of their own life.

Faith becomes a means to escape reality and functions as a device to manipulate the Haitian poor by distracting their attention from economic injustice, political oppression, and social exclusion. Salvation is strictly reduced to the personal and concerns only the inner self of the individual. It is intrinsically spiritual, internal, and offers no perspective for present life. Under these conditions, Haitian believers are disempowered, desubstantialized, and bereft of what used to give meaning to their world and shape the contours of their personalities. They develop a distorted sense of identity as mere dependent objects of pity by their "brothers" and "sisters" in the First World.

The challenges of understanding and applying holiness in the complexities of the Haitian context stem not only from marginalization and domination, but also from an individualistic understanding of the self that is inherent in the traditional interpretation of the doctrine. This understanding of holiness assumes a simplistic and inadequate view of self that is dependent on a philosophical tradition that fails to take into account its corporate dimension.

In contrast to this view, recent developments in philosophy and the humanities alike have shown that selfhood is not a static category, but a dynamic entity that emerges from a complex of social interactions and processes. The self is a social category; it does not exist prior to society and relies on social and physical reality for its own definition and existence.[151] As Albert Truesdale explains, the self "creates and is created by the structures in which it comes to expression."[152] However, the social structures in that we are a part and that serve to inform the sense of self are not always an expression of goodness and can be marked by sin and evil.[153]

In this light, sinfulness cannot be explained only in personal, abstract, and ontological terms. Sin is not as much a metaphysical reality as it is a relational category and extends to the very social structures through which individuality expresses itself. It is systemic, structural, and social, and it involves a corporate or collective dimension.[154]

---

151. Albert L. Truesdale, "Christian Holiness and the Problem of Systemic Evil," *Wesleyan Theological Journal* 19, no. 1

152. Ibid, 46.

153. Ibid, 47.

154. Ibid, 44.

Given this integrative understanding of sin, holiness must incorporate the same relational categories and social structures. Holiness cannot be defined in isolation from the social context in which it is embedded.[155] The self cannot be sanctified apart from the social structures of which it is a part. Holiness can only be defined inside the social reality through which the individual self-expresses itself.

Sanctification does not happen in a vacuum, but emerges from within a particular social context. Therefore, teaching about holiness that is indifferent to the socio-economic realities and cultural processes that affect self-consciousness is both irrelevant and participates—whether consciously or not—in structures that are used to justify oppression or exclusion.

Social conditioning also affects a peoples' ability to respond adequately to the full possibility of holiness. The possibility of total consecration to God is compromised and logically unimaginable in the absence of true consciousness. True consciousness involves the realization of both enslavement to and victimization from sin. In the Haitian context, true consciousness involves awareness of our condition of alienation and its distorting effects on every aspect of human life. The recuperation and recovering of selfhood is a prerequisite and parallel process to any meaningful and authentic devotion to God in Haiti.

The Haitian context requires us to move beyond an individualistic approach to holiness and compels us to embrace a more incorporative and responsible understanding of both holiness and the self. In the biblical worldview, holiness plays a crucial role and functions to bind creation and community together. Not only does holiness serve to establish the moral foundation of creation, but also to define the moral character of the Israelite community. A creation ethic of holiness reflects and is reflected in Israel's own understanding of identity and role in the world.[156]

Holiness does not start with the individual, but with the created order itself. It does not start with the personal, but with the communal and the social. It is not simply an individual experience, but a social and communal reality.

Thus, as long as the social reality and material condition of the people of Haiti is determined by unnamed and ongoing acts of violence, holiness cannot truly be a reality in the life of Haitians in all its fullness. As long as structural and physical violence continue to generate exclusion, disempowerment, and dehumanization, the possibility of holiness will always be illusive in Haiti. We cannot adequately represent holiness with teaching about holiness that focuses on a transcendent

155. Ibid, 51.

156. William P. Brown, *The Ethos of the Cosmos* (Cambridge: Eerdmans, 1999), 12,15,19.

self but leaves out the social and political structures that serve to exploit the poor and alienate their sense of self. An adequate understanding of holiness includes community and creation. Holiness is embedded in both space and time and is about integrity and fullness of life through the boundless love of God.

As a global community, our task within the church is to emulate God's holiness. Our call is not simply personal, but communal and cosmic; it includes the whole of creation and the entire human community. We can no longer claim holiness as the distinctive characteristic of our church while at the same continuing to ignore its communal and cosmic dimension, as well as our responsibility in the sanctification of both creation and community. The future of Haiti and other vulnerable places in the world depends on an understanding of holiness that invites the rich and the poor, the oppressed and the oppressors to name the violence of sin and to embrace a view of holiness that extends to all created things.

Sadrack Nelson is from Haiti, is married to Sarah, and has a seven-year old son named Metch. He has a B.A. from the Seminaire Theologique Nazareen D'Haiti and an M.A. from Trevecca Nazarene University. He is the pastor of Jessup New Generation Church of the Nazarene in Massachusetts and serves as Coordinator for Haiti-Mid-Atlantic Partnership Initiative.

Cosmopolitan Christianity:
Learning How to Eat and Dance
Gabriel Salguero

When I was a young boy, I often visited the comic book shop in the center of town with my brothers and friends. Our greatest find was purchasing an early issue of one of our favorite comics: Superman, Wolverine, or Batman. The idea was that you bought one and never took it out of its air-sealed bag. Why buy it and keep it sealed? Simple, the idea is that the issue increases in value as long as it is never let out of the bag.

Sadly, this is the view many have of holiness. Holiness, for some, decreases in value if it gets out of the bag. Tragic misinterpretations of Jesus' caution in John 15 of being "in the world but not of the world" have led many to believe that holiness is somehow a call to live like sealed comic books with no opportunity to be read or enjoyed. Ironically, many of us have missed the continuation of Jesus' farewell prayer when he says, "My prayer is not that you take them out of this world" (John 17:15). Jesus is unpacking the dialectic of holiness and the incarnation; we must live in this tension.

The truth is that the Christian gospel proclaims a holiness rooted in the incarnation. Incarnational holiness has always been at the heart of God. Through the Incarnation of Jesus, God demonstrates that he is radically committed to the messiness and concreteness of life. Our gospel is not so much an escape route to an other-worldly reality as it is a call to live in this world in a way that is profoundly redemptive and transformative. It is living out the prayer of Jesus in Matthew 6, "Let your kingdom come, and let your will be done on earth as it is in heaven."

For those of us living in the urban centers of "Late Modernity," this is lived-out in what I have come to call Cosmopolitan Christianity. We are, in the words of the Petrine admonition, "a chosen people and a holy nation" (1 Pet. 2:9), called to manifest God's marvelous light in the midst of a diaspora that requires incarnational living.

The term "cosmopolitan" presents some challenges. The etymology of the word points to two words that have not usually been associated with holiness namely "cosmos" (world) and "polis" (city). Usually, "cosmopolitan" refers to folks who see themselves as global-citizens or urbanites, people who love being in the centers of fashion, finance, and culture. Of course, like any stereotype, this misses much of the complexity and nuance of cosmopolitan living while highlighting some of its most prominent features.

Nevertheless, when they are also citizens of the Kingdom of God, this global and urban citizenry has to deal with the challenge of navigating their hybrid reality of faithful presence and prophetic imagination. What cosmopolitan holiness communicates is that Christians are committed to being present. We are not going anywhere. We love the city. Simultaneously, we are committed to transforming our cities with whatever is good and beautiful. Rarely, if ever, has adopting a mentality of a disengaged holiness been fruitful.

Cosmopolitan Christianity is not a new phenomenon for followers of Jesus. It was one of the core missional challenges for the apostles and early church planters. The books of Acts transitions from a rural church to the center cities of the Roman Empire from Ephesus, Philippi, Corinth, and even Rome itself. Jesus forecasted this as a move from "Jerusalem . . . to the utter most parts of the earth" (Acts 1:8). The apostles, and chiefly St. Paul, had to develop an ecclesiology and missiology with a methodology of faithful and fruitful presence. They were a holy people in a cosmopolitan context.

St. Augustine of Hippo, in his book *City of God*, dealt with the tension of living in the cosmopolitan centers when he tried to draw a framework for Christians living in the declining Rome Empire. Augustine underlined the places of consonance and conflict between what he called the "City of God" and the city of humanity. He was clear to point out that to be a follower of Jesus did not mean that you hated the city but that you sought—through loving and sacrificial service—to transform the city.

If it is true that there is no holiness without social holiness, then Cosmopolitan Holiness is at the very center of our holiness heritage. We are created to be in relationship, and this is where our Christlikeness ought to be most evident. It is through these relationships that our holiness is truly tested. Holiness at its core is relational and transformative. Holiness brings with it the virtues that seek the shalom of the city.

Holiness is an action. "Be ye holy" means that we actively pursue what is good, true, right, beautiful, and just (Phil. 4:8). Holiness demands that we both transform and are transformed by the city. The incarnation requires some profound self-emptying.

These questions have been asked in every generation since Jesus: How do we effectively engage our urban centers in ways that do not deny our Gospel-centered commitments? How are we to be a faithful and fruitful presence in the city while not uncritically assimilating to a *modus vivendi* inconsistent with the Gospel? Urban pastor Tim Keller clearly articulates this Christian negotiation: "Our stance toward every human culture should be one of critical enjoyment and appropriate wariness."[157]

St. Paul tried to find that balance of incarnational and holy living when there was a dispute about food in Corinth. Meals can often be a place where we unpack our best theology and practice. In the urban and multi-ethnic mecca of Corinth, the question of eating foods sacrificed to idols was no small matter. Jews and Gentiles had quite different cultural interpretations of how this was seen. Paul's now famous quote, "I become all things to all people" (1 Cor. 9:23), is not a simple assimilation into the idol-worship of Corinth but a discernment between what was essential and non-essential in a gospel-centered but culturally-sensitive presentation of Jesus Christ. Paul neither compromised the gospel nor alienated the urban-center of Corinth.

As a pastor in Manhattan, one of my principal tasks is to help people know how to live a Christlike life in the midst of urban realities. This requires discernment not disengagement. Holiness is not synonymous with weirdness. Holy people are neither uncritical nor hyper-critical of urban values; rather we are appropriately and biblically discerning. D. A. Carson explained that not all "cultural elements are morally neutral. Far from it. Every culture has good and bad elements in it . . . Yet in every culture it is important for the evangelist, church planter, and witnessing Christian to flex as far as possible, so that the gospel will not be made to appear unnecessarily alien at the merely cultural level." [158]

This learning how to eat and dance is at the center of Cosmopolitan Holiness. It is carving out this space where the Kingdom of God meets the city and transforms it. Cosmopolitan holiness is being incarnational enough that you earn a hearing while presenting a powerful "new creation" that brings the "oughtness" of the kingdom of God into view.

In Manhattan, at the Lamb's Church where I pastor, that means we engage art, culture, film, and architecture in ways that are both affirming and critical. Cosmopolitan holiness is profoundly unselfish; in Pauline terms, it's kenotic. It empties itself sufficiently to serve the world in transformative ways.

The question I most often get is, "To what degree do we become contextual without becoming compromised?" This is precisely the Christian missional task of discernment based in love. Wherever the essentials of the gospel are not

---

157. Tim Keller, *Center Church: Doing Balanced, Gospel-Centered Ministry in Your City* (Grand Rapids, MI: Zondervan, 2012), 109.

158. D.A. Carson, The Cross and Christian Ministry: Leadership Lesson from 1 Corinthians (Grand Rapids, MI: Zondervan, 2004), 120. In Keller, 111.

compromised, we can venture out in Christian mission without fear of losing our way. This, of course, requires that we have thought through the essentials of our Christian witness: love and truth, sin and grace, fallenness and redemption, repentance and forgiveness.

Conversely, holiness people must also provide a missional cartography of the city. Living in the city means really being a part of it: "Build houses and settle down; plant gardens and eat what they produce. Marry and have sons and daughters . . . Increase in number there; do not decrease. Also, seek the peace and prosperity of the city" (Jer. 29: 5-7).

The call of God for holiness people is not only faithfulness but also fruitfulness. Fruitfulness requires a faithful presence that does not flee from the most challenging places on the earth. Fruitfulness requires a careful negotiation of integration without removing the scandal of the cross. It is integration without capitulation. This means we must not just be present but transformative.

We cannot be the comic book in an air-tight bag. No, cosmopolitan holiness allows images and glimpses of the kingdom of God to break into every sphere of the city from art, government, education, media, and family. We cannot break-in if we are not truly present. Urban revival requires that we repent from the urban flight of bygone eras and return to our first-works of urban revival and renewal. That will require some holy dancing.

Entire sanctification must also mean the sanctification of the entire cosmos, including our cities. The God who began his relationship with humanity in a garden ends it in a city. The city is a part of God's eternal plan to bring the broad complexity, diversity, creativity, beauty, and messiness of creation into proximity with his holy people. It is in the beautiful concreteness of a city, the New Jerusalem, where God promises to sanctify all things or to make all things new (Rev. 21:5).

Gabriel Salguero is the president of the National Latino Evangelical Coalition and the pastor of the multi-ethnic Lamb's Church in New York.

Christian Holiness and the Restoration of Eden

Mark Mann

Many in the Wesleyan-holiness tradition have thought of Christian holiness as an essentially individual, personal matter. According to this view, sanctification is the process by which "I" become renewed in Christlikeness so that I might love God with my entire heart, mind, soul, and strength, and my neighbor as myself. While this is certainly a key aspect of holiness, Scripture actually provides us with a far grander picture of Christian holiness—one in which individual holiness is more properly understood within the context of God's work to redeem *all* creation.

One of the main reasons for our individualized misreading of Scripture is our focus on Adam and Eve in Genesis, but they are only a part of the story. Indeed, we don't find them created until day six, while God has already declared creation "good" six times. And, the seventh time that God announces creation's goodness—this time after humans have been created and using the phrase "very good"—it is after God sees *"everything* that [God] had made" (1:31). This means that the goodness of creation is derivative of its Creator. Anything that is good is so only because God makes it so. Put in a slightly different way, creation is good ultimately not for what it provides for human beings, but because God created it and loves it. Also, the ultimate value of humanity is in the way that we *complete* creation. This, then, also means that human goodness is tied up with the goodness of the entire creation as the harmonious whole that God created it to be. Simply put: creation is good without us, but we make it *very* good when we fulfill the role that God has intended for us.

While God's ultimate intention for us in creation, as laid out in Gen. 1:26-30, is to "have dominion" over creation, we often misunderstand what that means. We often interpret this to mean that God has given us creation to exploit for solely human purposes. God certainly intends for human needs to be met by creation, but God does not intend this to happen *at the expense of* creation. Christians have used this passage to defend so-called human progress at the expense of other species, failing to recognize that God commanded other animals to be fruitful and multiply, too (1:22). God's command that humans have dominion over the earth must always be read within the context of God's plan for all of creation to flourish.

Furthermore, God's declaration of human dominion over creation comes immediately after the announcement that human beings have been created in the "image" and "likeness" of God. God intends us to exert dominion, or lordship, exactly as God does. As Christians, we affirm that God's dominion is best expressed in the life of Jesus Christ. When we look to Christ as a model for lordship, we find one who took a towel and washed the feet of his disciples (John 13:13-17), laid down his life for his sheep (John 10:11), and did not "regard equality with God as something to be exploited, but emptied himself, taking the form of a slave" (Phil. 2:6-7). The dominion given to humanity in Gen. 1:26 is a call for us to *care for* all of God's creatures. Therefore, not only is human goodness tied up in the goodness of creation, but human goodness is in some sense best expressed when humans fulfill the divine mandate to care for creation.

We can also see that the holiness of humanity and creation are inextricably interwoven through the devastating consequences of the fall. Again, we often focus on Adam and Eve's actions and punishments, but there is more to the story. In Genesis 3, we find that, as a result of the first sin, the ground itself has been cursed, and humans now must toil against the earth—which now produces "weeds and thistles"—in order to survive (17-19). Sin not only disrupts the relationship between God and humans but also the originally harmonious relationship— which I call the "primal shalom"—between humans and the rest of creation. In other words, the original harmony of the whole of creation has been undone by *human sin*. As humans cease to serve God, so also do we cease to care for creation, only to find that creation becomes as much foe as friend.

We see such "cosmic" consequences of human sin manifest today in the countless ways that we are destroying creation, only to find human life and civilization threatened as well. Pollution has led to health problems. Ozone depletion has led to skin cancer. Global warming has led to melting glaciers and rising sea levels, which is already beginning to displace low-lying coastal populations in some areas of the world. In each case, our failure to care properly for creation by living harmoniously with it causes harm to people, especially the poorest and most vulnerable.

However, just as Scripture declares a close link between the goodness of humanity and creation and between the demise of humanity and creation because of sin, so also does Scripture declare that God's plan to save humanity is directly tied to God's plans for creation. Indeed, we find in both the Old and New Testament witness that God's final intention is to redeem creation by restoring the goodness of the primal shalom.

The story of Noah and the flood, for example, illustrates the interwoven destiny of humanity and creation (Gen. 6-9). God's decision to send the flood is based upon the fact that both the earth and all flesh on earth have been corrupted by wickedness and violence (6:11-13) and that God intends to "blot out... people together with animals and creeping things and birds of the air" (6:7). So, God chooses not only to save human beings and those animals that serve human needs, but to save "two of all flesh in which there was the breath of life" (7:14-15). Then, after the waters have receded and Noah makes a sacrifice, God forges a covenant with Noah and creation. In fact, four times God announces an everlasting covenant with all creation, including "every living creature of all flesh that is on the earth" (9:10, 15-17).

Isaiah 11 also points to the restoration of the primal shalom by describing the state of the coming messianic kingdom. In verses 6-9, we find a rather odd state of affairs: wolves, leopards, lions, and bears in immediate proximity to their prey but not consuming them and children playing with poisonous snakes without being bitten. Isaiah envisions a return to Eden where all of creation lived together in perfect harmony, or shalom. Violence and wickedness have disappeared, as the entire "earth will be full of the knowledge of the Lord" (11:9), and a "little child shall lead them" (11:6).

Among New Testament texts, the Pauline tradition mostly profoundly affirms that salvation ultimately includes all of creation. In 2 Corinthians 5:18-19, we find that "in Christ, there is a new creation: *everything* old has passed away; see, *everything* has become new," and "in Christ God was reconciling the world to himself." Paul is not merely talking about the human world here, as he clarifies elsewhere that this "ministry of reconciliation" includes *all* creation.

In Romans 8:18-23, we find that "the whole creation has been groaning in labor pains until now" and "waits in eager longing for the revealing of the children of God." While "creation itself was subjected to futility," through Christ and the redemption of the children of God, "creation will be set free from its bondage to decay."

Ephesians 1:9-10 further affirms that God desires to gather up "*all* things... in heaven and on earth." And Colossians 1:20 adds, "through [Christ] God was pleased to reconcile to himself *all things*, whether on earth or in heaven, by making *peace* through the blood of the cross."

The restoration of the primal shalom is also foretold in Revelation. This is especially evident in chapters 21 and 22 in which the New Jerusalem is seen "coming down" "prepared as a bride" and a "new heaven" and "new earth" are brought into being (21:1-2). A popular interpretation of the "passing away" of the first heaven and earth (21:1) is that they have been destroyed by God. However, note that a loud voice states that "the home of God is among mortals. He will dwell with them" (21:3). Then God states, "I am making all things new." The passing away of the old heaven and earth is not their destruction, but their wedding—the "destruction" of their separation. It is the final restoration of the primal shalom in which all things find their right place, and God rules over all. As if to drive this point home, in the center of the city we find the Edenic tree of life with the river of life running through it and with leaves for the "healing of the nations" (22:1-3). God's plan is to restore the reign of God so that the final shalom, just like the primal, becomes a reality.

Christian holiness concerns humans and human relations. About this, there can be no doubt. But if we *only* think of holiness in terms of our love for God and neighbor, then we are missing the fullness of God's intentions. True holiness is found not just in perfect love for God and neighbor, but also in perfect love for *all of creation*!

Mark H. Mann is Associate Professor of Theology and Director of the Wesleyan Center at Point Loma Nazarene University in San Diego, CA. He has been a pastor for churches in New England, New York, and southern California.

Holiness Gets Dirty
Megan Rae Krebs

In the creation epics of Genesis, God works as an artist, carefully molding the mud into a new form. Out of the dust, something unique is raised. Into this form, God breathes. In both Hebrew and Greek, the original languages of the Bible, breath and spirit are the same word. God breathes both life and spirit into these dusty creatures, and humanity is born. The unique status and nature for these creatures is called "the image of God" (Gen. 1:26, 27). This *imago dei* was imprinted upon the very fabric of human nature. Humanity was made to reflect God.

But then something unexpected and heartbreaking takes place in the Genesis narrative. Humans reject this God who had given them breath, instead turning toward sin. And much like an ancient masterpiece, covered by dust and filth over time, humanity dirtied the image. We tarnished ourselves, inhibiting our ability to reflect the God who loved us so deeply.

Theologians over the ages have referred to this marring as depravity. Many Calvinist traditions would even say that this "Fall of Humanity" irrevocably destroys the image of God. This has profound effect on the life of a believer, for if my life will be forever bound and dirtied by sin, there is no hope in real change. Life will always be defined by sin, even sin *covered* by the blood of Christ.

Holiness traditions, on the other hand, emphasize the far-reaching effects of a redemption that is not simply a change of eternal destination but a present and altering reality. Holiness theology is rooted deeply in hope—hope that sin does not have the last say in individual lives or in society at large. Salvation works itself out in our lives. Sin is not merely *covered* by Christ's shed blood; its power it broken. The grace of God is not helpless before sin but transforms the lives of followers of Christ into Christlikeness.

Moreover, holiness traditions spring up around issues of injustice, fighting for the oppressed and sinful. Many holiness denominations, like the Church of the Nazarene, trace their theological roots back to the ministry and thought of John and Charles Wesley. These brothers proposed a radical idea: perhaps, the claim to be Christian embodies a different sort of life. A life marked by a love for the other, the stranger, the sinner, the oppressed, those most despised. A life marked by the same all-accepting love that Jesus the Christ modeled and that the entirety of Scripture calls for. Perhaps Christians ought to look more like Christ.

This deep-rooted belief manifested itself not only in the teachings of John Wesley but also in his ministry. From schools for the poorest of children to orphanages to the clothing of the poor, John Wesley took seriously the instruction of Jesus Christ, that all of the Law and Prophets hang on two commandments to love, "Love the Lord your God with all your heart and with all your soul and with all your mind . . . And the second is like it: 'Love your neighbor as yourself,'" (Matthew 22:37-40). Holiness at its deepest core is a reflection of the loving nature of God. To love God truly entails what it means to love neighbor truly.

As the years passed, other groups began to embody the need for justice as well. Most famously, many holiness denominations came out of the cry for the abolition of the slaves. Likewise, most also pushed for women's equality. These groups knew that the image of God was not limited by gender or by skin color.

Steeped in such a brilliant heritage, it only seems natural that the origin story of Church of the Nazarene began in the dirty slums of Los Angeles. There, between addicts, the poor, and others in desperate need, holiness again became about loving and seeking out the other. People committed to holiness again realized that those made in the image of God must reflect God's nature—love. Love that seeks out the broken and dirty.

For the Wesley brothers and their theological descendants, holiness was not simply moral lines drawn in the sand. Christian Holiness was always deeper than simply not sinning. Holiness must do what God does. God chooses to reclaim the artwork of God's own hands. God chooses to restore. Grace abundantly poured out on humanity empowers those who participate to reflect the image of God once again. Such a beautiful collision of hope and restoration!

But as with all traditions, something went wrong. In the wake of the disillusionment brought on by two World Wars, the 1950s, 60s, and 70s led to many seeing the church and the world as a moral battleground. Having missed the spiritual impetus of their parents and grandparents, the next generation of torchbearers began to seek out the same passion instead in rules and legalism. For instance, rather than supporting the prohibition of alcohol because of its devastating impact on the poor, alcohol simply became a naughty thing. Holiness descended from the transforming work of God (restoring the *imago dei* in the life of followers of Jesus) into primarily avoiding sin. "We don't drink, cuss, or chew, and we don't go with girls who do." Movie theaters and dance halls were viewed as dens of debauchery to be avoided rather than mission fields full of people who were attempting to fill the void.

When holiness is centered in keeping the self-bleached white, it will only ever be legalism. For to be holy is to be like Christ, the God who enters the homes dirtiest and most despised. Tax collectors, women of ill-repute, and law-bound Pharisees alike all welcomed Jesus for dinner. If the Hebrew Bible kindles an imagery of God kneeling into the mud to shape and form humanity to reflect the Creator, that speaks about the kind of image we are to bear.

When I was a little girl, I would get dressed up for church and loved to bounce around in pretty dresses on Sunday mornings. Almost as soon as the car pulled into our driveway, my mother or father would quickly say, "Now go change into play clothes, so you don't ruin that dress." I was usually halfway down the yard at this point, chasing the dogs. Sullen, I would have to rush inside and change into ordinary clothing before returning to my fun.

Many pastors and teachers have peddled this image of "white robes" to describe holiness. A Christian's holiness must not be sullied by our dirty world! However, a sense of worry about the state of my "personal" holiness only leads to a refusal to be in community and solidarity with those who most need the hope of Christ. If holiness is truly rooted in the love of God, then it must constantly be found wading through the muck and mire, seeking to restore the paintings that God has made. It must constantly be seeking those to whom it may be a neighbor.

A beautiful piece of art, over time, can be lost under dirt and grime. Dust collects and bars the image from being seen. Without a clear image, it is impossible to guess the master artist who created the work. Humanity shares much in common with such art. Sinful choices that go against the will of God leave the image of the Maker in disrepair. God's love can seem almost completely lost.

However, much like a painting can be restored, so to God restores the broken life. Cleaning away the filth that has settled into the cracks of the paint and along the edges of the frame, something beautiful emerges: the image that was always present, the image put there by the loving Artist. This is holiness, not that we made ourselves clean, but that God is able to restore even the dirtiest of paintings, sending us back out to bring in the next piece.

Megan Krebs serves as the Associate Pastor at Euclid Community Church of the Nazarene in Boise, Idaho. A recent graduate from Northwest Nazarene University, she is passionate about reading the Old Testament in ways that show its heart of holiness.

Exodus and Holiness

Marty Alan Michelson

Holiness takes all of our commitment, partnered with all of the commitment of others, framed, focused, and led by the LORD in transforming the World to become on earth as it is in Heaven.

I am convinced that the central call of the Bible is found articulated in the story of the Exodus. This story (not the book, the entire story of the Exodus that extends through the Torah and into Joshua and beyond) is focused on becoming holy people.

Most people know the story usually called "The Story of the Burning Bush," found in Exodus 3-4. Most readers, though, miss out on its central tenants as the story is usually read as in introduction to the "signs and wonders" and "plagues" and contest with Pharaoh that become the focus of story-telling, and certainly this is the focus of narrations like those found in films like Cecil DeMilles' *The Ten Commandments* or Pixar's *The Prince of Egypt.*

When the LORD appears to Moses in Exodus 3, after addressing Moses by name, the very first thing the LORD announces to Moses is that he should not come any closer and must take off his sandals. Before addressing the cries and suffering that God has seen, and before commissioning Moses, Moses is first told that to stand in the presence of this God is to stand with the Holy in Holiness. Though Moses is simply at the back of the wilderness (Exodus 3:1), with the LORD now present, this wilderness takes on a new dimension, for the LORD brought holiness to this place.

Most people read the conversation between the LORD and Moses as a commissioning, and it certainly is that. Most read that this commissioning is about how Moses will become "as God" (Exodus 7:1) in the contest that takes place with Pharaoh and Egypt. And, most see the focus of the story on the signs and wonders that culminate in the death of the firstborn, and the miraculous water crossing and celebration that takes place in Exodus 12 to 15. In fact, most point to the "signs and wonders" and plagues as the "sign" of what this Holy LORD is doing with Moses and the Hebrew slaves. And yet, I think the focus on the signs and wonders misses the clearest sign of God's purpose, which God first narrates in Exodus 3.

144

When Moses is commissioned by God in Exodus 3, and when Moses first falters at his immediate acceptance of his call, the conversation is urgent. Moses states, "Who am I" to go before Pharaoh (Exodus 3:11) and God offers *the* sign of what God is doing. Before any "signs and wonders" or plagues, and even before the "magic" of Moses pushing God such that he would be able to have rod that becomes a snake a leprous hand (Exodus 4:1-9), God first says that the sign of this Holy LORD and the work of this Holy One will be that this community will get out of Egypt to become a "worshipping community" (Exodus 3:12). This sign, the sign of a community in worship to the Holy LORD is *the* sign of what the LORD would do. The rod to snake, leprous hand, and other signs and wonders (be they frogs, famine or darkness), serve a function, but these are not *the* sign. *The* sign of the LORD, first given and worked toward, is that this community comes to worship on this mountain.

Since most readers of the Bible focus on the "signs and wonders" and "plagues," they miss out on the fulfillment of the sign first given by this Holy LORD in Exodus 3:12. The agency of this LORD—who has freed Israel from service to Pharaoh so that these people might become servants to the LORD in holy work—comes in Exodus 19:1-6. It is here that this Holy LORD speaks again to Moses, again at the mountain and now with the people, in continued fulfillment of what the LORD has been doing. Now, gathered on the mountain, the LORD reminds these people that the whole earth belongs to the dominion of this LORD. All things fall under the authority of this Sovereign! Now, this Holy One in the midst of Israel wants them to become for God and for the world, a "priestly Kingdom and Holy Nation" (Exodus 19:6) as they listen to the LORD's voice and obey the covenant (Exodus 19:5).

The people here are reminded of what God had said before, about what God wants to achieve. God's holy presence previously made known to Moses, toward the goal of creating a worshipping community, now is made known to this treasured people, called out of Egypt to become God's treasured possess as a light to the nations and a beacon for the kingdoms of the world as "priestly" and "holy."

In order to become this unique people, the crowds prepare themselves with two days of preparation, separation, and making themselves "sanctified" for God's purposes (Exodus 19:10ff) so that on the third day they might stand in the holy presence of the LORD. Exodus 19:17ff reveal that the Holy presence of God is powerful and tangible, made known to Moses, priests, and people. They can come near the holiness that the LORD calls them toward and yet not come so near or so gallantly as to infringe upon this holiness.

And then, it happens, the LORD gives the provision of holiness, in the form of commandments. Exodus 20 is the announcement of God's holiness as the "sign" for this "worshipping community" (Exodus 3) who are becoming now "priestly kingdom and holy nation" (Exodus 19). Exodus 20 is the first record of the Ten Commandments. And, beyond Exodus 20, we read chapters of laws that govern food, civil duties, property boundaries, and more.

When the LORD calls a people to be holy, to become a priestly kingdom and holy nation, the LORD does not free people to do whatever they will in whatever way they like. Quite the contrary, the LORD gives specific, deliberate, and explicit provisions by which the people of God will manifest the lifestyle of God!

God's call to holiness in the story of Exodus frames the story of the Bible. God not only calls Moses, but he also uses Moses as a conduit for calling all the people. God does not free the Hebrew slaves to enable them to get out to the wilderness or into the land of promise where they can be idle, do as they please, or act like the empire of Egypt. Rather, the laws that God gives enable Israel to look different from other nations. They are laws that focus on care for others and concern for one another.

I often point out that the Ten Commandments carry prohibitions: "You shall not!" And yet, the function of the prohibitions is not to prohibit good life! It is a prohibition to say, "you shall not," yet when the prohibition is against stealing or lying, the purpose of the prohibition is to extend life and to make life more vibrant. This is a called out and holy community that is not shaped by taking from others; instead, they are to lead in their generosity for others. This is a called out and holy community that are not shaped by false words; instead they are shaped by words of life giving hope for each other.

In the Exodus, a Holy God calls a people who are not special to become special. They become special and take on the quality of being holy when their life identity becomes focused in worship—in the daily practices of life that make life not about lying but about truthful speech, coupled with genuine care of their neighbors, reflected from the life-giving connection to worship of the One True God. Worship, for ancient Isreal, was not about a few minutes of special singing on the Sabbath. Rather, worship was the total commitment of one's entire life to live in obedience to God's order made evident through a community of people to the nations.

The commandments that God gives become the means by which God intends for individuals, living in community, to reflect and embody the character of God in specific ways. The laws focus not just on the Ten Commandments; they extend beyond the commandments to all areas of life from food and diet, to sexuality and family relationships, to property lines and domesticated animals. The LORD intends that all of life be lived fully as a means to practice the disciplines of neighborly kindness with all of Creation: our bodies, our families, our animals, our property, our possessions, our neighbors, our enemies, and our God.

Holiness is worship that encompasses the totality of every aspect of our lives, and not just part of it.

Holiness is shaped by relationship to a Holy God who calls people out of the systems and structures of the world (Egypt) to become an alternative community who are "priestly" in extending God's order of benevolent care to the world.

Holiness is made manifest in human persons, whose whole bodies and relationships reflect a love of and with God and a love of and with others, such that all people come to know the LORD.

Marty Alan Michelson (Ph.D., University of Manchester) works for a world more intentionally at peace brought to fulfillment by Christian peacemakers. He is a professor and peacemaker at Southern Nazarene University.

Separation or Presence?
Reimagining Biblical Theology of Holiness
Arseny Ermakov

Our tradition has different ways of explaining holiness. One of the dominating discourses is built around the notion of holiness as separation. Biblical dictionaries told us that at the basic level of meaning the word "holiness" denotes the idea of "separation" or "withdrawal."[159] We have held these definitions as the self-evident truths throughout the twentieth century. This certainty of the word's meaning was cemented by some Hebrew lexicons and especially by Brown-Driver-Briggs, so loved by English-speaking evangelicals.

However, by the mid-twentieth century biblical scholars had to recognize that not only is the etymology of the word "holiness" uncertain, but even its meaning has to be defined contextually.[160] Recent studies have shown that "holiness" may refer to power, glory, wholeness, perfection, purity, goodness, morality, being set apart, and life. If so, holiness cannot be simply reduced to "separation," let alone "withdrawal." Jacob Milgrom even notes that "separateness" is a derivative notion of holiness and not primary.[161] Moreover, holiness in the Scriptures has never been equated with God's withdrawal or absence. *Au contraire*, holiness language constantly indicates divine presence and divine actions in the human or heavenly realm.

The book of Leviticus has often been perceived as understanding holiness as separation. This short essay will use Leviticus' themes to demonstrate that the picture is more complex than we used to think. Leviticus is at the heart of the Pentateuchal narrative of the creation of the people of Israel. As a part of this story, Leviticus paints a picture of establishing Israel's life in the *presence* of YHWH.

At the beginning of the book, the Israelites find themselves in a completely new situation. YHWH, who dwelt before on Sinai and spoke to Moses from the top of the mountain (Ex. 26:46, 27:34), is now in the *midst* of his covenant people and speaks to Moses from "the tent of meeting" (Lev. 1:1). Thus, the *presence* of the Holy God among the people of Israel is the *raison d'etre* for all of the Levitical

---

159. H. Ringgren, W. Kornfeld, "qdš." In TDOT, 12:523-543; F. Brown, "qdš." In BDB, 871-874.

160. W. Kornfeld, "qdš." In TDOT, 12:523.

161. Jacob Milgrom, *Leviticus 17-22* (New York: Doubleday, 2000), 3B: 1606.

laws that to follow. All the Levitical commandments—regarding the sanctuary and priests, festivals and sacrifices, ritual and moral purity, the land and covenant relationships—define the way the holy people of God should live in the presence of the Holy LORD. The happy co-existence of divine and human is guaranteed by following one simple instruction given by God himself: "Be holy, for I am holy."

"I will show myself holy" (Lev. 10:1-11).

A vivid example of the terrifying experience of God's presence and holiness is found in a very strange and enigmatic story of the death of priests Nadab and Abihu (Lev. 10:1-11). The priests were trying to bring an illicit flame into the sanctuary, and their offering of the unholy fire was met by the divine fire that came out from the presence of the Holy God.

The sudden death of Nadab and Abihu was explained by Moses as demonstration of YHWH's holiness (Lev. 10:3). In Torah, fire is often associated with the presence of God (Ex. 3:2), including God's dangerousness and power (e.g. Ex. 40:38; Lev 10:2; Num 9:1-2). God's holiness is "a consuming fire" that destroys all who profanes his glory.[162]

Leviticus warns the Israelites about danger of God's presence and restricts access to him; supreme holiness could be accessed only through divine regulations. But should anything profane or unclean enter God's presence, it gets consumed or destroyed. No one can approach the Holy God in an irreverent and profaning manner.

However, the holiness of YHWH has a positive effect when approached properly. Whatever comes into the presence of God becomes holy and pure.[163] When a person approaches God properly, divine holiness sanctifies, cleanses, imparts life, or inspires wonder (e.g. Is. 6:1-13). The contagious divine holiness is capable of both cleansing and destruction, danger and goodness . . . as Harrington explains:

> On the one hand, God is a powerful fire, seemingly unapproachable since he transcends human categories and forms of discourse. On the other hand, he is passionately involved in the affairs of his people. The exalted "Other" is at the same time an active Goodness within the community. He is giver of life, but he is also the most dangerous force in the world.[164]

---

162. Hannah K. Harrington, *Holiness* (London, New York: Routledge, 2001), 13.

163. J.E. Hartley, *Leviticus* (WBC 4; Dallas: Word Inc., 1998), 312.

164. Harrington, 44.

We see the same contagious power of God's holiness at work in Jesus' ministry. By contact with Jesus, the unclean become pure, the dead come back to life, the oppressed get freedom, the sick gain health, and the sinners receive forgiveness. The contagious holiness of Jesus transforms people around him and brings purification, wholeness, and liberation. In Christ's ministry. the Kingdom of Heaven breaks in, loudly manifesting God's holy and saving presence among his people (Matt. 1:21-23).

Jesus' practices and attitude are in stark contrast with the Pharisaic notion of holiness. For them, holiness is about separation and maintenance of purity boundaries; they stay away from the sinners and the unclean. Jesus crosses these invisible, but tangible, separation lines in order to bring those on the fringes of social and religious life to the center of the Kingdom of God. For Jesus, holiness is about this active and transformative presence. Jesus' disciples are called to do the same (Mark 3:13-19, 6:6-13), i.e. to practice contagious, transformative, and inclusive holiness that changes lives of others and manifests God's presence in this world.

"You shall be holy to me . . . I have separated you from other people to be mine" (Lev. 20:24b-26).

The language of separation indeed surfaces in Leviticus in connection to holiness, but it often refers to the *creation* of Israel. For example, Lev 20:24-26 uses the language of Gen 1 where "separation" refers to God's creative activity: separating elements in order to create the universe. Jacob Milgrom notes that the creation of Israel—by separating her from other nations—has brought order to the human realm and thus completed "the divine process of creation."[165] Structural anthropologist Mary Douglas also notes that YHWH's holiness serves as a principle of ordering of creation as well as social and religious life.[166]

Thus "separation" in this passage is *not* about withdrawal. On the contrary, YHWH creates his "holy people and priestly nation" (Ex. 19:6) with a special mission in mind: to manifest the presence of God to other nations and to represent the whole of humanity to him. They are both set apart *from* other nations and *for* a purpose.

In Leviticus 20:26, God has created the people of Israel to be his own possession. The holiness of the people is about *belonging* to God. This privileged relationship makes them different from "other people." YHWH's holy people are called to *counter-cultural life* that is radically distinct from the customs of

165. Milgrom, Leviticus 1-16, 3A:1397.

166. Mary Douglas, *Purity and Danger* (London, New York: Routledge, 1966), 53.

surrounding nations. The rest of Leviticus 20 calls the Israelites to say "no" to child sacrifices, to magic rituals, to weird sexual practices, and to eating unclean food.

This notion of holiness as *counter-cultural living* is very important for modern Christians. God's holiness often confronts human patterns of life and values. In the society that praises go-getters and worships success, live out servanthood. In the society that worships money, practice sacrificial giving and reliance on God. In the society that values individualism, create healthy communities of faith. In the society that encourages consumerism, exercise modesty and taking care of others. The holy people are called to an alternative way of living that reflects holiness of God.

"Be holy, for I the Lord your God am holy" (Lev. 19:1-2).

Chapter 19 is one of the key texts in Leviticus. It starts with the call to *all* people of Israel to be holy. Holiness is not exclusively reserved for ancient clergy. YHWH expects the common people to be holy as well. The whole nation of Israel has to maintain holiness if they want to enjoy the life-giving presence of the Holy God.

This is followed by the list of commandments giving us a clue to what it means to be holy. They cover a whole range of issues—starting with agriculture, cloth making, ceremonial rules, beard cutting, making tattoos and finishing with the issues of social justice, fairness, love, and respect. Some commandments from the Decalogue also were added to this mix.

But what does holiness have to do with all of this? First, the commandments represent the totality of life of ancient Israelites; they ought to reflect holiness in *all* aspects of their lives. YHWH requires nothing less but complete commitment to him. Second, these commandments somehow reflect the holiness of God himself. Holiness is not only a category of powerful presence or a special status; it also has ethical dimensions deeply rooted in the character of God. Israelites are called to have fair balances, to exercise justice, to take care of poor and disfranchised, to be honest, to be truthful, to be respectful, and most importantly to love both neighbors (Lev 19:18) and aliens (Lev 19:34) because this way of life reflects who God is.

The Israelites are called to be holy because YHWH is holy. It is a call *to imitate* God's holiness, imitate his character. They are ought to reflect *his* justice, righteousness, and love in all aspects of everyday life. The holiness of people is inseparably linked to the divine source.

Conclusion

A careful reading of Leviticus easily breaks down our perception of holiness as separation. Its emphasis on the presence of Holy God among his holy people is foundational for understanding holiness in both Old and New Testaments. Reimagining holiness around the concept of active and contagious presence takes us away from the logic of separation and withdrawal from the wider society. It forces us to embrace a more positive vision of holiness: living out the contagious, transformative, and inclusive holiness of God.

The holiness people are called to a counter-cultural life that is based on God's love, justice, and righteousness. They are called to be like the holy God in loving neighbors and foreigners, in bringing salvation, freedom, restoration, and life. Those who belong to God are called to imitation and manifestation of God's holiness in this world. Here the ancient notion of holiness happily meets the modern idea of incarnational ministry.

Originally from Russia, Arseny Ermakov currently serves as Head of Biblical Studies at Booth College, Sydney, Australia. His research interests lay the area of holiness and purity in the ancient world and the Bible. He is married with two lovely girls Maria and Kira.

Holiness As Priesthood
Eric Frey

> *Then Moses brought Aaron and his sons forward, and washed them with water. He put the tunic on him, fastened the sash around him, clothed him with the robe, and put the ephod on him. He then put the decorated band of the ephod around him, tying the ephod to him with it. He placed the breastpiece on him, and in the breastpiece he put the Urim and the Thummim. And he set the turban on his head, and on the turban, in front, he set the golden ornament, the holy crown, as the Lord commanded Moses. . . . He poured some of the anointing oil on Aaron's head and anointed him, to consecrate him. And Moses brought forward Aaron's sons, and clothed them with tunics, and fastened sashes around them, and tied headdresses on them, as the Lord commanded Moses. (Lev. 8:6-13, NRSV)*

It was a Sunday just like every other, except that on this particular Sunday, after fielding question after question from my youth group about how their Roman Catholic friends were different from themselves, I had decided to use the Sunday School hour to take my youth group to Mass. I arranged to have the priest meet with the group to answer their questions after Mass, and after that I made plans to have lunch together to help them unpack their experience.

As it turns out, the things they noticed first—the thing that stuck with them the longest—was their most profound realization of the day. When we arrived, their senses were immediately saturated. Christian symbols were etched into the glass doors. The windows brought biblical scenes to life in vivid stained glass. The saints were present, too—many of them portrayed in statues. The smell of decades of burnt incense exuded from the walls, which were themselves adorned with tapestries and banners. The soft melodies of the organ filled the air as people began filling the pews, genuflecting, kneeling and praying. The only thing missing was the chatter.

The first question posed by my youth group that day—and the question we spent most of our time later unpacking—was why the people came in quietly and genuflected before making their way into the pew where they knelt in silent prayer until Mass began. Why were the people doing this? Why was our church so full of busyness and noise? Young enquiring minds wanted to know!

What they discovered is that holiness always has a thread of transcendence running through it. As much as we emphasize holiness as presence and incarnation and even love, holiness must also always be understood as separation and otherness.[167]

Our Church of the Nazarene tradition tends to gravitate toward the God who is present to us and incarnate among us, but God is not that simple. God after all *is* holy, and the Hebrew term most commonly translated "holy" (*qodesh*) is literally "apartness." God is certainly present and incarnate, but God is also the God who is wholly other.

When speaking of God, this otherness is expressed in terms of transcendence. When speaking of human beings, this otherness is best expressed in terms of priesthood. Priesthood, however, is not something with which our tradition is comfortable.

The small town in which I minister is one heavily influenced by Roman Catholicism and Eastern Orthodoxy. One Thursday evening, a woman from my church was helping me greet the children who were coming into our children's ministry. A new boy came in and I introduced myself as Eric, the pastor. He looked at me confused. Then, a light came on in his eyes, and he replied, "Oh. You are the priest."

Knowing the culture of the area, I knew what he meant by his question, so I simply answered, "Yes."

The woman with me, however, was quite taken back that I would consider myself a priest. She quickly corrected me, saying to the boy, "Well, really, he is our pastor. We don't have priests here."

We just aren't sure what to do with priesthood. Whether talking about our clergy as priests or about the church as a priesthood, we get a little nervous when conversations turn toward the topic of priesthood. This presents a gaping hole in our theology of holiness if we cannot come to terms with a version of holiness that includes a strong sense of priesthood.

Peter Leithart helpfully articulates a theology of priesthood that gives us a framework for moving forward.[168] Consider the Old Testament priesthood. When

---

167. Allan Coppedge makes an excellent case in *Portraits of God: A Biblical Theology of Holiness* (Downers Grove: IVP Academic, 2001) that God's holiness cannot be reduced to any one of God's attributes or "roles." Rather each role is a unique portrait revealing one aspect of God's holiness. It is not problematic then to understand holiness in a variety of ways—even contradictory ways—as this project intends to do, but rather God's holiness is so rich and deep as to encompass all of the attributes and roles revealed in the Scriptures.

168. Peter J. Leithart, "Attendants of Yahweh's House: Priesthood in the Old Testament," *Journal for the Study of the Old Testament*, 85 (1999): 3.

people think about Old Testament priests, they tend to think first of a priest's work. Most commonly, people think of the liturgical work of offering sacrifices. Understanding the Old Testament priesthood, however, will be difficult, if not impossible, if it is viewed foundationally in terms of the work a priest does. There is far too much variety and diversity involved in priestly ministry to define a priest by his work.

Rather, to understand the Old Testament priesthood, we must understand the *context* of the priestly ministry. We must ask *where* and *for whom* did the priest work. Leithart argues that the context of priestly ministry is best understood by considering the Hebrew concepts of "stand" and "serve." It is here, at the intersection of standing and serving, that the priesthood takes root. A priest is one who first has a special standing before God, having been granted through Christ a privileged access to God. The priest, then, is one who stands before God, enjoying a unique relationship with God.

The priest is secondly one who serves. This service has a dual meaning best expressed in the notion of "the house of God." On the one hand, the "house of God" refers to the Temple; on the other hand, the "house of God" refers to Israel. The priest serves both in the Temple and among the people. The object of service is likewise twofold. The priest serves God; the priest serves the people. Relationship and service are thus the hallmarks of those set apart as priests.[169]

How then does this theological framework help us to understand holiness as priesthood? When we take this theology of Old Testament priesthood and apply it to the New Testament concept of a "priesthood of believers," things start to come into focus.

Aside from the usual texts (1 Peter 2:9; Rev. 1:6.), the key to understanding this priesthood of believers is found in Hebrews 10:19-25, "Let us approach with a true heart in full assurance of faith, with our hearts sprinkled clean from an evil conscience and our bodies washed with pure water" (Heb. 10:22). What is surprising it that this is a *baptismal* text. What is more surprising is that it is also a *priestly* text! According to Leithart, "Hebrews 10:22 describes baptism with imagery borrowed from ordination."[170] As ordination functioned for ancient Israel, baptism now functions for the church. Baptism makes priests![171] I am a priest. You are a priest. Through baptism we are brought into a new standing, or

---

169. It is worth noting that this same pattern of standing and serving is present as the author of Hebrews talks of the High Priesthood of Christ, though the posture of standing sees a subtle shift to a posture of "sitting."

170. Peter J. Leithart, "Womb of the World: Baptism and the Priesthood of the New Covenant in Hebrews 10.19-22," *Journal for the Study of the Old Testament* 22, no. 78 (2000): 54.

171. This line of thinking is prevalent in the work of the early Fathers (see: Tertullian, On Baptism; Ambrose, On the Mysteries; and Cyril, Catechetical Lectures).

relationship with God. Through baptism we are given a new ministry of serving God and serving God's people—the world. This is our context for ministry as the priesthood of the baptized.

Standing and serving: this is priesthood. This is holiness. The holy God is making a holy people. The God who is holy (wholly other, transcendent, far above and set apart) is making a holy people who are themselves wholly other and set apart to enjoy their unique and privileged relationship with God. The God who is holy is making a holy people who are themselves set apart from all creation and set apart for all creation, to love and serve all creation and bring all peoples to share in that special relationship with God. To be holy is to be set apart. To be holy is to be a priest.

> *To him who loves us and has freed us from our sins by his blood, and has made us to be a kingdom and priests to serve his God and Father—to him be glory and power for ever and ever! Amen.* (Rev. 1:6, NRSV)

Eric E. Frey is a graduate of both MVNU ('99) and NTS ('06) and is pursuing a Doctor of Ministry in liturgical studies at Trinity School for Ministry. He presently serves the Church of the Nazarene in Toronto, Ohio where he resides with his wife Antonina and their three children: Pax, Pierce and Pria.

Manna or Mammon:
Holiness as Economic Imagination
Hank Spaulding

In the modern world, the definition of value has shifted from character-based logic to monetary-based assumptions. For example, D. Stephen Long shows this shift in his fact-value distinction. This distinction suggests that the reality of a thing (character) can be boiled down to its economic accidents. Long illustrates this through a popular economics illustration involving a married psychologist that makes $50 an hour. This woman, Mrs. Harris, chooses to spend an hour cooking a meal for her family. The question then becomes, "what are the opportunity costs involved in her preparing the family meal?" Disconnected from character-based values, the answer becomes simply that the Harris family misses the net profit of $50 minus the cost of ordering out. Long argues this common example and its equally common solution means that family and individuals find their meaning primarily in their identity as producers and consumers. According to Long, the character of a thing is becoming slowly subordinate to economic value.[172]

Furthermore, this mentality has also taken root in our churches. For the Church of the Nazarene, this means that our doctrine of holiness has become increasingly exposed to "monetary values" of interpreting the faith and holiness. Large numbers equal value while small numbers equal unhealthy visions.

Two traditions in Scripture help us name what is at stake in the valuation of faith: *manna* and *mammon*. The former assumes possession of something while the latter reveals what possesses us. Understanding the relationship and the presuppositions of *manna* and *mammon* helps us understand our current situation and the way forward into the future of holiness theology.

Mammon: Economics as Hegemonic Captivation of Imagination

Mammon is the New Testament word for money used by Jesus in the Sermon on the Mount, "You cannot serve God and mammon" (Matthew 6:24, RSV). According to the textual footnotes in the RSV, "*Mammon* is a Semitic word for money or riches."[173] Something about *mammon* gets in the way of a Christian

---

172. See: D. Stephen Long, *Divine Economy: Theology and the Market* (New York: Routledge. 2006), 3-4.

173. *The New Oxford Annotated Bible: Revised Standard Bible*, Herbert G. May and Bruce M. Metzger, eds. (New York: Oxford University Press. 1977), 1178.

life, namely not just what you possess, but what possesses you. This, after all, is the wisdom of the rich young ruler parable: that God cannot possess one who is already possessed by wealth.

Thomas Sowell explains, "[Economics'] fundamental concern is with the material standard of living of society as a whole and how that is affected by particular decisions made by individuals and institutions."[174] The material existence of humanity is a necessity, but the depth of this statement begs the question, "What is economics" contribution to the good of material life?" For example, economics seems to be value-free, simply the relationship between producer and consumer within larger systems of economic structuring (i.e. capitalism, socialism, etc.).

However, this ordering of the world assumes a *mammon* understanding. The problem of what is possessed in the economic imagination of *mammon* has material consequences for the church.

Consider the following example from William Cavanaugh's book *Being Consumed*:

> Rosa Martinez produces apparel for US markets on her sewing machine in El Salvador. *You* can hire her for 33 cents . . . Transnational corporations are able to shop around the global for the most advantageous wage environments, that is, those places where people are so desperate that they must take jobs that pay extremely low wages, in many cases wages insufficient to feed and house themselves and their dependents.[175]

Cavanaugh asks whether this transaction is bad. On the one hand, Martinez chooses to lower her wages to 33 cents an hour. On the other, the company can choose to open factories that pay living wages rather than pay a lower rate to Rosa to increase profit. This economic exchange is free in the sense of absence of coercion.[176]

However, it is not free in another sense because of the involvement of consumers. Cavanaugh writes, the parties involved "feel as if they have no choice in the matter, because they assume that, given the prevailing logic of free exchange, consumers will want to want to maximize their own gain in any transaction by paying the lowest price possible for a product."[177]

---

174. Thomas Sowell, *Basic Economics: A Common Sense Guide to the Economy*. 3rd ed. (New York: Basic Books. 2007), 1.

175. William Cavanaugh, *Being Consumed* (Grand Rapids: Eerdmans, 2008), 21-2.

176. Ibid, 3.

177. Ibid.

Therefore, with the global consumer in mind, companies can pay extremely low costs in order to service the wants of the consumer. Thus, the producers of goods and services are caught in a vicious cycle of logic seeming to allow no solution outside the current dynamics.

Now Christians inhabit multiple roles within economic systems, namely, producers and/or consumers. The problem with the economic system taking over the Christian imagination is not just about buying and selling goods. The problem is that we accept limits on our imagination, which maintain the status quo for people like Rosa Martinez.

Anytime we begin to analyze this economic logic, the prevailing questions point to the current system offering the greatest good for the greatest number of people.

- Sure, the free market is an imperfect system, but isn't it the best we have?
- As good Wesleyans, are we not supposed to make all we can, save all we can, and give all we can?
- Do not the lower prices of resources create the conditions that allow us to be more charitable?
- If I had more money, couldn't I give more to people like Rosa Martinez?

The best responses to these questions are more questions.

- What actually possesses us when we ask questions like based on the existing economic worldview?
- What is necessary and what isn't?
- Does this line of thinking leave us with the rich young ruler who goes away sad because he has great wealth—or actually because great wealth has him?

Manna: Holiness as Economic Imagination

Distinct from *mammon*, *manna* is the bread from heaven. It is not a possession of the people, and they cannot control it. Its existence cannot be bought or sold, but arises from one thing: Israel's relationship to God. It would even come to define them as a people and name what possessed them. It is a sign of covenant, that the Israelites define their God through God's faithfulness. Because this God possesses them, they are given gifts like *manna*. In turn, they are given the means to live and to relate faithfully to others in the world.

In short, it is not enough for God to raise up a people out of Egypt. Instead, God wants a people that is *for* the other people. Isaiah understood this, "I will give you as a light to the nations, that my salvation may reach to the end of the earth". (Isaiah 49:6, NRSV) And what is God's salvation? "[T]o open the eyes that are blind, to bring out the prisoners from the dungeon, from the prison those who sit in darkness". (Isaiah 42: 7, NRSV) Justice accompanies righteousness, and this is essential for our understanding of holiness and entire sanctification.

Thus, entire sanctification is understood in terms the God who possesses us. Sanctification provides us with, as David Kelsey writes, "full disclosure and judgment of who we are."[178] We are not simply consumers, people possessed by *mammon*. Any understanding of charity that might keep individuals like Rosa Martinez in her prison is not charity. Rather, utilizing a *manna* understanding, we are possessed by God and understand the "other" as a gift also possessed by God.

By way of Conclusion: The Lord's Supper and the Sanctified Imagination

As it is written in Article X of the Church of the Nazarene on Entire Sanctification: "Participating in the means of grace, especially the fellowship, disciplines, and sacraments of the Church, believers grow in grace and in wholehearted love to God and neighbor."[179] What difference does taking the Eucharist make? The means of grace foster the sanctified imagination and yield practical wisdom toward how to love those run over by the train wreck of our culture's *mammon* shackled imagination. As Cavanaugh explains,

> The enacting of the body of Christ in the Eucharist has a dramatic effect on the communicability of pain from one person to another . . . The pain of the hungry person is the pain of Christ: therefore, it is also the pain of the member of Christ's body who feeds the hungry person.[180]

Partaking in the body of Christ is essential to the Wesleyan imagination of holiness. It is the lens through which we view the rest of creation, and it initiates us into the works of mercy. If we use the Wesleyan phrase, "Make all you can, save all you can, and give all you can" as a means to save structures of oppression, then its misused.

---

178. David Kelsey, *Imagining Redemption* (Louisville: Westminster John Knox. 2000), 82.

179. *Manual* (Kansas City: Nazarene Publishing House, 2013), 33.

180. Cavanaugh, 96.

Either God or *mammon* possesses us. For Wesley, this truth came before anything else: "And you cannot be faithful to God, if you trim between God and the world, if you do not serve him alone."[181] There can be no divide for the Christian. Holiness must be seen as a gift that God gives. Like *manna* it arises from the relationship that we already have with God and defines us as God's own. However, it is also a call to liberate the oppressed and to set free the captive.

Hank Spaulding is an Adjunct Professor of Theology at Mount Vernon Nazarene University. Hank is also a doctoral candidate at Garrett-Evangelical Theological Seminary in Evanston, IL. He earned an Masters in Theology Studies at Duke Divinity School and a Bachelors of Arts in Religion from Trevecca Nazarene University. He has published in various books and journals such as the Wesleyan Theological Journal *and* The Journal of Youth Ministry.

---

181. John Wesley, "NT Notes, Luke 16:13," in *Parrell Commentary on the New Testament*, Ed. Mark Water (Chattanoga: AMG Publishers, 2003), 236.

Orphanage #10

Teanna Sunberg

It was a late summer afternoon, and the kids from the orphanage were away at camp. That is August in Bulgaria, like a Balkan Sabbath, people find refuge away from Sofia. They migrate to the mountains or the seaside or a patch of land with a garden and primitive fixings. In the city, everything considered non-essential comes to a complete halt, and this thrusting, heaving entity returns to the village that it once was.

There, in that August pause, I was at Orphanage #10. Quiet. Empty. Clean. Like the Sabbath.

As I looked around, I missed the faces. My first friend from Orphanage #10 was a 16-year-old transvestite named Galin or Gallya, depending upon the day's drag choice. He actually had a father in the village, but Dad abandoned Galin to Orphange #10. Eastern Europe has a term for kids like Galin: social orphans. They are kids who have at least parent who cannot (or will not) function as the guardian, yet refuses to release them for adoption.

Orphanage #10 was full of social orphans. Kids nobody wanted but nobody would give up. And every single one had a story.

Galin prostituted himself dressed as a boy to make money for cigarettes, but he preferred to be a girl. Toni's Nigerian mom was dead, and his Bulgarian dad had contracted to sell him for organ harvesting. Lili tried to escape her hellish conditions via the 3rd floor window, fell, and laid in the snow with a broken back for several hours.

Lili's story made the national news. The other stories never did.

From a theological perspective, a God-forsaken place on planet earth does not exist, but walking through the halls of that orphanage, one stretches to find a word or a phrase that would better describe it. An Orphanage #10 teacher once said to me, "When the lights go off at night, every kind of hell exists here."

In the August pause, I closed my eyes and imagined what Hell must feel like in Orphanage #10.

Under the surface, there was a cosmic system at work. We know that devastating, powerful, evil, perilous, blood-letting, life-draining system. There is a spirit that is actively, systematically, comprehensively, and successfully devouring humanity.

And, what Hell #10's teacher did not voice, I must. Where was God? Where was God when every kind of hell was happening?

In Bucharest, Anna's grandmother died, and there was nobody left to protect her. Sent to the orphanage, the director noted her beauty and fed her better so that he could prostitute her for a fatter price. She was 13. Sold as a sex slave at thirteen. THIRTEEN.

And the words are so tragic, so ugly, so evil, so grotesque that the ink of our pens runs blood red for the pain of the torturous story told. Where was God?

I learned the word, *Habiru*, from Tim Green while sitting on a dairy farm in Croatia. As he talked about an ancient people group that nobody wanted and nobody liked, the *Habiru*, I recognized their faces. Dirty, stinking, nomadic wanderers: a scourge to every civilized, organized culture around them. *Habiru.* Not a name they called themselves, but one given by outsiders and said with twisted faces and a spray of spittle for the force of the disgust.

"I know them," I cried. "Here in Eastern Europe, they are derogatorily called Gypsy. There's a village just down the road."

Shaking his head, Dr. Green redirected me to Abraham and Sara. By other nations, they were called, *Habiru*, like a big, angry jagged X in the side of humanity's genetic pool.

Habiru. Hebrew. The people that nobody wanted. The slaves. The social orphans of the gods.

And while the prophets of Baal and Ashera danced for fertility, and the Pharaohs became gods, and the Greeks wove mythologies, the *Habiru*—the people that nobody wanted—became a cherished possession in the heart of a Holy God.

Holy. The word that the non-*Habiru* grabbed to explain this Israelite God. This God like no other that the dominant nations had experienced. A God who loved, interacted with, spoke to, and protected—a God who dwelt with his people.

A Holy God. "A God like none we have ever seen before," they said, grasping for words. Prostituting did not motivate him to give a plentiful harvest. He was not vindictive, easily angered, self-serving, or unjust. He was not stoic, removed, or distant. A Holy God, different, full of love. Nations watched the deity of a despised people and saw a God that was powerfully present in the lives of the nomadic *Habiru*.

For the first time in the span of my theological life, the word "holy" had been rescued from the tombs of books.

Because, there has to be a word that breaks into the tortuously pregnant silence made by 27 million blood-curdling screams today: 27 million modern day slaves, marketed for prostitution, for slave labor, and for organ harvesting.

Because, there has to be a response to the tortured in-take of a heaving sob in North Korea.

Because, there has to be a peace-giving response to the ragged death rattle of war zones across our planet.

Because there has to be medicine for the devastation of disease in Africa, and bread for the starving, and a well for the thirsty.

Because there has to be an answer to the question, "Where are you God when the night is long and every kind of hell is here?"

Only holiness can answer that accusation. Only holiness can bring words that have healing. Only holiness knows what it means to become *Habiru* for love. "We have never seen a God like this before."

Holy. A Love that is present in brokenness. A Love that is assaulted, hungry, thirsty, abandoned, tortured. A God who chooses to be powerfully present through every dark night. Holy love.

And how I wish, Oh God, how I wish that my fingers could stop typing. How I wish that our story ended with a God who was risen and waved the pains of our world away with his magic wand. How I wish that my question did not boomerang back to me, "Where were you in the dark night of Hell #10?"

It is convenient to blame God for the hell happening in our world. To stand with our toes on the barrier of time and point our fingers of accusation: "Why didn't you? Where were you? God."

Into the vast expanse of history and time, Jesus speaks, "Be holy, for I am holy." And hearing those God-words, we check that our skirts are low enough and our necklines are high enough and our language is clean enough. We hide our sins, and we lock secrets behind doors because somewhere we learned that holiness is a judgmental, vindictive, and legalistic god who smacks us with a bolt of lightning if we sin. Our version of God is so Greek.

But, God is *Habiru*: despised and homeless and present. And we, we are to be like him, to join him in his presence through the dark night of Hell #10.

"We have never seen a God like this," they said stretching for words to grasp this *Habiru* God's powerful love.

Orthodox theologian, Bishop Kallistos Ware, reflects, "it is not holiness, but evil that is dull."[182] He means that the Holy Spirit's work in us is a continual

---

182. "Excerpts from *The Orthodox Church* by Bishop Kallistos Ware, Part II: Faith and Worship," http://www.fatheralexander.org/booklets/english/history_timothy_ware_2.htm, accessed Aug. 15, 2014.

becoming of what we already are. A redeeming, a perfecting, a reclaiming of who God already made us to be.

To be holy, is to be vulnerably broken and poured out for the love of the world.

To be holy, is to be a beautifully obedient movement towards God.

To be holy, is to be becoming a sharpened image: a reflection of the *Habiru* God.

To be holy, is to be present so that the unique creation of what it is to be me is poured out in the night of Hell #10. And to believe, in faith, that this is the will of God and the mystical victory of the Cross.

Sometimes, I worry that the Church has entered into an early Sabbath. As if we have decided that the work here is done and that the saints are gathering in for that final hymn. Or maybe we have just decided that the sin out there is too powerful, too evil, that hell is bigger and stronger and more terrifying than we ever imagined. Or maybe we prefer the refuge of a quiet and empty sanctuary to the thrusting, heaving entity of the world in the night.

It is a rainy Tuesday afternoon in June when we push twenty college students through the open doors of an average house in the middle of a Bucharest neighborhood. The people who live there have been waiting, and to be honest, they are a little unsure. Afraid. The divide between American students from a Christian college and the women who now call this place home is wide.

With pizza and Cokes teetering on knees, the awkward silences of broken languages and broken bodies and broken lives works its way into games and laughter. I stay in the back and watch Anna. She is careful, much too careful for a 13 year old. Hanging out in the doorway, hesitating to enter the room, sometimes she laughs with the group, but she shields her body behind Betty, the counselor at the Open Door.

Twenty minutes later, Anna has moved inside the doorway and is perched on the edge of the chair.

And I look around the room at the faces: missionary kids and college students, Romanian men and women committed to rescue, and women who are escaping a life of sexual slavery. I see a 13 year old who survived a nightmare. And the Spirit whispers to me, "This is holy ground."

My toes wiggle in their summer sandals as I think about Moses trudging down a mountain with two slabs of rock on his back. Ten commandments, and one of them says to remember the Sabbath and to keep it holy. Funny, how I have always limited the Sabbath to Sunday afternoon naps and church.

The Sabbath was the day that God took a seat in the garden and savored the good of his creation. Sabbath was the day in the desert when the slaves celebrated the end of their captivity and the beginning of their freedom.

The Sabbath is a Tuesday in Bucharest when a thirteen year old whose body was sold for sex finds a home. The Sabbath is God present in his people.

Remember the Sabbath and keep it holy.

Teanna Sunberg has spent a good portion of her life in Eastern Europe experiencing the rhythms of God's grace in the face of challenges and the embrace of diverse cultures. She lives with her husband, Jay, and their four daughters in Budapest, Hungary, where they serve the Central Europe Field as missionaries. She is a writer and a teacher of literature and missions.

Holiness Now:
Resurrection and Shalom on the Big Island
Eric Paul and Ryan Fasani

Hanu (hah-noo), an unwed mother of two young children, is a "local here." She's of Polynesian descent, grew up in Hawaii, and considers the culture of the Big Island normative. Hanu conceived her first child as a teenager. Under the pressures of motherhood, part-time employment, living in a multigenerational home, and being single, she chose to complete a GED rather than high school. Her current boyfriend (and father of her second child) works for a hotel when not serving scheduled, three-month stints in jail. Cost of living here is beyond their means, and they suffer from health complications and family dysfunction.

We have found Hanu's story very common. As pastors on the Big Island of Hawaii, we ask: What does holiness look like for Hanu?

The *doctrine* of holiness is the church's articulation of Christ's life being enacted, through the power of grace, in the world. The *life* of holiness is the embodiment of that truth. However, our observation is that the doctrine has largely ignored the Christ who came preaching the Shalom Community as the Kingdom of God, and thus has not been helpful for realizing embodied holiness.

We contend that holiness is the embodiment of Shalom in a particular place with particular people—where Christ's life has become our own. Consequently, holiness is both contextual (to a particular place) and communal (to a particular people). We find it helpful to use the biblical vision of the Shalom Community (Micah 4) to understand embodied holiness, which is to say that the biblical vision of a particularly placed people will help us better understand how we ought to envision holiness for Hanu here and now in our community.

Hanu and the Holiness of Our Past

Holiness has been taught as a moment of entire sanctification rendered by the grace of God in an individual's heart. The Church of the Nazarene's understanding of where sanctification occurs is indicative of where we locate sin: in the heart of the individual. This is why the familiar adage is so fitting: "Justification is what God does *for* us. Sanctification is what God does *in* us." Sin is rooted *in* the human heart; therefore, sanctification also takes root *in* the human heart. Unfortunately, with this understanding, holiness can only be understood in contrast to an individual's (non-communal) breech of (non-contextualized) faithfulness.

In this way, the Church of the Nazarene has focused on Hanu and her boyfriend's litany of personal sins: premarital intercourse, criminal activity, poor financial stewardship, etc. The Good News for Hanu, from this perspective, is that God forgives and can do a sanctifying work in her. The bad news is that it leaves unaddressed a majority of Hanu's life and, therefore, a majority of the healing God desires.

The scriptures are clear that God alone is a holy, self-giving God, and God desires to sanctify Hanu's whole realm of existence (Colossians 1). Locating sin and sanctification in the heart of the individual certainly offers the potential for a narrow "inner cleansing," but it ignores the totality of God's desire for reconciliation, which includes the breeding ground of Hanu's sin.

We simply cannot separate the experience of holiness from all that is implicated in the holy self-giving of God. We contend that this self-giving and the Kingdom preached by Christ are all-encompassing, implicating the complex web of relationships and influences in Hanu's life. Where Hanu lives, her social and familial network, and the cultural structures that govern her life are all environments of influence and sinfulness. Sanctification, then, must be dislodged from the very limited locale of the heart so that it can be realized as broadly as God desires.

But just as Hanu's life (and sinfulness) is unlike anyone else's, so too should sanctification be unique to her experience. Sanctification must be conceived broadly enough to include Hanu's whole sphere experience and particular enough to be realized in her immediate, unique context. Hanu's story teaches us that holiness is necessarily both communal and contextual.

The Shalom Community of Micah 4

Holiness, far from only being the state of a believer's heart, is God's move to restore the intricate web of relationships in which we all participate: personal, social, political, economic, etc. But if God is actively restoring these relationships, then we must be able to speak in terms of restoring concrete interpersonal, socio-political and even economic relationships. Inversely, we must speak of the brokenness needing healing in each of those relational arenas. We must speak of both communal brokenness and the communal context of restoration.

Scripture is ripe with such articulation. Take for example Micah 4:1-4:

> *In days to come . . .*
> *many nations shall come and say:*
> *'Come, let us go up to the mountain of the Lord,*

to the house of the God of Jacob;
that he may teach us his ways
and that we may walk in his paths. . . '
He shall judge between many peoples,
and shall arbitrate between strong nations far away;
they shall beat their swords into ploughshares,
and their spears into pruning-hooks;
nation shall not lift up sword against nation,
neither shall they learn war any more;
but they shall all sit under their own vines and under their own fig trees,
and no one shall make them afraid;
for the mouth of the Lord of hosts has spoken.

In general, the prophets proclaim words of disaster and optimism, grief and comfort, apocalyptic end and future hope. But they refuse to divorce "spiritual health" from the totality of health in communities. When we read and engage prophetic literature, we must read it through a holistic "lens of life." No aspect of the human experience is excluded from the blessings and ultimate judgment of God. As such, three important aspects of Shalom are apparent in this prophetic vision.

First, this is a religious text. God, judgment, and a divine voice along with particular references to "the God of Jacob" and "Lord of hosts" are all clear references to a religious tradition known as Israel. But the vision itself is hardly "religious," as if religion were a sector of life distinct from economy or politics. Instead, God's restoration is concrete and practical, a matter of worship *and* work.

Second, Micah gives us a broad picture of what the Kingdom will look like, and it's not only the restoration of individuals. The restoration encompasses individual estrangement from creation, poverty, starvation, and violence. God's sanctifying power reaches into every facet of communal existence.

Third, the prophetic vision is a universal hope but not a universal reference. In other words, the particularities of a this-world communal context are evident. Though there are references to "nations far away" and "many peoples," the peaceful community envisioned is not like every community. It is a particularly placed people. They are familiar with an agrarian lifestyle ("ploughshares"), which is to say they are not nomadic and make a living through cultivating soil. They have a history of combat and wield a particular arsenal of weapons ("swords and spears"). Among them are orchardists (requiring "pruning-forks") and vintners or winemakers ("sitting under their vines"). They may have a history of being the underdog, likely a reference to their small size ("strong nations far away . . . [making] them afraid"). We get the image of an agrarian community with a non-aggressive foreign policy or expansion tactic, relieved to finally put up their weapons to more fully invest in peaceful and satisfying pursuits of stewarding creation.

The holiness vision of Micah 4 is not limited to God's sanctification of the human heart; instead, it is a holy restoration of all the complex facets of a particular community, in and between the concrete lives of neighbors in a particular place. Holiness is communal. Holiness is contextual.

Holiness Now

So how does Micah 4 help us understand sanctification for Hanu? Micah clearly understood the distinctions of the envisioned community. In order to envision redemption and sanctification, we need to know that which is broken (needing healing) and unholy (needing to be sanctified). We can start, then, by better understanding unique brokenness and sin in Hanu's context.

Many of Hanu's relationships are strained or broken, creating immense stress, anxiety, and fear. The consistency necessary for marital health is abruptly interrupted every few months when her almost-husband is in jail—vacillating between single parenthood and dual parenthood. Her living environment is not conducive to conflict resolution because of the proximity to multiple adult family members, who are themselves unhealthy. Discussions often turn to arguments, arguments to abuse. And each sphere of relationship is negatively affected by her material poverty.

She also suffers from multiple failed socio-political systems in Hawaii: a food system that promotes disease and unhealthy bodies, a punitive criminal system that dismembers families, an education system that cannot accommodate unique family needs, an economic system that exacerbates poverty, a governmental aid system that serves as a disincentive to gainful employment, and a cultural system that is often ethnically oppressive.

As we learn more about the complexity of Hanu's brokenness, we begin to see multiple interlocking spheres. When one sphere is stressed or broken, the pain (or sin) reverberates into all other spheres. We believe that God cares and longs to restore the brokenness in each of these interrelated spheres so that Life and sanctification may be fully expressed.

The question of holiness could be posed thusly: What if these relationships could be healed? We contend that this is the abundant, shalom life that God desires. When we abandon the belief that sanctification addresses the sinful heart alone and begin to believe that the self-giving holy God that we worship desires the complexity of our existence to heal and be made new, then we begin to harness the imagination of Micah and the Shalom Community. Sin, we believe, is a "heart issue" *and* a "systems issue" *and* a "relationship issue" (Ephesians 2), thereby making sanctification holistically relevant and necessary.

For years, the local church created specific programs to heal suffering in each sphere (i.e. food pantry or ESL classes). But, in Hanu's case, her experience and suffering from sin is unique to her context, rendering generic programs partially effective at best. Because Hanu's sin is both internal and systemic, she suffers from a web of brokenness, rendering charitable, one-dimensional solutions too narrow and mostly unhelpful. The only "solution" we can imagine for Hanu's convolution of sin is the slow and gentle inclusion into a worshipping body that takes seriously God's call to Life and holiness in every facet of existence.

As is the case in Micah 4, only a self-giving community bent toward holiness can envision and ultimately realize a holiness for Hanu's broken context. Only a community of Shalom can realize a radically different (set apart, holy) way of life together—from the way we consume and clothe ourselves to the way we interact with the broader market economy, from the way we nurse our babies to the way we adopt unwanted children, from the way we embrace a diversity of cultures to the way we worship one God, from the way we use our ploughshares for farming to the refusal to bear arms. These are part of the Shalom Community. These are all part of Hanu's sanctification. We find that we cannot talk of Hanu's holiness apart from the holiness of the community in which she lives. Imagining and enacting such a community contextualizes Hanu's life while caring for both individual and communal growth in Christ.

Ryan Fasani and Eric Paul (Senior Pastor and Missionary-Pastor at Kona Coast Church of the Nazarene) see and work toward a unified Kona Coast where the Gospel is uniquely embodied in diverse communities.

The Powerful Helper:
The Holy Spirit in the Prologue of Mark
Nabil Habiby

Entirely Sanctified—Say What?

The sun had set, and night was upon us. I was walking silently with my college friend, surrounded by the beautiful mountains of Lebanon. The time was ripe for a deep talk, "We believe in a second experience of being filled completely with the Holy Spirit—entire sanctification," said I to my Evangelical friend.

"Say what?" he replied, his voice showing a distinct fear of heresy. I was not able to explain what being "filled" with the Holy Spirit means.

Turning to the Bible does not always give easy answers about who the Holy Spirit is or what being filled with the Spirit actually means. C. K. Barrett questions the limited mention of the Spirit in the life and words of Jesus in the Synoptic Gospels in light of the fact that the early church believed itself to be experiencing the rule of the Spirit in a unique and moving way.[183] I will reiterate the same questions as we look into the beginning of Mark: Where is the Holy Spirit? What role did the Spirit play in the ministry of Jesus, and consequently, what role does the Spirit play in our lives today as Christians?

Understanding the Holy Spirit in Mark—How Shall We Go About It?

Like R.T. France, when considering the narrative character of the Holy Spirit, I prefer to read Mark as on unified story rather than as separated sections.[184] Moreover, Mieke Bal argues that only actors who are related to functional events should be selected. He defines "functional events," a term borrowed from Barthes, as events that create a choice, fulfill a choice, or reveal the consequences of a choice, thus, leading to other events.[185] Hence, I shall highlight only those passages where the Holy Spirit is mentioned, then consider whether or not the Spirit is a functional actor in the story.

---

183. C. K. Barrett, *The Holy Spirit and the Gospel Tradition* (London: SPCK, 1966), 1-2.

184. R.T. France, *The Gospel of Mark* (NIGTC; Grand Rapids: Eerdmans, 2002), 1-2.

185. Bal, Narratology, 184-5.

Functionality of the Holy Spirit in Mark's Prologue—
What Does the Spirit Do?

The Holy Spirit is mentioned six times in Mark, but since the Spirit's role is more prominent in the prologue (and space does not suffice), only the three mentions there will be discussed. The prologue of Mark stretches from verse 1 to 15.

As the passage itself proclaims in verse 1, it is the "beginning of the gospel of Jesus Christ" (Mark 1:1, ESV). These 15 verses can be seen as this beginning, or preparation for the Lord. After that, from verse 16 and onwards, we see Jesus forming disciples, casting out demons, healing, and teaching.

The Holy Spirit is first mentioned in verse 8. In verse 7-8, Mark shows the difference between John and his successor in terms of might, value, and manner of baptism.[186] We have a clear contrast being made between water and Holy Spirit.[187] The phrase "Holy Spirit" points to the eschatological hope of God pouring His Spirit, of Him coming down and dwelling upon His people.[188] Thus, baptism in the Spirit has eschatological connotations and is a fulfillment of Old Testament hopes (Is. 44:3, Ez. 39:29, Joel 3:1f).[189]

The Holy Spirit, in this first mention, is related to a functional event: the fulfillment of an eschatological hope. This event will—using Bal's language—create a choice for people whether or not to participate in this baptism, and it will enact a change, a movement from water to Spirit. The new baptism will be done by/in the Holy Spirit. Hence, we can conclude that in this verse the Spirit is a functional actor inasmuch as the Spirit is vital to the coming ministry of Jesus.

The second mention of the Holy Spirit in the prologue comes in verse 10, when the Spirit descends on/into Jesus. We are invited in 1:9-11 to focus on the minute details of the baptism—the movement of Jesus, the opening of the heavens, the descent of the Spirit, and the voice from heaven—rather than the act of baptism itself. This is the epitome of the revelation of the identity of Jesus in the first section.[190]

The Holy Spirit appears again on the scene in verse 10, this time using the parallel verbs "came up" and "descending."[191] The opening of the heavens draws

---

186. Morna D. Hooker, *The Gospel According to Saint Mark* (BNTC; London: A & C Black, 1991), 37-8.

187. Kent Brower, *Mark: A Commentary in the Wesleyan Tradition* (NBBC; Kansas City: Beacon Hill Press, 2012), 56.

188. R. T. France, *The Gospel of Mark* (NIGTC; Grand Rapids: Eerdmans, 2002), 72.

189. Hooker, Mark, 38.

190. Brower, Mark, 57.

191. Guelich, Mark, 31.

from similar language seen in Ez. 1:1 and Is. 63:19.[192] The descent of the Spirit on Jesus is the anointing of Him. This anointing serves to point to Him being the Son of God.[193] Hence, through the Holy Spirit, God now takes full control of Jesus.[194] Jesus carries the Holy Spirit and is God's presence on earth. He is also the way through which people can be baptized in the Holy Spirit.[195] The gap between heaven and earth is crossed in Mark 1:10.[196]

If the Spirit was functional as an instrument of baptism in the first mention, here the Spirit is the carrier/authenticator of the Divine proclamation and the in-dweller of the Messiah. The Spirit's role is securely tied to the Spirit's functional event, one in which a choice is fulfilled: the Father's choice to proclaim His son as Messiah and Jesus' choice to accept this anointing. This event gives Jesus His identity and launches him on his mission.

The third and final mention of the Holy Spirit in the prologue comes in verse 12. The Spirit is the driving force behind the temptation scene.[197] Interestingly, Jesus is a "static" character, while the active verbs are attached to the Spirit and the angels.[198] The verb used by Mark to describe the Spirit's leading of Jesus is strong,[199] and Mark uses it to speak of exorcising demons!

As for the wilderness scene, the peaceful dwelling of Jesus with the wild beasts echoes the peaceful Eden of God's original plan. Similarly, the temptation, the character of Satan, the wild beasts, and the angels all speak of a cosmic conflict between God and his agents and the agents of evil.[200]

Once more, the Spirit is a functional actor in the prologue. The Spirit is the one who leads Jesus into the wilderness, thus enacting a change in the events and bringing about a functional event: Jesus accepting the anointing of the Sprit and finding himself in conflict with Satan.

The prologue gives us a glimpse of the movement of the Spirit.[201] The Spirit is functional as an instrument/means of baptism, as a conveyer of the divine

---

192. France, Mark, 77.

193. Tom Wright, *Mark for Everyone* (London: SPCK, 2001), 5.

194. Ira Brent Driggers, *Following God through Mark: Theological Tension in the Second Gospel* (Louisville: Westminster John Knox, 2007), 15.

195. Gabrielle Markusse-Overduin, "Salvation in Mark: The Death of Jesus and the Path of Discipleship," (Ph.D. diss., The University of Manchester, 2013), 41-2.

196. Elizabeth Struthers Malbon, *Narrative Space and Mythic Meaning in Mark* (The Biblical Seminar 13; Sheffield: JSOT Press, 1991), 82.

197. C. K. Barrett, *The Holy Spirit and the Gospel Tradition* (London: SPCK, 1966), 49.

198. France, Mark, 83.

199. Robert A. Guelich, *Mark 1-8:26* (WBC 34A; Dallas: Word Books, 1989), 38.

200. Brower, Mark, 63-4.

201. Hooker, Mark, 31-2.

proclamation, as a leader of the Messiah, and also as an instigator and helper in conflict with the powers of evil.

The Holy Spirit in the Church—Is the Spirit Functional?

Where is the Holy Spirit, or where should the Spirit be, in the Church today? The Spirit is a powerful presence, but the Spirit works in the background, ever pushing Jesus forward on His mission of spreading the Kingdom of God. The Spirit is the "creative activity of God which calls into being the conditions of the Messianic era."[202] The Spirit is the one through whom the followers of Jesus are to be baptized, and we see the Spirit in Mark aiding the disciples as they stand in front of the authorities (13:11) much as Jesus stood.

Perhaps the Church today needs to remember that the mere presence of the Holy Spirit in Jesus, in our world, speaks of a God of active holiness. Mark is telling us that Jesus wants to baptize each disciple and the collective Church, by the Spirit, so that they too may go out and preach the kingdom of "boundary-shattering" holiness.[203] We, as modern day disciples, are called to receive the help of the Spirit. We are called to be—like the Spirit and with his aid—helpers of God, challenging all that is dark in our world. We are entirely sanctified in working to sanctify the entire world.

Nabil was born in Kuwait to a Lebanese father and a Jordanian mother. However, he grew up in Lebanon. He serves in the Church of the Nazarene in Sin el Fil as well as with Youth for Christ. He also works as a Student Supervisor at the Church of the Nazarene School in Beirut.

---

202. Barrett, The Holy Spirit, 45.

203. Hanson, *Endangered Promises*, 177-89.

Everyday Holiness:
Meditations on Identity & Calling (Mark 1 & 2)
Heather Ardrey

My call into ministry was very strong and yet vague in the details. As a teenager at family camp on the Metro New York District, I was only half listening to the sermon. Then, out of nowhere, I paid full attention. The speaker was saying something about how the churches all around the world were growing, but in the United States they were not. As soon as he finished that sentence, I heard God speak in what is, to this day, the closest thing to God's audible voice I've ever experienced: "That is what you are going to do." I knew then, without a doubt, ministry was my path.

But what kind of ministry? Was I to be a missionary, a pastor, a youth pastor, or a teacher? I knew of many others who had received specific calls—pastor, doctor, missionary, and teacher. I felt like I was the only person in the history of the world whom Jesus had called in such a vague fashion. As I grew up, I continued to ask for clarity. "What are you calling me to, Jesus? If you would only tell me, I would go."

Time after time, as I asked and searched scripture, I was brought back to the same unspecific calling: "Follow me."

If I'm honest, I was very unsettled by the vagueness of this. "Follow you where? To do what? Give me some clue, please!"

In the first two chapters of Mark, Jesus begins to call his disciples. It turns out that I'm in good company; Jesus seems to call these disciples with the same vagueness with which he called me. Rereading these passages recently, I noticed a pattern that clarifies the substance of this calling even though the direction is still uncertain. Mark tells the stories of three different callings with this same pattern. Mark names the people and gives them an identifying feature. Then, Jesus shows up and calls them, and they leave their identifying feature behind. Finally, they follow Jesus right back to their own life arenas.

First, in Chapter 1, Jesus sees Simon and Andrew, who are identified as fishermen. Jesus calls them, "Follow me." They respond by leaving their identifying feature (their fishermen's nets).

177

As Simon and Andrew begin to follow him, they first go to their neighbors' boat. There Jesus sees James & John, identified as Sons of Zebedee. Jesus calls them, and they respond by leaving their identifying feature as well (their father and his hired men). They then follow him, not to Jerusalem, but right back to their own synagogue, their own houses, and their own town.

In chapter 2, we see a similar pattern when Jesus calls Levi. Jesus finds him at a tax booth (his identifying feature). Jesus gives Levi the same calling, "Follow me," and Levi leaves the booth behind to follow Jesus. They leave his tax booth and go to Levi's own house for a dinner party he's hosting with his friends.

Jesus is calling these people (and therefore us) out of the things that we humans cling to for identification. This relationship between calling and identity is difficult to swallow. Our identity is deeply ingrained. It is challenging to leave that aside for the sake of answering this call.

Our identity is shaped from the moment we're born. Our parents have a large influence over the ways we identify ourselves. Going to college, trade school, or graduate school further shape us into a certain identity—cook, philosopher, engineer, or auto mechanic. We label ourselves and construct a precise identity for our lives on Facebook and in our interactions with others. There are some identifying labels we want—wife, friend, lawyer—and others we would rather live without.

Here in Mark, through the simple act of calling, Jesus seems to make it clear that those identities don't matter quite as much as the calling placed on our lives. In fact, it seems that answering his call requires leaving those identities behind. How we are identified doesn't matter as much as the interaction between Jesus' invitation ("Follow me") and our response ("Leave everything and follow").

This is not to say that, once we follow Jesus, suddenly everyone around us only sees us as some sort of amorphous being, unidentifiable in any way. In fact, the story in Mark seems to suggest that whatever the men Jesus called were when he meets them, they continue to carry the same labels. In fact, at the dinner party at Levi's house, we see that people labeled as tax-collectors and sinners (by themselves? by others?) seem to keep their label even after they answer Jesus invitation to follow! Identifying features are important because they make up who we are. Jesus is not inviting us to forget who we are. He's just inviting us to anchor our identity in something more stable.

Following Jesus is not an easy calling. It means not having control of my own life. It means the labels I cling to for myself aren't that important in my pursuit of this Holy God. It also means the labels I assign others don't bear much weight. It means I'm tasked with prying the anchor up from the places I want so desperately to put my identity, and being content with one identifying feature—Jesus Follower. This calling is not just for pastors or evangelists or missionaries. I am in good company as I heed the call of Jesus to "follow him" because it is the call he gives to all of us—every woman, man, and child, both today and throughout history.

As we watch the Jesus followers in the first two chapters of Mark, we see that when they leave their identifying features, Jesus takes them right back to their own spaces. The fishermen and the sons leave their nets and fathers only to head to their own synagogues—where Jesus teaches in a way they had never heard before. They leave their places of work to head back to their home—where Jesus heals their ailing families. They go to the city gates, where Jesus calls Levi. Once Levi leaves the tax booths, he throws a dinner party and invites all his friends to meet Jesus as well. There, the followers of Jesus dined with people whom the religious establishment of the day considered to be outsiders, unclean—when, in fact, Jesus considered those very outsiders his followers as well!

After receiving a call like "Follow me," we might expect that the result would be leaving behind every known thing and going off to doing something amazing somewhere else. Instead, we see that following Jesus does something that can sometimes be more difficult. Once we answer the call, we find ourselves entering into our own lives more fully and engaging the world that we find there, the world of parenting and friendship and neighborhood. Following Jesus leads us to intentionally forging friendships with people who are different from us in every way—including spiritually. Should we find ourselves living next door to an atheist or agnostic, we would not avoid them in case they would pull us away from God, but befriend them deeply in case Jesus would pull them closer!

When we follow Jesus, he does not lead us out of the world—just out of ourselves. As we follow him, we are following the Holy God who desires to care for us and everyone we come in contact with. It gives us freedom and boldness in life that we might not have had otherwise. If we are too busy trying to hone and protect our own identities, we will miss out on the amazing things Jesus desires us to participate in throughout the everyday parts of our lives.

The stories of calling in Mark 1 & 2 paint a picture of a way of holiness, and a group of holiness people that feels very different than what I gleaned growing up in this denomination. Mark paints a picture of a way of holiness determined only by one defining question: **How do you respond when Jesus calls you to follow?**

Mark paints a picture of a holiness people who are set apart. But rather than being set apart from others, we are instead set apart from our claim of determination of our lives. Jesus does not send us away from our families, our communities, our friends, our neighborhoods—he brings us back—but without the baggage of living up to the expectations we place on ourselves.

The way of holiness is not about roles and rules. It is about putting our identity in its rightful place so that we are willing to ask for direction from, to be led by, and to follow Jesus. The life of holiness is about attentiveness to Jesus—where he is, what he's doing, and where he's going. This is a holiness that can translate into every life circumstance and every space where we find ourselves. It is discipleship that is not divorced from the everyday living of life but engaged in that life and attentive to Jesus' work in it. As we follow Jesus, instead of finding ourselves separated from a "sinful world," we find ourselves separated from our sinful selves, immersed in a fallen world, following a God who wants to influence, to guide, and to shape our world and us.

After having worked at Harvard for Intervarsity Christian Fellowship for the past seven years, Heather now has the opportunity to practice living out everyday holiness in the middle of the Pacific Ocean. Moving for her husband's work, her family will be living in the Marshall Islands for a few years, and Heather looks forward to partnering with what Jesus might be up to there. She also has plans to raise her two kids, take up drawing, work on some writing she's not previously found time for, and finally get a tan.

Discipleship as Dynamic Identification in Mark 8 and 9

Edgar Baldeòn

I want to start by proposing that, after the fall, God has left the capacity of identification in human beings because this is the indispensable element to establish the kind of relationship that God wants to have with his children. This capacity is the cause of adhesion to singers, soccer players, models, politicians, thinkers, and social activists. People use extremely creative ways to identify themselves with other people whom they admire and who serve as their models for life.

The commission of the Lord for his disciples was to make more disciples. It is understood that discipleship is a relationship that has a beginning but continues to grow each day. So it happened with the Twelve, and so it happens with us.

Seeing our relationship with God and with Christ as a dynamic discipleship that gets better each day and looking at this relationship from the perspective of identification, it is natural to think of discipleship as a process of dynamic identification. Total identification with Jesus is unquestionably required in discipleship. However, we need to know who Christ really is to be able to identify ourselves with him.

Mark 8 & 9 close the final stage of Jesus' teaching to his disciples about who he is. Mark starts and ends this section with those who believe in him. In the middle, the theme of the identity of Jesus and his disciples stands out.

The first group that Mark mentions is the multitude. They believe in him as a prophet. Next are the Pharisees. They haven't believed in him. They are with him only to disprove him. They ask him for a sign only because they think he cannot give one. Finally, Mark identifies his disciples as a distinct group.

But suddenly Mark tells the story of the blind man of Bethsaida. This is the only miracle in which Jesus' healing happens as a process rather than instantaneously. Jesus has to touch him again, so he can see with clarity, with his total vision restored.

This miracle is an illustration of what is going on in the larger narrative of Mark. Jesus has taught for a while, and his work is bringing some results. Yet neither the multitude, nor the Pharisees, nor even the disciples see who he really is. In the rest of this section, Jesus teaches again till they can see clearly.

This second part of the section presents the clearest teaching that Jesus can offer to his disciples about himself. Jesus is clarifying who he is, who they are, and what they will do.

Who is Jesus? Peter answers famously, "You are the Christ." Although Peter answers well, the rest of the story lets us know that really he doesn't have a clear idea of who the Christ is. Jesus increases and clarifies Peter's concept of the Christ. He must suffer, be rejected, and be killed—though he will rise after that.

Peter doesn't want to accept what Jesus has just said. Jesus rebukes Peter. Surprisingly, it seems Peter has aligned with the same Satan who wants Jesus to avoid his mission of going to the cross. Peter doesn't think according to the concerns of God but according to human concerns. Jesus is the Christ who will die and be raised for the healing of the world.

Who are the disciples? They must also deny themselves, take up their cross, and follow Jesus. Here Jesus establishes the unquestionable principle of identification. Total identification with Jesus is unquestionably required in discipleship. At the same time, Jesus declares that this kind of disciple will receive the Kingdom of God.

Who is Jesus? Jesus took Peter, James, and John and transfigured himself before them. They listened the voice of God saying, "This is my Son, whom I love. Listen to him." What else could Jesus do to make them understand who he is?

Who are they? Mark says that Jesus' disciples cannot cast out a demon. Once safe at home, the disciples ask Jesus why they couldn't cast out the demon. Jesus says that they need to pray more. They don't have power in themselves to cast out demons. This teaching is key to understand who the Christ is and who his disciples are.

Working from this passage, we see the importance of making space in discipleship for this struggle over denial. The question of denial is set in a deeply human context. We see this struggle in Peter. We see it in Jesus himself, and of course we see it in ourselves.

Peter is uncomfortable with the idea that his master has to suffer and die on a cross. He cannot accept grief and death—not even as a means to achieve a happy ending.

The problem is that Peter doesn't have in mind the concerns of God. Identification with human concerns seems more secure because in that way you safeguard what is nearby: family support, possessions, food, clothes, a peaceful future—even life.

Identification with God's concerns, on the contrary, is a leap into a vacuum. It requires an exercise of faith. It is a dangerous, risky, unpredictable venture. It is the debate between the rational and the irrational, between unbelief and faith, between what is known and unknown.

Jesus rejects completely the suggestion to avoid his mission. He rebukes Peter, discerning the voice of Satan laced in Peter's words. It is against this subtle temptation to security that the Lord highlights the principle of total identification with him and the gospel, "Whoever wants to save his life will lose it." This doesn't mean that the struggle is not intense. Jesus will experience the utter depths of human struggle in Gethsemane. In fact, Gethsemane was neither the first nor the last time Jesus entered into the denial of his own desires for safety.

The struggle of Jesus at Gethsemane is described vividly. To his disciples he says, "The spirit is willing, but the flesh is weak." Jesus understands well the tension between the disposition of the spirit and the disposition of the flesh. His advice is to watch and pray.

When we think of our own struggles, we have to admit that they are not all the same. It is not possible to think of Christian life, in each of its different stages of maturity, as a single path that all Christians must walk. Life is far richer than this. Conversion, growth in grace, and maturity stages achieved by personal victories are all particular to individuals and different for each one of us.

We can talk of equality in terms of what is asked but not in terms of how we fulfill what is demanded. Our personal circumstances and surrounding environment determine the texture of our personal struggles: overcoming sin or bad habits, an interpersonal relationship with a troublemaking boss, accepting God's nudge to leave a comfortable situation. The possible variations are infinite.

However, one commonality remains. In our particular personal struggles, our interests and God's interests contradict. We are required to deny ourselves, to identify with Christ in his obedience to the purposes of the Father, and to fulfill our calling without limitation, even to the point of giving life.

As an example, we can take the disciples' circumstances. First of all, the Lord asks them to be inclusive. They want to prohibit someone from preaching in the name of Jesus because he isn't part of their group. Here you have the manifest group interest. The Lord commands them not to prohibit it. This is a wakeup call from the Lord to stop thinking about our own kingdoms, even though collective, and to think of His kingdom.

Secondly, the Lord calls them to humble service. When they are thinking about who will be the greatest, each one looking for the first place, the Lord says that the greatest must be the servant of all. He calls them to follow his example of being one who has come to serve.

Inclusion and service are just two particular examples that may touch our lives. In what sense are we inclusive? How are we serving others? In some cases, inclusion and service will demand that we sacrifice much of what we have and much of who we understand ourselves to be. It is in this kind of personal confrontation where holiness must shine. This is discipleship.

Practical holiness means total identification with Jesus. This is the foundation of true discipleship. It is a process is ever growing and ever progressing as we are always experiencing new challenges in life.

Edgar is married, with two grown daughters and two wonderful grandchildren. He was a pastor, but now he is the Vice-Rector at the South America Nazarene Theological Seminary in Quito. He earned his Doctor of Ministry at NTS in Kansas City. His university work focuses on enterprise administration and human resources.

Reflecting God:
Holiness by Loving Those Who Do Not Love You
Kenton Lee

The greatest commandments: Love God, love others. There is simplicity in that statement. But when it intersects with life, it becomes much more complicated. For followers of Jesus who are committed to walking in His steps, it is paramount to wade into the deep waters of this commandment. And for those who are pursuing holiness of heart and life, these words are the center from which everything grows. Often, the conversations around holiness focus too much on the relationship with God and not enough on the relationship with others. Renovating holiness must include a renewed emphasis on the role of loving others.

So who are the "others" in our lives? Friends? Family? Co-workers? Jesus tells his followers in very plain terms who the others are. In Matthew 5:43-48, during the amazing Sermon on the Mount, Jesus says, "You need to love your enemies and those who persecute you. If you just love those who love you—what good does that do? Be holy as God is holy." Christians are not called to love only those who love them back; Jesus commands us to love *everyone*.

Holiness is the pursuit of loving God and loving others. It is not just a two way street back and forth between you and God. You share an epic journey with God as you go into the world and into the lives of others. As we renovate and enrich our understanding of holiness, we must highlight the importance of loving the "others" in our lives who are not easy to love. Holiness is not made complete in us until we love our enemies, those who annoy us, those who do not like us, those who we do not understand, and everyone else. Loving others—everyone in our circles, communities, and cities—is a central component of renovated holiness.

Anthony the Great is considered the first of the Desert Fathers. Around 270 AD he sold his possessions, traveled out to the desert, and committed to a life of complete solitude. I used to think that this was the ultimate peak in holiness. But the role of others in our lives and the teachings of Jesus demand that we include relationships in our understanding of faith and pursuit of holiness.

Shane Claiborne is a Tennessee-born author and speaker who lives with an intentional community in Philadelphia sharing his life with all kinds of people around him. He has made it his life's work to become as connected to others as possible. Here are three points to consider why a renovated holiness should look more like Shane Claiborne than it should Anthony the Great.

First, holiness has to include loving others because that is the example that God has set for us.

Matthew 5 finishes with the conclusion that we should "Be holy as God is holy." This statement is used frequently when talking about holiness. When understood in the context of the passage, it highlights that God is a God of loving others—even those who do not love Him. He exemplifies holiness for us, and we are called to reflect the loving nature of our God.

Second, holiness must be experienced by loving those who do not love us.

Jesus called us to love our enemies and those who persecute us. But it is also a call to love those who have no reason to love us: those we do not know, those we just recently met, those we work with, those we see at the coffee shop. Jesus explains that our calling to love others means loving those who do not love us because just loving our best friends and moms isn't going to change the world or bring us closer to reflecting our incredible God. We need to love *everyone*. That will change the world and make us closer to a life of holiness.

Third, we can understand God better when we focus on loving others.

Anthony the Great was able to commune with God at an extreme level through his solitude. But we are also able to commune with God at an extreme level when we love others. We see the diversity of God. We can be surprised by connecting with unique people. Through the conversations and interactions with others, we learn how big and wide are the loving arms of God. Loving others does not distance us from loving God; it empowers us to love and understand God even more.

Consider the parable of the Good Samaritan. A man is badly beaten and left on the side of the road. Two religious men see their fellow man, but pass him by without helping. The final man to come along is a Samaritan. Traditionally, Samaritans and Jews were enemies. However, the Samaritan man stops to help the beaten man and cares for him. There is power in loving each other. There is a challenge to all of us to love one another as the Samaritan man chose to love, by caring for the man who should have been his enemy.

God does not want His followers to pass by the other people in our lives—as we are in a hurry to get to our small groups, prayer meetings, and hangouts. He calls us to love more than just those who love us back. He calls us to follow the example of the Good Samaritan. He calls us to a deeper understanding of holiness that includes both commandments to love God *and* love others.

How can you renovate holiness in your own life? Do you need to reflect God more through loving others who do not love you? And how can we renovate holiness in our churches? Can we focus on ministries, services, budgets, and opportunities that emphasize loving others? One of the most vital movements in our lives and in our churches will be our commitment to loving others—especially those who do not love us. That is where the rubber meets the road.

Jesus laid out the calling to His followers in his Sermon on the Mount—a calling to love those who do not love you because this is the true nature of our holy God. For all readers here who commit to the pursuit of holiness in your heart and life, I encourage you not only to love God but also to love others, especially those who don't "deserve" it. This kind of love will change your life—and maybe theirs, too.

Kenton Lee is the pastor of The Table Church of the Nazarene in Nampa, Idaho. He is also the Executive Director of Because International—an organization focused on practical compassion for those challenged by extreme poverty (BecauseInternational. org). He is most excited to be the husband of Nikki and the dad of Kenny.

A Kingdom-Centric Holiness

Donnie Miller

"Everyone knows the Jayhawks are God's team."

It was a bold declaration that my best friend, Brandon, loved to say. As someone who grew up in a small Kansas town, the Jayhawks had always been his team. I grew up, however, in a small Iowa town where the Hawkeyes were clearly the "good guys." While our small towns had a handful of Kansas State Wildcat fans or Iowa State Cyclone fans, it wasn't until we moved away from our small towns and enrolled in a Church of the Nazarene university that we were exposed to large groups of people who cheered for other sports teams.

Our friendly banter about which team Heaven preferred was simply that for the first two years of college, as it wasn't until our Junior and Senior years that the two teams actually met on the basketball court. In 1998, the Hawkeyes broke the Jayhawk's 62-game home winning streak by beating the Jayhawks in legendary Allan Fieldhouse. While Brandon and I didn't sit together at the game, his seat in the bleachers gave him a clear view of us running out onto the court to celebrate the Hawkeye victory. The next year, in Iowa City, the Hawkeyes were again victorious. While neither of us was at the game, our apartment was a bit tense as we watched in different rooms with different groups of friends. Unfortunately, Brandon also found himself on the losing end of a bet that resulted in him walking around campus the entire next day in Hawkeye gear that we graciously lent to him. People on campus were shocked to see such a big Jayhawk fan sporting the logo of a team that had just defeated "God's team."

While Brandon and I moved onto campus as committed members of our respective team's fan bases, we knew that neither team found itself in better standing before our Creator than the other, though we may have secretly hoped that was the case. We had both been exposed to plenty of people who were both Christian and—gasp—fans of another team that our worldview was larger than Brandon's humorous statement would suggest.

The same cannot be said, however, of the national loyalties held by many well-meaning Christians. While I know enough of history to be aware that the problem I'll be addressing in this article exists in other countries too, I will be speaking with a distinctly American voice in this article, though feel free to substitute your own nation for "America." Whenever we make the declaration, or even simply operate under the assumption, that God somehow favors our nation over other nations, we are committing the same narrow-minded fallacy of which Brandon and I were guilty.

It breaks my heart to realize how many times we have made this mistake. All throughout my lifetime, I have heard statements about how the United States is a "Christian Nation" or the "New Israel." I have heard Christian economists argue that capitalism is taught in scripture or that democracy is God's plan for the world.

Of course, I'm not denying that the United States has brought some light into the world or that democracy and capitalism have had positive results. I am trying to demonstrate that whenever we make the assumption that God is on our side— that God has uniquely blessed our political, economic or military endeavors— we are simply fashioning God after our own image. We are assuming that God prefers what we prefer. We are confusing the familiar with the holy. After all, many Americans throughout all walks of life and throughout history have been on "God's team," so doesn't it make sense that God would prefer our nation to other nations? Isn't there enough evidence to show that God is on our side? Can't we assume that the global actions that favor our nation also favor the Kingdom of God?

Those assumptions are simply wrong. Historical examples abound in which our nation's leaders have pursued policies that have advanced our own interests while harming citizens of other countries. A history lesson, however, is not the main point of this article. Of all the different aspects of holy living expounded upon in this book, this particular essay seeks to add to the discussion a Kingdom-of-God-centric approach to our earthly citizenship.

To be entirely sanctified is to be set apart from the world for the purpose of serving the Kingdom of God. Holiness is about separation and re-attachment: separation from the Kingdom of the World and attachment to the Kingdom of God. As citizens of God's Kingdom, our allegiance transcends any national loyalties, and our corporate worship, political actions, economic activity, and even our support of our earthly nation's military must reflect this reality. Jesus said of the disciples in John 17:16, "They do not belong to this world any more than I do." An important part of a lifestyle of holiness is laying aside our nationalistic fervor for the sake of the Kingdom of God.

This isn't to say that we ignore our responsibility or our identity as citizens of our earthly nation, but it does mean that said responsibility and identity is to be redirected from a mentality that puts our nation's interests above the interests of other nations. Instead, we embrace a mentality of calling our nation's leaders always to put the needs of our global community above the needs of our particular nation. The Kingdom of God transcends national boundaries; as citizens of that Kingdom, we are to do the same. We are not American Christians; we are Christians who happen to live in America. For this reason, our ultimate allegiance is not to our earthly country, but to the Kingdom of God.

There will be times in which advancing our nation's interests on a global scale is in accordance with the broader interests of the Kingdom of God. There will also be times in which global policies that benefit our nation (one of the wealthier and more powerful nations in the world) actually harm the weaker and poorer nations. One of the values of God's Kingdom is that the rich are to serve the poor, so whenever a conflict arises between the "haves" and the "have-nots," the scriptural expectation is that the "haves" will sacrifice their own interests for the benefit of the "have-nots."

Our global economy provides endless opportunities to live with a Kingdom-first perspective, but the following are just a few examples.

Debt: Affluent western nations and global banks have helped to put developing countries into hopeless situations. The interest on loans to developing countries intended for building up that nation's infrastructures have created a crippling cycle of debt, which has a direct impact upon their poorest citizens. In many cases, over half of these nation's budgets are spent just servicing their debt to more affluent western nations. Following the example of the "Year of Jubilee" teachings in the Old Testament and forgiving the debt of developing nations would undoubtedly hurt the bottom line of some of the "haves." However, when this happens, the "have-nots" have significant new economic opportunities.

Coffee: Are the coffee producers we are supporting providing living wage to the farmers who produce their coffee beans? Or are they paying a bare minimum that keeps the farmers in a continual state of subsistence living? Free Trade coffee may be more expensive at the cash register, but it allows the farmers who grow the beans to provide their families with education, healthcare and other things most of the people buying the coffee take for granted.

Clothing: Are we willing to pay more for the clothes we buy to purchase clothes made by workers receiving a fair wage? Or are we supporting companies that perpetuate the virtual slavery of sweatshops? Are we willing to do the research necessary to discover which clothing companies are actually using ethical production practices?

Politics: Do the politicians we support take an "America first" approach to global politics? Or are they willing to sacrifice our nation's interests for the benefit of weaker, developing nations?

Worship: Our times of corporate worship are meant to affirm our collective citizenship in God's Kingdom. Bringing national symbols and national hymns into our worship space brings a false legitimacy of our nation being "God's team," while simultaneously minimizing our primary citizenship in the global Kingdom of God. Celebrating our nation during corporate worship is an idolatrous act that harms the witness of our churches.

War: What criteria do we use in choosing to support our nation's declarations of war? Christian Just War Theory has been the criteria throughout history for a Christ-follower's decision to support their nation's wars. Whether it is bombs that miss their target and land upon hospitals or wartime governmental budgets that redirect funds from serving the poor to the serving military interests, war has horrendous consequences that stand in direct contrast to the Kingdom of God. We can live out our identity as Kingdom people by carefully considering if the proposed (or existing) war passes all the criteria of Christian Just War Theory. That our national leaders deem the war necessary must never be enough for us as Christians.

Derek Webb said it best in the lyrics of one of his songs, "My first allegiance is not to a flag, a country, or a man/ My first allegiance is not to democracy or blood/ It's to a King and a Kingdom."[204] As Christ-like people, our citizenship in God's Kingdom guides our citizenship in our earthly nation and not the other way around.

Donnie and Erin Miller, along with their son Dawson, have just finished a year of serving as Mission Corps Volunteers on the France District and are moving to Büsingen, Germany to work on the European campus of MidAmerica Nazarene University. Before serving in France, the Millers planted and pastored a church in Gardner, KS where they started ministries to reach the marginalized of their community.

---

204. Derek Webb, "A King and a Kingdom," Mockingbird, Ino/Epic, December 27, 2005.

How the Fire Fell:

Rethinking Pentecost as Power Rather Than Prescription

Nathaniel J. Napier

> *Thus it is written that he Messiah should suffer and rise again from the dead the third day, and that repentance for forgiveness of sins should be proclaimed in His name to all the nations, beginning from Jerusalem. You are witnesses to these things. And behold, I am sending forth the promise of My father upon you; but you are to stay in the city until you are clothed with power from on high (Luke 24:45–49).*

Much earlier than these words of the resurrected Jesus, Luke tells us of the words of John the Baptist, "As for me, I baptize you with water, but One is coming who is mightier than I and I am not even fit to untie his sandals; he will baptize you with the Holy Spirit and fire" (3:16). In chapter 3, the prophetic words of John the Baptist didn't make much sense, but now Luke is bringing his Gospel message full circle. What Luke began in his Gospel he is bringing to completion in his telling of Pentecostal fires in Acts.

But what is Pentecost? If we follow the life of Jesus, Pentecost marks its culmination. After Pentecost, we enter Ordinary Time in the Christian calendar and Witness Time in the biblical narrative. It is a time where nothing supernatural happens in the life of Christ: no "hark the herald angels sing," no wise men, no miracles, no resurrection, and no more Pentecost. What does this mean that our journey ends with paranormal descriptions of divine empowerment from the heavens? The graduation of Jesus via the Ascension begins the downward commencement of the Holy Spirit.

If we follow the text closely and pay attention to the themes and motifs at work within the entire scope of Luke/Acts, one discovers that despite the fact that we celebrate the big three events (Easter, Ascension, Pentecost) in the life of Jesus separately, they were never understood theologically as separate moments that could be divorced and still understood as isolated textual wholes. Together these events are the theological apex that occurs in the Gospel, statements of the Gospel's dénouement, not historical niceties that prove creedal historicity. These three function together in order proclaim one singular message: the Lordship of

Jesus as disclosed through the Gospel of Easter. The Lordship of Jesus is on the line, and the Resurrection is the catalyst that gives birth to the Ascension and Pentecost. Christ is raised; Christ returns to God; and Christ returns to us again, as promised.

What this means is that to try to understand Pentecost apart from Easter is misleading and to understand Easter without an empowering Spirit would be an empty proclamation. This needs to be understood because we often separate these events to such a degree that days like Pentecost become removed from their Easter context and Pentecost becomes a time about my experience with God rather than my experience for God.

In other words, Pentecost is essentially the capstone event that began via the incarnation, seemed doomed at the Passion, and brings to completion the promises of a physically absent Christ. The disciples are passive recipients to a divine coming of God to them so that they may proclaim the story Luke has just told us in his Gospel, of one Jew named Jesus who lived, was crucified, was resurrected, and has returned to God in order that God may return to us. Pentecost is part of the journey that makes Easter proclamation possible. Yet this is not how we often read the Pentecost event.

Our tradition has often deemed Pentecost a prescriptive personal experience. It has been preached as a hallmark that guarantees our personal holiness before God, not as the continuation of Easter that empowers our witness. Our Wesleyan/ American Holiness and broader Pentecostal heritages have encouraged us to seek Pentecostal experiences, to speak in tongues, and to be ecstatic—all as the demonstration of the indwelling presence of the Holy Spirit. Some of us may even remember with fondness that members of the Church of the Nazarene were often referred to as "noise-a-renes" since our tradition has been so influenced by Pentecostal fervor and forms of worship.

All manner of folks have used Acts 2 to describe the type of experience we ought to have with God—all the while, this particular experience is unique to this text. Where similar manifestations occur later in Acts, for example at the home of Cornelius in chapter 10 or when Paul is in Ephesus in chapter 19, these events are best understood not as prescriptions of a necessary prerequisite along the way of salvation, but as extensions of the Spirit via Pentecost. Pentecost happens to Jews and proclaims the Gospel to Jews; Cornelius and the Ephesus experience are repetitions of God already moving to the Gentiles. These are extensions of Pentecost, not proof text paradigms.

For Wesleyans who value a holistic hermeneutic, there is simply no textual mandate for understanding Acts 2 as a prescriptive event that demands strict salvific adherence. It is the witness that the Holy Spirit is here, and has fallen, not that it must fall "afresh" on us in Pentecostal caricature. A canonical reading of other New Testament literature will also find us vainly looking for texts that make Acts 2 a normative event. Acts 2 still has an important place for a deep understanding of and appreciation for the work of the Holy Spirit, but we have turned the text into something it clearly is not. We have made it what we want, not allowed it to be itself.

In addition, our tradition has linked this event to sanctification. We have taken Acts 2 as a paradigm or a model for what it means to be sanctified by God (an act completely harmonious with Article X in our *Manual*), set apart for his purpose, and granted the indwelling presence of the Holy Spirit. There are some particular problems at this point, however.

First, Acts 2 says nothing of sanctification. The Greek is absent the Pauline language we find elsewhere in the New Testament. Not only is "sanctification" language absent this text, the passage does not say anything about sanctification as a "grace" or workout a theology of sanctification as one might find in 1 Thessalonians. Further, it says nothing about our personal spirituality being God's primary interest in sending the Spirit. Hymns such as "How the Fire Fell" have been hugely influential in shaping our faith, perhaps even taking precedent over sound biblical exegesis.

Secondly, by forcing a prescriptive rule from Acts 2, our tradition has made normative a particular type of experience and dictated its shape. We have turned this divine encounter (a New Testament Theophany, no less) into an experiential formula that allows us to contain the Spirit and to control its dissemination. By inappropriately using biblical texts to determine doctrine, we have neglected the very subjective reality that is our individual and communal experience with God.

However, the most troubling of these modest protestations is perhaps that we have divorced Acts 2 and the narrative of Pentecost from its broader textual contours in the New Testament, and therein been even less biblical than we would like. Traditionally Resurrection, Ascension, and Pentecost were all closely celebrated together because they are all movements of one unified narrative. By separating them on the calendar, we have unfortunately lost what Luke/Acts is doing with this text.

Pentecost has become a unique experience for us, rather than an outpouring of power in spite of us! Pentecost is not a domesticated experience to be conjured by pastor's preaching. According to the text, it is about the descent of the Spirit in order for Easter proclamation to take place. It is not a prescriptive part of a mechanical spiritual walk that Luke/Acts wants all people to emulate. It is the description of an event that empowers the church to proclaim perpetually the impossible, because the Spirit is already present in the church.

Pentecost offers us the story of why the Spirit came, how it came, and what it came for! Pentecost came to fulfill the words of Jesus, "It is written that Christ should suffer and rise again from the dead the third day and that repentance for forgiveness of sins should be proclaimed in his name to all the nations. *You are my witnesses.*" We are witnesses of what? We are resurrection witnesses!

In the Gospels, we do not see mass spreading of the stories of Jesus after his resurrection. Mark even leaves us without a post-resurrection narrative. The community of faith keeps this reality to itself. Resurrection sounds crazy, even impossible. The disciples do not have the power, the unction, or the witnessing ability to do tell this impossible story. They are stuck in fear, amazement, thankfulness, but lost about what to do now that the proof that Jesus is not dead has just ascended into the clouds. Who's going to believe them?

Pentecost is the event that sets this faith in motion and empowers the disciples to take the Gospel to places it would not have otherwise reached. Pentecost is an extension of Easter in that it is the event that enables the Easter proclamation to go forth into creation.

It's not about a new experience for me or you or the disciples. It is about empowering our ability to proclaim what we have already experienced by rushing into the tomb and finding it hollow and empty, the body of Jesus the Christ no longer there. Yet, if we continue to interiorize a text that was meant for divine exteriority, we have to ask ourselves, "What is it we are being filled with, and how selfless is our idea of being filled with the Spirit after all?"

A graduate of Trevecca Nazarene University and the McAfee School of Theology, Nathan is pastor of Christian Education at Cleveland First Church of the Nazarene, Cleveland, TN. A member of the Church of the Nazarene raised in East Tennessee, he has authored recent articles on Wesley's theology, Arminius, economics, popular Christian topics, and several academic book reviews. He is currently exploring the interstices of nihilism and biblical interpretation.

Holiness in Relation to Purity/Impurity in Ephesians

Svetlana Khobnya

The author of Ephesians[205] is convinced that those in Christ are holy and blameless and that no impurity should come from them (Eph 5:3). Impurity is a characteristic of the former life without Christ (4:19). It is closely associated with sin (2:1-3) and immoral practice (4:17ff, 5:1ff). Those in Christ have to be cleansed from their past allegiance to sin. They are to put away a former way of living and to become a dwelling place and a temple of God through Christ's election and the renewal in the spirit of the mind. This is described as becoming children of God, new self and new humanity created according to the likeness of God in true righteousness and holiness (2:15, 4:24).

Based on this brief sketch, it is evident that the identity of Christians and their holiness is expressed in Ephesians in additional terms of purity/impurity (employed in the rich vocabulary of *blameless, without blemish, fornication,* and *unclean* and conceptually by the image of the holy temple). The interconnectedness between the terms leads some scholars to associate holiness simply with "cleanness" or as the "bond" with Christ that has no "fellowship with wickedness and impurity."[206] Others relate purity/impurity to the human response to divine holiness, "the awareness of holiness brings consciousness of impurity."[207] Yet, others specify purity/impurity in the light of the anthropological findings as patterns of order/ disorder in the society, as descriptions that communicate the specific values of that society and its contraventions.[208] That is to say that the characteristics of holiness are defined by the society's system of purity.[209] So, an object (person) or

---

205. The authorship is not focus of the discussion although I do recognise that Ephesians is written within the Pauline tradition.

206. O. R. Jones, *The Concept of Holiness* (New York: Macmillan Co, 1961), 100; W.T. Purkiser, *Exploring Christian Holiness* (vol.1; Kansas City: Beacon Hill Press, 1983), 24; P. P. Jenson, *Granted Holiness: A Key to the Priestly Conception of the World* (JSOTS 106; Sheffield, JSOT Press, 1992), chs. 2-3.

207. James D. G. Dunn, "Jesus and Holiness: The Challenge of Purity" in *Holiness: Past and Present* (ed. Stephen C. Barton; London: T&T Clark, 2003), 172.

208. Jerome H. Neyrey, *Paul in Other Words: A Cultural Reading of His Letters* (Louisville: Westminster/John Knox Press, 1990), 33.

209. Peter Oakes, "Made Holy by the Holy Spirit: Holiness and Ecclesiology in Romans" in *Holiness and Ecclesiology in the New Testament* (ed. Kent Brower and Andy Johnson; Grand Rapids: Eerdmans, 2007), 167.

action is pure when it conforms to the specific norms or order of the society that "make up the symbolic system of a particular social group."[210]

If we take this latter explanation as a working model for studying Christian holiness in Ephesians, the question of how the language of purity/impurity communicates the patterns of order/disorder or specific values of the Christian community becomes particularly crucial. In Ephesians, two types of order (Christian and non-Christian existence) are outlined and set in opposition.[211] This essay suggests that the language of purity is used to urge the Christian audience to share views and practices corporately as a holy community created in Christ and, in Christ, to live differently from the outside world. The language of purity/impurity in describing believers' status as being holy and blameless (1:4) and in the metaphor of the temple (2:11-21) is especially illuminating.

Ephesians refers to those whom God has chosen in Christ before the foundation of the world corporately as holy and blameless in love (1:4). Both concepts describe a new status for those in Christ. God's election in Christ provides "cleansing" and adoption of those who were previously outside of God into his family, thus into a close relationship with him and into his holy presence. This election is not of temporal predestination but of "the election of Christ and what is destined to happen to those, whoever they may be, who are in Christ."[212] The key note in establishing this new order is Christ as the center or head of this new order.

Although both terms "holy" and "blameless" have a background in cultic language (cf. Num. 6:14; 19:2; Ex 29:37), they imply the inner or moral purity.[213] This corresponds with 2:3, 10, where it is said that God prepared Christians for good works. The terms have both cultic and ethical overtones. The idea that God in Christ cleanses and sanctifies (also 5:26-27) confirms the status of those before God. But God also equips those whom he cleanses and sanctifies for tasks appropriate to their status: specifically, to do good. Thus, the status of Christians in Christ bears moral consequences. The new order established in Christ is the life of purity that implies doing good.

The transfer to this state is a matter of divine ordination described in terms of love. This love can be interpreted first as God's love toward humankind (cf. 5:2) and then also as an outcome of those who are standing fully in God's presence and fully belong to him (1:15; 3:18; 4:2, 15-16; 5:2; 6:23). Living in love is the

---

210. Neyrey, 23

211. Ernst Best, *Essays on Ephesians* (Edinburgh: T&T Clark, 1997), 139.

212. Ben Witherington III, *The Letters to Philemon, the Colossians, and the Ephesians: A Socio-rhetorical Commentary on the Captivity Epistles* (Grand Rapids: Eerdmans, 2007), 234.

213. Being holy and blameless is part of a liturgical usage here in 1:3 and rather cultic in 5:26. See Best, 122, 542.

distinctive conduct and identity of the believers as explained more fully in 5:2. Christ loved humanity and gave himself up as a fragrant offering and sacrifice to God. His costly and sacrificial love is the ground and the norm for the community; they are to be imitators of God and to live in love. Love is emphasized over and over as a necessary context of the community formed holy and blameless in Christ (4:ff.).

The present situation in Christ (who himself is above all, 1:21-23) is superior to being outside of Christ. It includes abiding in the heavenly realms (1:3), renewal in the spirit of the believers' minds, being equipped with the armor of God, being filled with the Spirit, and having confidence in the face of opposing evil powers and principalities (6:10ff). This language is used to persuade the community to hold on to the life in Christ and to be his obedient children compared to the sons of disobedience (2:2) and the children of wrath (2:3). The audience is called to live as holy and blameless citizens and members of the household of God (1:19) in a non-Christian environment whenever they respond to Christ. The insiders are to embrace the code of conduct of the insiders (4:17-32) and be different from the world, for they have learned Christ (4:20). Their belonging to God in Christ inevitably should lead to godly practices that mark them as insiders once more.

The new order in Christ is clearly seen in contrast to the past situation of Christians without Christ. The contrast is expressed in antithetical language between "then" and "now" (Eph 2:11-22), "once" but "now" (Eph 2:1-10), were dead, now alive (2:5), old person versus new humanity and new self (2:15: 4:22-24). The past situation of Christians is a condition of death and sinfulness, desires of flesh and of solidarity with evil. Andrew Lincoln describes this past life as "sinful activities" alongside "the norms and values of a spatio-temporal complex wholly hostile to God." [214] This perception of before and after implies a sense of "bad" and "good" or "impure" and "pure" that corresponds to a sense of a sinful state of being outside of Christ and a holy state in Christ that results in abstinence from all sort of impurity.

In fact, impurity as immoral and sinful behavior is not only inappropriate for the saints, it somehow excludes a person from God and Christ and consequently from the context of the new order that Ephesians describes (5:5ff). Dunn explains this in terms of preventing divine holiness from having an effect, "It is the negative, inhibiting effect of impurity, as preventing access to or relation with the holy, which sets impurity, as the effective antithesis to the positive, outgoing power of the divine holiness."[215] This absolute contrast between purity/

---

214. Andrew T. Lincoln, *Ephesians* (WBC 42; Dallas: Word Books, 1990), 95.

215. Dunn, 172.

holiness and impurity/life without Christ is set up to establish a different way of looking at things (renewal of the mind) and a different set of values and norms of the Christian community within society as a whole (4:20-24). Since the world outside is evil and its organized system of values is opposed to God (although not necessarily ethically wrong in its particularities), those outside could and "must be won into the community from it," and those inside are warned not "to fall back into its ways."[216]

The community as a new temple is the key move in the view of the new order in Christ. Clear physical boundaries that mark holy people of Israel and the temple where God dwells are being remade through Christ. The community of the believers is "a fellowship made up of people—Jews and Gentiles—whom traditional notions" of the holiness kept apart.[217] Even though, at the beginning of the letter, the author refers to the Jews (as the saints) and Gentiles (the faithful ones in Christ) separately,[218] in chapter 2 the whole structure (all the believers) is joined together into a holy temple and his dwelling place. "Holiness as separation— of life and death, male and female, priests and lay, Jew and Gentile, purity and impurity—is displaced by holiness as solidarity: the solidarity of Jesus."[219] Christ bridges the former Gentiles with Israel making them together God's temple, thus opening the door for the world to join in the temple through himself.

The temple language (supplied with additional descriptions of the household of God, structure, dwelling place, body of Christ, his fullness, and Christ being the cornerstone) is used most likely to elucidate community self-understanding as an entity united in Christ. If God's dwelling was expected to be in a special place in the OT (in the holy of holies in the Temple in Jerusalem and among Israelites), the letter speaks of the temple as all people in Christ, thus, obliterating the physical space and barriers between Jews and Gentiles. The unity of the believers and their center in Christ is the sacred space that constitutes a true and holy temple of God. God is present where those in Christ are. In fact, the author insists that the division should be not among Christians themselves but between Christians and evil forces of the world (6:12) or between their former pre-Christian life and their present life in Christ.

To conclude, the language of purity in Ephesians shapes the identity of a newly-formed community as the holy members joined in unity and love by Christ. In a sense, the author calls Christians corporately to be and to live the life

216. Best, Essays, 154-55.

217. Stephen C. Barton, "Dislocating and Relocating Holiness: A New Testament Study" in *Holiness*, 201.

218. Witherington, 225-26.

219. Barton, 206.

of who they already are in Christ (in purity) in contrast to who they were before Christ and in contrast to the evil world with its immorality and sinfulness (in impurity). This means not a withdrawal from the world of impurity but keeping the integrity of the community and living together as a social unit in the power of God and Christ, practicing godly actions and abandoning all sorts of impurity, thus pervading and challenging the world with its views and values.

Svetlana Khobnya holds a degree in Linguistics (Volgograd State University), a B.A. in Theology (EuNC), an M.A. (NTS), and a Ph.D. (University of Manchester). Svetlana and her family live in Manchester, where she is Lecturer in Biblical Studies at NTC. She is author of The Father Who Redeems and the Son Who Obeys *and several academic articles.*

When Slavery Is Freedom:

Toward a Servitude of Love

J. Gregory Crofford

It was time for social studies. The unit was on the U.S. Civil War, and the second grade teacher asked the class, "Does anyone know what the word 'Emancipator' means?" A shy girl gathered her courage and raised her hand. "An 'Emancipator' is someone who sets you free," she replied. The surprised teacher had no idea where the young girl had learned such a big word, not knowing her pupil had often sung the hymn "Glorious Freedom" with others at church. The lyrics were catchy and spoke of a liberator far greater than Abraham Lincoln, "Jesus, the glorious Emancipator, now and forever, he shall be mine!"[220]

Scripture is replete with references to liberation. Some within the Wesleyan-Holiness tradition have viewed these through the lens of soteriology, the study of salvation. In comments on Isaiah 61:1 and the promise of the Messiah to proclaim "liberty" to the captives, John Wesley observed, "This applies to Christ's Kingly office, whereby he proclaims liberty from the dominion of sin and the fear of hell."[221] In his 1734 sermon, "One Thing Needful," Wesley speaks of "miracles of love" made possible by the incarnation, life, and suffering of Christ, miracles that have no other end in mind than "to restore us to health and freedom."[222]

Yet there is a parallel motif in Scripture sometimes overlooked. While the Bible clearly speaks of Christ as the one who frees us from the bondage of sin (John 8:32-36, Romans 6:17-18), Scripture also speaks in positive terms of what may be called a "servitude of love," a voluntary surrender of one's own newfound freedom in order to become a slave of Christ in service to others.

It's small wonder that this message is rarely touched upon by contemporary preachers. The word "slave" today evokes human trafficking or forced child labor. Yet Scripture must be read on its own terms and not be colored by the tinted glasses of modern usage. In fact, the same Bible that celebrates our liberation from sin calls us to a different attachment, to move away from what is devilish

---

220. Music and lyrics by Haldor Lillenas, 1917 (public domain).

221. G. Roger Schoenhals, ed., *Wesley's Notes on the Bible* (Grand Rapids, Michigan: Zondervan, 1987), 337.

222. *The Works of John Wesley, Bi-Centennial edition* (Frank Baker, ed. 35 vols. projected. Nashville: Abingdon Press, 1984 to present), 4:356.

in order to be bound to all that is divine. Whereas before we pursued a freedom that only enslaved us, now we submit to a bondage that sets us free. Such is the paradox of the holiness message.

Pierce My Ear, O Lord My God

When I was a university student, the music group *Glad* came to campus. Their up-tempo beat and innovative sound packed out the house. One lyric had all of us thinking in new ways:

Pierce my ear, O Lord my God.
Take me to your door this day.
I will serve no other gods.
Lord, I'm here to stay.[223]

This song is incomprehensible unless one knows the background from Exodus 21:1-11. The passage provides regulations regarding the purchase of a Hebrew slave. Such a purchase entitled the master to six years of faithful service, but in the seventh year, the slave must be set free. However, sometimes the master would provide the slave with a wife, and the slave may have children with this wife provided by his master. In this case, the slave had the option of voluntarily indenturing himself to his master for life, "But if the servant declares, 'I love my master and my wife and children and do not want to go free,' then his master must take him before the judges. He shall then take him to the door or the doorpost and pierce his ear with an awl. Then he will be his servant for life" (vv. 5-6, TNIV).[224]

In this scenario, it is important to underscore two points. First, this is a far cry from the chattel slavery common in the 19th century. The master was not cruel but benevolent. It was he who provided a wife for his slave that led to children. It was the master's love that engendered in the heart of the slave affection toward his master. Secondly, committing himself to the master's service as a life-long slave was not required but freely chosen. Victor Hamilton compares the slave's decision to that of Ruth, who out of love chose to accompany for life her mother-in-law, Naomi.[225] It is the same kind of loving relationship that led Paul to call himself and Timothy "slaves of Christ Jesus" (Philippians 1:1).[226] Love cannot be coerced, only evoked.

---

223. "Pierce My Ear," lyrics by Steve Croft, Dayspring Music, as sung by "Glad" on the 1980 album, Beyond a Star.

224. All Scripture citations are from Today's New International Version (2005).

225. Victor P. Hamilton, *Exodus: An Exegetical Commentary* (Grand Rapids, Michigan: Baker Academic, 2011), 374.

226. The Greek word "slave"—douloi—can also be translated as "servants." See Hamilton, 371. For an argument that slavery in the Graeco-Roman world was a means of upward mobility, see Dale B. Martin, *Slavery as Salvation: The Metaphor of Slavery in Pauline Christianity* (New Haven and London: Yale University Press, 1990).

From "Slaves to Sin" to "Slaves to Righteousness"

Moving to the New Testament, one of the most captivating passages considering both liberation from sin and servitude to God is Romans 6:15-23. Verse 18 clearly states, "You have been set free from sin and have become slaves to righteousness" (TNIV). Compare this to the misery of sin's slavery:

> Just as you used to offer yourselves as slaves to impurity and to ever-increasing wickedness, so now offer yourselves as slaves to righteousness leading to holiness. When you were slaves to sin, you were free from the control of righteousness. What benefit did you reap at that time from the things you are now ashamed of? Those things result in death! (vv. 19b-21)

Then in verse 22, Paul celebrates the happy alternative. His readers have now become "slaves to God." And why exactly should such slavery be celebrated? Paul explains that those who are indentured to God benefit from both "holiness" and "eternal life," God's "gift" through "Christ Jesus our Lord" (v. 23).

Frank Matera concludes, "For Paul, there is no absolute freedom. Human beings live in a cosmos of competing lords, who demand their allegiance. True wisdom is to align oneself with the Lord who makes one truly free."[227] The life of holiness becomes a life of grateful and joyous service to the Christ who broke the chains of sin and drew us to God with cords of love.

Holy Slaves of God in a Pagan Society

Though other passages from Paul address the same theme, words from Peter also beckon us. 1 Peter 2:13-17 calls the people of God to a life of love for God and fellow believers as well as submission to human authorities. To "live as God's slaves" is to live as "free people" (v. 16), not to be confused with a life of license, an "anything goes" mentality. Freedom is never to be a "cover-up for evil" (v. 16). Instead, our goodness will "silence the ignorant talk of the foolish" (v. 15). Here is a vision of integrity that commands attention yet points beyond oneself to the Holy One, the Christ who suffered for us, setting us an example to follow (v. 21).

Moving Godward and Outward

All three Scripture passages we've considered point to one conclusion: There is a slavery that is freeing, a voluntary submission to a master that springs from a relationship grounded in love. Yet to this point, the direction is only vertical, i.e.

227. Frank J. Matera, "Romans," in Mikeal C. Parsons and Charles H. Talbert, eds., *Paidea: Commentaries on the New Testament* (Grand Rapids, Michigan: Baker Academic, 2010), 155.

between the person and God. It takes Paul's instructions in Galatians 5:13-14 to define what freedom from sin and attachment to God look like horizontally in terms of our human relationships, "You, my brothers and sisters, were called to be free. But do not use your freedom to indulge the sinful nature; rather, serve one another humbly in love. For the entire law is fulfilled in keeping this one command: 'Love your neighbor as yourself.'" Likewise, John Franklin Hay in the novel *What Saved Grace?* observes, "You cannot have an authentic personal faith that does not express itself in ways that positively impact the social order. Holiness cannot be holy if it is just about one person claiming to be pure in heart. Holiness is expressed in community."[228] The servitude of love is directed both Godward and outward.

Toward a Servitude of Love

Holiness is always a journey. We are being made holy, being set-apart for sacred use, serving one another in loving community, being cleansed as God's slaves, and being tethered more-and-more to God's heart by the bonds of affection. To call Jesus "Lord" is not a mere affectation. It describes the loyalty and service that are his due, a life-long expression of gratitude for the salvation and liberation from sin powerfully enacted by Christ for our sake. In response, may we remain joyfully bound to this glorious Emancipator, in whom alone is true freedom, and may we be wonderfully yoked together in loving service to one another.

J. Gregory Crofford (Ph.D., University of Manchester) is Coordinator for Education and Clergy Development on the Africa Region, Church of the Nazarene. His writings include Streams of Mercy: Prevenient Grace in the Theology of John and Charles Wesley *(Emeth Press, 2010) and* The Dark Side of Destiny: Hell Re-Examined *(Wipf & Stock, 2013). Greg's blog, "Theology in Overalls," is found at gregorycrofford. com.*

---

228. John Franklin Hay, *What Saved Grace?* (Smashwords.com: Kindle Edition, 2013), location 2384.

Is Love Enough?

Behavioral Holiness in Paul

Jason Matters

Movie theaters. Dancing. Wedding rings. For many members of the Church of the Nazarene, these keywords trigger memories of sweaty preachers railing against the evils of a worldly culture while loudly exhorting listeners to live a holy life. This practical articulation of holiness often sounded more like a list of restrictive rules than holy living. In response, some rejected the ideal of holiness while others sought the purity beneath the rules. Those who longed for a motivating, joyful spirituality often found refuge in a positive, relational vision of holiness that that sought the ideal of perfect love described in 1 John 4:18.

For over one hundred years, every generation in the Church of the Nazarene has debated the particulars of a holy lifestyle, delicately balancing external conduct with internal motivation. At the same time, theologians have expanded the language of holiness to include broader biblical and theological themes. Ron Benefiel, noting the diversity in theological language, suggested that holiness is understood primarily through four theological images: purity, love, power, and character.[229]

These emphases are not, however, given equal attention, especially among younger leaders. I recently served as the pastor co-leader for a Senior Integrative Seminar at Nazarene Theological Seminary. In this particular group, every student described holiness in terms of perfect love, almost to the exclusion of the other three images. During his research at Asbury Seminary, Bill Kirkemo found that younger pastors in the denomination predominantly preferred the relational perspective that emphasizes love over the American-holiness perspective that emphasizes cleansing from sin.[230] It is no stretch to suggest that the dominant image and language of holiness preferred by young leaders is that of "perfect love."

But does the language of perfect love provide comprehensive instruction for a life of holiness? I suggest that it does not. Love, even when modified by the

---

229. Serrao, C. Jeanne Orjala. "Truth In Any Language." *Holiness Today.* https://www.ncnnews.com/nphweb/html/ht/article.jsp?sid=10005075&id=10013275 (accessed July 6, 2014).

230. William M Kirkemo, "Substantialist and Relational Understandings of Entire Sanctification Among Church of the Nazarene Clergy," DMin. Diss. Asbury Theological Seminary, 104 & 121. http://place.asburyseminary.edu/cgi/viewcontent.cgi?article=1316&context=ecommonsatsdissertations. Accessed July 7, 2014.

adjective "perfect," is not sufficient to inform and guide a Christian in the pursuit of the holy life. Love is perfected only when complemented by a focus on behavior. Behavior and love are mutually dependent as they balance, support, and inform each other to produce the fruit of holiness of heart and life. It is appropriate and necessary for pastors and other disciplers to teach holiness in terms of both love and behavior.

In the discipleship conversations that we call the epistles of the Apostle Paul, we find that he skillfully guided his disciples into the holy life by emphasizing both love and behavior. He regularly qualified "love" with adjectives that kept it from misunderstanding. He consistently illustrated love with descriptions of loving behavior. Paul did not stop with mere descriptions of loving expression, though. He regularly commanded his readers both toward and away from specific behaviors, to keep them living the holy life.

For Paul, however, holiness does not begin with love or behavior. God, who is holy, justifies and sanctifies humans as a gift of grace, received through faith. Paul's favorite description of the Christian's life and identity is "in Christ." Holiness is a mere expression of one's union with Christ and identity in Christ.

In the short letter to the Galatians, Paul argues for the freedom that is found in living the holy life by faith in God rather than by human effort. Paul beautifully concludes his argument by proclaiming that, "the only thing that counts is faith expressing itself through love" (Gal. 5:6, NIV). As he calls for action and outward expression, he grounds this desired behavior in terms of love. As he warns against taking freedom to the point of selfish indulgence, he repeats his conviction that, "the entire law is fulfilled in keeping this one command, "Love your neighbor as yourself" (Gal. 5:14, NIV). He then contrasts two lifestyles, listing specific behaviors that are inconsistent with a holy life, followed by a list of virtues found in the holy life. This pattern can be found throughout his writings.

In Romans 12:1, Paul transitions from his explication of righteousness that is experienced only "in Christ," to the practical expression, or application, section of his letter, and what remains in the final chapters are directives related to previous teaching. In two places within these chapters, Paul describes the Christian life in terms of love. In 12:9, he begins with a simple directive, "Love must be sincere." While not a grammatical imperative, the simple structure suggests that it functions as an implied imperative.[231] He then follows with over 25 directives, using various verbal constructions, but each with the force of an imperative.[232] His commands include prohibitions and prescriptions ("Do not repay anyone evil

---

231. James D. G. Dunn, *Romans 9–16* (Dallas, Tex.: Word Books, 1988), 737.

232. Dunn, 737-752.

for evil," and "Mourn with those who mourn."), and his directives are both broad and specific ("Hate what is evil," and "Share with the Lord's people who are in need.")

In Romans 13:8, Paul transitions to the letter's grandest explication of love, extolling "the continuing debt to love one another." He affirms the teaching of Jesus that the Old Testament social laws are "summed up in this one command: 'Love your neighbor as yourself'" (v. 9). He then boldly declares that "love is the fulfillment of the law" (v. 10). However, even within this grand vision of love, Paul explicitly illustrates the converse of the law of love, "Love does no harm to a neighbor" (v 9). Rather than cast a simple, broad vision of love, assuming that his readers would understand and apply it, he immediately illustrates love in terms of behavior.

In his first letter to the church at Corinth, Paul advocates for unity within the church, and in chapter thirteen, he argues for the priority love over gifts. We do not find Paul assuming a shared definition of love. Rather, he illustrates the attitudes and behaviors that are consistent with love and contrasts the behaviors that are inconsistent.

Paul's usage of the term "love" expands in the shorter epistles. In the letter to the Ephesians, Paul deftly describes the holy life in terms of love, commanding his readers to behave in love, as received from God, flowing from the believer's identity "in Christ." This compelling vision of love is found, however, in the middle of a lengthy section of prohibitions and specific behavioral directives. Similar expressions are found in the letters to the Philippians, Colossians, and others.

We also discover that Paul sought to model the holy life for his young disciples, through his love for them and his behavior in front of them. It is not difficult to sense the deep relational affection between the Apostle and his disciples. He regularly writes of the thankfulness with which he prays for them, and recalls his joy as he recalls the actions and love that grow out of their faith. He even commends the troublesome Corinthians! From this relational connection, he boldly calls them away from sinful behavior into the sanctified life. (1 Thessalonians 4:3-7 is a great example of a call to holiness described in terms of behavior.)

While we can affirm that Paul described the holy life in terms of love, we cannot miss how he laboriously qualified love and illustrated its application so that his readers could imagine love as enacted in their own behavior. He boldly prohibited his readers from specific behaviors and commanded them, often using the strongest grammatical constructions, towards behaviors consistent with faith in Christ. Grounded in an identity found in Christ, Paul discipled believers to be empowered by Christ to love deeply and to behave appropriately.

At this point, one may object, arguing that genuine love naturally results in behavior. "Love, and do as thou wilt," a favorite quote from Augustine, suggests that behavior naturally flows from love. Teachers, preachers, and spiritual guides need only expound on love and behavior will eventually result. Unfortunately, this plan often fails. It simply assumes too much. The Apostle Paul did not subscribe to this theory. Even as he wrote of love as the summary of the law, he was not content merely to state the summary. Love grows from immaturity to maturity and is perfected only within the boundaries provided by a behavioral covenant (or rules).

In the end, the holy life is a synthesis of love and behavior expressed from our identity in Christ. Love exists in a relationship of mutual pursuit; behavior exists in a relationship of hierarchy and authority. Our need for growth in love invites God, "who sees the heart," to speak personally. Our need for growth in behavior invites accountability from the Church. Perfect love illustrates what we are saved *for*; behavioral holiness illustrates what we are saved *from*. Perfect love meets our need for a positive vision for life; behavioral holiness meets our need for clear boundaries and restraint.

The theological images of perfect love and holy behavior are inseparable. Neither is primary, relegating the other to secondary status. Both are necessary for vital, growing relationship with God. Perfect love and behavioral holiness synergize to express the image of God in us and to propel us to work the mission of God.

The work of the pastor and discipler is complex. The temptation is great to over-simplify holiness into one image that can address all concerns. The difficult but wise path is to teach and to model holiness in terms of the believer's identity in Christ, the motivation of love, as well as observed behavior.

Jason Matters serves as pastor at New Vision Church of the Nazarene in Raymore, Missouri. When he is not preaching and teaching, he can usually be found at home with his family or deep in the woods sitting in a tree stand waiting for unsuspecting deer, with a bow in one hand and good book in other. He especially enjoys studying the intersection of New Testament studies with strategic evangelism and church growth.

In Christ:

Holy-Being and Holy-Becoming by Our Continuous Belonging

Rob A. Fringer

"What do you do for a living?" It is an inescapable question in today's society, and strangely it has become intricately connected to identity and thus to self-worth. While the phrase is usually employed as a simple discussion starter or to fill an awkward moment of encounter, the recipient often hears "Who are you and what value do you have?"

In such a world, it is no wonder many of us find ourselves busier than ever, caught in the endless cycle of doing in an attempt to gain value in our own eyes or in the eyes of others. Sadly, the church has not escaped this busyness, and many Christians continue to seek their identity in our doing rather than in our being. Even those of us who identify as holiness people have defined our holiness in terms of what we do and do not do.

Please hear me. I am not saying we should sit back and do nothing, quite the opposite. In many ways, we are not doing enough—at least, not enough for the lest of these. However, we must begin by accepting our identity, self-worth, and holiness as grounded in our being in Christ and belonging to him. The challenge comes in the fact that we must *already* embrace our new identities even though we have *not yet* lived into them. This dissonance is difficult because it feels hypocritical. We have been trained to believe we must "do" before we can "be" when in reality our "doing" comes out of our "being."

The Apostle Paul's correspondence with the church in Corinth provides us with an important example of this. If we take 1 & 2 Corinthians along with Acts 18:1-17, we know more about this church than any other. It was a struggling church, a divided church, a dysfunctional church, a church which no doubt tested Paul's resolve on more than one occasion. This is why the opening verses of 1 Corinthians (1:2-9) are so perplexing. Paul describes the Corinthians as,

- the church of God
- those who have been sanctified in Christ Jesus
- those called to be saints (holy ones)
- those who have been given the grace of God

- those who have been enriched in Christ in every way, in all speech and knowledge
- those who have had the testimony of Christ confirmed among them
- those not lacking in any spiritual gifts
- those whom God will strengthen till the end so they might be blameless
- those called by God into the fellowship of his Son

At first glance, these descriptors do not resemble the Corinthian church. So why does Paul say these words about them and to them? Some scholars believe Paul was simply moving through the customary niceties of the traditional Greek letter. Others believe Paul was buttering them up before sticking them in the frying pan. Both of these hypotheses are unsatisfactory. Rather, Paul sought to shape their identity around the *already/not-yet* Kingdom of God in which they now belonged.

Paul affirmed that all believers, through their faith in the faithfulness of Christ (Gal 2:16; Phil 3:9), become part of a new reality, a Kingdom reality. In Paul's words, "If anyone is in Christ—new creation; the old has passed away; behold, the new has come!" (2 Cor. 5:17, my translation). While many have over-individualized this verse, Paul is not primarily speaking about the individual becoming a new creation but rather about how union "in Christ" transports a person from one sphere of reality (*not yet*) to a new sphere of reality (*already*). The individual becomes a new creation not by being individually transformed but by entering into a "new creation" community known as the Body of Christ. In this way, there is an immediate transformation that takes place to such an extent that a new believer can *already*, like the Corinthians, be holy, sanctified, and not lacking in any spiritual gift, while simultaneously *not yet* exemplifying such transformation. This is because the Body has taken on the merits of Christ through their union with Him.

Notice the strong connection between the new Christ-identity and the Body. In 1 Corinthians, Paul explains to the Corinthian church that together:

- they have the mind of Christ (2:16),
- they form a single temple where God's Spirit dwells (3:16),
- they are washed, sanctified and justified (6:11),
- they must give up their rights for the sake of others (8:13),
- they must discern the Body as part of their worship (11:29),
- they have been baptized into one body through the one Spirit (12:13),
- they are the Body of Christ (12:27).

Here we learn that an inseparable part of our new identity is union with one another. As we belong to Christ, we simultaneously belong to one another. In fact, we first take on the attributes of Christ corporately, and only later, in our continuous belonging to him and our continuous belonging to his Body, do we begin to personalize this new identity in tangible ways.

The next step in the transformation process of both the community and the individual is not first ethical engagement ("doing") but the embracing of this new identity ("being"). In other words, we do not need to start acting a certain way in order to become what we already are in Christ. Rather, as we understand and accept who we already are in Christ, then we will begin to live out of this new being. Paul's words are not mere complements but truth statements waiting to be embraced and then actualized.

When this truth is applied to our understanding of holiness, we are again reminded that it is both *already* and *not yet*. Likewise, we are reminded it is first and foremost about "being" in Christ and belonging to one another, and only then, and from this being, about "doing." Another way of saying this is we must embrace Holy-being before we can embrace Holy-becoming.

The implications of this are far-reaching and can transform not only the way we understand ourselves but also the way we read and understand Scripture and interact with our world. If we understand Scripture as only giving us a list of ethical imperatives, then our understanding is limited to the few topics and situations Scripture addresses. The Word quickly becomes archaic, and so does our faith and witness. Likewise, if Christians see themselves primarily as ethical police teaching others the difference between right and wrong, we will likely continue to spend more time fighting amongst each other and missing important opportunities to live out the love of Christ.

However, if Scripture is primarily concerned with revealing the identity of the Godhead and helping us understand our identity in Christ, then the ethical outcomes are endless. This does not mean we become a law unto ourselves. Rather, filled with the Holy Spirit and guided by the Scriptures, we are able to discern the ethical demands of any given situation, not as individuals but as part of the Body of Christ. In this way, we see that our new Christ-identity gives us a Christ-authority that moves way beyond just pointing out others' sins.

The reality is that most people, whether Christians or not, do not need to be told when they have done something wrong or when they have sinned. Most experience the guilt and shame of their actions almost immediately. Rather, they need someone to tell them their sin ("doing") does not define them. They need someone who will speak a new world of possibility and hope into their lives, someone who will see them as Christ sees them—New Creations!

The same hope drives the Bible's consistent declaration that we are holy while also calling us to be holy. As we continue to reside in Christ and thus in his new age, we are indeed changed and made new, but more than that and more importantly, we are people who are helping to make all things new. We have been tasked with the great responsibility and the great authority to reveal the *already/ not-yet* Kingdom to the world around us, first in our Holy-being and then in our Holy-becoming.

Rob A. Fringer is Associate Lecturer in Biblical Studies and Biblical Language at Nazarene Theological College, Brisbane, Australia. He has 15 years of pastoral ministry experience in the areas of youth and adult discipleship and community outreach. He is co-author of The Samaritan Project *and* Theology of Luck: Fate, Chaos, and Faith *(forthcoming). Rob and his wife Vanessa have two children: Sierra and Brenden.*

The Holiness Gift of Languages:
Reclaiming Cross-Cultural Evangelism in America
Mark Montgomery

> *"All of them were filled with the Holy Spirit and began to speak in other tongues as the Spirit enabled them" (Acts 2:4, NIV).*

Our confusion about the flat-line of church growth for the last 50 years in North America has only been exceeded by the shroud of mystery that covers the face of holiness evangelism and its lack of traction here in comparison to "over there." Many veils of excuses layer our discussions from the materialism and individualism of America to the virginity of foreign soils with their rampant poverty and disease of mind and body. Those banners no longer fly. *Translation: We all know something is missing; just can't say what.*

Our sanctified envy of foreign fruit drives us to ask some good searching questions and to accept the humble position of being taught from the harvest field itself. Overseas, the absence of some luxuries (such as debating the finer points of everything, impressing our professors with our ability to detail and annotate our position, and reviewing our peers mercilessly) can be accounted for by the necessity to spend the lion's share of our time "cracking the missional code." *Translation: No time to split hairs; there's a dying world to win! High time to get that here at home.*

The holiness family of denominations finds itself staring down the wrong end of the twin barrels of post-modern thought and a rapidly changing demographic in America. The powdery smell of disengagement threatens to implode what is left of our confidence, relevance, and influence. *Translation: The fish have moved; time to fish where they're biting.*

Perhaps, the great challenge of the modern American Holiness Movement (if it can be still called a movement) is to develop a continuing capacity to translate the biblical message of Holiness in the heart language of every generation and culture in America. *Translation: Speak their lingo; talk to them, not over them.*

The real problem is that we have no missiology that adequately addresses the accelerating rate of change in America. We still act like it is 1950's monolithic America, and like canned holiness sermons distributed to every Church of the

Nazarene pulpit will get the job done. *Translation: Good news is no good unless it is today's news to today's people.*

May I suggest a fresh, comprehensive examination of New Testament missiology, in terms of our holiness heritage? In the full counsel of the Bible, the relationship between "holiness" and "mission" is seamless and peerless. Divorcing the two concepts disables the church, and creates what Alan Hirsch calls a "crisis of infertility."[233]

Let's start with the birth of the Church itself on the Day of Pentecost and investigate one key ingredient to God's Movement Chemistry, "diversified translation." Sadly, the typical holiness sermon seldom advances beyond Acts 2:4a, and the Pentecostal Mission is poorer for it. This case of "creative cropping" is a loss of cross-cultural strategy.

Lost on the perennial debate over "speaking in tongues" (Pentecostal vs. the Corinthian misunderstanding and malpractice) is the strategic advantage of **Diversified Translation,** as an act of the Holy Spirit. To be sure, the spiritual gift of languages is best defined by its inception on the Day of Pentecost rather than its abusive counterfeit in the sick, immoral, divided, and carnal church of Corinth. Allow the impetus define the true character of the phenomenon.

During that Pentecostal event described in Acts 2, visitors to Jerusalem from fifteen world areas heard the gospel in their own heart language as the 120 believers, newly filled with the Holy Spirit, spoke in languages that they had never learned.

Therefore, the content produced by the authentic gift of languages is an intelligible language of an actual people group in our world. It is not a heavenly language or prayer language. The gift of languages, in this context, is a sign of the universality of the Gospel, and by extension, it is an enduring cross-cultural evangelism gift.

Career missionaries know that indigenous people are most receptive to the Gospel when it is presented to them in their own heart or "first" language. Thus, one of the greatest needs of our day—when world missions have come to us in America and really in every major city around the world—is to translate the timeless truths of God's Word into the languages of the people of cultures and subcultures around us.

"Love is . . . not rude" (1 Cor. 13:5, ESV), says the greatest missionary of the early Church, Paul. In ancient and modern multilingual church settings, the message should be spoken in a language all present can thoroughly understand, or a translator should provide a translation. The reason for the cascading "yawns"

233. Alan Hirsch and Tim Catchim, *The Permanent Revolution* (Hoboken, NJ: Jossey-Bass, 2012), xxvii.

across our congregations during Sunday sermons may be more than the late Saturday night on the town. We preachers miss the mark and, therefore, sin against our people when we unwittingly bore them with jargon and tedium.

Have you ever spoken "factory rat rant" or "soccer mom muse" or "coffee club jawing" or "Goth-speak"? We love the people in the pew—as well as the unreached in our cities—by speaking their heart language.

The Holy Spirit often provides the miracle of translation through His instruments. The miracle can be in the speaker or the hearer. Scripturally, abuses of this gift are to be handled by the shepherds/elders privately, discreetly, and lovingly. We have those rare church splits over the counterfeit of the genuine largely because of our fearful silence on the subject, *and* in the meantime, we sacrifice missional power.

As a point of contrast, according to Muslim-background believers in Isa (Jesus), the Qur'an does not read the same in other languages as it does in its original Arabic. The Holy Spirit has an uncanny ability to translate the Word of God into every language and cultural context with no loss in meaning or potency. He does the same through His modern-day prophets—if they are sensitive to the need to communicate with contextualization.

Moreover, as David Garrison, Alan Hirsch, and others have noted, the Holy Spirit guides and propels the church in accomplishing its mission of translating the Good News into the heart language of every people group and sub-culture *in a way that can be rapidly reproduced throughout that culture.* The key to jumpstarting the Holiness Movement is diversified translation.[234]

The Gutenberg Press and the German Bible translation, John Wycliffe and the English Bible and his namesake modern translators, as well as the JESUS Film Project with nearly 1200 languages and dialects are all testimonies of a spiritual gift of languages "known to hearers," previously "unknown" to the speakers. Whether it occurs instantaneously like at Pentecost or through the "wrinkle" of learning a culture/language and *at the same time* witnessing and loving them to Jesus, the miracle is the same in essence, and the purpose is clear. Speaking in tongues is, first and last, a cross-cultural evangelism gift, not a heavenly language nor a self-indulgent status symbol.

What does that mean for our local churches?

First, we leaders must realize that we can no longer see the abundant, ripe harvest from behind our pulpits. We have to enter the harvest fields.

---

234. David Garrison, *Church Planting Movements: How God Is Redeeming a Lost World* (WIGTake Resources, 2004); Alan Hirsch, *The Forgotten Ways: Reactivating the Missional Church* (Grand Rapids, MI: Brazos, 2009).

Second, we cannot assume that we know what the people in our communities are really like. We have to do the hard work of missional research that cannot be gathered through arm's length transactions with a few representatives. We must mix covertly with the culture and really see the people and listen to their expressions and hearts beat.

Then, we must use the pictures, allegories, and similes from their unique workplaces, marketplaces and neighborhoods that communicate the timeless truths of the Gospel, including holiness, in their heart language.

Finally, the best translation of holiness is the walking, "living epistle" of our own lives and the lives of our people, "known and read by all men" (2 Cor. 3:2, NIV). Do we really live and move and speak as Jesus did? This is only possible through reading the Gospels with fresh eyes and receiving fresh Pentecostal outpourings of the Holy Spirit upon our own lives.

I began by demonstrating the contrast between the way we talk and write in scholarly circles and the way many of ordinary Americans need to hear it. My goal was to provoke the reader to embrace what we all instinctively know. Loving proclamation touches the heart of the hearer. The heart is where real spiritual business is done with God. With effective contextual communication, our words can be powerfully delivered to the target area.

Indeed, it is time to reclaim cross-cultural evangelism for the Holiness Movement. Preciseness and accuracy in our doctrines will matter little if the message is delivered in a way that does not communicate within the frame of reference of our hearers and thereby touch their hearts. Speak the heart language of the unreached, and the Good News will sound to them like a language from heaven. They will be changed, and we will light a fuse that burns through their web of relationships in life-giving ways.

R. Mark Montgomery leads BreakThrough—a network of church-type missions in the Greater Lansing Area. He serves as regional representative of the Nazarene Organic Church Network Taskforce and as Tri-District Church Planting Conversation Facilitator in Michigan. He studied at Olivet Nazarene University and Nazarene Theological Seminary.

Remembering the Role of the Gifts of the Spirit in the Pursuit of Holiness

Robert S. Snow

I am currently Associate Professor of New Testament at Ambrose University College in Calgary, Alberta. I have grown up in the Church of the Nazarene and continue to serve in our Canadian Nazarene school and at Calgary First Church of the Nazarene, where I teach and preach quite regularly. I have an increasing interest both intellectually and spiritually in what Paul calls the "spirituals" (e.g. 1 Cor. 12:1). In this short paper, I contend that practicing the spiritual gifts is indispensable for living a holy life, characterized not only by purity but also by power. However, in my experience growing up in the Church of the Nazarene, many are largely uniformed about these gifts, a situation about which the Apostle Paul would surely disapprove (1 Cor. 12:1).

While we as members of the Church of the Nazarene rightly seek the cleansing work of the Spirit for purity of heart and mind, we must also ask God for the manifestations of his Spirit, or the *charismata*, so that he might work through us by means of his power and wisdom to edify (or to build up) the church (1 Cor. 14:12). Paul himself realizes the importance of both moral purity generated by love *and* the necessity of the spiritual gifts for growth, "Pursue love *and* strive for the spiritual gifts, and especially that you may prophesy" (1 Cor. 14:1) The Greek verb translated "strive" expresses the pursuit of something with passionate zeal or ardor. Paul uses this same word in Phil. 3:6, "as to zeal, a persecutor of the church." Paul is exhorting the Corinthians to pursue the gifts with ardor, passion, and enthusiasm, using the same word to describe the level of intensity by which he persecuted the earliest followers of Jesus!

Some may object to such a pursuit of the gifts, as we do not see it as often as Paul's exhortations to pursue love and other virtues. However, in a couple of other epistles, we see evidence that Paul and others regularly practiced them (i.e. 1 Thes. 1:4-5 and Rom. 1:11). Furthermore, we see descriptions of Paul's charismatic ministry in the book of Acts.

One of the first things to realize about the spiritual gifts is that they ultimately serve, as Paul says, "the common good" (1 Cor. 12:7). They are for the betterment of the church, the body of believers. In some conversations I have had with members of the denomination, I have found a hesitancy to pursue the gifts because they can be used for self-serving means, which is not a baseless concern as Paul had to deal with precisely this issue in Corinth.

There is a level of messiness that comes with congregations and groups who seek the gifts, as there will be abuses, but Paul never uses this as a reason not to seek the gifts including tongues, "So, my friends, be eager to prophesy, and do not forbid speaking in tongues (1 Cor. 14:39)." We members of the Church of the Nazarene who pursue heart purity (lives filled with the love of God in Jesus Christ) are in a very good position to seek the gifts as we have a doctrine that denounces selfishness and calls believers to live lives totally at the service of God and others, empowered by the purifying work of the Spirit in our hearts. We must, however, seek not only the Spirit's purity but also his power and other manifestations of the Spirit, given their purpose of building the church!

So, how do the gifts build up the church? As we zealously strive after the gifts of the Spirit, the presence of God is made manifest through us in very specific ways so that others can receive a touch from God that addresses particular issues or concerns in their lives.

This is most evident in Paul's description of prophecy and the effect that this gift has on the unbeliever when exercised in the worshipping community, "But if an unbeliever or an inquirer comes in while everyone is prophesying, they are convicted of sin and are brought under judgment by all, as the secrets of their hearts are laid bare. So they will fall down and worship God, exclaiming, 'God is really among you'" (1 Cor. 14:24-25). Here we see that the gift of prophecy, through the revelation of that which is unknown by means of the natural senses, enables the heart of an unbeliever to be laid bare in the presence of God leading to that person's salvation. When the gift of prophecy is active in the church, God will speak in very specific ways to those who do not know him that will lead them into God's kingdom.

Paul is likely alluding to Zechariah with the phrase, "God is really among you." In Zechariah 8, the prophet describes the restoration of the presence of God in the Jerusalem temple, "Thus says the LORD of hosts: In those days ten men from nations of every language shall take hold of a Jew, grasping his garment and saying, 'Let us go with you, for we have heard that God is with you'" (Zech 8:23). Through this allusion, Paul makes the point that the gift of prophecy unleashes the presence of God in tangible ways in the worshipping community to which the unsaved will be drawn, leading to their salvation.

As indicated above, the gifts have a specific function and always lead to growth or the building up of those who are on the receiving end of their ministry. With the gift of prophecy, we see that the prophetic word leads to conviction of sin and salvation, and earlier in 1 Cor. 14 the prophetic word, more generally, leads to "upbuilding and encouragement and consolation" (1 Cor. 14:3).

When we think about the gifts as the means by which the Holy Spirit is made manifest in the worshipping community (1 Cor. 12:7), it is natural that believers grow in holiness. When the Holy Spirit is active, holiness is the result, which is clearly demonstrated in the ministry of Jesus in Luke's Gospel.

According to Paul's list of the gifts (1 Cor. 12:8-10), the Spirit desires to manifest himself in a variety of ways.

- A *word of knowledge* gives insight into a particular issue related to a person or a situation.
- A *word of wisdom* provides a solution to deal with the revealed situation.
- The *gift of faith* is given for the exercise of an expectant faith for a specific and miraculous move of God.
- When it comes to *healing*, there is more than one gift available likely reflecting the different areas in which people need to be healed: emotional, physical, spiritual, etc.
- The next gift is the *working of miracles*, which is a general designation for any work of God that is not explainable by means of rationalism or science, such as the dead being raised after an extended period of time.
- After prophecy (we will skip this, since I've discussed it above) is the *discernment of spirits*. This gift enables the one who possesses it to see past outward appearances to the spiritual state of an individual. For example, one can detect the presence of persistent and tormenting thoughts in a person or the presence of evil spirits or demons. We see Jesus exercise this regularly with his religious adversaries, the demon possessed, and the disciples.
- The last two gifts, *various kinds of tongues* and the *interpretation of tongues*, are the lightening rod gifts! Because of the historically hostile stance of some segments of our denomination toward the gift of tongues, many members of the denomination have written off all the gifts! This should not be, especially in light of Paul's explicit injunction not to forbid speaking in tongues. In informal discussions with blue-blooded Pentecostals, there are few instances of the utterance of tongues by one individual in a worship service that is then interpreted. I believe it is quite uncommon, and if I

were to choose between tongues and prophecy in the worship service, I would advocate for the prophetic word. However, tongues is still a gift that must be zealously and earnestly sought after in keeping with 1 Cor. 12:1. For Paul, this gift builds up the one who exercises it (1 Cor. 14:4a), which, as we have seen, is the case with all of the gifts.

Unlike the gifts of prophecy, knowledge and wisdom, which are expressed in intelligible speech, the gift of tongues comes in the form of unintelligible speech because the Spirit is not ministering to the believer's mind but to his or her spirit and that one then speaks "mysteries in the Spirit" to God (1 Cor. 14:2). From God's perspective, there is nothing odd or foolish about this gift, contra the assessment held by far too many Christians.

Paul clearly asserts in 1 Corinthians 2 that "those who are unspiritual do not receive the gifts of God's Spirit, for they are foolishness to them, and they are unable to understand them because they are spiritually discerned" (1 Cor. 2:14). These gifts, including tongues, come from the wisdom of God and cannot be understood apart from the Spirit which makes known God's wisdom, "Now we have received not the spirit of the world, but the Spirit that is from God, so that we may understand the gifts bestowed on us by God" (1 Cor. 2:12).

Let me give an honest confession of my own experience. One year before I wrote this essay, the gift of tongues was completely weird, foolish, and unnecessary in my estimation. However, as I began to seek the Spirit on his terms, looking not only for the fruits of the Spirit but also for the gifts of the Spirit, I subsequently received the gift of tongues. I can testify that this gift builds me up in Christ providing another means by which the Spirit of God ministers to me. I believe that if my generation takes seriously the task of recovering the forgotten gifts of the Spirit, the Church of the Nazarene will see a revival in North America that will exceed the exponential growth of its earliest days.

Postmodern culture places a high value on experience. We serve a God who desires that we experience him and all that he has for us, but this will only happen if we accept his Spirit on his terms and not our own. We must, therefore, not only pursue love and purity but also zealously strive after the spiritual gifts—those things that manifest the power and wisdom of the God. We must no longer harbor prejudice or bias against the gifts as a whole or against any gift in particular. In his infinite grace, God wishes to pour out both his Spirit and his spiritual gifts on his people so that our worshipping communities will be unmistakably characterized by the realized presence of our holy God. This is *the* way to Scriptural Holiness.

Rob Snow is Associate Professor of New Testament and Chair of the Christian Studies program at Ambrose University in Calgary, AB. In 2007, he earned a Ph.D. in New Testament from The University of Manchester. Rob is currently writing a commentary on Mathew 1–16 for the New Beacon Bible Commentary series. The desire of his heart is to share and live out the transforming power of Holy Spirit whenever and wherever he can.

Working Because God Works:
Philippians 2:10-11 as a Level for Crooked Conceptions of Responsibility for Holiness
Ryan K. Giffin

Renovations to the doctrine of Christian holiness are necessary for younger generations in the Church of the Nazarene in part because of confusion over who is responsible for holy living. Much of the holiness preaching and teaching I have heard has left me with either one of two opposing impressions.

The first common impression from holiness preaching is that living a life of holiness is entirely dependent on *me*. If I muster enough determination and will power to make the right choices, then and only then can I be described as "holy."

The opposite impression I have received is that any holiness in me is entirely up to *God*. If I just trust in God's grace alone, then I will be holy. My determination, willpower, and choices have nothing to do with it.

And so holiness is either all about *my* work for God, or it is all about *God's* work in me. My contention is that this prevalent "either-or" understanding of divine and human responsibility has resulted in a skewed view of the doctrine of Christian holiness among the majority of Gen-X and millennial Christians. Younger generations in the denomination are often either hesitant to embrace holiness with the gusto that characterized previous generations, or disinterested in holiness altogether. My strong hunch is that mixed messages concerning who is responsible for holy living is partly to blame. In order for the doctrine of holiness to find some stability among future generations in the denomination, this contorted understanding must to be straightened out.

My younger brother Matt is an exceptionally gifted professional builder. I, on the other hand, know only enough about physical renovations to be able to identify a few tools. One of the few things I remember as a junior high student in wood shop is being somewhat fascinated with one tool in particular: the carpentry level. The level is a long rectangular-shaped tool used by builders to establish true vertical and true horizontal measurements. What caught my middle school attention about the level is the key element inside it: a small clear sealed tube with two parallel lines drawn at its center, containing water with an air bubble. When the bubble is aligned between the two parallel lines at center of the tube, the builder knows that their work is "level" and therefore straight, firm, and secure. If the builder of a house could not establish a clear measurement of "level," the walls of the house would be crooked, and the house would not stand for long.

I want to propose that Philippians 2:12-13 are able to do for the doctrine of Christian holiness what a carpentry level is able to do for the builder of a house. The apostle Paul's instruction and assurance in this text offer some helpful straightening out of cockeyed understandings concerning divine and human responsibility for holiness. Shortly after encouraging the Philippians to have the same mindset as Christ Jesus, Paul writes:

> *Therefore, my dear friends, as you have always obeyed—not only in my presence, but now much more in my absence—continue to work out your salvation with fear and trembling, for it is God who works in you to will and to act in order to fulfill his good purpose.* (NIV)

These two short verses contain much that can level out our understanding of who bears the responsibility for holy living. First, Paul clearly indicates here that salvation is something that must be "worked out" by Christians. Salvation from sin has been fully provided for us by the atoning death of Jesus, and this salvation must be "worked out"—actively and continually responded to—in a life of holiness.

Some want to embrace a doctrine of hyper-grace and argue that being made holy is entirely dependent on God, yet the unavoidable truth of this text is that holiness does indeed have something to do with *me*. My determination, will-power, choices, and behavior do matter in my pursuit of Christlike discipleship. If there were any doubt about this, notice the connection Paul makes here between working out salvation and *obedience*: "just as you have always *obeyed* . . .continue to *work out your salvation* . . ." Being holy requires a daily life of disciplined obedience to the will of God, exhibited in the choices we make and the actions we embrace or neglect. We are not saved by any work we do, but there is some "working out" to do on our part when it comes to living a holy life.

At the same time, Paul clearly teaches here that *God works in us*. Just as it is unavoidable that holiness has something to do with *me*, it is also gloriously true (to the chagrin of those who understand holiness as entirely dependent on human effort) that the holy life does have something to do with *God* as well. My choices and behaviors may matter, but they are certainly not *all* that matters. In fact, God's work in us is the sturdy foundation that enables us to live a life of holiness.

Paul makes this clear in a number of ways by his careful choice of words in this passage. To begin with, the word "for" toward the front of v. 13 indicates that we can work out our salvation precisely *because* God is working in us at the same time. Because God works, we can work.

Secondly, "God" appears at the front of this part of the sentence in the original Greek, which gives God a special emphasis here. The full force of Paul's Greek would look something like this in English, "***GOD*** *is the one working in you . . .*"

Finally, you might have noticed Paul's play on words: Christians are instructed to "work out" their salvation because God is "working" in them. Any "work" we have to do is bolted together by the reality of God's simultaneous "work" in us. John Wesley captured this well in a sermon he preached on this text when he said, "God works, therefore we *can* work; God works, therefore we *must* work."[235]

This text also teaches that the work of God in us takes place at the level of both our *will* and our *action*. Through the Holy Spirit, God works in us to *will* to please God, increasing our desire to live a holy life. God also works in us through the Holy Spirit to *do* what pleases him, helping us to act in ways that are in harmony with the character of his Son.

These verses conclude by acknowledging that God works in us on behalf of his good purpose. God has a *motive* for working in us, and that motive is his own good purpose and pleasure. This is one of the reasons why our salvation is to be worked out "in fear and trembling." We tend to associate such things as "fear" and "trembling" with dread or being scared. Here, however, the idea has to do with the awe and reverence that should come from knowing that we are living out our salvation in the presence of God, with God's power, all for God's good purpose.

In the end, Paul's instruction and assurance in Philippians 2:12-13 offers a helpful leveling out of skewed understandings concerning who is responsible for what in the life of holiness. What my generation might have understood to be an "either-or" scenario is, according to Paul, actually a "both-and." We have work to do in the pursuit of holiness, and we can do this work because God is working in us. As we work out our salvation as individuals within Christian communities, we can rest assured that God is working in our lives and in our churches for his good purpose. Only when our understanding of Christian holiness is renovated in a way that gets all of this measured to level will holiness among Gen-Xers and Millennials be built to last.

Ryan K. Giffin is Lead Pastor of Paris Church of the Nazarene in Paris, Kentucky and a Ph.D. Candidate in Biblical Studies at Asbury Theological Seminary. Ryan has served with his wife Kendra in pastoral ministry at Mason First Church of the Nazarene in Mason, Michigan and in campus ministry at MidAmerica Nazarene University. Ryan holds a Bachelor of Arts in Youth and Family Ministries from MNU, a Master of Science in Education from the University of Kansas, and a Master of Arts from NTS.

235. John Wesley, "On Working Out Our Own Salvation" (1785), in *John Wesley's Sermons: An Anthology*, ed. Albert C. Outler and Richard P. Heitzenrater (Nashville, Abingdon, 1991), 486-92.

Perfect Love
Tara Beth Leach

When I was a 21-year-old Bible student, I ran into a Church of the Nazarene evangelist that boldly professed to me that he "was indeed living a perfect life without sin." I sat there rather perplexed. I was young, I was cynical, I didn't buy it.

The word "perfect" carries a lot of meaning in Wesleyan-Holiness circles. Many might ask, does perfection mean sinlessness or maturity? As a Millennial, such a concrete word makes me squirm immediately.

John Wesley, no doubt, had a thing or two to say about perfection. He admits, "The word 'perfect' is what many cannot bear. The very sound of it is an abomination to them. And whosoever 'preaches perfection' (as the phrase is) i.e. asserts that it is attainable in this life, runs great hazard of being accounted by them worse than a heathen man or a publican."[236] And yet, "Christian perfection" has been a chief principle the Wesleyan-Holiness tradition. Wesley continues, "We may not therefore lay these expressions aside, seeing they are the words of God, and not of man. But we ought to explain the meaning of them . . ."[237] The Greek word for perfect, *teleios*, is used throughout the New Testament[238] and is even uttered from the very lips of Jesus in the Sermon on the Mount when Jesus says, "But you are to be perfect, even as your Father in heaven is perfect" (Matthew 5:48).

With its striking call to radical discipleship, the Sermon on the Mount is one of the most beautiful discourses in the New Testament. In the Sermon, Jesus speaks with an authority that is revealing, piercing, and commanding. In a section known as the "antitheses" (5:17-48), Jesus demands more of His followers, more than almost anyone would expect. Jesus's teachings are not practical advice for beneficial living or a list of virtues, but prophetic implications because of the coming, and already present, kingdom of God.[239]

In the final antithesis, the greatest commandment emerges from the lips of Jesus. Jesus commands the listeners that it is no longer enough to love our neighbor

---

236. Albert C. Outler, Richard P. Heitzenrater ed. *John Wesley's Sermons: An Anthology* (Nashville: Abingdon, 1991), 476.

237. Ibid.

238. See Matthew 19:21, Romans 12:2, 2 Corinthians 12:9, 1 John 4:18

239. Leander E. Keck, *The New Interpreter's Bible: Matthew—Mark*, vol. 8 (Nashville, Tenn.: Abingdon Press, 1995), 177.

and to hate our enemies; rather, we must now love our enemies and pray for those who persecute us. In doing this, the Christ follower becomes a daughter or son of the eschatological kingdom of God. As children of the kingdom, then, we are to have a boundary-breaking, indiscriminate, counter-cultural, and a cross-cultural love for all.[240]

In the final sentence of the sixth antithesis, Jesus utters the culminating words, "Be perfect, therefore, as your heavenly Father is perfect" (Matthew 5:48). Still, what exactly does Jesus mean by "perfect"?

In many holiness circles, we often equate this word "perfect" with "sinlessness." Others are tempted to soften the word "perfect" because of its seemingly impossible standard. They may prefer translations such as "maturity," "wholeness," or "completeness."

But when we look at "perfect" through the hermeneutic of Jesus (love God, love people), we can see that we are called to love *all people* just as the Father has loved *all people*.[241] In context, then, "perfection" means "loving all." Loving our neighbors is not limited to the easy-to-love or the-people-like-us, but we are to also love our enemies (Matthew 5:47). To be perfect, then, is to love in the same indiscriminate way that the Heavenly Father loves (Matthew 5:45).

As King and Messiah, Jesus becomes the ultimate authority for the ethical life for the Christ follower. Therefore, perfection is imitating the way Jesus loves the sinner, the Gentile, the woman, the man, the child, the desolate, the prostitute, the tax collector, the poor, the rich, the broken, and even the enemy.[242] Jesus is every bit of serious about the conduct of His disciples mirroring the greatest command. As Scot McKnight explains, "To respond to the Sermon is not to respond to an ethical vision. To respond is to respond to Jesus. The proper response is to declare who he is by the way we live."[243]

Therefore, we can conclude that the way of perfection—or what we members of the denomination lovingly call "holiness"—is love. Holy perfection is indiscriminate love, love for all, even when it is difficult and demanding.

Mildred Bangs Wynkoop, holiness scholar and Church of the Nazarene preacher, describes this with great depth in *A Theology of Love*:

---

240. See for example, Matthew 8:5-13, Matthew 9:9-13, Matthew 15:21-28, John 4:1-26.

241. Scot McKnight and Tremper Longman III, eds., *Sermon on the Mount* (The Story of God Bible Commentary) (Grand Rapids: Zondervan, 2013), 145-147.

242. See for example, Luke 7:36-50, Matthew 8:5-13, Matthew 15:21-28, Matthew 5:2-11, Matthew 8:28-32, Matthew 9:9-13.

243. McKnight, 277.

The love which we call Christian love, then, is not a substitute for the other loves, nor is it an addition to those loves, but it is a quality of the entire person as it is centered in Christ. The distorting self-orientation, which flaws all other relationships because it uses them to personal advantage . . . is brought into wholeness by the abiding presence of the Holy Spirit. In this relationship all other relationships of life are enhanced and beautified and made holy.[244]

Even so, loving indiscriminately is difficult when the loving is for those who are hard to love. Personally, I have had quite a challenge in loving those who have been very outspoken of their view of complementarianism and thereby denigrating God's calling in my life. Although the Church of the Nazarene affirms women in ministry, it seems we have some in every local church who do not affirm the calling of women to preach.

Several years ago, while serving as a pastor in a Church of the Nazarene congregation, I built a relationship with an elderly man in our congregation. "Joe" had an intense desire to study the scriptures and was always full of questions on Sundays. However, one day Joe had a change in perspective.

One Sunday morning, while I was preaching a message, Joe made his way down the center aisle and sat gruffly in the front row. I almost thought he was going to stop me from preaching. At the end of the service, Joe was quick to jump up and hand me a sheet of paper with various scriptures written in red ink. "This is the Holy Word of God," he said. "I can't argue with God."

When I looked down at the paper, I noticed that it was saturated in passages similar to 2 Timothy 2:12. Then, Joe announced, "Since you are a woman, you have no business preaching and teaching." As I attempted to walk Joe gently through some of the passages, I quickly realized that I was getting nowhere and that he was only getting angrier.

Joe's words were piercing and left me feeling wounded for days. They were echoes of other harsh words at other times through emails, letters, and phone calls similar in content.

Five days later, Joe had a severe brain aneurism and almost lost his life. As a single man with hardly any family in town, Joe didn't have many people to visit him. Since our other pastor was on vacation, I was on hospital visit duty. Knowing that our last conversation left me wounded, I struggled with the thought of visiting Joe. It was difficult to love Joe indiscriminately. As I arrived at the hospital, I stopped for a moment to whisper a prayer. I prayed for the Spirit

244. Mildred Bangs Wynkoop, *A Theology of Love* (Kansas City: Beacon Hill, 1972), 33-34.

to propel and impel me to love Joe with the same self-sacrificial of God that Jesus explained in the Sermon on the Mount.

When I walked into the room, I was overcome with sadness for Joe. I saw him slumped over in a wheel chair with his head down, sadly staring at the floor. He sat alone and helpless; it hurt my heart. I had never before felt such loneliness and brokenness as I did when I looked at him that day. I sat next to him, and he was even well enough to know who I was and carry on a conversation.

About halfway through our talk, I placed my hand on his hand and said, "Joe, we've been praying for you at church, and we love you." As those words came out of my mouth, his body shook with emotion as he began to weep uncontrollably. At that moment, I knew I had meant it; I loved Joe. The Spirit had indeed propelled me and impelled me to love him with the indiscriminate love of the Father.

It was a holy moment. Love is, after all, holiness.

In their book, *Relational Holiness*, Thomas Jay Oord and Michael Lodahl explain, "Divine love outpoured through Jesus Christ in the power of the Spirit can so fill our hearts that in this very moment—and in the next—we can truly love God, our neighbors, and God's creation, including ourselves."[245] They continue, "Christian perfection is, in its essence, *perfection in love*."[246] The way to holiness is love—divine love that comes from the indwelling of the Holy Spirit that gives us the ability to become conduits of God's love to a world that so desperately needs it.

Tara Beth and her husband, Jeff, were married in 2006 and now reside in the Western Suburbs of Chicago with two toddler sons, Caleb and Noah. Tara Beth serves as the Pastor of Women's Ministry at Christ Church of Oak Brook. She graduated from Olivet Nazarene University in 2004 and is now finishing her Masters of Divinity through Northern Theological Seminary, where she is also a Teaching Assistant for Scot McKnight.

---

245. Thomas Jay Oord and Michael Lodahl, *Relational Holiness: Responding to the Call of Love* (Kansas City: Beacon Hill, 2005), 107.

246. Ibid.

Reclaiming Entire Sanctification

Tim Crutcher

Just how "entire" is "entire sanctification"? That's always been a difficult question for me. On the one hand, I read in Scripture the call to "Be perfect, therefore, as your heavenly Father is perfect" (Matt 5:48, NIV). I have also inherited a tradition that tells me that God can completely and decisively "fix" the problem of sin, either by eradicating the root from which it springs (an American Holiness emphasis) or by filling the heart so full with love that there is simply no room for sin anymore (John Wesley's emphasis).

On the other hand, my own experience—indeed, the experience of all the people I know—tells me that the battle against sin isn't something that just "goes away." Furthermore, it just doesn't make sense to think that, in this world filled with distractions and pleasures, we could ever rise above the level of temptation and reach some state where sin is no longer an option. After all, look at Jesus. Surely he had no "root of sin" in him, and surely his heart was completely filled with love, and yet he was tempted.

And so I'm still left with my question: *Just how "entire" is "entire sanctification" anyway?*

To begin with, let's think about how we think about sin. Given the biblical affirmation of the goodness of God's original creation, it is hard to imagine that sin was a part of that. The story of Adam and Eve seems to indicate that sin gets introduced into the world by human action. Sin is not there in the beginning, so in some sense it's a foreigner to God's good creation. On the other hand, sin is not some new "thing" that invades God's good creation from the outside—because there is no such place outside God's creation. Nor do Adam and Eve create this new "thing" called sin when they eat the fruit of that forbidden tree. Nowhere in their story—nor in our own—do we find them (or us) invaded by some outside "thing" that, like a bad seed, gets introduced into our lives, takes root there, and now makes us constantly mess up our relationship with God and with other people. Adam and Even sinned because they choose to prioritize themselves over God, and when we sin, we do the exact same thing. The "root" of sin, in that case, is nothing more than our "self," the center of our desires and identity, which—simply by existing—is always pulling for our best attentions.

Now, if that's the case, it sounds like we could only get rid of sin "entirely" by getting rid of our "selves" entirely, and that solution seems to be a bit too radical. Additionally, we have to affirm, with the Scripture, that Jesus was tempted in all the ways that we are tempted, and he did not sin (Heb 4:15). Jesus seemed to have clear desires and a sense of identity, so it must be possible to *be* a "self" and never to prioritize one's "self" over others. But the fact that we never get rid of our "selves" would also mean that the possibility, the opportunity, the temptation to focus on that "self" will always be there. Jesus's own temptations demonstrate that whatever "entire sanctification" Jesus had—and I doubt we could hope for any better—did not release him from all temptation, though it did empower him to always overcome it. So, it would seem, then, that "entire sanctification" cannot mean "entirely free from the possibility of sin," at least if we take Jesus's experience and the reality of his temptations seriously.

Now, if the possibility of sin stays around as long as we do, does that not imply that actual sins are probably going to happen eventually? Can we reasonably expect that broken human beings who are deeply conditioned to focus on themselves can ever get to the point that they just don't focus on themselves any longer and so never sin? Would it not be better if we just started being honest and talk about being "mostly" sanctified instead of "entirely" sanctified, since we all know that we are all going to mess up anyway?

No, actually, I don't think it would. Not if we really understand what sanctification means.

We usually think about sanctification as the avoidance of sin, but the idea actually has different orientation. The word "sanctification," in both English and in the original language of the New Testament, means "the process of being sanctified." "To sanctify" something is to make something "holy," that is, to make it more like God or to use it to point toward God or to set it apart for God's use (all of which are important). And God—at least if the Scripture is to be believed—is not a big fan of divided loyalties. When something or someone is set apart for God's use, it is not to be used for anything else. As we have often said in our tradition, when it comes to a person's life, God will be God "of all" or God won't be God "at all." There does not appear to be any middle ground.

In this light, the idea of being "mostly sanctified" sounds a lot like the idea of being "mostly faithful" to one's spouse, and that doesn't make any sense. To be faithful at all is to be faithful entirely; anything less doesn't count. Of course, failures in fidelity can be forgiven and overcome, but one cannot justify them by saying, "But I was faithful all the rest of the time; doesn't that count?" No, frankly, it doesn't. No one is going to marry someone who simply commits to loving them 99.99% of the time; even one breach in fidelity every 28 years is one breach too many.

If sanctification is much more about our relationship to God than it is about our relationship to sin, we cannot talk about sanctification at all unless we are willing to talk about "entire sanctification." In fact, it strikes me that we cannot really even call ourselves "Christian" unless we intend by that label a life completely oriented toward God. The idea of a "part-time Christian" makes as much sense as a "part-time pregnancy." If God expects and empowers undivided loyalty, then the orientation toward some kind of "entire sanctification" is entailed by our acceptance of Christ's offer of salvation-and-radical-transformation (which is really just one idea in Scripture).

Now, this does not mean our sinning has nothing to do with it. Of course it does. As we allow God to make us more and more like God and to make us more useful for God's redemptive project in the world, this will entail an avoidance of sin. We cannot claim Jesus as our Lord and tell him, "No." Willful and knowing violations of our relationships to God and others—marked out by those boundary lines we know as God's laws—have no place among Jesus's followers.

And yet such violations occur anyway; we all know that. They shouldn't, though, and that's the point. Keeping the idea of "entire sanctification" before us helps us to keep that in mind. If we thought sin was inevitable, we would, indeed, just give in to it. However, we believe that God empowers our complete devotion. We affirm that, at every given moment, God always provides enough grace and strength to avoid the temptation to prioritize our "selves" over God and God's will. That's what it means to believe in "entire sanctification."

Fortunately, we know that if we mess up our relationship with God, God wants to fix it even more than we do. "If we confess our sins, he is faithful and just and will forgive us our sins and purify us from all unrighteousness" (1 John 1:9, NIV). So the fact that we don't always live up to our entire sanctification does not sink our ship, thanks be to God! But we should never get comfortable with the fact of those failures; if they happen—and since they are unnecessary, they don't have to happen—if they happen, they are always tragedies and should be dealt with as such.

So, then, perhaps sanctification is best thought of as that which orients us away from sin and toward God, allowing us to become more like God so that we can be a more effective part of God's work in the world. And if that orientation is an all-or-nothing proposition, then we must think of it as an "entire sanctification" if it is going to be any sanctification at all. This is the life that God empowers, and so it is entirely appropriate for us to pray for the grace to live it out for this next minute, this next hour, this next day, and then hopefully the one after that and the one after that as well, and so on for as long as God lends us breath.

Tim is a professor of theology and church history at Southern Nazarene University. A fourth-generation Nazarene himself, Tim has spends his time equally thinking and publishing about the history of his tradition (mainly about John Wesley) and ways to help chart a course for that tradition's future.

Crisis, Process, and Diversity in Holiness

Adam Jantz

Understanding holiness seems to elude much of the church today. One would expect that growing up in a "holiness church" would help one understand holiness, but the opposite is often true. Diversity of generations, perspectives, and vocabulary can create a muddled picture of holiness.

Holiness has many names in the Christian church: sanctification, pure love, second blessing, Christian perfection, etc. Yet, the essence is the same: giving ourselves fully to God. Holiness is when God has permeated our thoughts, our ideas, and our lives to the point that we live for God, only God. We have become slaves to Christ in every aspect of our lives. We are constantly working to live for Christ, without sinning willfully. God's grace is continually purging us of our pull to sin. God has inhabited our lives fully.

For many, the traditional, accepted view of holiness is a defining moment, a crisis experience, with a date, time, and place. It is an instantaneous change, after which we are never the same.

For others, especially among younger generations, the emphasis is more on a slow moving learning of who we are and where God is taking us. It is not so much a recognizable moment, but an understanding that can take years. Over time, we begin to see that we are intentionally giving our entire lives to God and trying to do God's will in every aspect of our lives through the help of the Holy Spirit. But it is not instantaneous. There is no *Aha!* moment. We cannot put a date on when this happened. It is a slow journey that may take years.

The traditional view of holiness through crisis experience became popular through the Holiness Movement in the USA in the late 19th century. Over time, a defined crisis experience became a requirement for holiness people. One might even say that this emphasis on crises took the shape of a folk religion for many traditional holiness people. Without a crisis moment, they could not believe that a person had experienced or even understood holiness. The crisis moment became a legalistic standard.

However, slowly we are learning that holiness is not a legalistic matter. Holiness cannot be defined with definite parameters. Claiming a specific moment of sanctification is not a legitimate sign of holiness, and not knowing a particular crisis experience does not indicate a lack of holiness.

In fact, our tradition's emphasis on the instant attainment of holiness has created clashes among generations and instigated anger from younger Christians who do not experience God's sanctifying work in the same ways as their grandparents. Younger Nazarenes tend to see the traditional view as narrow-minded and discriminatory. Many feel a great sense of frustration that older leaders are unwilling to accept their different experiences of God's grace and inward action. More than a few young Nazarenes have left the denomination and even the Church because of this conflict.

On the other hand, our understanding of holiness cannot become so loose that it has no substance. We must also have a rich relational and theological understanding of who God is and what God truly wants from us. We must be rooted in the Biblical story of the Trinitarian God of holy love who calls us to live in holy love:

- "But anyone who does not love does not know God, for God is love" (1 John 4:8).
- "You must be holy because I, the Lord, am holy. I have set you apart from all other people to be my very own" (Leviticus 20:26).
- "So think clearly and exercise self-control. Look forward to the gracious salvation that will come to you when Jesus Christ is revealed to the world. So you must live as God's obedient children. Don't slip back into your old ways of living to satisfy your own desires. You didn't know any better then. But now you must be holy in everything you do, just as God who chose you is holy. For the Scriptures say, 'You must be holy because I am holy'" (1 Peter 1:13-16).

In my work at Korea Nazarene University, I am blessed to teach a class on folk religions to students from all over Asia. As we discuss our varying backgrounds, it has become abundantly clear that for each of us our idea of holiness is very culturally biased. Our home cultures color our perspective both on the definition of holiness and on the methods of attaining it. Identifying and moving past those biases is extremely difficult. Many who have soaked in the Scriptures for decades remain blindly entrapped by their own cultural lenses.

And yet, however arduous, seeing beyond our biases is crucial for hermeneutics. We approach the Bible with filters based on our generation, culture, socio-economic status, and family backgrounds. If we ever hope to understand—much less to apply—the Scriptures effectively, then we must fully understand ourselves and the contours of the lenses that color how we see the Bible and the world. Once we acknowledge our own lenses, we take a step closer to seeing the text for what it truly is.

Holiness is actually not about us. It's not about what we did or what we will do. Holiness is about God, God's love, and the loving presence of God in our lives today. How we understand the transition into loving holiness depends both on our cultural backgrounds and upon our personal experiences.

For some, it takes a crisis to experience the depths of God's grace. It literally takes God knocking us to our knees before we see what he has to offer us. We may try to follow God for years, only to come face to face with our own failure time and time again. Finally, God "whacks us over the head" spiritually and overwhelms us with grace. It is an instantaneous transformation.

For others, it is a process of time and understanding. We take time to understand who God is, who we are, and what God means to us. We take three steps forward and two steps backward, but all the while we are steadily climbing. For many of us, if we were forced to identify a single predominate moment of sanctifying grace, we simply couldn't decide where to put the pin in the map. The progress of the journey stands out far beyond the individual directional changes.

We are all different, the kaleidoscope of God's design. We are introverts, extraverts, Type A, and Type B. Our differences do not make one personality right and another wrong. In the same way, we must be careful to avoid judgmentalism over our different pathways into holiness. To create a narrow criteria of what "counts" as a holiness experience runs the risk of pushing many out of the church and denying the work of grace in their lives.

In the end, God defines holiness, not us. One plants, another waters, but God makes us grow. Let us be careful to look for the one fruit of holiness that God values most: love.

Adam Jantz serves as a professor at Korea Nazarene University and as an associate pastor at KNU International English Church of the Nazarene in Cheonan, South Korea. He is currently working on his second book in the Annyeong English *series for university students. He is married to the amazing Hwang YunKyung.*

Holiness as a Process: Means of Grace

Mark A. Maddix

While attending the Church of the Nazarene's Global Theology Conference in Guatemala City, Guatemala, I was invited to lead a small group at the conference. The members of my group included Nazarene leaders such as a General Superintendent, college professors, pastors, and missionaries. One of the themes of the discussion was holiness and sanctification. As we talked around the circle, it became evident that most of the members of that small group had struggled with the doctrine of entire sanctification.

One professor said, "I teach about entire sanctification as a second work of grace, but I have never experienced it myself." Another long time professor and administrator, who grew up in the church said, "Through-out my life I have head the message of entire sanctification as an instantaneous act, and I went to the altar and sought the experience, but I have never had the experience what was taught and preached throughout my life."

As the discussion continued, it became evident that these Nazarene leaders from all around the world were expressing the same thing. They had simply not experienced the doctrine of sanctification as an instantaneous work of grace.

This quiet conversation at the Global Theology Conference is representative of what many faithful Christians have experienced. The doctrine of entire sanctification that grew out of revivalism and camp-meetings seems to have faded over time, and it is being replaced with new language and expressions of how Christians can become holy and sanctified. This is most evident with younger Christians who have grown up without any memory of these revivalist and camp-meeting experiences.

Does this mean that the doctrine of entire sanctification and the life of holiness are not relevant today? Does this mean that God is not working to transform persons into Christlikeness? Does it mean that holiness is no longer relevant for this generation of Christians? Many young adults have asked these questions as they learn about the doctrine of holiness and entire sanctification. They confess that the words "holiness" and "sanctification" need to be translated in order to be understood and experienced in their contemporary context.

I believe that living a holy life is still possible and that God is still transforming Christians to live a holy life. I believe the content of the message is the same while the process into holiness is very different today. I believe that Christians are being sanctified and are becoming holy through their participation in the "means of grace" as they seek to live a life of holiness.

Whereas previous generations focused on an "experience" or "event" as a means of sanctification, today many young adults seek the sanctified life through the practices of their faith. The spiritual growth and development of young adults takes place through their participation in a variety of Christian practices—what John Wesley called "the means of grace."

The "means of grace" are channels through which God conveys grace to his people. In Wesley's sermon "The Means of Grace," he explains, "By means of grace I understand outward signs, words, or actions, ordained of God, and appointed for this end—to be the *ordinary* channels whereby he conveys to men, preventing, justifying or sanctifying grace."[247] These means in themselves do not save or sanctify, but they are channels by which the Holy Spirit works in extraordinary ways for Christians to respond to God's grace.

Wesley divided the "means of grace" into three divisions: instituted means of grace, the prudential means of grace, and the general means of grace. The **instituted** means of grace are practices given directly by Jesus Christ. They are: prayer, searching the Scriptures, participating in the Lord's Supper (Eucharist), fasting, and Christian conferencing (spiritual conversation). The **prudential** means of grace are practices that are wise and beneficial to do. They include obeying Christ, small groups, special prayer meetings, visiting the sick, doing all the good we can to all the people we can, and reading from the devotional classics of the rich tradition of two thousand years of Christianity. The prudential means of grace were designed to meet the person at his or her point of need; thus, they are adaptable to a person's particular historical situation or context. The **general** means of grace include: watching, denying ourselves, taking up our cross daily, and exercising the presence of God.[248]

Wesley didn't confine God's grace to just these practices. Because he understood grace to be God's loving, uncreated presence, he believed many other activities could be means of grace. Thus, grace is still active even among those who have no access to specific means like Christian baptism, the Eucharist, or the study of Scripture.

247. John Wesley, *The Works of John Wesley*, Richard P. Heitzenrater and Frank Baker, eds. (Nashville: Abingdon Press, 1975-2003), 1:381.

248. For a further discussion on the means of grace as it relates to catechesis and discipleship see Dean Blevins and Mark A. Maddix, *Discovering Discipleship: Dynamics of Christian Education* (Kansas City: Beacon Hill Press, 2010).

However, Wesley believed that through participation in the instituted means of grace a person can be made aware of God's pardoning and empowering presence of Christ on a regular basis. Wesley's therapeutic focus is evident in his invitation for his people to meditate regularly on the affirmation that Christ "sealed His love with sacraments of grace, to breed and nourish up in us the life of love."[249] Thus, all who need further empowering by God's grace should faithfully participate in the instituted means of grace.

The means of grace can be closely associated with spiritual disciplines or practices that are central to the process of spiritual formation. It is not the practices themselves that change us, but the Holy Spirit uses these practices to transform us. Participating in spiritual practices is the way we cooperate with God. The participation in the means of God's grace shapes and forms us in the image and likeness of Christ.

A new generation of Christians is appropriating Wesley's "means of grace" through a return to more historical Christian practices.[250] Some have a fresh new appreciation for Scripture by reading Scripture for formation instead of information.

An example of this is the practice of *lectio divina* (sacred reading).[251] This practice is a series of prayer dynamics that has roots in the religious orders of St. Benedict of Nursia in the sixth century. This process moves the reader of Scripture to a deep level of engagement with the text as the Spirit enlivens the text to the reader.[252]

Others are engaging in contemplative practices such as solitude and silence. These simple practices are helping Christians grow in grace and become holy.

Many congregations are practicing the Eucharist on a weekly basis. Participation in communion is a means to encounter Christ and to receiving God's healing and renewal.[253] Christians are becoming holy as they gather around Word and Table on a weekly basis.

---

249. Randy L. Maddox, *Responsible Grace: John Wesley's Practical Theology* (Nashville: Abingdon Press, 1998), 200.

250. See Diane Leclerc and Mark A. Maddix, eds. *Essential Church: A Wesleyan Paradigm* (Kansas City: Beacon Hill Press, 2014). Mark A. Maddix and Diane Leclerc, eds. *Pastoral Practices: A Wesleyan Paradigm* (Kansas City: Beacon Hill Press, 2013).

251. See Joel B. Green, *Seized by Truth: Reading the Bible as Scripture* (Nashville: Abingdon, 2007); Mark A. Maddix and Richard Thompson, "The Role of Scripture in Christian Formation," *Wesley Theological Journal* 46, no. 1 (Spring 2011): 134-149.

252. See Tony Jones, *The Sacred Way: Spiritual Practices for Everyday Life.* (Grand Rapids: Zondervan, 2005); Diane Leclerc and Mark Maddix, eds. *Spiritual Formation: A Wesleyan Paradigm* (Kansas City: Beacon Hill Press, 2010); Diane Leclerc, *Discovering Christian Holiness: The Heart of Wesleyan-Holiness Theology* (Kansas City: Beacon Hill Press, 2010).

253. See Brent Peterson, *Created to Worship: God's Invitation to Become Fully Human* (Kansas City: Beacon Hill Press, 2012); Rob Staples, *Outward Sign, Inward Grace* (Kansas City: Beacon Hill Press of Kansas City, 1991), William Willimon, *The Service of God: Christian Work and Worship* (Nashville. T.N.: Abingdon Press, 1983); James F. White, *Introduction to Christian Worship*, 3rd ed. (Nashville: Abingdon, 2000); Susan J. White, *Foundations of Christian Worship* (Louisville: Westminster John Knox, 2006).

Others are engaged in acts of mercy. These acts of mercy include social justice, serving the poor, and advocating for the outcasts of society. They are concerned about the planet and are active in preserving and renewing creation. They view the redemption of persons and creation as central to a life of holiness.[254] The associated social and practical disciplines are helping younger adults experience God and enter the process of becoming holy.

The practices and experiences of young Christians may look different from the previous generation of revivalism and camp-meetings, but God is still calling and forming a new generation of Nazarenes into holy persons who are engaged in living out God's mission in the world. These expressions of God's working may cause some to think that we are losing our doctrine of holiness and sanctification, but a closer look will show that young adults are as deeply called and committed to holy living as previous generations.

Likewise, perhaps the key denominational leaders from my small group who shared their struggles with the doctrine of sanctification had, in fact, experienced sanctification and are actually living a holy life. Maybe their experiences of God's grace in their lives are genuine but different from the testimonies of yesteryear who emphasized the dramatic and sudden alter experience. Around the globe, many of our young people today are living the holy life in deeply significant ways as they allow God's holy means of grace to transform their daily lives.

Mark A. Maddix is Professor Practical Theology and Dean of the School of Theology & Christian Ministries at Northwest Nazarene University. He has written and edited six books in the areas of Christian discipleship, spiritual formation, ecclesiology, and online education. Most recently, he edited Essential Church: A Wesleyan Paradigm *(2014).*

---

254. See Mark A. Maddix and Jay R. Akkerman, eds. *Missional Discipleship: Partners in God's Redemptive Mission* (Kanas City: Beacon Hill Press, 2013).

Sin in the Sanctified:

Holy Living in Broken Creation

John M. Bechtold

Creation is the beginning and end of Christian theology. It is no accident that, as the Bible as we know it has been developed, the Scripture as a whole begins with the story of divine creation and ends with a vision of new creation. Creation and eschatology bookend the entirety of the relationship between God and humanity. Creation is not just a bookend, however, but truly essential to any theology that should be called 'Christian'. The story of God begins with an understanding of God as Creator. The universe, including this world and all of its inhabitants, is Creation.

It is exceedingly rare for a doctrine of holiness to begin with the notion of God as Creator. Rather, it is usually the case that God's transcendence receives more focus than God's relatability. A focus on God's transcendence often goes hand in hand with a focus on the subjective individual.

One common way of speaking of the Wesleyan doctrine of entire sanctification has been to use the phrase "sinless perfection." The idea behind this term is that the sanctified individual, through the sanctifying God, transcends sin in word and action. While John Wesley himself did not originate this phrase, his understanding of sin certainly made it possible.

Wesley argued that there should be a distinction made between sin "properly so called" and sin "improperly so called," which is to say between that which is actually sinful and that which is not. Wesley believed that properly-so-called sin could be described as an intentional transgression of a known law of God. He wanted to distinguish this sin from accidents or mistakes stemming from human weakness. In making this distinction, Wesley made sin purely volitional, and therefore individual. When sin becomes only the intentional wrongdoing of the individual, it would certainly be possible to speak of the sanctified as sinless. Yet, to speak of sanctified individuals as living without sin leaves the possibility that they could, unintentionally or accidentally, cause immense damage to the created order around them.

At face value it is obvious that even those believers who claim the term "sanctified" for themselves repeatedly act in ways that are damaging to their relationships and to the world at large. There is a term that is currently being debated in scientific and various intellectual circles, *Anthropocene*, to describe the world on the brink, if not over the brink, of self-inflicted destruction. Regardless of one's opinions about the scientific validity of this term, in an increasingly globalized world it is no longer possible to take refuge behind volition to pretend that actions do not have far-reaching consequences in ways that are unplanned, unexpected, and generally unknown.

While these consequences are certainly not unique to the sanctified, neither is the church exempt from them. Something as simple as eating breakfast has become a complex and multifaceted ethical dilemma. Choosing coffee means deciding whether to purchase organic/non-organic, shade grown/sun grown, and whether to pay a premium for fair trade coffee. Even a consumer that does a lot of research into the economics and ethics of coffee production and distribution may be unaware the extent to which a particular fair trade certification does or does not benefit the lowest level employee in the production chain. Even the purchase of a single cup of coffee is multiplied exponentially by a corporate-industrial complex that expands indefinitely by creating and consuming customer demand. Nor is coffee alone as the breakfast time ethical dilemma.

Something as simple and healthy as a banana also must be considered. How far and upon what means of transportation has this banana travelled to reach my plate? What level of carbon and pollutants has been emitted in bringing this fruit? Do the producers of this fruit pay protection bribes to criminal gangs that participate in violence, drug distribution, and human slavery? What level of chemical pesticides are applied to this fruit while in the field, and does this have actual or potential links to health problems for workers in the field? These are but a few of the questions that could be, but rarely are, asked by banana consumers.

And, of course, ethical purchasing power goes beyond coffee and fruit to meat consumption, clothing, jewelry, electronics, transportation, energy consumption, etc. The list goes on and on. The point here is not to argue that the sanctified individual must research extensively and always make ethically justifiable purchases, although this is certainly a goal to strive for. Rather, the reality of the situation is that no consumer has access to the entire production chain for every product or service that they use.

The more that is learned about international trade and globalized consumer chains, the more clear it becomes that it is nearly impossible to make a purchase that is entirely ethical. That is, nearly every decision that is made results in non-livable wages, ecological destruction, negative health impacts, or the furtherance of an economic system that places a higher value on profit than on human flourishing.

Indeed, each of these effects, to varying degrees of efficacy, serves to counteract the very creation that is so central to the Christian faith. Human consumption, particularly but not exclusively in the developed world, violates the spirit of the Christian faith to bring about life abundantly. If even a single person is hurt through a particular act of commerce, the essence of creation itself has been violated. Inevitably this is the case, and unfortunately this is usually invisible to the consumer.

Returning, then, to Wesley's understanding of sin, it is now more than ever the case that sin is not merely volitional. As in the American judicial system, ignorance is no excuse for wrong action. In a globalized world, Christian holiness, or entire sanctification, ought not to be described as "sinless perfection." If this were the definitive description of a doctrine of holiness, then no one whatsoever would ever be entirely sanctified.

As individuals, as the church, as socio-political nation-states, in all these ways and more, sinfulness—the breaking down of God's creation—is practiced consistently. Sin is not merely the result of a single action, but a vast and inescapable web that has ensnared the very structures of God's good creation. Entire sanctification cannot remove a believer from the possibility or reality of this sin because the believer continues to live within the brokenness of the world. To proclaim entire sanctification as equivalent to "sinless perfection" is ethically irresponsible.

Sin, from the beginning, has always been as much a social phenomenon as it has an individual action. The fruit from the Tree of the Knowledge of Good and Evil was not eaten in solitude. The stories of Genesis and beyond also make it clear that the consequences of this socially enacted sinfulness go far beyond a punishment of the individuals involved. Christian Scripture makes clear that sin is never solitary. This is precisely the problem with the language of "sinless perfection."

To speak of "sinless perfection" overlooks the truly insidious nature of sin. Within the Arminian-Wesleyan tradition great value is placed on the importance of living well. John Wesley himself strongly emphasized the importance of doing justice, loving kindness, and walking humbly before God. Wesley was wrong to make the concept of sin dependent on volition, yet even he recognized that the sanctified would continually act in ways that would require atonement. Wesley believed that these actions, what he called "sin improperly so-called" were the result of ignorance and human frailty. Indeed, he also explicitly rejected the language of "sinless perfection" despite the fact that he did believe it possible for the sanctified to forever after live without intentionally transgressing divine laws. Even so, it is important to reject Wesley's definition of sin because it fails to account for the transgressive and structural nature of sin in the world.

Rather than following Wesley here, a more apt description of sin in a globalized world would be something along the lines of this: "Sin is any action or inaction which counteracts the well-being of creation and the flourishing of humanity." Creation is, after all, the cornerstone to Christian theology. Sanctified believers, just as all humans, consistently counteract the well-being of creation.

Entire sanctification, then, is not the utter removal of sin nor the removal of the sanctified from sin. Rather, sanctification is better understood as a purification of love, of being made one with the mind of Christ. To live a holy life is not to live outside of sin, but to recognize fully one's own continuing sinfulness. Living a holy life is to live a life in which creation is celebrated, in which constant repentance leads to ethical growth, and in which love reigns supreme. Sanctification is not life without sin, but the overcoming of sin with life.

John is a PhD candidate in the University of Denver/Iliff School of Theology Joint Doctoral Program with an emphasis in theology, philosophy, and cultural theory. John's academic work involves exploring the interplay between German idealist philosophy and contemporary Christian theology. John serves as youth pastor at Gracia y Vida Iglesia del Nazareno in Denver, CO.

Second Blessing?

Brent Dirks

The Church of the Nazarene has traditionally explained entire sanctification as "a second definite work of grace." As with other aspects of entire sanctification, people have taken various positions on this issue. I have wondered at times, myself, what this aspect of entire sanctification means. In this essay, I invite the reader to take a journey with me to rediscover and to retain this element of the doctrine of entire sanctification.

Although I grew up in the Church of the Nazarene, I attended a Bible college in a moderate Calvinistic tradition. I remember hearing a former Methodist say in passing, 'When I was a Methodist I heard them talk about a second blessing. I don't know why they stop at a second blessing. I'm on my 50th blessing." That was the clearest way I had heard people talk about this definite work of grace related to entire sanctification. The irony was that it was someone outside of the tradition.

Of course, I heard about entire sanctification before that. My clearest memory of the subject from within the holiness tradition was when I was in high school and an evangelist spoke of the second blessing. Had it just been me, I would have simply overlooked this as technical preacher's jargon for living a meaningful life. But my youth leader, coming from a different tradition, called this into serious question with the senior pastor. Of course, the senior pastor wasn't fazed by the question, but his well-informed response wasn't satisfactory to my youth leader.

These experiences, combined with my own faith struggles, caused me to call into serious question whether a definite second work of grace was indeed true. I had also heard of other Wesleyans that put more emphasis on the process than on the crisis.

Looking back on a long journey, the person who cleared this up for me was not my senior pastor affirming the doctrine of the Church of the Nazarene, my youth leader calling this into serious question, or that former Methodist preacher. It was the well-known Nazarene theologian, Mildred Bangs Wynkoop, who explained the doctrine of entire sanctification in *A Theology of Love*.[255]

By the time I got a hold of Wynkoop's book, I was thoroughly confused about theology in general. I had completed a three-year intensive Bible program at the

---

255. Mildred Bangs Wynkoop, *A Theology of Love*, (Kansas City: Beacon Hill, 1972).

Reformed Bible college. Although I never affirmed what the school believed on paper, I knew I had been influenced by the notion that we can only experience imputed righteous not imparted righteousness.

The first light that came on regarding a clearer understanding of this second work of grace was when I read in Wynkoop that the secondness is metaphorical. Its meaning is of a deeper work. By stating it in this way, she cut to the chase of the second work of grace.

Although this helped some, I still had many questions about the claim that entire sanctification is a second work of grace. Even if it were indicative of God doing a greater, yet distinct work in a person's heart, I still questioned whether this view is really taught in Scripture. This struggle followed me not just through my university experience, but even beyond my seminary experience, just prior to my ordination interview.

In preparation for ordination, I began reading the Bible from the very beginning. I had read the Bible through before, but I had taken so many classes that interpreted the Bible for me that I wanted to see for myself from a fresh perspective what the Bible "really" says. I began to see that the Bible has numerous references of God calling people into deeper relationship. This is explicit in the story of Abraham, the pinnacle being Abraham's offering his son Isaac as a sacrifice.

But this was not the first time God pursued Abraham. It was also not the second time in the literal sense. By the time the reader of the Biblical text gets to this account, God has appeared to Abraham multiple times. God has called Abraham to go to a foreign land (Genesis 12), and God has established God's covenant with Isaac (Genesis 17).

But Genesis 22 shows us that Abraham's commitment had not yet reached the depths of his heart. God told Abraham to sacrifice his son, Isaac. Although contemporary readers wonder how Abraham could have gone so promptly without reservation, the text doesn't tell us about Abraham's doubts but only that he walked in obedience. Even when it came to Abraham raising the knife to slay his son, we aren't told what was going through Abraham's mind though we can certainly imagine. But an angel of the Lord came to Abraham and prevented him from killing his only son. And the words of the angel, or more specifically, of God, were, "for now I know that you fear God, since you have not withheld your son, your only son, from me" (Genesis 22:12, NRSV).

Reading this passage made me think about entire sanctification as a second work of grace in a whole new light. Although this was not the last thing that happened between God and Abraham, it seems to have been the most significant.

Abraham continued to grow in his relationship with God, but this experience was the pinnacle. But if one got hung up on the sequence of events in Abraham's life, one would miss the significance of this moment. Likewise, it would also be a misunderstanding if one took this story to mean that Abraham had "arrived" in the sense that he no longer needed to engage in spiritual disciplines.

But that is the tone that some people have taken to this notion of entire sanctification that has become almost a form of "eternal security" which has turned others off. Some have seemingly bragged about the "fact" that they haven't sinned since their experience of entire sanctification some ten, twenty, thirty years ago. And yet, the "mistakes" they committed were beyond unintentional behavior in any sense of the word.

Because of the abuses of the language of the second work of grace in the experience of entire sanctification, questions of the significance or reality of a second work of grace have arisen to the point that some, even in holiness groups, have dismissed or undermined the meaning or the possibility that one could experience complete heart-transformation at any moment in this life.

The former Methodist pastor who celebrated his "50th work of grace" had a good point. It would be a tragedy if someone were to experience entire sanctification in that sacred moment and think that there were no need for further growth.

And that is where simply teaching entire sanctification as a second work of grace could set up those who have experienced such grace for failure. Teaching "secondness" in isolation from progress, as it seems we've been doing, naturally leads to confusion about secondness itself as well as the other aspects of entire sanctification. This confusion, if left unresolved, could very well lead us to abandoning the whole doctrine.

The Bible, human experience, and theological literature lead me to one simple yet clear conclusion. The depth of the experience matters far more than the numbering of the experience. The bottom line is not whether someone has had their "second" experience, but how deeply they have been transformed. Jesus echoes the Old Testament's summation of the law: to love God, to love others, and to love ourselves. The question of entire sanctification is not whether or not one has experienced an emotional "high" in a moment of prayer. The evidence of entire sanctification is simply walking on the path of loving God and others.

I am convinced of this second work of grace, and I believe God's Spirit has testified with my spirit that it is true. For me it came at an altar call in a church of the same tradition as John Wesley. I had been attending for several months, but I couldn't participate in communion with a clear conscience. I had explored the depths of the questions in my head, and I finally came to a point of decision.

I made the step of faith that Jesus was in fact my Savior and that I trusted him to cleanse my sins, all of them. Upon receiving that holy bread and wine, it became the spiritual presence of Christ in me, and I had an overwhelming since that God really loved me. And that experience has stayed with me, with many subsequent prayers of consecration and God's response of filling me anew with God's Spirit.

Yes, we believe entire sanctification is a second work of grace. However, don't get hung up on the number and miss out on that "G" word, grace. That's what it is—all grace.

Brent has been teaching English Conversation in South Korea for over six years, fat Korea Nazarene University and at Myongji University Science Campus. He was ordained in the Church of the Nazarene in June 2014. He is eclectic in his interests in philosophy, theology, and issues that concern the marginalized. In his free time, he likes to travel and meet local people.

Sanctifying Vision:

Towards a Wesleyan Integration of Imputed Righteousness

Chad A. Maxson

Martin Luther spoke of how, when God looks at redeemed humanity, God looks at them through the lens of Christ. This meant that instead of seeing redeemed humanity in its sinful state, God instead sees them through Christ's righteousness. A thoughtful person might be concerned at this notion that instead of seeing humanity as it really was, a humanity in the clutches of sin, God is misled to see humanity as righteous. It is almost as if God is being fooled!

God cannot be fooled, and a Wesleyan might reframe Luther's insight to acknowledge that, when God sees us through Christ, God sees us as we *really* are. That is to say, sin is not truth. It is not human identity, and it does not reflect the purpose of God in creation. In contrast, Christ is God's purpose for human beings, and he has always been that purpose. Humanity was created in the image of God, which is Christ (Col. 1:15). Jesus is human identity—what human persons are to be. Unlike sin, Jesus is truth (John 14:6).

Luther's insight for us is that God sees the truth of us in Christ, as we really are, rather than the lie that is sin. This is not being misled. This is seeing truly rather than through the warped lens of sin.

This represents a challenge and a hope for Wesleyan doctrines of sanctification, which all too often focus on sin rather than on Christ. Many Wesleyans think that the doctrine of sanctification is a doctrine about sin. It is not and should not be. Having confused the American Holiness Movement's emphasis on instantaneous sanctification with John Wesley's, many Nazarenes have widened the "credibility gap" identified a generation ago by Mildred Bangs Wynkoop. This gap is a result of the expectation that humans will be saved in an instant from all sin. Luther's wisdom helps to re-establish credibility because it focuses attention on Christ (where it belongs), and, therefore, it provides a hopeful model for a Wesleyan doctrine of sanctification.

God's Vision Is Reality

It may sometimes appear to Wesleyan Christians as if the reality of human life is that we human beings are incurable sinners. While John Wesley insisted that the core of holiness was being perfected in the love of God, most of the preaching that came out of the holiness movement in the twentieth-century focused instead on freedom from sin. While freedom from sin is important, making that the main point of sanctification is a serious error. When we do so, we shift our gaze from God to the human person. In sermon after sermon, Wesley insisted that nothing good comes out of such a shift of attention to the human. Real, genuine, Wesleyan Christianity keeps the gaze solely on God.

God's vision challenges ours. When God looks at us and sees Christ's righteousness, that vision *is* reality. It is not an illusion. It is not a mask or filter. It is reality because it is what God sees. Is there a better descriptor of what is real?

Luther's doctrine of imputed righteousness might be more meaningful to us if we really believed that God is Creator. Many Christians struggle with that belief. We can see evidence of our struggle here in our deep insistence in attacking alternative creation accounts like evolution. This belies an insecurity within many Christians. It is like children fighting over who has the biggest toy. It means a lot to children, but as we become more secure as adults, such debates lose their significance. If we Christians were truly secure in our belief that God is Creator, we would be much less bothered by evolution and other scientific theories. We would simply affirm that God is the only Creator, no matter the mechanisms.

Similarly, we may have difficulties with Luther's doctrine because we may not really have faith that God is Creator. God is the Creator who brought forth creation out of nothing. When the Creator sees us through Christ's righteousness, then we are, in fact, recreated into Christ's righteousness. Human beings were created to be in Christ, the image of God. Therefore, when we are recreated in Christ's righteousness, the image of God is restored. God's purpose in creation is fulfilled. Salvation and creation have always been closely linked.

God's Vision Is Christocentric

It is important that God's vision is Christocentric rather than anthropocentric. Human righteousness is not the construct of a heroic effort on the part of individual human beings. It is not brought about because human beings have finally consecrated themselves sufficiently to God and have the necessary faith that God can sanctify them in an instant. Such a process makes sanctification all about the human will, choice, and decision.

Christianity teaches that something about Jesus' death and resurrection makes salvation and sanctification possible. In practice, many sermons, teachings, and study groups put a lot more emphasis on what we human beings do rather than on what Jesus does. God is formally necessary, but for all practical purposes, sanctification in this model become entirely dependent on human will. This causes our spirituality to become increasingly secular, as the significance of the Redeemer is reduced to practically nothing.

Luther's wisdom saves us from that error by insisting that if we are to be sanctified, Jesus will do it. It will not be by human works. When our sanctification is entirely accomplished by God through Christ, this reflects the gospel message. It keeps the human gaze focused exactly where the divine gaze is focused—on Christ. God sees humanity through Christ, the one who gave himself for us out of obedience to the Father.

God's Reality Is Sanctifying

Part of what makes God's vision and God's reality sanctifying is that relationships are central to God's purpose in creation. God created for relation, and God saves and sanctifies through relation. When God sees humanity through Christ, God sees us the way we were created to be. This is the restoration of the divine-human relationship, which is the restoration of the image of God.

In his book, *Reflecting the Divine Image*, Ray Dunning identified four constitutive relationships of the human being: God, self, human others, and creation. With the restoration of that primary relationship to God, the other constitutive relationships are also prepared for restoration.[256]

The human relation to God is restored when God sees us as we truly are, in Christ. Likewise, as human persons come to see themselves as they truly are, in Christ, the relationship to self is restored. That person's identity is no longer defined in terms of sin, but rather in terms of Jesus who emptied himself in obedience to the Father. This is a challenging image of ourselves, and it is sanctifying.

It is equally challenging to begin to see other people as they truly are, in Christ. We see broken, dysfunctional, obnoxious, beautiful, successful people all the time. We craft images of ourselves and others. We live our lives through these images, but they are not Christ. When we see others through Christ, the relationship to the human other is restored.

The same is true for the cosmos. It is not there for our consumption or our economic prosperity. It is also created for Christ and for the glory of God (Col. 1:17).

Conclusion

The promise of the Wesleyan doctrine of sanctification is that the human person can be entirely sanctified in this life. That is to say, the love of God can be perfectly manifest in the human being. It is the perfection in divine love

---

256. H. Ray Dunning, *Reflecting the Divine Image*, (Eugene, OR: Wipf & Stock, 2003), 45.

resulting in restored relationships that frees humanity from sin, not the reverse. Martin Luther's doctrine of imputed righteousness has been rejected in popular teaching by Wesleyans who prefer a stronger doctrine of imparted righteousness. We Wesleyans have been slow to recognize that it is precisely Christ's imputed righteousness that is the hope for imparted righteousness.

Perhaps the greatest gift of Luther's insight is that it may finally makes other people necessary for salvation. As Wesleyan doctrines of salvation and sanctification currently stand, there is almost no reason for the Church. There is no need for other human beings. The emphasis is usually on the personal relationship between oneself and God. This does not reflect the New Testament's role of other people or the Body of Christ. Luther's insight can help us Wesleyans recognize the absolute necessity of those New Testament roles once more. This may rejuvenate our own spirituality and our church experience. This is our sanctification.

Chad is currently the Associate Dean of Academic Integration for Olivet Nazarene University's School of Graduate and Continuing Studies. His academic work focuses on the intersection of culture and theology. This has led to concerns about how Nazarene spirituality reflects some of the very secularizing tendencies of modern culture that it often seeks to resist.

Be Human, For Christ Is Human

Dick O. Eugenio

Holiness involves transformation. But such a transformation does not entail an ontological metamorphosis that makes gods out of humans.

Although Wesley was indebted to Eastern Orthodoxy, including his understanding of holiness, he did not interpret *theosis* (becoming like God) in the way Western theologians translated it as literal deification.[257] The holy life does not entail an escape from our creatureliness or humanness into becoming celestial beings or children of Krypton. As Randy Maddox succinctly summarized, "Wesley's affirmation of entire sanctification is not a claim that humans can embody the faultless perfection of God in this life."[258] The absurdity of Christians becoming gods may be easily discernible, but I suspect that—in reality, consciously or unconsciously, because of high moral demands and expectations—in the minds of holiness people, the image of the holy life is the deified life, whether we care to admit it or not.

This is evident in how holiness people relate with human weaknesses, particularly in those who are serving as leaders, ministers, and workers in the church and seminaries. Because of the demand for a holy testimony, the temptation for Christian workers is to hide or even deny our weaknesses. People perceive that it is unbecoming for the servant of God to be publicly admitting his or her thorn in the flesh, weaknesses, and struggles. In front of others, we must act strong and never reveal our own spiritual battles. Because of social, ministerial, and ecclesial pressures, we are forced to wear a mask that functions both to announce our supposed spiritual-ness and to hide our own weaknesses.[259]

Colorful neckties wrapped around brand-name long sleeve shirts become the veil to conceal our weaknesses. Academic degrees, political position (whether

---

257. The Eastern theologian Georges Florovsky writes: "The term *theosis* is indeed embarrassing, if we would think of it in 'ontological categories.' Indeed, man simply cannot become 'god.' But the Fathers were thinking in 'personal' terms, and the mystery of personal communion was involved at this point. Theosis means a personal encounter. It is the ultimate intercourse with God, in which the whole of human existence is, as it were, permeated by the Divine Presence." See "St. Gregory Palama and the Tradition of the Fathers," in *Bible, Church, Tradition: Eastern Orthodox View* (*Collected Works*, vol. 2; Houston: Nor and, 1972), 115.

258. Randy Maddox, "John Wesley and Eastern Orthodoxy: Influences, Convergences, and Differences," *Asbury Theological Journal* 45 (1990), 39.

259. For an insightful sermon related to this, see Russell V. DeLong, "Shedding Our Masks," in *Why Be Moral? And Other Sermons* (Kansas City: Beacon Hill, 1962), 95–98.

ecclesiastical or whatsoever), economic status, and the like make our human failings nearly invisible. Then, we vindicate our acts by saying to ourselves that we are doing this for the sake of the weaker brothers and sisters (who we also assume are Donatists[260]). The desire to be a blessing eclipses the need to admit that we need God's blessings too. We try hard to project ourselves as super-pastors, supra-human, and almost infallible. In reality, however, we become modern day trying-hard-but-epic-fail "super-apostles," like white-washed tombs who look clean on the outside but are full of suppressed feelings and secrets inside.

In one sense, it is the expectations of our church members, of our leaders, and even of the world that force us to hide our vulnerabilities as a holiness people. But this external reason is not the only source of blame. Underlying our desire to hide our weaknesses is an incipient pride. This is ironic because pride is an evidence of self-centeredness, which in turn is antithetical to the life of holiness. Is it not arrogance when we wear a mask intentionally to hide our own weaknesses and unintentionally to announce our spiritualness? Is it not an act of deceit if we deny who we really are and erect a pseudo-self or an illusory façade to make others esteem us with higher value than we deserve?

We seem to have forgotten that our theological ancestor, John Wesley, was very clear that absolute perfection is not possible in this life and that the life of holiness does not entail freedom from ignorance, mistake, and human infirmities.[261] For Wesley, we remain human, with all our human bodily and intellectual imperfections and limitations even after the experience of entire sanctification.

The Scriptural command to be holy is directed to finite humans, who shall be holy as humans. To be human is to be imperfect in knowledge, which leads sometimes to terrible decisions, misconceptions, doubts, and even a self-interrogating unbelief. To be human is to suffer physical pain and emotional turmoil, which lead sometimes to exhaustion, discouragement, anger, and temptations of the flesh (gluttony, lust, etc.). Holiness people suffer and struggle with these things, perhaps on a daily basis, but we are too proud to accept them, because we are a holiness people!

---

260. The Donatists were a breakaway Christian sect in the 4th century who believed in a church and especially a clergy made only of saints and not sinners. This sect was widely rejected by councils throughout history because no person is fully morally pure.

261. John Wesley, "Christian Perfection," in *The Works of John Wesley*, vol. 2, *Sermons 37–70* (ed. Albert C. Outler; Bicentennial Edition [henceforth, BE]; Nashville: Abingdon, 1985), 100–104. Wesley wrote in *A Plain Account of Christian Perfection* §15: "There is no such perfection in this life, as implies an entire deliverance, either from ignorance, or mistake, … or from numberless infirmities… We cannot find any ground in Scripture to suppose, that any inhabitant of a house of clay is wholly exempt either from bodily infirmities, or from ignorance of many things, or to imagine any is incapable of mistake, or falling into divers temptations."

As a concrete example, I recall when I attended the Global Theology Conference of the Church of the Nazarene in 2007. We had a Covenant Service in one of the worship gatherings, but after the service, several people complained because they felt that it was inappropriate for us to have a time of confession as part of the liturgy. They felt that holy people must not engage in confession! It seems that many of us have also forgotten one of Wesley's important teachings: the importance of the repentance of believers.[262]

Of course, I am not saying that we should lower our holiness standards. What I am arguing is that we should be realistic. Since we do not agree that entire sanctification entails a transformation to become divine beings, then we must admit that we are holy as human beings, full of limitations and vulnerabilities. The acceptance of this fact allows us to be more accountable and communal. Because we have our own struggles, all of us are in need of guidance, assistance, and even rebuke. No one is beyond edification, reproof, and correction. If we are honest to ourselves and to one another, perhaps growth is more realistic, and we can be more sympathetic than judgmental and condescending to others.

What is wrong with admitting and accepting our own weaknesses? Paul's response is simply: "Nothing." Paul was actually quite open about his own speech, personality, and physical limitations. But the Lord promised to Paul, "My grace is sufficient for you, for my power is made perfect in weakness" (2 Cor 12:9). God empowers us, showers us with his grace, protects us, teaches us, and guides us, precisely because we are weak. No wonder why Paul responds, "*Therefore,* I will boast all the more gladly about my weaknesses, so that Christ's power may rest on me. That is why, for Christ's sake, I delight in weaknesses, in insults, in hardships, in persecutions, in difficulties. For when I am weak, then I am strong" (2 Cor 12:9-10).

Biblical Christology may be the antidote to our deifying tendencies and notions. The writer of Hebrews wrote that Christ became human by "sharing in [our] humanity" and that "he had to be made like his brothers in every way" (2:14, 17). Therefore, he added, we have someone "who is not unable to empathize with our weaknesses, but we have one who has been tempted in every way, just as we are" (4:15). Although he was God, Christ became fully human sharing our finitude, limitations, and weaknesses. To have weaknesses is neither something to be ashamed of nor something to be hidden.

Like Paul who relied on God's sufficient grace, the human weaknesses of Christ actually became the reason for his humility and dependence upon the Holy Spirit throughout his whole human life. He was born of the Spirit (Matt 1:20;

---

262. Wesley, "Repentance of Believers," in BE 1: 335–52.

Luke 1:35); baptized by the Spirit (Matt 3:16; Mark 1:10); led by the Spirit into the wilderness to be tempted (Matt 4:1; Mark 1:12; Luke 4:1); anointed by the Spirit (Luke 4:16–21); mobilized by the Spirit (Luke 4:14); drove out evil spirits by the power of the Spirit (Matt 12:28); and even rose from the dead in the power of the Spirit (1 Pet 3:18). The Holy Spirit permeated the whole life of Jesus. Christ lived his life without recourse to his divine powers and privileges; rather, he chose to live in weakness and in need, utterly dependent upon the Spirit's help, guidance, and providence. Throughout his entire life, Jesus lived as *Christos*, the Anointed One.

By looking at the life of the human Christ, we realize important holiness synonyms such as dependence, selflessness, humility, and Spirit-fullness. In particular, we appreciate better what Christlikeness means, because just as Christ lived a holy human life, we too can be holy as humans. When we are summoned to imitate Christ, we are not encouraged to imitate his divine life.

This is not only impossible; it is also idolatrous. There is a type of human imitation that goes against the purposes of God for humanity. There is a godlikeness that humans are prohibited to attempt to attain. The story of the Fall illustrates this. When the serpent tempted Eve to eat from the forbidden tree of knowledge, he told her that eating the fruit would result in them becoming "like God" (Gen 3:5).

God created us to be humans, and sin is the attempted undoing of humanity to become godlike or gods. Holiness involves "an affirmation of the essential finitude of human nature, not an escape from it."[263] In imitating Christ, holiness, therefore, is to be who we were intended to be, as finite human creatures dependent on God.

Dick O. Eugenio (Ph.D., University of Manchester) is Assistant Professor of Theology at Asia-Pacific Nazarene Theological Seminary in the Philippines, and Research Fellow of Manchester Wesley Research Centre, United Kingdom. His primary interests are the early church, worship, the doctrines of salvation, and the Trinity.

---

263. David H. Kelsey, "Human Being," in *Christian Theology: An Introduction to its Traditions and Tasks*, eds. Peter C. Hodgson and Robert H. King, 2nd ed., (Philadelphia: Fortress, 1994), 170.

Logotheandric Witness as Incarnate Christlike Presence

Larnie Sam A. Tabuena

Christian truth is essentially a life-changing discipleship process. It's far more than religious tenets in the form of metanarratives and metaphysical propositions. "Confession of faith" per se constitutes performative statements tantamount to the words "I do," uttered by the bride and groom in a wedding ceremony. Marriage vows do not fundamentally embody objective expressions of research conclusions achieved but an actual personal engagement in the act itself. Thus, the message is indeed the person himself/herself.

Jesus Christ declares, "I am the Truth" (John 14:6). For the gospel to be existentially authentic, it must be a "mode of being," effectively engaged in interpersonal communion with other selves. In this manner, each redeemed personality—as a bearer of divine grace and unconditional love—dynamically represents such divine likeness to fulfill the ideal ontological *telos*. God, as the supreme influential agent, calls us to share in the holy life and its ethical dimensions of acting and being acted upon by virtue of Christ's exemplary life. Being so, "we can and may share in and emulate the perfect immanent power of becoming and perfect transitive power of influence."[264] Sanctified life encompasses the incarnate state of a transformed being, the synergy of gracious influence within the scope of interrelationship, and the ethically responsible reflection of *imago Dei* to the present age.

From the socio-ethical perspective, living a holy life means practicing mutually Christ's incarnate presence as *logotheandric* witness. "*Logotheandic*"—derived from *logos* (word), *theos* (God), and *andros* (human)—presupposes a certain conceptual compatibility to the oriental holistic mode of thinking. Truth in Christianity does not exclusively dwell in the epistemological domain, but it is in its essence a subject to subject encounter.

In Western thought, the word *theandric* has referred to the union of the human and the divine without confusion. It is analogous to the incarnation of Jesus Christ who has both divine and human natures. In Christian theology, it can be called "the incarnational model."

---

264. William L. Power, "Imago Dei- Imittio Dei," *International Journal For Philosophy of Religion* 42 (1997): 140.

On the other hand, *logos* is from the verb meaning "to say" or "to speak." No single English equivalent quite captures its richness, so it is best in many cases to leave the term untranslated. The frequently common concepts associated with this rational order are "word," "reason," and "wisdom." Thus, its basic meanings entail representing the divine in concrete terms, the creating-recreating agent of all that there is, the integrating principle of existence, and the sustaining force of life.

Thus, St. John's Gospel conveyed the most comprehensive Christological account on the logos: "The Word became flesh and made His dwelling among us. We have seen His glory, the glory of the One and Only, who came from the Father, full of grace and truth" (John 1:14). Christ is the personification of God's wisdom, and without Him humanity will never experience ontological significance, life's meaning, authentic relationships, a transformed self, or eternal validity. Christ has restored the image corrupted during the Adamic fall, and he has reunited us to himself after we had been made partakers of the benefits of His atoning sacrifices, by participating in His grace and imitating His life.[265]

This amalgamated word, "logotheandric," bears the essence of what it means to live and to grow in Christlikeness. By embracing the "Personal Truth" and taking the resolute responsibility of representing all the redemptive and sanctifying attributes revealed in Christ, who is the perfect image of the Father, we become *logos Christos/theos*, incarnate presence of the "Living Word" to both the world and the community of faith.

Holiness, then, means "Word-conformed." We are living according to the standard of the written word (Bible) as well as to the model of the Incarnate Personal Word (Jesus Christ). In other words, logotheandric witness is a distinct nomenclature for the creative practice of human-divine presence as meaning-bearers within the context of everyday lives.

Such incarnate Christlike presence expresses concretely the missional character of holiness that fulfills both the redemptive value of the gospel and the edifying potential of *theos corpus*. Thus, it implies a "sacramental presence," actualizing agape through intersubjective communion. "This work of sanctification finds its principal source in the grace of Christ, who is both the Son of God, perfect Image of the Father, and Son of Mary, truly human like us. But this grace requires human collaboration, above all though faith, hope and love."[266]

---

265. Leo the Great, *Sermons*, introduction by Jacques Leclercq, Trans. Rene Dolle, Sources Chretiennes, vol 22 (Paris: Cerf, 1949), 44. For a lengthy discussion see Servais Pinckaers, *The Pinckaers Reader: Renewing Thomistic Moral Theology*, edited by John Berkman and Craig Steven Titus, Translated by Sr. Mary Thomas Noble (Washington, DC: The Catholic Press, 2005), 132-133.

266. Pinckaers, 135.

The communion of the saints could be possibly realized within the nexus of incarnational living. The God-Man participates in our nature, so we can participate in the divine nature. Hence, we participate in one another's life in a common way. Sharing the totally redeemed nature in the same life of the God-Man resonates through the common spiritual DNA in each Christian self.

Mutually practicing the Christlike presence together requires an in-depth understanding of what the nature of the "subject" is in relation to the process of growth in sanctification. Marcel explains that the term "ego" does not mean an isolated entity with precise boundaries but a part of myself that I focus on and present to others for their recognition and approval.[267] Designating one's ego as the privileged center of the cosmos leads to the idolatry of making one's ultimate concern to safeguard itself from all external threats. However, one's own ego is the most valuable gift to others. Authentic communion, then, is recognizing each other as unique, free, and intrinsically valuable.

Furthermore, authentic communion constitutes a mutual enrichment of selves by influencing each other at the ontological level. Such onto-ethical interpenetration of autonomous individuals enables each subject to experience relaxation rather than threat because there has been reciprocal openness[268] The analytic isolation of Cartesian, "I think; therefore I am," is replaced by *a* Marcelian metaphysic of 'We are.' The goal is neither to obliterate individuality nor to establish dichotomy totally but to enhance "suprapersonal unity," which creates a "vital milieu from which each subject draws its strength."[269]

Genuine community is realized in the vocation of self-donation, participation, and I-thou commitment to the fullness of presence that. Authentic communion is a willful engagement of spontaneous familial intimacy that fosters a kind of fertile indistinction of persons.[270] Nobody primordially exists in monadic state, since all bearers of *imago Dei* are seized by an inner need to form community.[271]

God establishes a viable structure for finite I-thou relations. The different images of ecclesia involve the covenant of God's special people under the internal motivation of grace to form a messianic community. Thus, the Holy Trinity offers an understandable paradigm for human community. No divine Person exists alone for its own sake; they are always and eternally in relationship with one another. God's communion seeks above all the intimacy and freedom of the heart.[272]

---

267. Gabriel Marcel, *Homo Viator*, trans. E. Cruaford (New York: Harper & Row, 1962), 14-20.

268. Marcel, Mystery I, 177-81.

269. Ibid., 182; Gabriel Marcel, *Creative Fidelity*, trans. R. Rostal (New York: Fordham University Press, 2002), 35.

270. Varghese J. Manimala, *Being, Person, And Community: A Study of intersubjectivity in Existentialism With Special Reference to Marcel, Sartre and the Concept of Sangha in in Budhism* (New Delhi: Intercultural Publications, 1991), 173.

271. Leonardo Boff *Trinity and Society*, Paul Burns, trans. (Great Britain, Burns & Oates, 1992), 131

272. Boff, Trinity, 132-133.

So then, if even our social relationships have such a theocentric trajectory, we should no longer consider God as the highest priority but actually "our all." "For in Him we live and move and have our being" (Acts 17:28). Therefore, holiness simply means "God is my all." By living out the character of God, we are staying true to our own nature as the *imago Dei*.

Practicing God's incarnate presence produces a creative impact upon human life and ethical relationships as we all journey together toward Christlikeness. Functionalized existence in a technocratic milieu treats everyone else objectively as a mere tool to achieve our own desired outcome. However, if the Other is a genuine person, then the Other offers a creative participation that makes us more fully ourselves than we would be if we were not exposed to its impact.[273]

Holiness is a lifestyle of authentic communion with the Other, in order to carry out our mission to be the salt and light of the world. Indeed, Christ's incarnate presence indicates the noble function of the renewed *imago Dei* that is at work in the world as well as in the body of Christ. Jesus is the original logotheandric witness.

Holiness is essentially a dynamic growing relationship of transformed selves who are mutually committed to participate in each other's spiritual journey and life toward Christlikeness. Indeed, authentic communion, which internally affects each other significantly in the bond of divine love and fidelity, creates their ideal selves in response to an invocation emanating from the I-thou relationship.

Logotheandric witness is a holiness lifestyle of mutually practicing Christlikeness as sacramental presence to edify each other within the faith-community and to reflect the redemptive character of the gospel outside the church. Our ethical interaction ought to represent effectively the messianic life of Christ to the world as well as to the ecclesiastical body. Our sacramental presence represents the mediatorial function of the God-man who renders life's meaning in the midst of the present technocratic milieu of uncertainty. In the final analysis, the Christian message is performative statement reflected in our very being.

Larnie Sam A. Tabuena is an assistant professor of Philosophy and Ethics and the Director of Supervised Ministry Experience program at Asia-Pacific Nazarene Theological Seminary, Philippines. He is also Associate Director of the Bresee Institute Center that facilitates the Ph.D. in Transformational Development. He finished his B.A. in theology and M.A. in Religious Education at Asia-Pacific Nazarene Theological Seminary and M.A. in Philosophy at Dela Salle University. He is also a Ph.D. candidate at the University of Santo Tomas.

---

273. Marcel, Mystery I, 205.

Holiness to Come

Eric M. Vail

The Bible opens with a lone character—God, who creates all there is. Given the opening verse of Scripture, it is so easy to read the Bible as a story between that lone character and each individual thing God creates. Christian theologians have, from early in the tradition, thought of God as having immediate, solitary causation in establishing each and every part of creation. In turn, each thing has its own direct line of connection back to God.

That Creator-creature connection is not only viewed as primary (over connections among creatures), but it is viewed as coming first in a sequence, before relations with fellow creatures are established. This fosters a weak interconnection between love of God and love of neighbor. It is easy to understand in this framing of things how creatures should respond lovingly toward God. All God's creatures are left standing awkwardly side-by-side as we all individually face God. Love toward neighbor seems like an awkward addendum that must be done simply because it is a way to love God through obedience.

This framing of the opening biblical narrative does not fit the narrative itself. We are not created first by God to relate subsequently to everything else God creates. Rather, we come into existence in relation to God and neighbor. God is indeed Creator, but God creates by calling creation to support the unfolding existence of other parts of creation. For example, plants are supported by resources from the ground, air, and sun so that they can grow and be sustained—possibly giving themselves, then, as food for something else. Plants do not come into being relative to God alone (*ex nihilo*), but in relation to God and neighbor. If the soil lacks nutrients, or if the air is saturated with airborne pollutants, a plant will be negatively impacted—regardless of having great genetics and unbroken life from God.

Humans are no different. We too come into the world in relation to God and neighbor. The world and our fellow creatures are called by God to nurture us into the wholeness of life in the communion of love. Yet tragically, we are born into a world steeped in practicing evil. Not all things in the world are working in the fullness of God's love, even before we are conceived. In the best circumstances, there are still the subtle disfiguring effects of sin at play. God's love is not perfected in the way the world interacts with us; we do not stand in the wholeness of divine love in relation to all things.

To clarify, our life and existence is a complex relational interaction with both God and neighbor. Love of neighbor is not an afterthought to how we love God. As Genesis 1 puts it, we are day-six creatures—creatures of the land, among the other creatures of the land, and eaters of the land's plants. We have a relation with creation that is fundamental to our existence and vocation.

At the same time, we are uniquely related to God as ones who are to image God in the world. As Genesis 2 puts it, we are dust, and we are divinely breathed-into. We are inseparably tied to the soil and to God. We do not volunteer to have a relationship to God; we are related by our very life-breath.

Similarly, we do get to choose whether or not to have relationships to all of God's creation; we are related by our very composition. The question is the nature or quality of those relations, not whether we have them. The fact that we stand in relation to God and all things is a given.

The standard for assessing our relatedness is love. Is there reciprocal love or a love-denying relationship at work there?

If all creation is going to come to God's full purpose for it—which is that God's love would radiantly shine among every facet of creation—then there must be reciprocity in love being expressed among all parties. If any of us tangibly act with love toward someone who then replies with a kick in the shin or a dismissive waive, the fullness of God's purposes have not yet come for us or that other person. We may bear witness bodily to the truth of God's own character, purposes, and in-breaking salvation (and with it, the lie of the world's ways). However, the most holy people and the most just, right fellowships of believers have more that awaits them when Christ returns and finishes his work of New Creation. All creation will then express other-nurturing love in relation to all other parts of creation.

Too often the holiness tradition has overemphasized the relationship between God and an individual. Where that person is fully yielded to God, the fullness of God's redeeming work for that person might be imagined to have come. It is true that there is ever increasing beauty expressed in the life of continually maturing believers. They may have the love of God shed abroad in their hearts. They may have divine-like love, excluding all wayward affections, as their primary impulse in all they do. Faithful cooperation through the Spirit's prompting fosters sanctified dispositions in believers. They continually grow and mature in their actions toward others, out of this Spirit-fostered life. God continually reorders and rehabituates their steps, purifying them of the world's false wisdoms.

All of this sanctification, nevertheless, does not remove believers from their fundamental interconnections within the world. No matter how purified believers may become in their primal inclinations and habits of life, they still are not related to the entire world in a fully redeemed way.

On the side of believers, the manner in which they live in the world is not yet uncorrupted by sin. They may not treat their bodies well through diet, sleep, or physical activity. They may be living in oversized houses that took more resources to build and now to maintain than what is truly needed. This manner of life over-harvests from the earth and limits financial resources that could have been used for the care of others. The ways that sin has corrupted our forms of life and thought are legion; we can hardly imagine living in relation to all of God's creation freed entirely of sin's corrupting effects on those relations. We can (and should) spend a lifetime identifying and repenting of these corrupted expressions. Even then, we will never erase our need for God's work of making all things new when Christ returns in glory.

On the side of the world's manner of relating, mature Christians still have greater salvation yet to experience. Not only may the world hate Christians and/or express itself in dis-creative ways toward them, but the holiest of Christians are not yet experiencing from the world the perfect nurture God intends. We still live with locks on our doors and passwords on our accounts. We still clothe our nakedness against harsh environments, ridicule, or lustful ogling. We still vaccinate our bodies and warily open up to strangers. With the love of God for others ripening within, Christians ought to be grieved (like Christ in John 1:11 and Luke 19:41) that their love is met with inhospitality and that the world further languishes in alienation. We must bear faithful witness to God's coming kingdom while its full expression by all creation is not yet realized.

An entirely sanctified life (this side of Christ's return) does not require that Christians abandon prudence in their engagement with a world deadened in its love (or dimmed in reflecting God's glory). Christians should not be stingy or selective in their love. At the same time, the form that love takes is important. Becoming a passive doormat for others is unloving to those people and oneself. Christians actively seek to foster wholeness of love in others. They seek to establish justice, righteousness, and peace in creation's communities.

Christians are active in their love because we are not without hope. The universality of the world's corruption under sin is not the most absolute truth that should be said about the world: past, present, or future. Righteous response to the Father can happen through the work of the Spirit and the Word at any point in the midst of the world marred by sin. Even though the ultimate, universal healing of creation is coming with Christ from over the horizon, we are already tasting the bounty from Christ's banquet table.

We must remember in our holiness theology that we are fundamentally related to both our Creator and all creation. Our life has its many textures as we live in relation to God and all else. Our salvation, then, entails full reconciliation with not only God but also with our estranged world. We do not live in resignation to the corrupting consequences of sin in the world. The power and radiance of God's love stands before, above, and beyond any expression of sin. Believers can experience profound growth into God's love as they cooperatively respond to God's restorative work.

Nevertheless, we must await God's ultimate salvation when our systems of interacting with others are fully redeemed and all creation expresses itself in self-giving love toward others. Until the work of new creation is finished, we all await with earnest petition, the full salvation of the Church and the entire world, for which our lives are poured out in caring service.

Eric Vail is Assistant Professor of Theology at Mount Vernon Nazarene University. He is the author of Creation and Chaos Talk: Charting a Way Forward. *Prior to his current ministry position, he served as senior pastor in St. Joseph, Missouri.*

Green Eggs and Holiness

David E. Bartley

For decades, a peculiar book has captured the hearts of children and intrigued the minds of parents from generation to generation. The short narrative unfolds cleverly with twists and turns that draw the reader in. The reader initially resonates quickly with the plight of the main character. Beyond the reading eyes, the story also captivates the senses of taste and touch and smell. Page after page the plot thickens, creating a dilemma that the reader actually feels deepening phrase after phrase and sentence after sentence.

When the final page is turned, the greatest twist of all reveals the protagonist as the antagonist and the antagonist as the protagonist, and the entire narrative turns upside down. This peculiar book, with such depth of plot, revolves entirely around two sentences: "I do not like green eggs and ham. I do not like them Sam I Am."

Think about this with me. The story begins innocently with a cat-like androgynous figure presented with a simple dish that seems so unappealing, even revolting. With crude artwork in childish cartoon style, the display of the food causes readers of all ages to bristle at the sight of it, while then imagining the stench and taste that must come with green eggs and ham. Within a few pages your entire being is pulled in—senses and thoughts and all.

As I read it repeatedly with my daughter several years ago, this narrative enthralled me in a new way as an adult. Through foxes and boxes and boats and goats, I found myself agreeing with the figure that seemed to stand up for all that is good and right, to proclaim the obvious truth that no one in their right mind would like green eggs and ham. I felt as if this was more than just a cute nursery rhyme, more than a simple poetic anecdote. The truth of the matter rang clear in my heart: "I do not like green eggs and ham. I would not like them here or there. I would not like them anywhere." Agreeing with every retort to each scenario, I became unnerved by the antagonist known as Sam I Am as he persistently stretched for bizarre situations and drastic forms of delicacy enjoyment.

Yet, turning the last pages, I watched the world of the cat-like character come crashing down into the sea around it. Then, surrounded by a mess of boxes and boats and foxes and goats, he surrenders to the query of Sam, saying, "Sam, if you will let me be, I will try them. You will see." Then comes the biggest twist of all. In a moment of revelation, he tastes and sees. Suddenly, the plot turns upside down as he proclaims, "Say, I like green eggs and ham. I do! I like them, Sam I Am!"

A Holy Narrative

The story has connected with all ages, not only for its creative rhyming, but also for its plot that thickens with every twist and turn. This is the formula for every great narrative, especially the ones we upon which we build our lives.

Consider our narrative of life and creation where another I Am character brings goodness out of a formless void and shapes a people in His image—a people who will be holy as He is holy. Through every twist and turn, the plot thickens, revealing a new scenario and another retort, until the holy narrative culminates in the biggest twist of all, turning the plot upside down, leaving the characters involved speechless at what they witness.

This culminating twist has been captured best in Philippians 2:5-7: "Your attitude should be the same as that of Christ Jesus: Who, being in very nature God, did not consider equality with God something to be grasped, but made himself nothing, taking the very nature of a servant, being made in human likeness."

For those first century witnesses, the plot of God's narrative thickened as the definition of Divinity received a major twist in Christ. Those first disciples walking side by side with the Son of God. They learned that Jesus had not merely released his Godliness in order to become human. On the contrary, they realized that Jesus was completely redefining Godliness by purposefully becoming human, in the image of God, taking on servanthood.

Through the incarnation, Christ declares that being God is not a title of higher distinction to boast of and lord over others; it is an existence of selfless sacrifice in servanthood to all. The very nature of God is the very nature of a servant. In grasping this huge twist in the narrative, the disciples understood that Godliness should not be considered something to grasp for and cling to. Jesus exemplified Godliness as a way of giving life away, thereby defining humanity, the image of God, as a life of giving. And the plot thickens.

Christ taught this repeatedly: "The last shall be first," "To save your life you must lose your life," "Whoever wants to be great must be a servant," "Freely you have received, freely give."

We so often speak of blessings we receive as items we acquire, like the car we needed or the home we wanted or the ministry building we raised for or the converts we prayed for. What a blessing from God, we say. In the American spirit, we consider God and faith from our consumer mindset: if I give then I will surely get.

Yet, in the spirit of Abraham, Jesus understood blessings not as gifts from God to hold on to, but as opportunities to give to others. As God covenanted with Abraham to bless him so that he would bless others, Jesus took the life He was blessed with and used it, gave it away, to bless others. To be Christ-like, to have the same mind as that of Christ, must involve this understanding of Godliness as a servant, giving life away rather than attaining a life of blessing. To be holy, as He is holy, is a call to surrender your life in order to live a life of surrender, an invitation to give with a challenge to live.

A Holy Mission

American pastor Hugh Halter has said that the average Christian does not want to be a consumer, a materialistic individualist who lives by the mantra, I give, therefore, I should receive. The average Christian wants to be a kingdom advocate with a holy heart and a holy mission to affect the world with the mantra, I give therefore I am. Our message has never been one of a disembodied heaven in some eternal distant future. The message of holiness is a message for here and now, of seeking first His kingdom come on earth as it is in heaven.

The thick plot of a simple Dr. Seuss rhyme grabbed my attention like never before and pulled me in through a story of a cat-like, androgynous creature that, being tormented by the persistent and relentless Sam I Am, consented to taste, and in surrendering thereby discovered a new exciting view of life ahead. It's a simple plot pulled right out of the holy narrative of God, where all creation is hounded by the persistent and relentless love of the Great I Am, until surrendering we taste and see a new exciting view of life and humanity in creation.

To surrender our lives and our agendas, in paradoxical twist, means we will find new life so immense it cannot be contained in our simple lives or agendas. As we give up our lives, abundant Life fills us and expands in us until we simply must offer it to others. And when they taste holy love through us, they will see life anew and join in the extravagant forms of servanthood and compassion.

Godliness, in his image, is neither something to hold on to, nor something to gain from. Being holy as He is holy means living a life of surrender. Giving life away, not to get blessings but to simply bless, not to retreat from the world but to go boldly into the darkness, to give the message of hope and a future to the lost and dying in darkness, to truly be an expression of the kingdom of God that becomes a light on a hill that draws men and women to the saving and sanctifying grace of God our Father.

Together, let's give that Godliness away. Let's give it here and give it there; let's give it away anywhere. We can give it in a boat or with a goat. We can share it in a box or with a fox. We can give it with green eggs and ham, because we rely on the Great I Am. Let's partner together in whatever ways possible to reach out to the millions in our own backyard with our taste and see holiness while we partner to reach billions around the world with the same.

David Bartley serves as District Superintendent of the Northwest Indiana District. Before his election, he served as senior pastor of South Bend Church of the Nazarene. He is a graduate of Olivet Nazarene University and Nazarene Theological Seminary, and he is currently pursuing his Doctorate of Ministry at Northern Seminary. He and his wife Jolyne have four kids.

Getting Back to Our Roots:
Realigning Our Doctrines with Our Standards
Megan M. Pardue

In the application for ordination in the Church of the Nazarene, question twelve asks the following, "Are you in full sympathy and hearty accord with the standards, doctrines, and government of the Church of the Nazarene?"[274] This is a "yes" or "no" question. It seems that before requiring our ordination candidates to answer this question, we members have some work to do to get our "doctrines" and our "standards" aligned with one another.

One of the most poignant and alarming examples of the discontinuity between our "doctrines" and our "standards" relates to the Manual's explicit doctrinal statements regarding the nature of Christian holiness and the standards with which we embody Christian holiness in many, if not most, Church of the Nazarene congregations in the United States.

In the Covenant of Christian Conduct, the Manual explains what the doctrine of Christian holiness requires (article 28.3). This explanation occurs *before* any specific instructions for what is to be avoided in the holy way of life.

> The Church of the Nazarene believes this new and holy way of life involves practices to be avoided and redemptive acts of love to be accomplished for the souls, minds, and bodies of our neighbors. One redemptive arena of love involves the special relationship Jesus had, and commanded His disciples to have, with the poor of this world; that His Church ought, first, to keep itself simple and free from an emphasis on wealth and extravagance and, second, to give itself to the care, feeding, clothing, and shelter of the poor and marginalized. Throughout the Bible and in the life and example of Jesus, God identifies with and assists the poor, the oppressed, and those in society who cannot speak for themselves. In the same way, we, too, are called to identify with and to enter into solidarity with the poor.

---

274. "Ordination Recognition Questionnaire," 2014, District Forms, http://nazarene.org/Document_Library/

We hold that compassionate ministry to the poor includes acts of charity as well as a struggle to provide opportunity, equality, and justice for the poor. We further believe the Christian's responsibility to the poor is an essential aspect of the life of every believer who seeks a faith that works through love. We believe Christian holiness to be inseparable from ministry to the poor in that it drives the Christian beyond their own individual perfection and toward the creation of a more just and equitable society and world.[275]

This is what Christian holiness is all about? Our churches are supposed to be simple, free from an emphasis on wealth and extravagance? The church gives itself above all else to the care, feeding, clothing, and shelter of the marginalized? Christian holiness is "inseparable from ministry to the poor?" Christian holiness is about more than what I *don't* do?

That's the problem, isn't it? For too long, we in the Church of the Nazarene have told our members what holy people *don't* do. I know the list backwards and forwards. Holy people, people transformed by the sanctifying power of the Holy Spirit, don't do many things—swear, smoke, sleep around, etc. The list goes on and on.

There is also the list of what holy people are to *do*, but it consists primarily of individual requirements, relating to one's "personal relationship with God" and having few implications for the life of the community or acts of justice and mercy with our neighbors. For countless members of the Church of the Nazarene in the United States, the short *do* list along with the long *don't* list make up the sum total of the life of holiness. We are left with the denominational standard for what constitutes Christian holiness as it's understood and embodied in so many of our churches in the United States. It can be boiled down to a list of boxes needing check marks, a kind of application for the sanctified life. Do you pray? Check "yes." Do you smoke? Check "no."

Our doctrinal statements about Christian holiness call us to something else entirely, something deeper and relational, beyond ourselves. Jesus spent his time with those on the margins, the struggling, the oppressed, and the outsiders. As holiness people, we believe we are called to follow the life of Christ, specifically in this regard according to the Manual. Unfortunately, not only have we failed to empower people to live into what holy people *do* beyond our individualized perfection, many members of the denomination are not even aware that our church holds such strong commitments to social holiness, to caring for and being

275. *Manual*, 2013-2017 (Kansas City: NPH, 2013), 46-47.

in solidarity with the poor. If Christian holiness is "inseparable from ministry to the poor," then we are in need of a renewal of our holiness identity and a commitment to realign our doctrines with our standards.

How does a living body of people go about renewing our holiness identity? Perhaps one place to start is education. How will our congregants ever know about that we believe Christian holiness to be inseparable from ministry to the poor if we never tell them or *show* them? When I wonder what such renewal of our identity might look like, I find inspiration in the words of Dr. Phineas F. Bresee on October 30, 1895, from an organizational meeting at First Church of the Nazarene in Los Angeles:

> We seek the simplicity and the power of the primitive New Testament Church. The field of labor to which we feel called is in the neglected quarters of the cities and wherever else may be found waste places and souls seeking pardon and cleansing from sin. This work we aim to do through the agency of city missions, evangelistic services, house-to-house visitation, caring for the poor, comforting the dying.[276]

If we want to be constantly reminded of our denominational identity, maybe we should commission an artist to inscribe these words above the doors leading out of the church or in the room where our church board convenes. Bresee's words remind us who we are. Our identity as holiness people is much richer and more relational than a list with boxes to check.

Another way to educate ourselves for the renewal of our identity is to visit churches and to talk with pastors that are already living into our doctrinal understanding of Christian holiness. We can ask questions, seek their wisdom, heed their prophetic voices, and invite the Holy Spirit to transform us through their stories and witness. We can elect the pastors of these churches to be District Superintendents, to help point out where we've made a misstep. In my experience, these churches and pastors are often overlooked, shadowed by the fancy gymnasiums, the well-balanced and cushioned budgets, and manicured grounds of neighboring congregations of the Church of the Nazarene. Yet, we have witnesses of our denominational identity in our midst, those who have given themselves "to the care, feeding, clothing, and shelter of the poor and marginalized."

---

276. First Church of the Nazarene, Los Angeles, California. *Minutes of the Organizational Meeting.* October 30, 1895.

A further step in education is submitting to our holiness identity, allowing our identity to *reeducate* us. I was recently at a meeting of Church of the Nazarene pastors where one pastor suggested, in a matter of fact tone, that the financial crises of churches are easily remedied if only you win more people to Jesus. More people in the church results in more tithers, hence solving financial problems. It seems that this might be true if you are winning people to Jesus from a particular socio-economic class. As members of the Church of the Nazarene "called to identify with and to enter into solidarity with the poor," however, can we expect those that we welcome into our churches will be excellent tithers with money to spare?

Such reeducation also challenges the "Field of Dreams" church-growth mentality. Many churches and pastors are convinced, "If we build it, they will come." In all actuality, our denominational commitments to simplicity, to be free from wealth and extravagance, encourage us to imagine our use of resources beyond the standard building campaign. Our holiness identity can reeducate us, exposing the platitudes and even lies that have seeped into our practices, while helping us realign our doctrines with our standards.

In addition to education, we need to hold each other accountable to getting back to our roots. For many churches, such renewal will require serious changes in values and priorities, how we think about and spend money, and how we understand and live into our commitments to the life of holiness (i.e. Christian holiness is about more than what I *don't* do).

Accountability could begin with a simple list of questions that pastors could go through with neighboring pastors or that pastors could discuss with their local church boards annually.

- In what ways does our church adhere to the standards in article 28.3 of the *Manual*? In what ways do we not?
- How often have we preached on Scripture that shows how "God identifies with and assists the poor, the oppressed, and those in society who cannot speak for themselves?"
- If our church closed the doors tomorrow, who in our neighborhood would realize we were gone?
- How is our church engaged in compassionate ministry?
- Are these ministries primarily focused on acts of charity or the struggle to provide opportunity, equality, and justice for the poor?
- What are the top five expenses in our church budget, and do they reflect the standards of article 28.3?
- Who is not welcome at our church?

These questions and others provide opportunities for concrete reflection and evaluation, a step forward in renewing our identity. The questions are a means of accountability only insofar as they move us to act, to have hard conversations, to confess where we have been wrong, and to dive into our rich heritage of Christian holiness.

A renewal of our identity will help us to realign our doctrines with our standards, but it will require an enormous amount of commitment, education, energy, accountability, and prayer. People transformed by the power of the Holy Spirit actually *do* a great deal. Justice, mercy, friendship, and charity mark their lives, as does walking alongside those who are poor, oppressed, and marginalized. If we aligned our standards with our doctrines, imagine what an example the Church of the Nazarene and our distinctive doctrine could be to the denominational landscape of the United States.

Enough with the list of boxes to check. Christ invites us, through his example, to participate in God's redemptive acts of love for the souls, minds, and bodies of our neighbors.

Megan Pardue the Lead Pastor at Refuge in Durham, North Carolina. Megan was born and raised in Portland, Oregon. She holds Master of Divinity from Duke Divinity School and a B.A. in Theology and Ministry from Southern Nazarene University. She loves preaching, international travel, and backyard bonfires.

Holiness, Polity, and Politics

Andrew J. Wood

Communities must make decisions. As an island, individuals might set their own course without reference to another's needs, preferences, or opinions, but communities of various kinds—neighborhoods, congregations, denominations, governments—cannot operate in this manner. Decisions are corporate business or the work of the "body" (Latin: *corpus*). How we make decisions—and, in particular, how we conduct ourselves in the often messy and contested conversations such corporate decisions require—is a vital matter.

One might assume that communities committed to a high ideal—say, for example, the religious ideal of holiness or the political ideal of a "more perfect union"—would not have messy and contested conversations. But this is not the case, and it seems such disagreements should be expected precisely in communities with such high ideals and commitments. It is *because* we aspire to holiness in our churches and denomination—and *because* we hope for a public sphere where goodness and honesty are the norm—that we have such disagreements. We are deeply interested in, and invested in, the future shape of our communities. We want them to be all they should be. Since achieving any such goal requires decisions made together often with limited resources, all that commitment is conducive to debate and discussion about what specifics we should commit ourselves to and exactly what we should do in order to achieve those ideals. Because Christians care about the church and because citizens care about the state, debate is to be expected.

So, if it is the case that decisions are necessary and that we should expect disagreements, how might we best participate? How should we engage the often messy, shrill, and contested worlds of church polity and secular politics?

First, we should humble ourselves and pray.

We are not infallible. We are not lords, emperors, or dictators. We are children of God—all of us. Do we pray over our opinions and decisions? Do we pray about our reactions to the opinions expressed or decisions made by others? How often do we pray, not that someone else might get wise to our favored program, but that we might hear them and harbor no malice in our hearts?

274

Second, we should remember the faith resources God has given us.

The Scriptures provide abundant advice to us. Galatians 5 reminds us that the fruit of the Spirit includes forbearance, kindness, gentleness, and self-control. The Ten Commandments include a prohibition on bearing false witness. Matthew 5 reminds us that Jesus declared we are light, salt, and a city on a hill that cannot be hidden. James reminds us that we have opportunity in each discussion to bless or to curse, to honor or to shame. Our opinions may be ignored; the manner and spirit by which we express them may not be.

Third, we should engage one another respectfully, graciously, and honestly.

How we make decisions is often as important for our witness as the decisions we make themselves. So, too, is the way in which our decisions are perceived. This seems clear enough. But what about the way in which we express our opinions about church matters or about politics? There, too, we are being watched.

We should carefully avoid disrespect. All too often, decision-making discussions and debates devolve into disrespectful personal attacks. It is beneath us to treat those we disagree with disrespectfully. Being wrong is not proof of malice or even ignorance, nor are good intentions and knowledge of the subject at hand adequate proof a person has the right or best position. Most of us can remember an encounter where we were treated poorly because someone didn't like our opinion. Hopefully, we can also remember a time when we were treated with respect by someone who did not favor our opinion but still valued our person.

Likewise, we should avoid dishonest ways. We should be honest about own motives for our opinions. We should also be honest about the motives of others. We might be slower to declare confidently the supposedly despicable motives of others, especially those we do not know personally. We might be slower, too, to declare someone stupid or dangerous because we think their proposals are stupid or dangerous. They may well be wrong and their ideas poorly thought-out and unwise. But history provides many examples of well-meaning, intelligent, honorable, and even godly people who made serious mistakes.

When we encounter someone with a position that we don't agree with, often it is helpful to ask what is at stake. Why are they worried, and what are they worried about? We may find that we agree more than we think we do. Affirm the agreements. Then, having been honest and respectful, work out the (actual) differences. We live in a world that encourages us to believe we have nothing in common with "those people." But we do not have to play along. Expose and affirm the agreements.

Wisdom will be honest and gracious, and honest in both the sense of stating what may be critical and honest in the sense of refusing to bear false witness against someone even if that false witness is already widely circulated. Some of us will have opportunity to defend the falsely accused, most nobly when we defend those with whom we disagree.

Part of being honest entails being precise. This is especially important with decisions that are more complicated. I may disagree strongly on a few points, but avoiding blanket declarations of opposition is best. State what you disagree with and why you disagree.

Additionally, a word should be said about means and "levels" of decision making. Decisions made in smaller groups where regular in-person meetings are possible—say a local church board—can often happen directly. Decisions made at a wider level—a district, a city, a nation, or a denomination—frequently require a medium.

For many years, denominations and political units have relied on periodical publications, e.g., newspapers or magazines, to share news and further discussion. In more recent years, internet resources have become increasingly common. This latter development has many advantages, but it also has downsides. Decision making requires that information or facts be shared in common or at least debated in common. Publishing has been and will remain vitally important to a shared discussion. But the diversity of sources of information has increased the opportunity to talk past each other. If we desire to convince, we will have to find—and support—ways to engage directly and together.

In the Church of the Nazarene, we must remember the importance of the task of working together. Polity is not just how we are organized. Polity is how decisions are made and who will be involved in making those decisions. Polity is how visions are enacted and furthered and how prioritizing, institutional and communal will, and missional focus are displayed and achieved. Polity is how doctrine is spread, changed, and reinterpreted. Polity is how denominational identity is shaped, remembered, and reshaped.

We are bound together. We are connected in a "connectional" system. We cooperate and thus do more together than we would ever do apart. We embrace a vision of organizing ourselves for ministry that attempts to embody Psalm 133, "How good and pleasant it is when God's people live together in unity . . . for there the LORD bestows his blessing."

Finally, we would do well to remember that in political matters we are heirs to a prophetic tradition wherein our forebears believed they had a broad responsibility to bear truthful witness to the surrounding society and the state. They understood that hypocrisy was a serious threat to the church's witness and mission and that in order to bear that witness effectively the church itself needed to be, and remain, free from sin if not from temptation. A worldly church, regardless of its reputation, could not successfully bear prophetic witness to a sinful world. It was not just a reputation for hypocrisy that they wanted to avoid. They believed true spiritual forces were at work. Even a church widely praised by the world, if it were not truly faithful, would still be lacking in the spiritual power and vitality necessary to fulfill its mission of bearing a truthful witness.

Prophetic ministry, then, had its internal and external aspects. In order for the church to be a sanctifying force, it needed to be sanctified or holy itself. In order for the church to be a civilizing force, it needed to be a civilized church. Even in difficult ages past, our forebears embraced what they understood to be the call of God to speak truthfully about social and political matters. They aspired to be part of a righteous church ministering to a world (including both state and society) that was being transformed, remade, reformed, and even sanctified by the power of God. And they understood that such a great mission would require a great cooperation.

Could we not, should we not, confer *together*, respectfully, graciously, and honestly?

Andrew J. Wood is a Church of the Nazarene historian and former lecturer at Auburn University and United Theological Seminary. He has published with Holiness Today, Grace and Peace Magazine, Cambridge University Press, *and several academic journals in the fields of history and religion. He lives in Dayton, Ohio.*

Renovating Holiness Includes Renovation of Leadership

Erik Groeneveld

The renovation of holiness is a metaphor, similar to the biblical metaphor of pruning. Both metaphors acknowledge, in essence, there is something good or valuable present. But in order to release that value, it requires work to be done. In this article on the renovation of holiness, I argue work needs to be done to our Church of the Nazarene concept of leadership.

The denominational model of leadership is clearly described in our *Manual*. This description, however, is a vertical one. Take, for example, the role of the pastor in a local church. The *Manual* draws a top-down perspective by saying the pastor is "the president of the church" (paragraph 113.5). From a bottom-up perspective the pastor is accountable to the Annual Meeting. In this vertical view, both the pastor and the congregation are described as static entities. They each have their responsibilities; they each know their position. As an exaggeration, all year, the pastor delivers the "content," and once a year the Annual Meeting reviews the content . . . as well as the pastor.

Although this picture of local leadership and the balance of power is a legitimate one, the picture is too limited. A more helpful picture would pay more attention to the "process" of leadership, rather than just the "content." So, if we want to renovate the picture of local leadership, what has the picture of holiness to say to us? Let's take holiness as displayed within the Trinity as our point of departure.

First, the picture of holiness among the members of the Trinity shows us not a static but a dynamic relationship between Father, Son, and Holy Spirit. Second, the interaction is based on love, mutual respect, and trust. Third, the purpose of the interaction is the promotion of overall well-being, inside and outside the Trinity. In contrast to the vertical leadership model in the *Manual*, the "model" in the Trinity suggests a horizontal, relational approach based on cooperation. To accomplish the divine mission and vision, the Trinity works together to achieve the goals. This approach requires letting go of unilateral power, and it requires a willingness to share the blessings of contributing towards a common goal.

This horizontal approach, transposed to a local congregation, has several strong credentials. From a biblical perspective, it does justice to the view of cooperative congregational leadership. For instance, the selection of deacons in Acts 6 shows us the multiple blessings of cooperation in a congregation. Justice is given to specific groups in the congregation that require attention and care, and the apostolic leadership team is freed from a heavy responsibility. Also, new leaders are encouraged to use their Spirit-given talents. From a Wesleyan perspective, Acts 6 displays an application of relational holiness, since it contains the characteristics of cooperation within the Trinity. Entities are working together in love, mutual respect, and trust towards the promotion of overall well-being.

Other credentials come from organizational theories that recognize that the church in general does not meet the criteria of an archetypal hierarchical organization. Although some denominations have stronger hierarchical authority lines than others, on a local level at least, a part of the ministry is done because of loyalty and commitment, rather than top-down instructions. For that reason, the church is seen as a hybrid organization, in which instructions and cooperation go hand in hand.

My experience—both as a pastor and as a student-researcher—is that cooperation on a local level often takes place more accidentally rather than intentionally. More in particular, as in Acts 6, cooperation is sought only after situations of crisis. Individuals or united church members start to express their opinions or frustrations, and by that time the local leadership team is more or less forced to listen to them and to work with them. Applied to the Church of the Nazarene, in situations of problems or dilemmas, it is often not helpful to rely on the vertical leadership structure of the *Manual*. Claiming your rights, either as pastor or as church member, based on the power granted to you by the *Manual*, can do more harm than good. As one pastor told me, "If you pulling out the Manual, you might win the battle, but you won't win the war."

In this brief discussion, I argued that in most situations, and based on the *Manual*, congregational leadership is vertically oriented with the pastor overseeing the flock. Intentional cooperation within the leadership team and with the congregation at large seems to be an exception rather than the rule. Cooperative leadership rarely occurs out of the necessity of crisis. Research and experience suggest, however, that congregational leadership should be horizontally oriented. Are there renovation possibilities as a way forward in this dilemma? There are, and surprisingly enough, it is the *Manual* itself that directs us towards its own renovation proposal.

In addressing the leadership structure of the denomination, the *Manual* differentiates the global level of leadership, the district level of leadership, and, as discussed, the local level of leadership. And although the vertical structure stands out in all three levels, there is a clear hint of horizontal leadership on the district level.

On the district level, the *Manual* states the district superintendent can appoint a *zone facilitator*, whose role it is to assist in building a sense of community and camaraderie among the pastors, promoting the cause of Christ by encouraging and strategizing, and serving as a communications bridge between the local congregations and the district (paragraph 200.6).

It is striking that the legal document of the Church of the Nazarene, with its emphasis on vertical leadership responsibilities, suddenly refers to an "assistant" to facilitate in horizontal relationships. The verbs clearly indicating this horizontal approach are, "the building of community and camaraderie," "encouraging," "strategizing," and "serving as a communications bridge."

In my thesis, I have not elaborated on the actual role of zone facilitators, which is a separate area research in itself. In the context of relational holiness and leadership, however, it is an interesting paradigm to consider the local pastor and the church board as local facilitators rather than local overseers.

Fortunately, some pastors and church boards already function this way. A broader practice, supported by the *Manual*, will be a tangible application of our faith and doctrine. It will immediately highlight the focus of local leadership: relationship building in order to co-labor for the cause of Christ. Rather than cooperation as an afterthought in situations of crisis, cooperation within the church board and with the congregation at large can be intentional.

A congregation with this ethos will reflect the divine cooperation within the Trinity. Creaturely cooperation, however, will involve the pruning of egos and personality styles, since it is not always easy to work alongside others. However, did we not define "renovating" and "pruning" as a metaphor for a work that needs to be done in order to bring to the surface something that is valuable and holy?

Erik Groeneveld is from the Netherlands and is currently working on a D.Min. thesis on "congregational leadership" at Nazarene Theological College in Brisbane, Australia. Erik is co-pastor at the Redlands Church of the Nazarene in Brisbane.

Holy Love Making

Greg Arthur

In the West, we live an era of overly sensitive political correctness. Whenever others place us in a category that causes us the slightest bit of discomfort, we push back and reject that categorization. We don't want to be told who we are. Our fierce independence slams into the perceived barriers we encounter within categories. It is infuriating to have others assume they understand us based on an arbitrary designation they have created. We don't want anyone to assume they know us or can define us in generic terms. Each of us is a complex being yearning to be truly known.

In the church this spirit of independence can cause us some heartache. Being part of the Body of Christ is by definition an act of submission. We submit who we are to God. Our inclusion in the family of God gives us a new identity. Our lives in Christ are a struggle to take on this new identity and to let go of our old identity. In Colossians 3, the Apostle Paul four different times uses the image of taking off old clothes and putting on new ones. The identity that we wore before Christ is exchanged for a new one. This is an act of submission. It can make us uncomfortable. Our old clothes are worn and familiar. They have been shaped to fit us. The new clothes can feel very unfamiliar. We put them on, look in the mirror and feel like we are just wearing someone else's outfit. We don't shape these new clothes, they shape us.

Our new God-given wardrobe has some articles of clothing that can make us very uncomfortable. Many women struggle because some of these new clothes are men's clothes. God adopts us into his family as his children, but Paul tells us that we are specifically adopted as sons. This means not that God doesn't also have daughters, but that we are given the identity of first-born sons. This is great news for all of us. Paul wrote in a culture where first-born sons received the bulk of their father's inheritance and were given highest status. To be made the sons of God is not about gender; it is about full inclusion as heirs with Christ.

Galatians 3:26 makes this very clear. It says, "So in Christ Jesus you are **sons** of God through faith" (NIV, emphasis mine). The word for sons is often translated as children to convey that this is not a gender specific reference. (This if further emphasized by verse 28, which says there, is neither male nor female in Christ.)

This translation misses some of the point, however. We are wonderfully adopted as first-born sons who inherit the best of their father! This is good news, but it makes some of us uncomfortable to put on these clothes of first-born sons.

Whatever discomfort this may cause, it pales in comparison to discovering that our new wardrobe also includes a wedding dress. There aren't too many men who relish the imagery of being the Bride of Christ. But this role of the people of God as the Bride is a dominant theme of scripture.

In the Old Testament, we find the powerful imagery of husband and wife assigned to God and his people. Isaiah 54:5 says, "For your Maker is your husband—the Lord Almighty is his name—the Holy One of Israel is your Redeemer." In Isaiah 62:5 the prophet tells Israel that God will rejoice over them as a bridegroom rejoices over his bride. God commands the prophet Hosea to marry a promiscuous woman as an elaborate illustration of the difficult marital relationship between God and his people. The great love of God is demonstrated in his willingness to forgive his promiscuous bride for the sake of her redemption.

The Apostle Paul uses this same language to talk about Christ and the Church. Our example for the love of a husband and wife is the sacrificial love of Christ who gave himself up for his bride (Ephesians 5:25-33). Our job as the Bride of Christ is to remain faithful and pure until he returns (2 Corinthians 11:2). Our ultimate hope as the bride of Christ is to be reunited with our groom at our wedding feast (Revelation 19:7-9, 21:1-2). The culmination of the work of Christ will be his wedding to his bride for which he has sacrificed so much.

Why does all of this imagery of Christ and his bride make so many of us uncomfortable? Well, the answer of course is sex. The union of a bride and groom is consummated in the marital bed. That is part of the great joy of the wedding feast. The two shall now become one flesh in an act of love that perfectly demonstrates and seals the covenant bond. It is not very often, however, that you hear someone talk about their desire for God to make love to them.

Our sexuality is a part of us that we hold back from our relationship with God. We are uncomfortable with God having a place in our sex life. At best we reluctantly submit the *dos* and *don'ts* of our sex life to God. At our core, we are still influenced by the Platonic philosophers who believed that the flesh was evil or less valuable than the spirit. This philosophy led to the heresy of the Gnostics and Marcians who struggled with God taking on flesh. They separated the physical and spiritual worlds. In their view of God and the world, flesh and spirit are pitted against each other.

Many Christians still carry on this false dichotomy of the flesh and the spirit. We want holiness to be a merely spiritual reality. The work of Christ, however, shows us that flesh is not evil. God cares about our physical lives just as he cares about our spiritual lives. Jesus came as God in the flesh. He showed us a redeemed life in a physical body. Jesus even shows us our ultimate hope for a resurrected body. God is working to redeem our whole beings, flesh and spirit. Our flesh and our spirits are intertwined and inseparable. We cannot seek the redemption of one without the redemption of the other.

God cares about what we eat, our health, our physical suffering, and yes our sex life. All of these different functions of our body are to be submitted to Christ. All of these parts of us are to be united with Christ. God wants all of us.

When God chastised the Israelites for worshiping idols, he often did so with a sexual description. Worshiping an idol is an act of adultery. It is giving away an intimate part of us. In a covenant relationship, our sexuality is reserved for our covenant partner. Giving this away to someone outside of that covenant is betrayal. This is why Paul declares in 1 Corinthians 6, "The body, however, is not mean for sexual immorality but for the Lord; and the Lord for the body." Paul makes it clear that sexual immorality is a betrayal of our spiritual and physical union with Christ. Adultery is a violation of the two becoming one flesh. So too is idolatry a violation of our union with Christ.

Our sanctification then is as much a physical reality as a spiritual reality. God wants every action we take to be an act of faithfulness to our covenant with him. A life of holiness requires a holy sex life. It requires submitting our sexuality to God far beyond limiting sex to the covenant relationship of marriage. It means that within marriage our sexual activity should be an act of worship. It should demonstrate the sacrificial love Christ displayed for the church. If we are to be a holy people we must learn to have holy sex.

So long as we allow our sexuality to be separate from our worship we will miss out on the blessing of our union with Christ. If we seek to understand our worship as sex and our sex as worship, a whole new world of union with God is available to us. Worship should be personal, intimate, and exclusively reserved for God our husband. An act of worship should feel like sex. It should be filled with anticipation, joy, and ecstasy.

Sex should be worship. At its best, sex should function in the same way as worship. Worship encourages us, reaffirms our covenant with God, reminds us of our identity, and invites us to submit ourselves to God. We come to worship to give back to God the praise his faithfulness deserves. A holy sex life will mirror these acts of worship. It will be an act of mutual submission with our spouse. It will be an act of reaffirming our covenant bond. It will be an act of love expressed in thankfulness to them. It will encourage us and bring us joy.

The idolization of sex has taken these intended outcomes and destroyed them. Sex has become about the individual rather than covenant partners. Even within the bonds of marriage, sex is not holy so long as it is anything other than affirming to both spouses. It cannot be an exercise of power by one spouse over against the other. It must be a mutual submission of thankfulness and praise. That is holy sex.

Many of us are uncomfortable with this idea of worship as sex and sex as worship. We are uncomfortable with images of our wedding night with God. When we celebrate this union, however, and become fully one with Christ, then we discover levels of intimacy with our Redeemer we never before thought possible. Our pursuit of holiness must include a redeemed sexuality that fills our bedrooms and our sanctuaries with holy lovemaking.

Greg Arthur is the Senior Pastor of Duneland Community Church in Chesterton Indiana. Since finishing his studies at Wheaton College and Denver Seminary Greg has served on staff at churches in Colorado, North Carolina and now Indiana. An avid blogger, Greg spends his time writing about holiness and the mission of the church at his website holinessreeducation.com. In addition, Greg is passionate about the fight against human trafficking and serves on the board for Free the Girls, a non-profit organization helping trafficking survivors (www.freethegirls.org).

The Practice of Biblical Forgiveness and Holiness

Frank Mills

The Bible clearly supports the practicing of forgiveness among fellows. Matthew 6:14-15 says, "If you forgive those who sin against you, your heavenly Father will forgive you. But if you refuse to forgive others, your Father will not forgive your sins."

One of Jesus' disciples asked him to teach the disciples how to pray (Luke 11:1). Jesus responded by teaching them what has been called the Lord's Prayer (Luke 11:2-4). The third petition of the prayer is this: "Forgive us our sins, for we also forgive everyone who sins against us." In this prayer, Jesus emphasized humans' need to receive the forgiveness of God and to express forgiveness to one another. For disciples of Jesus, being forgiven by God makes it necessary to be forgiving of one another.

Most people consciously or unconsciously cause wounds to themselves in the way they handle forgiveness and unforgiveness in their daily walk. However, not all wounds are self-inflicted. In many cases, wounds are caused by the decisions and actions of people we come into contact. The injury from such unexpected wounds can be very painful especially if the wounds are deep and were deliberately inflected—whether by friends or enemies. Many of us are constantly struggling with the hurt caused by people who, at one time or the other, were near or dear to us, perhaps a relative, classmate, teacher, co-worker, pastor, parent, child, husband or wife.

Christians who have been thus wounded usually claim to have forgiven our offenders, but in reality we are often unable to bring ourselves to forgive sincerely those who inflicted the wounds upon us. In our hearts, we are still bitter and angry at what happened to us and at those who caused it. In our minds, we find many reasons to justify keeping a record of the wrongs afflicted against us.

But as painful as our wounds may be, the constant reminder of those wounds only makes our wounds worse. The more we think of past hurts, the more we cause present pain to ourselves. Instead of healing, the wounds are fresh every day. Such painful reminders, with time, eat us up emotionally, psychologically, physically, and spiritually. We eventually cause great damage to our whole being and to our relationships.

I do not believe that unforgiving spirit is from the Lord. Forgiveness is a major characteristic of Jesus, and therefore, forgiveness must be evident in the lives of all followers of Jesus. Jesus taught and practiced true forgiveness.

Both forgiveness and unforgiveness are willful choices we make in daily life. The word *forgiveness* is used many times in the bible. Forgiveness is to cease to blame or hold resentment against someone. It also carries the idea of canceling a debt. We choose either to forgive or not to forgive. We can forgive if we intentionally choose to forgive, and the opposite is same. Unforgiveness is a poison to our soul, our body, and our relationships with God and fellow brothers and sisters.

Unforgiveness is as dangerous as cancer or Ebola. It eats away at us from the inside until it clearly shows on our outside and we die. It steals our peace of mind; it holds us in perpetual bondage to the person who wounded us. To the extent that we choose not to forgive—not to let go of—something that is eating us up, we consciously or unconsciously continue to commit spiritually suicidal wounds to ourselves. How can we be set free from the sin of our unforgiveness? The answer involves a painful choice. But it is a choice that sets us free and secures our own forgiveness.

It is said that people who have been forgiven should be the most forgiving people. And yet we find the opposite in the church today. All Christians have experienced forgiveness of sin several times in their walk with Jesus. Unfortunately, some of us who claim to be children of God and flowers of Jesus are too hurt to forgive those who have wounded us.

If you want to know why you have to forgive and show kindness to the person who has terribly hurt you, look at how King David treated Mephibosheth, the grandson of Saul, and why he did so. Then, you will get a glimpse into the heart of God, and this will challenge you to forgive even your worst enemy.

Forgiveness is possible when you understand and have experienced God's own forgiveness. Refusal to forgive as Christ has forgiven us is an indication that we have not truly experienced the life-changing work of God's forgiveness or that we selfishly want to be forgiven but are never ready to extend the same grace to other who offends us.

You may not have had a choice over the actions of the people who inflicted painful wounds upon you. But you do have a choice over how you respond to those who have hurt you. You can choose to forgive them. An unwillingness to forgive suggests that you yourself have not been truly healed.

It is true that you are hurting from the wounds that others inflicted upon you. However, as painful as your wounds may be, there is another wound that is worse than those that have been inflicted upon you by others. The worst wounds that can ever be inflicted upon you are those inflicted upon yourself by your decision not to forgive your offender. The sin of unforgiveness can be fatal to the quality of your life now and can affect eternal destiny.

Is your present life being controlled by the hurts of the past? Have you allowed the past hurts to continue to steal the joy of your present life? Are you still wondering why you must forgive and forget? The story of David and Mephibosheth teaches that the most compelling reason to forgive is not because that individual deserves it or because the person has asked for it. David forgave for Jonathan's sake. Forgiveness "for Christ's sake" is the healing ointment for our past wounds.

Scars of Hope

Remember, our Lord Jesus Christ Himself bears some scars in his hands, side, and feet. His scars are reminders of wounds inflicted upon him when he came to save us and to die for us. But in the scars of Christ, all who carry ugly scars can find healing and hope.

On that Good Friday—the day of his crucifixion—evil men drove nails into His hands and feet, and they thrust a spear into his body. When he rose triumphantly from the dead on the third day, his glorious body still bore the scars of his past suffering, pain and death. But instead of feeling angered and hiding those scars because of shame, Christ displays them to give us victory, comfort, assurance and hope.

Yes our risen Savior also carries some ugly scars, but he did not hide his scars. When he appeared to doubting Thomas, Christ invited Thomas to see his hands and to put a hand into the scar in his side (John 20:27). Through the scars he identified with the disappointment, fears, doubts and pain of Thomas and every other follower of Christ. In the scars of Christ, every human scar can find healing.

But there's more. Even when we get to heaven, the scars of Christ will be an eternal reminder of what he did to save us. We turn now to the words of the Old Testament prophet Zechariah to describe what will happen one day when we also see our loving Savior: "If someone asks, 'What are these wounds on your body?' they will answer, 'The wounds I was given at the house of my friends'" (Zech.13:6). From Calvary to all eternity, we discover why our Lord would not let go of us. The imprint of the nails—the scars of Christ—will tell the story of our wonderful redemption and the dear price by which it was purchased.

If we have repented of our sins and accepted Christ as our Savior and Lord, then we need not continue suffering shame, guilt, and pain from our ugly past. In the scars of Jesus, we find hope and healing for all our pains and scars. Therefore, in the words of Isaac Watts, let us go back to Calvary and "survey the wondrous cross on which the Prince of Glory died." Let us "see from Jesus' head, his hands, his feet" and ask why He suffered so much. When we do so, His scars will transform our own ugly scars of pain and regret into scars of hope and love.

Frank wears many hats: pastor, District Superintendent for Ghana North District, NCM Coordinator for Africa West Field Anglophone, and teacher at Nazarene Theological Institute for West Africa. He earned his B.Th. from Africa Nazarene University and an M.A. in spiritual formation from Northwest Nazarene University, and he's currently pursuing a D.Min. from ANU. He and his wife Hanna have three boys and one girl.

Holiness and Health:
Cultivating a Flourishing Life
Joe Gorman

My interest in holiness and health emerged from a clinical depression I experienced several years ago. One of the enduring fruit from that season of depression is the firm conviction that God is concerned not with the kind of holiness that is related only to our spiritual well-being, but with the kind of holiness that leads to the flourishing of our entire lives—mentally, emotionally, physically, and spiritually.

The apostle Paul speaks of this dynamic interrelationship of spirituality, psychology, and biology when he writes to the church at Thessalonica, "May God himself, the God of peace, sanctify you through and through. May your whole spirit, soul, and body be kept blameless at the coming of our Lord Jesus Christ. The one who calls you is faithful and he will do it" (1 Thes. 5:23-24, NIV).

Holiness and the Whole Person

Holiness, as renewal in the image of God, extends to the total person. Because holiness is holistic, it cannot be divided into parts, inward or outward. Genuine holiness embraces heart *and* life, spirit *and* body. Neglecting or underemphasizing one part of our humanity leaves us diminished persons. To live fully flourishing lives in Christ, every aspect of our life must be nourished.

The root meaning of health provides important clues about the vital relationship between holiness and health. As Wendell Berry notes, "The concept of health is rooted in the concept of wholeness. To be healthy is to be whole. The word *health* belongs to a family of words, a listing of which will suggest how far the consideration of health must carry us: *heal, whole, wholesome, hale, hallow, holy.*"[277]

John Wesley, Holiness, and Health

Wesley's insights into the relationship of holiness and health are particularly important for those of us within the Wesleyan-Holiness tradition. In his *Primitive Physic*, a collection of home remedies for various illnesses, Wesley made accessible to the poor what he believed to be the safest, most effective, low-cost therapies

---

277. Wendell Berry, "The Body and the Earth," in *The Unsettling of America: Culture and Agriculture* (San Francisco: Sierra Club Books, 1977), 103.

of his day. Among the various "medicines" Wesley prescribes were prayer ("that old unfashionable medicine"), "the love of God" ("the sovereign remedy of all miseries"), adequate sleep, a "plain diet, and daily, rigorous exercise."[278] By teaching a holistic, pastoral approach of prevention and cure, Wesley refused to minimize the importance of the body in God's redemptive purposes.

Even though Wesley was a preacher and not a physician, he observed throughout his long ministry how physical health or disease influenced the spiritual lives of those to whom he ministered.[279] He was adamant that we must do all we can to care for our health. His pastoral counsel in a letter to Ann Bolton included the urgent admonition, "At all hazards get [medical help]. It is your bounden duty. You are no more at liberty to throw away your health than to throw away your life."[280] Wesley's pastoral concern for health also extended to emotional wellness.[281] Throughout his sermons, letters, and other writings, Wesley weaves together a unique tapestry of holiness and health.

An Invitation to Flourishing Life

God's offer of flourishing life occurs in the midst of life as we actually live it. It is a gracious invitation to integrate into one all the elements of life: worshipping, praying, playing, loving, limited, laughing, fixing and eating meals, working, going to school, exercising, sometimes exhaustion and illness, cleaning the house, traveling, talking, sleeping, aging. All of these are part of what it means to live a fully human, fully alive in Christ. Holiness as human flourishing acknowledges the very quotidian nature of our lives as well as their possibilities and limitations.

Jesus put such a life in the form of an invitation: "Whoever believes in me, as Scripture has said, rivers of living water will flow from within them . . . . I have come that [you] may have life, and have it to the full. . . . Come to me, all you who are weary and burdened, and I will give you rest." (John 7:38; 10:10; Matt. 11:28, NIV).

Jesus' call to overflowing, abundant life has repercussions for every aspect of our lives. His invitation may not usually be heard as a call to holiness, but that

---

278. See John Wesley, *Primitive Physic: Or, An Easy and Natural Method of Curing Most Diseases, in The Works of John Wesley,* Third Edition, Thomas Jackson, ed. (London: Wesleyan Methodist Book Room, 1872. Reprinted edition, Kansas City: Beacon Hill Press of Kansas City, 1979), 14:313-316.

279. See Randy Maddox, "John Wesley on Holistic Healing and Health," *Methodist History,* 46:1 (2007), 5. Maddox has counted close to 100 medical works Wesley cites or mentions during his lifetime.

280. John Wesley, "Letter to Ann Bolton, July 13, 1774," http://wesley.nnu.edu/john-wesley/the-letters-of-john-wesley/wesleys-letters-1774/. Accessed July 7, 2014.

281. For one example of Wesley's integrative approach to emotional disorders, see "Thoughts on Nervous Disorders; Particularly that which is Usually Termed Lowness of Spirits," *Works* (Jackson), 11:516-19.

is exactly what it is. It is a call to fully integrated, flourishing lives in relation to God, others, ourselves, and all creation.

Suffering and Limitations

While holiness and health are intimately interrelated, there is no simplistic relationship between them. Cultivating a flourishing life does not ignore or minimize the pain of others or our own. Many of us are deeply wounded people. Part of the human predicament is that our lives sometimes include inexplicable suffering. Some of us are healed and others of us experience chronic illness or even death no matter how Christlike or fervently we seek health through every available means.

Flourishing in life is about rising up as we are able. It is "doing what we can, with what we have, where we are."[282] By God's grace we seek to cultivate the health of which our bodies are capable as well as to accept those limitations over which we have no control. Moment by moment we discern, guided by the Holy Spirit and wise counsel of others, what can be healed and what cannot, where we can nourish health and where we cannot.

This is the unavoidable underside of holiness, health, and flourishing that must be acknowledged or else everything else said here is a neo-gnostic denial of the embodied conditions in which we and our loved ones live.[283] The Wesleyan optimism of grace shines rays of hope and healing into whatever dark corners may exist in our lives. Whatever limitations we or our loved ones may face, there is indeed a flourishing of life that is possible and appropriate to each of our capacities in whatever circumstances in which we find ourselves.

Flourishing Life and Love of Neighbor

Cultivating a flourishing life is a form of neighbor love. When we flourish, we bear fruit. When there is an abundant crop, there is enough for others. Well-meaning Christians may say that self-care is selfish, but the truth is this: when our bodies are exhausted, hurting, or sick, we cannot love well. For this reason alone, holiness as flourishing is not a self-centered project. We care for ourselves because we are the beloved of God, but also because we seek to be good stewards of the one and only life we have been given.

A healthy life has clear missional implications. We can't engage in mission—"make Christlike disciples in the nations"[284]—for example, if we're dead. Healthy

---

282. This quote is often attributed to Theodore Roosevelt, "Do what you can, with what you have, where you are."

283. For a hopeful, but yet realistic discussion of holiness, weakness, and limitation, see Diane Leclerc, *Christian Holiness: The Heart of Wesleyan-Holiness Theology* (Kansas City: Beacon Hill Press of Kansas City, 2010), 244-252.

284. This is the mission of the Church of the Nazarene. See http://nazarene.org/ministries/superintendents/mission/display.html. Accessed July 5, 2014.

minds, emotions, bodies, and relationships are essential to living well our divine vocation in the world. Holistic health enables us to live as fully alive participants in God's reconciliation of all things in Christ.

Healthy, whole lives mirror the abundant life of the Trinity. A genuinely healthy life is a call to be the eyes, ears, hands, and feet of Jesus in the world. As we participate in the generous nature of the triune God, we reflect God's presence in the world by living overflowing lives of faith, hope, love, joy, peace, gratitude, and generosity.

How Do We Cultivate a Flourishing Life?

Flourishing human lives do not happen by accident. Healthy habits require intentional cultivation, hard work, self-discipline, and encouragement from others. Holistic practices that nurture a flourishing life expand our understanding of the scope of salvation to include elements of life we may not immediately connect with spiritual health but are essential to being holy and healthy people. Such practices include, but are not limited to, setting aside time to play, getting adequate sleep, regular exercise, eating healthily, cultivating an emotionally healthy life, learning to manage depression and stress, constructing a theology of success and failure, balancing care for ourselves with care for others, participating in Christian community, and living a life of service to others. These practices are not reducible to human effort alone, but they are very similar to what John Wesley referred to as "means of grace."[285] Assisted by grace, such practices, when developed into mature habits, form us into the kind of persons who live more fully in every facet of our lives, wholeheartedly loving God, others, ourselves, and all creation.

May God help us and our churches to develop the habits that enable us to be worshipping communities in which holiness, health, and genuinely flourishing lives are rooted and nourished. As we wholeheartedly love God, others, ourselves, and all creation, we will reflect the glory of God to the world in healthy, well-rested, holistic mission.

Joe is Associate Professor of Practical Theology at Northwest Nazarene University. He is also the executive director of Compassion for Africa, a non-profit organization that partners in mission with local communities in Africa. He was a pastor in Golden, Colorado for almost twenty-one years. He is currently writing a book: Soul-Flourishing: Cultivating a Fully Alive Life. *A few of the activities that help him to flourish are gardening, backpacking, and getting eight hours of sleep a night.*

---

285. See Wesley's sermon, "Means of Grace," Sermon 16 (1746), in Albert C Outler, ed. *The Works of John Wesley* (Nashville: Abingdon Press, 1984), 1:376-394.

Alcohol and the Holy Church in the 21st Century:

Moving Beyond the Confines of the Past Century

Kevin Lambert

Timmy is a member of the Church of the Nazarene. He is 44 years old, but a birth defect impaired his cognitive development so that he never matured into adulthood. When Timmy was a teenager he had just enough social awareness to recognize he was different, but never knew how or why. Like all teenagers Timmy longed for friendship and acceptance, but often felt isolated and alone.

When he turned 21, he finally found acceptance at a local bar. His former high school classmates quickly realized that if they took Timmy drinking with them and got him drunk, he would entertain them for hours. Twenty-three years later they still take him drinking whenever possible so that they can watch Timmy act out ridiculous antics for their amusement.

Unfortunately, Timmy's self-control completely collapses after a few drinks. More often than not his drunken ways involve hitting on and groping local women who then press charges for sexual harassment. Timmy has spent a fair share of time before a judge and in a jail cell. Yet he still gets drunk most nights, knowing that alcohol is the only way to get the acceptance he so desperately craves.[286]

Peter is a board member of a Church of the Nazarene congregation. He is an insightful leader who devotes his wealth and time to the underprivileged in his community. After a hard day of work he enjoys a drink with liquor. It helps him relax and sleep well. He would never dream of giving up that "hot drink" because it is as much a part of his life as his tractor or his cell phone.

David recently joined a Church of the Nazarene congregation. He is a recovering alcoholic and single dad. David's family and friends all drink alcohol, many of them to excess. David has never known a time in his life when alcohol was not present, but it recently played a part in several abusive spats with his girlfriend who was the mother of his children. She finally left him and the

---

286. This story and the following stories are all of true people whom I know. I changed the names out of respect for them.

children. David is committed to becoming sober, but he has never gone more than a month without getting drunk because his friends and family do not support his sobriety.

Rick is a committed Church of the Nazarene layperson. As he was growing up in church, he was taught never to drink. However, in college he was convinced by a mentor that Christians need to enter into bars in order to engage in friendship evangelism. With mixed feelings Rick went to a local bar and talked to people about Jesus. To his surprise he found they were quite receptive to the gospel, so he continues to go a few times a week where he shares a few drinks and discusses God with any who will listen.

Then, there is my story. I am a 1st generation member of the Church of the Nazarene but a fifth generation teetotaler. My grandfather was a minister, as was his grandfather. Both of them ministered among alcoholics over the course of their lives and thought that complete abstinence from alcohol was the most compassionate form of evangelism to that community. I have continued in that vein by ministering in an inner city Rescue Mission and then pastoring in my current parish where the alcohol flows as freely as firearms (a dangerous combination to be sure).

Such a diversity of stories among these members of the Church of the Nazarene might surprise the parents of The Holiness Movement who considered abstinence from alcohol an essential component of their teaching and practice. For example, in the late 1800s, Phineas Bresee's prohibition efforts in Pasadena earned him death threats from local saloon owners. At the time he also claimed the Church of the Nazarene had a twofold mission, "holiness and temperance."[287]

The century between Phineas Bresee's prohibition efforts and Rick's friendship evangelism in local bars has been a long one, as is well documented in Mark Quanstrom's *A Century of Holiness Theology*. Quanstrom describes a doctrine of sanctification that was born out of the cultural optimism of the late 19th century but was forced to change as society became more cynical throughout the 20th.

He argues that the founders of the Church of the Nazarene optimistically believed the sanctification of individuals would lead to the sanctification of society.[288] The thinking was that, as individuals lived holy lives, society would become perfect. Concerning alcohol, this meant it was the Christian's responsibility to abstain from buying and selling alcohol in hopes of enacting societal reform.

287. Bangs, Carl O. "Pasadena." *Phineas Bresee: Pastor to the People* (Kansas City: Beacon Hill, 2013) 103-16

288. Quanstrom, Mark R. "Perpetuating the American Ideal." *A Century of Holiness Theology* (Kansas City: Beacon Hill, 2003) 13-25

This understanding was lost in the 20th century as an increasingly pessimistic society lead the heirs of the Holiness Movement to redefine sanctification as a matter of individual purity. This change is illustrated by what I was taught in a Nazarene Sunday School class in the late 1990s. My teacher explained that alcohol was a substance that corrupted the individual, so I should not drink alcohol in order to keep myself pure for heaven.

Twenty years have passed since that lesson, and most in my generation have flatly rejected the idea that alcohol makes one impure. Furthermore, the notion that abstinence from alcohol will effect greater societal change is thought to be as antiquated as the optimism that gave rise to it. Instead, as a recent article in *Time Magazine* made clear, the common belief is that prohibition led and still leads people to over consume alcohol.[289]

In the past 20 years, I have also become convinced by the arguments of several prominent Christians who locate the realm of holiness and ethics not in the individual but in the church. Simply put, I believe holiness flow out of ecclesiology.

In such a view Christians are not the 20th century individuals who are keeping their souls pure for heaven, nor are they the Holiness Movement and social gospel optimists who are seeking to perfect society. Instead, they are members of Christ's body, the Church. Christians are called out of the world by a loving God to become members of a community whose relational structures witness to the call of God to "be holy as I, the Lord your God, am holy."[290]

In such a formulation, holiness is less about the individual's choices and more about the community whose individuals love each other in a way that models the love displayed in the Trinity. This means holiness is not the pessimism of keeping individuals pure for heaven while the earth goes to hell. Neither is it the out-of-control optimism that seeks to sanctify all society through the private choices of individuals. Instead, it is about how the worship and sacraments of the Church form and shape the community into a body that expresses the love of the Trinity.[291]

Regarding alcohol, this means that holiness is about how Timmy, Rick, Peter, David and myself worship together in the church. Our congregation cannot be like Timmy's group of friends who only accept Timmy when he is drunk and

---

289. Paglia, Camille, "It's Time to Let Teenagers Drink Again" *Time Magazine*, May 19th, 2014.

290. See Leviticus 19:2 and 1 Peter 1:15-16

291. For a more detailed understanding of this view see Hauerwaus, Stanley. "A Community of Character." (Notre Dame: University of Notre Dame Press, 1981). Or Wilson, Jonathan R. "Why Church Matters" (Grand Rapids, MI: Brazos Press, 2006). Or Harink, Douglas. *Paul Among the Postliberals: Pauline Theology Beyond Christendom and Modernity* (Grand Rapids, MI: Brazos Press, 2003).

entertaining. Neither can the Church join with David's family in telling David he is worthless and unacceptable because he cannot drink moderately and so refuses to drink. Instead, the Church must be willing to understand David and Timmy's stories and respect the boundaries they need for healing and community.

At the same time, the church cannot shame or alienate the moderate drinkers in its ranks like Peter and Rick. Doing so would only set up a structure that alienates instead of loves.

Practically, this means that holiness is less about Peter's choice to enjoy a "hot drink" every evening and more about whether Peter is willing to sacrifice his drink on the evenings when David comes to dinner. And holiness would certainly demand that Rick be a responsible Christian brother who leaves the bar with Timmy before Timmy becomes the evening's amusement. However, it also means the church should rejoice when Rick brings a new friend from the bar to church, and the church should not shy away from being associated with Peter's compassionate efforts in the community.

In all such cases, the Church becomes holy as its members are willing to listen to each other's stories and then act lovingly in light of those narratives. When we do so with alcohol or any other issue, the community of faith will be made perfect as God the Holy Trinity is perfect.

Kevin Lambert is a Senior Pastor in a small town in Northeast Oregon. He graduated from NNU in 2008 and from Nazarene Theological Seminary in 2012. He is a long distance runner who also coaches the local high school's Cross Country and Track teams.

Positive Holiness

Rustin E. Brian

"I'm a Nazarene, and so I don't_____."

Fill in the blank: drink, smoke, chew, play cards, go to movies, go to public swimming pools, wear certain types of clothing, or hang out with "those people."

I do not want to downplay the value of abstinence or not conforming to the ethics of the world. At their best, such practices help the Church to be the Church and also help the world to know itself as the world. Such practices can positively testify to our identity as followers of Christ. The Gospel is not the good news of Epicureanism, after all.

However, there are some very insidious side effects to such a negative self-identification unless coupled with a heavy dose of grace and strong attention to the positive aspects of holiness. It is true that at the heart of the call to holiness is a call to be set apart—to be different. But intimately tied to this call is a positive purpose: for the sake of the world.

Consider the Scriptural witness to our positive calling as a holiness people, "Now therefore, if you obey my voice and keep my covenant, you shall be my treasured possession out of all the peoples. Indeed, the whole earth is mine, but you shall be for me a priestly kingdom and a holy nation" (Exodus 19:5-6, NRSV). And again, "But you are a chosen race, a royal priesthood, a holy nation, God's own people, in order that you may proclaim the mighty acts of him who called you out of darkness into his marvelous light. . . Conduct yourselves honorably among the Gentiles, so that. . . they may see your honorable deeds and glorify God when he comes to judge" (1 Peter 2:9-12, NRSV).

Remember that God's promise to Abram was that all the families of the Earth would be blessed through him (Genesis 12:5). Opening up the blessing does not way degrade their status in any way. If anything, the opening up of the covenant with Israel reaffirms and secures their place as blessed.

Unfortunately, many Israelites lost this sense of the purpose of the covenant, at least as it extends beyond the house of Israel. The same might be said for "Holiness people," for whom the calling to be holy or set apart is central to our understanding of the *Missio Dei* or the mission of God.

A recent survey of the "Religious Landscape" in the US reveals that holiness churches fare extremely poorly at retaining their young people.[292] The survey reports that only 32% of those who were raised in the holiness tradition remained in the same tradition as adults. That's 20 percentage points lower than the average Protestant retention rate. Within the grouping of "evangelical families," the holiness tradition scores the lowest retention rate by far. Anabaptists are next, retaining 40% of their childhood members, with Baptists coming in the best with a whopping 60% retention rate.

While we must be careful when assessing statistics, these numbers should be cause for great concern. Perhaps we have spent so much time negatively defining ourselves that we no longer know how to live graciously or to articulate the positive reasons for our distinct tradition.

For example, one of my former parishioners was heavily involved, one of the most spiritually mature men in the congregation, and a very faithful tither. Despite all of this, though, the previous pastor denied him membership in the church on the grounds that he smoked cigarettes and that the *Manual* forbids such a practice. In fact, smoking is strongly discouraged in the *Covenant of Christian Conduct* (29.5), but is this a requirement, or a suggestion? The *Manual* calls the code of conduct a "help and guide to holy living" (28.2).[293] After prayerfully considering the matter, I encouraged him to attend the first membership class I led, and I happily welcomed him into membership soon after. Do I think that his smoking is a healthy habit? No. But I certainly don't think that it should keep him from membership.

I've heard similar stories involving other social issues from each of the various churches that I have attended over the years. What is it about our polity and/or our theology that renders this sort of thing common? What would be wrong with this man joining the church and continuing to smoke? Perhaps with time he would quit. Perhaps not. What do we have to lose? Perhaps the better question is what do we have to gain?

I remember with great joy the many cigarette butts outside the front door of another church I pastored. We would often find an entire carton of cigarettes in our welcome area, waiting for one particular member who was battling homelessness. While I am in no fan of cigarette smoke, I was thrilled that we

---

292. "US Religious Landscape Survey," Pew Forum on Religion and Public Life, 2013. http://religions.pewforum.org/pdf/report-religious-landscape-study-full.pdf. Accessed 06/11/2014. (See page 31, in particular.) Of course, there are many different traditions of holiness people. Nonetheless, for the purposes of this essay, all those in the holiness tradition will be grouped together in the style of the Pew study.

293. Throughout the history of the Church of the Nazarene's existence, we have not always agreed upon what is a rule and what is a suggestion. This was especially true of the early Southern groups that merged into the Church of the Nazarene. While we agreed on doctrine, we sometimes differed on social practices. The same is true today.

had people in recovery, people who were homeless, people who were living their difficult lives in the midst of our congregation. That congregation got a lot of things wrong, but it sure got this right: holiness is about loving God and loving people—regardless of their choices.

I wholeheartedly affirm the suggestion to abstain from tobacco use. It is an unhealthy, destructive habit, stemming from one of the most oppressive industries of all time. That said, refraining from using tobacco products has no direct connection to the Gospel and little indirect connection.

In the case of the man who was denied membership, the evidences of his dedicated discipleship to Jesus were clear. He was living a Christ-like life. He could not check the "do not smoke" box, however. Meanwhile, there were many other people in the congregation who were allowed into membership, who did not smoke, but for whom the evidences of their dedicated discipleship to Jesus were less apparent, to put it mildly. The embrace of negative holiness, in this instance, had a negative effect on the congregation and the man denied membership.

On the other hand, in the second situation, where a man's addiction to tobacco was accepted by the congregation, and where people were welcome to smoke near the entrance to our building, positive holiness was being modeled by welcoming those in recovery from serious addictions. The fact that they smoked was far less important than the fact of their progress. We cared more about where they had been, where they were going, and the One whom they were following.

Our *don'ts* don't make us holy unless they are coupled with what we actually do. That's one reason I like Lent so much. During the season of Lent, we encourage parishioners not to simply give something up, but to give something up so that they will have more time to replace that practice or item with loving God and others. Thus, one should not simply give up Facebook for Lent, but she should replace her time spent on Facebook with time spent in prayer and in service of others. In this way, Lent, which is often viewed as a negative season and practice, is actually quite positive. I think it is time to view our tradition in the same way.

It is undeniably true that, as a holiness church, there are certain things from which we abstain. I fear though that we have lost the ability to articulate and, even more importantly, the ability to live out the reasoning behind such a stance. We must recover, embrace, and intentionally articulate the positive reasons for abstaining if we are to retain any sense of intelligibility in the world in which we live. Moreover, this positive identification must be coupled with positive social engagement with those around us. We must embrace a positive holiness rather than remaining stuck in the logic of negative holiness.

The consumption of alcohol is perhaps the greatest example for us. Historically, members of the Church of the Nazarene do not drink. However, early members did not abstain from drinking alcohol because they believed alcohol is inherently sinful. (Remember Jesus turning the water into wine?) Our historic tea-totaling stance emerged because early Nazarenes were actively engaged in ministry to those whose lives had been torn apart by addiction. They chose to abstain because of their desire for solidarity with the broken, as a social witness against the destructive power of alcohol, and as a voice against the alcohol industry. It was a social stance.

Over the years, though, the fading of our social understanding of abstention has rendered our historic stance practically unintelligible. Unofficial polls and personal experience tell me that the Church of the Nazarene's historic stance against alcohol is not something shared by younger generations.

Unfortunately, though, alcohol may have an even more widespread and destructive hold on society than it did in the early 1900's. I contend that we still need a collective ecclesial witness against alcohol, but this stance must be coupled with a deliberate and gracious ministry to those who are in the grips of addiction and in recovery if it is to be both faithful and effective. People can accept a socially responsible policy, such as abstaining from alcohol, when clear and positive examples are evident as to its importance.

While what we choose not to do matters, it is imperative that the world know what activities we intentionally choose to do and why. Just as much, we must embrace those who do our *don'ts*. Our unconditional love may be their strongest means of grace to move them toward holiness. We are called out, set apart, part of a kingdom of priests, a holy nation—not for our own sake—but for the sake of the world.

Rusty is the Lead Pastor of Renton Church of the Nazarene and Adjunct Professor of Theology at Northwest Nazarene University. He earned a Ph.D. in Theology & Ethics in 2011 from Garrett-Evangelical Theological Seminary. He is the author of Covering Up Luther: How Barth's Christology Challenged the Deus Absconditus That Haunts Modernity *(Cascade, 2013) and* Jacob Arminius: The Man From Oudewater *(forthcoming T&T Clark/Bloomsbury, 2015).*

Holiness Is Reaching Out

Kazimiera Fraley

As one who has grown up in the Church of the Nazarene, the concept of holiness has always been before me. I have heard holiness preached since I was a small child counting pages in the hymnal to entertain myself during evening services. I can remember desiring to receive what seemed to be the ever elusive gift of sanctification as early as the age of eight, always desiring all of what God had to offer so I could be the person God wanted me to be. I spent much time concentrating on what the *Manual* told me to do and how to live according to the rules. I sought God's best in all that I did and all that I was, as a preacher instructed me. And even when I realized that my efforts were not what made me holy and gave myself over to the will of God, I was continually deeply concerned with what it meant for me to be holy.

As a pastor, my desires changed somewhat. I was no longer concerned solely with being a holy person. I became more and more concerned with how to lead a holy people. How does this congregation—we as the people of God in this place in this time -reflect God's holiness in our city and in our world?

In coming to understand what it means to be a holy people, I explored what it means to say that God is holy. There are all the typical characteristics. God is separate, other, pure. God is light, and in God there is no darkness. God is good, and in God there is no evil. But these definitions did not really help us figure out how to be holy as a people.

So I began to explore what it means for God to be holy by looking at what God does. God lives in Holy Triune Community. The Trinity lives in eternal loving relationship, and that eternal loving relationship seems to propel God outside of God's Self. The holy Triune God of the universe is always reaching out to be in communion with us, with humanity. From the beginning of Genesis to the end of Revelation, the heart of the whole Bible is: *God so loved the world—each and every one of us—that God sent the only begotten Son to us, to draw us into relationship, to restore communion. And that same Son says to us, "Be holy as I am holy," and "Be holy as the Father is holy."*

And so we created a list? That seems to fall short on some level—many levels.

How do we, the people of God, a community of faith, a congregation in the Church of the Nazarene, strive to be holy as God is holy? Do we create walls saying who is in who is out? Do we create lists saying who is good enough and who is not?

Well, in some ways, we did. But being a holy person of God has to be something better, something more profound, something holier than that. If the holy community of the Triune God of the universe is eternally reaching out to us in love, then it seems only logical that a community of faith attempting to be holy as God is holy should also be continually reaching out to the world with the love of God. We should continual do everything we can to show our world, our community, and our city that God loves them.

When the First Church of the Nazarene in Cambridge began to envision what this looked like, for us to be continually reaching out, continually sharing the love of God with our world, we began by looking at the very first disciples. After all, they seemed to do a pretty good job getting this whole thing started. We spent a season in Acts, looking at them and seeing what they did.

On some level, we wondered if the church had things "all wrong." In our experience, the church threw an event and said to the world around it, "Come." But that is not what the early disciples did. They went out. They went to hilltops. They went to synagogues. They hung out near the women down by the river, in the streets, and the city squares.

So we decided that we would do something radical. One Sunday a month we would leave our sanctuary behind, and we would go out into our neighborhood, into our city, and do something to reach out to the people in the world around us. How will they know unless we tell them? How can we tell them unless we are where they are—wherever they are?

We also liberally translated the idea of "speaking in tongues" to see that not only on Pentecost did the disciples speak to the people in languages they could understand, but that every time they went out, in everything they did they were using "languages" which spoke to the people to whom they were ministering. To the needy, they gave clothes. The hungry, they fed. They spoke to the Jews about Abraham and Isaac and to the Philosophers about "the unknown" God. Wherever they were, whatever they were doing, they used the language that was needed to speak to the people around them.

We thought about it and realized that people have a hard time *hearing* about Jesus. But if we lived God's love before them, if we spoke in the language of giving and serving, if we hosted family events for our neighboring families, if we offered food to hungry people, or if we hosted something that put people in the place of honor who would not normally find themselves honored, then this could be what it truly means to speak to the people of our community and our city in languages they would understand.

It began as an experiment. We called it "A Summer of Serving." Between May and September, we went out every three weeks. We began by reaching out to the families to whom we minister through a baby pantry, throwing a brunch in the courtyard across the street, but really we served anyone who stopped by. We then spent the next three serving Sundays throwing "Family Fun Days" in the park. We offered crafts, snacks, and family friendly games to the families who gather on Sundays in a nearby park. We closed our Summer of Serving by hosting a community cookout to which everyone was invited.

We did so without any expectation. We had no "agenda." We just talked to our neighbors and got to know them. If they decided to ask us who we were and why we did this (and they did ask), we told them that we were the church around the corner and just wanted provide something nice to our community.

The idea was originally something to explore who were and who God was calling us to be as a community. We were searching for what it meant to be the holy people God was calling us to be. It was an experiment; it was "just for the summer."

But at the end of the Summer of Service, we could not imagine going back. Our old way of being the Church seemed empty and self-serving. If all we did was worship and offer activities for those in our congregation, how did we expect to be a people who were continually reaching out to our community? How could we live God's holiness before the world unless we were coming in contact with the world around us? If we wanted to be the holy people God was calling us to be, we had to continue to reach out to our community, to our neighbors, and to our city.

So once a month for the last year, we have taken at least part of one Sunday to practice what it means to be holy by reaching out with God's love to our community. Sometimes, that means handing out coffee at a busy pedestrian intersection. Sometimes, that means putting together kits for families in our city displaced by a fire in their homes. Whether it meant gathering and collecting items to give others in our community or actually going out and doing something in and for our community, we always did *something*.

In the process, we have come to a new understanding of what it means to say that—as a local congregation of the global Church of the Nazarene—we are a holiness people. It means reaching out. It means giving. It means becoming a part of the world around us, instead of insulating ourselves from it. It means loving as

God loved following God's example of going out, and following the examples of the early Christians by going to where the people are and speaking in languages that they can understand.

Kazimiera I.H. Fraley pastors the Nazarene Church in Cambridge, Massachusetts, where she lives with her husband and two school-aged daughters. She also serves as a barista at a nearby Starbucks where she makes way too many cappuccinos before 5:30 in the morning. In her spare time, she enjoys cycling with her husband and backpacking with her best friend.

The Economics of Sanctification

Ryan Quanstrom

In the summer of 1999, I took a life changing trip to NYC 99 in Toronto. I attended helpful lectures, spectacular worship services, and incredible concerts. While I had fun crowd surfing to "We Want to See Jesus Lifted High," the service learning experience stands out as quite poignant.

I was put on a team that cleaned out a creek in Toronto. We pulled out hundreds of bottles and plastic bags. I spent nearly an hour digging out a plastic shopping cart. I thought this all incredibly strange. Why was all of this garbage in a creek? It kept human beings and other wildlife from enjoying fresh water, which is a gift from God. I asked the leader why it was there; he said laziness. This also seemed odd to me. Why spend time and money cleaning up another person's mess? Wouldn't it be easier if we found a way to keep people from throwing their trash in the creek? That would prevent wasted time and energy. I'm fairly certain I threw a bottle out the charter bus window two days later.

This one creek, however, is not unique. Earlier this year, officials discovered that one of Duke Energy's coal ash ponds leaked more than 82,000 tons of ash into the Dan River in North Carolina, where I live. The ash ponds contain arsenic, selenium, chromium, thallium, mercury, and lead. These are now in the rivers that provide drinking water to thousands of people. Why is this watershed polluted? Duke Energy ignored problems and did not properly line its coal ash ponds. Why did they chose to do that? Perhaps it was simply sloth; maybe it was greed. Most likely it was a combination of the two.

While I would like to push all the blame on Duke Energy, I cannot. I use a smart phone and other electronic devices, so I use Duke Energy's electricity every day. I want to pay as little as possible for electricity. In the name of customer satisfaction, Duke Energy has polluted the Dan River and endangered thousands of lives, all for me and other consumers like me. What is worse, they are using mountain top removal techniques to get the coal that they burn. I pay Duke Energy to level mountains, a non-renewable resource.

My involvement in the degradation of God's creation is not limited to Duke Energy. Large scale beef farming is absurd. First, we gather natural gas from any number of sources, including fracking. We then process this into ammonia based fertilizer. We spread this on land through a petroleum based machine. Then, we use petroleum based machines to plant and harvest corn. These machines increase soil compaction and erosion. We then feed corn to cows, but since cows do not naturally digest corn, they are fed antibiotics. The cows are held in CAFOs (Concentrated Animal Feeding Operations). This means that they often live in pens barely larger than themselves, often in piles of feces and urine. This waste is typically collected in ponds that become toxic. Usually, manure is useful as fertilizer, not with CAFOs. Beyond disrespecting the animal as a part of God's good creation for which we are to care, the cow is typically shipped in vehicles that use petroleum and processed using electric machines that are powered by coal. The emphasis of this entire process is efficiency. The goal is a "cheap" burger. While this burger may not cost the consumer much money at the register, its costs are degradation of the land and the animals that inhabit this land.

But what can be done? Who really wants the land destroyed and animals disrespected in such manner? Could those who were created to tend God's garden actually allow such destruction? Can we rationalize this system by looking at the jobs it creates and the number of people who are fed?

In his essay "The Purpose of a Coherent Community," Wendell Berry answers these questions: "It doesn't make any difference that we mostly don't have an alternative to doing as we do; we still share the guilt. In a centralized, specialized, commercialized, mechanized society such as ours, we are all necessarily; and in considerable measure, helping to cause the problems we are helping to deplore, and trying to solve."[294]

This should be distressing to us holiness people. We believe that the God of truth is sanctifying us. We believe that love of neighbor is essential to loving God. How can we properly say that we love neighbors when we are willing to pollute and destroy the world in which our neighbor lives?

The response of many Christians has been similar to cleaning up the creek. We see the rivers polluted, the inner cities full of crime, the rural areas full of poverty. Our response is to create inner city ministries, migrant farmer ministries, after school programs, literacy programs, and pack the bus programs. Churches create soup kitchens, free stores, and food banks. Yet all of these compassionate ministries are not quite adequate. They are always fixing back end programs. They are band aids on broken systems.

At this point many might be willing to admit that a band aid is the best we can do. We will always have the poor among us. We must content ourselves by being the balm in Gilead.

---

294. Wendell Berry, *The Way of Ignorance and Other Essays* (Berkeley, CA: Counterpoint, 2006), 75.

Forgive me if I am too bold, but the God I serve is not that small. The God that I have heard about created the entire universe and called it very good. The greatest enemy to life—death—has been put to death. Death has no victory. Death has no sting. We are the people of the resurrection. We are willing to do the tough work of knowing the disease, so that we might know the cure.

As Church of the Nazarene moves forward, we are going to have to do a better job at defining sin. Wendell Berry gives us the questions we must ask ourselves, "How can we work without doing irreparable damage to the world and its creatures, including ourselves? Or: How can we live without destroying the sources of our life?"[295]

Perhaps we have failed to deconstruct our systems because we prefer to let our systems do the sinning for us. To be certain, we recognize that we are justified by Jesus' faithfulness. We cannot earn our salvation. We cannot even bring the kingdom by force. But if we are going to participate in an economy that destroys God's creation and this world, then we are challenged by Paul: "What then are we to say? Should we continue in sin in order that grace may abound? By no means! How can we who died to sin go on living in it?" (Romans 6:1-2).

The way forward is both simple and complicated. As we work in the world and participate in the economy, we are either providers or purchasers of commodities.

The first move is on the purchasers. When we buy things we must do our research. Does this widget pollute the earth? How are the wages shared? Are the workers given a livable wage? Do the business owners intentionally manufacture in a location that does not have labor laws? What has motivated this business? Does it align with the kingdom? If these answers are negative, then we should not be willing to purchase. The scriptures tell us that God takes care of the sparrows, that God knows our needs. They also tell us that we are not to store up treasures where moth and rust break in and steal. On another occasion, God even told a young ruler to sell everything. If we have truly died with Christ, then this act is not so revolutionary.

When we are the providers, we must broaden our view. How are we defining profit? Is profit found in cash? Do we consider our business successful when we can get rich, or is it successful when the earth and our employees are made to prosper? Put differently, does this business promote the Kingdom of God?

Throughout all of this we must remain Christian, Holiness, and Missional. We are guided by the sixty six books of the Bible, the history of the church, God's gifted reason, and our experience. We cannot except ourselves to have some special status. God has gifted the church in incredible ways.

---

295. Ibid, 59.

We must measure our actions to the rule of faith. We must be holy, because this is the goal we are seeking. We do not let anyone cut in our race that we are running. We do not give up on doing what is right. We must constantly rely on grace knowing that the marathon is a gift.

Finally we must understand that this is our mission. Our original purpose was to tend the garden. We should make every effort to continue tending it. In so doing, we will once again anticipate the heavenly city's descent to earth.

After graduating from Duke Divinity School, Ryan worked with Durham Resurrection Community, a Church of the Nazarene. He is currently working with The Anchor, a Methodist church plant in Wilmington, NC.

How The Monastic Tradition Informs Our Discussion of Sanctification

Rick Lee James

Most of us are pretty far removed from anything resembling monasticism in our culture. After all, monasticism is a form of religious life characterized by abstinence from various worldly pleasures. Our world doesn't abstain from much of anything. The majority of us indulge in the fastest and fattest foods we can find. We pay top dollar to have the fastest internet providers bring information into our homes at lighting speeds. We strive to have the best that we can possibly afford, and if we can't afford it, we simply use credit cards. We don't do very well at abstaining from anything.

Many of our churches have become proponents of this American gospel of extravagance with mega-church pastors preaching a gospel of wealth and health. Most of us can't even abstain from coffee for the hour it takes to hold a worship gathering so we accommodate by building Starbucks style coffee shops right into our houses of worship.

Over the centuries of church history, we have seen our houses of worship change from holy places of reverence to casual, non-offensive, concert style community centers where God is there to high five us and help us to indulge in our appetites. Even God wants us to have it all, right now. No longer do we have to wait upon the Lord. He now comes to us riding on delay filled dotted eights notes from loud electric guitars, soaring in the flashing lights, and projected on video screens.

It seems no pleasure is off limits in our American landscape. The gospel of America virtually makes it a sin to abstain from our desires. We want our best life and we want it now. We are free in this land, free to do whatever we want, free to be ourselves no matter what it costs anyone else. If there is a law blocking what we desire, then it is our right to have those laws repealed. Whatever it takes to have the best high, the wildest sex, and the biggest guns then that's the price that must be paid.

This is what's so revolutionary about monasticism in the midst of a culture that has forgotten how to wait. The life of a monk is characterized by vows of celibacy, poverty, silence, and obedience. A person who lives a monastic lifestyle is noticeably set apart from the rest of the world by the way they live and interact with it. Monks weren't born monks, they had to a choice to follow the call of the world or the call of God, and they chose God. For the sake of knowing Christ, they've forsaken everything to follow the call of Jesus.

Monasticism doesn't just happen; it's a discipline that has to be learned and embrace. I've always been told a person is set apart for Christ not by the things they won't do but by the things they will do. Monastics are actually set apart for both reasons. What makes monastics different is both their willingness not to participate in the capitalistic machine and their willingness to embrace spiritual disciplines of the ancient faith. Remember, by the way, that the goal for a monastic is to become a saint, to be set apart by God, sanctified, and holy.

One of the most well-known and highly regarded monastics of the 20th century is Thomas Merton. In addition to being a Trappist monk who resided at the Abbey of Gethsemane in Kentucky, Merton was also a writer, an ordained priest, a poet, a social activist, and a student of comparative religions. His classic book, *Life and Holiness*, was a guide for monastics (and laity) on incorporating holiness into everyday life while facing the worries and frustrations of the modern age. Merton writes:

> The final step on the way to holiness in Christ is then to completely abandon ourselves with confident joy to the apparent madness of the cross. . . . This madness . . . means a kind of death to our temporal selves. It is a twisting, a letting go, an act of total abandonment. But it is also a final break-through into joy. The ability to make this act, to let go, to plunge into our own emptiness and there find the freedom of Christ in all fullness—this is inaccessible to all our merely human efforts and plans. We cannot do it by relaxing or by striving, by thinking or not thinking, by acting or not acting. The only answer is perfect faith, exultant hope, transformed by a completely spiritual love of Christ. This is a pure gift of his: but we can dispose ourselves to receive it by fortitude, humility, patience, and, above all, by simple fidelity to his will in every circumstance of our ordinary life.[296]

Merton's final sentence in the above quote could have been written by any one of our Church of the Nazarene theologians as a way of describing the work of entire sanctification in the life of a believer. They believe, like Merton, that

---

296. Thomas Merton, *Life and Holiness*, (New York: Image, 1963), 119.

perfect faith can only happen in cooperation with the transforming love of Christ in the Holy Spirit. When Merton is instructing his fellow monks in the way of attaining holiness in this life, it's clear that it can only be done in and through the living Lord.

When members of the Church of the Nazarene talk about being free from original sin, we aren't saying that we no longer have the capacity to sin. We are saying that in Christ, and only in Christ, we have the freedom to do what is right. A life marked by holiness is not a life that can't sin but a life in a state of choosing not to sin. Holiness, the infilling work of the Holy Spirit in the life of the believer, is what allows us to do the impossible in our culture and live holy lives without having to move into a monastery. Holiness is not given as a reward for waiting upon God, rather it is the presence of Christ in us, helping us to overcome.

Members of the Church of the Nazarene and monastics have a common heritage of holiness. Both the sanctified monk and the sanctified Nazarene have an unquenchable passion to be faithful to God in every circumstance of life. We both have a desire to wait upon the Lord, laying aside whatever things may hinder us from pleasing Him. We both believe that daily dying to ourselves by denying many of our natural desires is a path that will lead us to joy. We both believe that total abandonment is both the result of and the path to holiness.

When Merton speaks to his fellow monastics of abandoning self to the cross he's speaking of total surrender of our lives to Christ. Surrender will not make us holy. Only God can do that, but surrender puts into a place where holiness can be received more fully. Monastics are people who are willing to take up their cross, abandon their lives, and follow Jesus. From what I've seen as a lifelong member of the Church of the Nazarene, many of our people are willing to do the same.

Whether you call it Christian perfection, entire sanctification, or monastic holiness, I believe we are speaking of the same thing. From the Catholic scholar Thomas Aquinas to John Wesley, the greatest evidence of holiness was a life that had been changed. Both Nazarenes and monastics agree that human beings are a canvas upon which God is creating His masterpiece. God is the master artist who can bring even the most tattered canvas to life. Holiness seems to be the paint God uses to make the human canvas into a work of art. When we see a human lay down his life to seek the good of others, we see the hand of the Master Artist, the Painter of holiness at work.

Monastics understand that holiness, like good art, takes time. This is why the monastery is such a helpful center for so many on their quest for holiness. It allows the time and space to wait upon the Lord with others who share the common goal of becoming saints.

Likewise, members of the Church of the Nazarene are coming to understand that holiness is an ongoing work in the life of the believer. It may start with total surrender to God, but that's only the start. The way of the cross—the path of surrender—seems to be the way that God chooses to cleanse the canvas for the work of art He has prepared. At the point of total surrender, the Master Artist has only begun laying his first brush strokes upon the canvas. The masterpiece will take a lifetime to perfect.

Rick is a professional singer, songwriter, speaker, author, worship leader, and podcast host. He has worked with Jason Gray, Andrew Peterson, Sara Groves, Michael Card, Brian Zahnd, Tripp York, Brett Mccracken, Ian Morgan Cron, Paul Baloche and many more. In 2013 Rick released his first live album of original songs called, Basement Psalms Live, *and its companion book in 2014:* Out of the Depths: A Songwriter's Journey Through The Psalms. *For more information about Rick's ministry visit his web site at www.RickLeeJames.com.*

Reflecting God:
Empowerment in Holiness and Feminism
Deanna Hayden

I set down the phone, dropped my face in my hands and slowly let the tears fall. As my husband sat nearby, holding our baby boy, he waited for me to settle down enough to explain. A year before, I had felt the Lord's call on my heart to become a senior pastor. Following months of communicating with districts around the country, I had finally interviewed. The leadership of the church had been enthusiastic toward me, and—even as the voices of some were raised questioning the validity of having a female pastor—my responses seemed well received. Several people told me they expected favorable congregational vote. After the vote, however, those questioning voices had carried enough weight to turn down my opportunity to come as their pastor. The apologetic phone call informing me of the decision left me heartbroken and confused.

In a holiness denomination that has ordained women since its inception, how could women be refused the opportunity to fulfill their call simply because of their gender? And from a broader perspective, what is it in the soul of the Church that seems inclined to deny the full equality of men and women? Can the call to a life of holiness speak to the work of feminism? Are they two contrasting theories, or might they relate to each other?

Feminism Defined

Simply defined, feminism is "the theory of the political, economic and social equality of the sexes." Looking through theological and biblical lenses, we could add "religious" to the categories of equality advocated by feminism. In a variety of cultures, this term has taken on negative connotations. Within religious circles including some areas of Christianity, feminism is often assumed to have specific political agendas, and is quickly written off as being irrelevant and even oppositional to a life of Christian faith. The work of feminism is then something to be ignored, if not opposed.

And yet, how can we ignore the difficult realities of inequality that lead to oppression? Examples abound from the whole spectrum of global cultures: sex trafficking, female genital mutilation, "honor" killings, early marriage, prohibition of mobility, limited education, and prohibition of property ownership. In some of these cultures, men use Scripture itself as justification for oppression. At its most foundational level, feminism seeks to free women from oppressive practices and to move toward equality and mutuality of the sexes.

Feminism in Wesleyan-Holiness History

Women in John Wesley's England (1703-1791) faced oppression that seems nearly unfathomable in many developed nations today. Unable to own property, be formally educated, or professionally employed, women were completely dependent upon their fathers or husbands for their livelihood. However, Wesley's mother, Susanna, had a profound impact on him. Despite her own society depriving her of a formal education, she educated all of her children in several languages, including the language of the Holy Spirit. Her theology is evident in the legacy left through Charles and John, as well as her other sons and daughters. Specifically, she encouraged John to empower women to minister alongside of men as leaders, and he did to a great degree.

During the lifetime of Phineas Bresee (1838-1915), the feminist movement—though it wasn't called that yet—began to experience progress. More countries began allowing women to receive a formal education, develop vocations, and to some extent to own property. Somewhat of a contemporary to Bresee, Phoebe Palmer (1807-1874) did the work of a feminist in calling for all people, men and women, to seek the experience of entire sanctification. As part of this experience, people were exhorted to testify publicly. This was perhaps one of the most marked areas where the holiness movement empowered women, as now they were being encouraged to speak in public. The movement sought to include and to empower all people, even and especially those on whom society looked down.

In this sense, holiness and feminism shared similar work of empowerment and inclusion. Bresee continued this empowerment in his ministry. At the prodding of a women's prayer group, he assisted them in opening—and later became president of—a school that welcomed men and women equally. It eventually became known as Point Loma Nazarene University, an institution representing the equality of the Wesleyan-Holiness tradition.

Theological and Biblical Reflections on Holiness and Feminism

One of the things I love most about the doctrine of holiness is its relentless commitment to God's Love being the ultimate power that overcomes sin, and this isn't something we have to wait to experience at the second coming. It is a claim and hope we can hold to now! The Love that was present and working at creation, that journeyed with God's people through their desert wanderings, and that filled the believers at Pentecost is the same Love that seeks to empower us today. When Christ came to earth and took on human flesh, he came to die for our sins, but not only that! He came to show us how to live! His life of holiness shows us how we can live holy lives. As we look at biblical and theological themes in holiness, it is not difficult to see ways where holiness and feminism mirror the same ideas and goals.

In our pursuit of holiness, we seek God's power—available to us through the gift and grace of the Holy Spirit—to help us live in the image of God. When God created people, the story in Genesis tells us they were created after the image of God. The Hebrew word adam used in Genesis 1:27 is best translated "humankind" or "humanity," so it would read, "God created humankind in his image, in the image of God he created them; male and female, he created them." All people have been created in God's image. In that same creation account, God blessed both the man and woman; God gave them both the mandate of overseeing the earth. And as they were both created in God's image, there was no hierarchy in the marriage relationship originally created by God. Some theological perspectives focus on the fallenness of humanity that takes place in Genesis 3 (which describes a hierarchical marriage as part of a curse).

These perspectives believe people will be controlled and dominated by their sinful nature for all of life on earth. But the perspective guiding Wesleyan-Holiness theology proclaims our call to allow the Holy Spirit's power to restore us to God's image, as we were created in the beginning.

Another interesting perspective to glean from men and women being made in God's image is the way God's character reflects both masculine and feminine traits. The God portrayed in a masculine way as a shepherd in Psalm 23 is further imaged in Psalm 22:9-10a as a midwife attending a birth. Yahweh who is called "Father" in Isaiah 64:8 is also described in Isaiah 66:13 as a mother who comforts her child. While God is not male or female, but a transcendent Spirit with no physical body, Scripture uses metaphors of both genders to portray God's image to us.

The deeper we look into the theology of sanctification, the more we see the work of the Spirit empowering people through love to be reflections of the image of God. It is a theology that includes the mutuality of all persons. The work of feminism seeks similar avenues of mutuality between men and women. As we follow the call to be restored in holiness to the image of God, we are not just sanctified as individuals but as the Body of Christ, called to submit mutually to one another out of reverence for Christ.

In these relationships of unity through holiness, all people are recognized equally. We all are in need of God's grace. We all are invited to live holy lives of redemption and restoration. We all are to exercise the gifts given to us by the Holy Spirit. We all are called to minister within the holy priesthood of believers. We all have equal value before God in this: all are invited to receive the grace of sanctification through the power of the Spirit.

What heartbreaking news that phone call brought as I tried to obey the call to pastoral ministry. Just months later, my phone rang again inviting me back to that same church. Eventually, a second vote took place, this time inviting me to be their pastor. In the months and years that have followed, the empowerment of love brought through God's Spirit has broken down walls of bias and bitterness. Holy love has transformed hearts and lives in the church and reached outside the church. What a magnificent reflection of the redemptive power of God's love!

As the empowering work of holiness and feminism continue to come together, may the image of God reflected in the face of the Church be a transforming power that brings the world to know the perfect love of our Lord!

Deanna lives in Raytown, MO, with her husband Ben, and their two children Josiah and Hannah, where she is the Lead Pastor at Southwood Church of the Nazarene. Born and raised in San Diego, she also spent time living and teaching in South Korea. She loves culture and coffee shops, being silly with her family, and serving the Lord in the never-dull adventure of life in ministry!

Sanctification and Addiction

RJ Strickland

A few years ago, while leading our "Compassion Sunday" church service, something life changing happened. On this particular Sunday, a homeless man named Jason gave his heart to the Lord. Later that week, I went to the shelter to lead a Bible study for him and his friends. I remember his eyes lighting up as we read through the whole book of John in a paraphrase, Hawaiian Pigin, version of the bible called "De Jesus Book." We laughed, we cried, we hugged, and we prayed.

Afterwards, he came to me saying he felt convicted to make changes in his life. For the previous 30 years he had been living homeless on the beach with his long-time girlfriend. They were both severely addicted to drugs and alcohol and had five kids. Jason told me, "God wants me to quit drugs and marry my girlfriend." I was so excited! We even made plans to surprise his girlfriend with a wedding that Saturday morning.

I woke up Saturday to a terrible phone call. Late the night before, while Jason's 17-year-old son was driving, their car hit a telephone pole. Jason died instantly. They were both drunk and high. I was devastated. Hadn't he just given his heart to the Lord? Hadn't he just committed to stop the drinking and drugs?

Situations like this can be frustrating, confusing, and ultimately defeating to those in ministry. Many times over the past 18 years I have questioned God's sanctifying power—especially within the context of addiction. I believe the answers to this questioning lie in a better understanding of both addiction and sanctification.

Often, addiction is erroneously viewed as a purely behavioral issue. I've heard phrases such as, "If they were serious about their salvation, they'd just quit," or "If they really cared about me, they'd stop."

The reality is that addiction begins within the human brain. "Altering brain chemistry is at the heart of what creates and sustains addiction."[297] Changes in the brain lead to physical dependence. (The addict cannot "simply stop.") But

---

297. Ohlsclager, G. & Shadoan, J. M., "Alcoholism, Substance Abuse, and Other Addictions: A Comprehensive Christian Approach," *Christian Counseling Today: Addictions in the 21st Century*, 16.1. 12-18 (2008).

addiction also hijacks the attachment center of the brain, ultimately inhibiting one's ability to have joy-filled relationships with God and others.[298]

The cycle of addiction further exacerbates relational issues. Engaging in the addictive behavior (acting out), leads to feelings of despair, guilt and isolation. Over time, relationship to the addictive substance/behavior becomes the primary release from isolation and takes the place of relationship with peers and God. Thus, addiction seems to be primarily a relational problem.

Sanctification is also often misunderstood as a behavioral issue. Many people equate sanctification with behavioral perfection and judge a person's sanctification by focusing on his/her actions. I would posit that, just as addiction is a relational issue, sanctification is also intimately connected to relationship.

Ultimately, sanctification describes the process of becoming holy, the process of "God forming us spiritually into the likeness of Jesus Christ."[299] In its essence, the likeness of Christ is love, and therefore the core of holiness is love. More specifically, holiness is *relational* love. In their book, *Relational Holiness*, Oord and Lodahl write, "To be holy is to love . . . We are holy as God is holy when we love as God loves."[300] In the forward of the same book, Greathouse writes, "By relational holiness, they mean that we are born into a cosmos of relationships. To be human is to be inescapably related to God, creation, and others . . ."[301] Sanctification leading to holiness centers on relationships—people growing by the grace of God in loving relationships, loving God with their entire being and loving others as themselves. Thus, the end goal of the process of sanctification is best described as *relational* holiness.

Because sanctification and addiction are both inescapably relational, addiction necessarily affects the sanctification process. So, how do we understand sanctification in the context of addictions?

When working with addicts, many people in ministry encounter feelings of frustration and defeat because the outward behavioral changes we expect aren't evident. We make the assumption that the addictive behavior will stop at the moment of sanctification. However, addiction is physiological and emotional as well as spiritual. Rewiring and healing of the brain takes time. This is a process in itself, just like sanctification. Therefore, the outward actions of the addict do not necessarily reflect the inward state of his/her heart.

---

298. Khouri, E. & Wilder, E. J. "What is Addiction? How Can Thriving: Recover Your Life Help Me?" (2006). Retrieved from: http://www.lifemodel.org/download.php?type=article&rn=93, June 16, 2014.

299. Leclerc, D & Maddix, M. *Spiritual Formation: A Wesleyan Paradigm* (Kansas City, MO: Beacon Hill, 2011), 13.

300. Oord, T. J. & Lodahl, M., *Relational Holiness* (Kansas City, MO: Beacon Hill, 2005), 72.

301. Ibid, 15.

Let me give you an example. Several years ago, a visitor arrived early to our church. He joined in as we unloaded our sound equipment and began church set up. Then, he disappeared and didn't return for the service. Through a later conversation, I discovered that he had left because after set up he saw our sound man (Let's call him John.) outside smoking a cigarette. The visitor told me that God couldn't possibly work through John because John was engaging in the sin of smoking.

Little did the visitor know that when John first started attending church, he was a drug dealer and an addict. But since then, John had given his heart to the Lord and was slowly changing. He sacrificed his time to be on the worship team. He had given up drugs and his life as a drug dealer, and he was now holding down a regular job and had led over 15 of his friends to the Lord.

Yet all the visitor could see was that John was engaging in a "sinful" act and thus was not in correct relationship with God. It was impossible for this visitor to see John's heart—to see his love for the Lord, to see God's sanctifying power at work. The visitor did not understand sanctification and addiction. Sanctification is an internal process, leading to restored relationship with God and others. This internal "heart change" will eventually manifest in behavioral changes as well, but this takes time. We must take care not to judge the internal state of the heart by outward actions alone.

Better understanding addiction and its relationship to sanctification can help us minister to and support addicts along their recovery process. Essentially, the two move in opposite directions. Addiction destroys relationship while sanctification strengthens relationships with God and others.

In my 18 years of pastoral ministry working with addicts, I view addiction as a relational battle that thrives on despair, guilt, and isolation. In working with people with addictions, I try to circumvent this cycle of addition by:

- helping them gain an understanding of God's incredible love for us and our being made in the image of God (relieves despair)
- teaching them about God's grace and helping them through repentance to receive it (relieves guilt)
- spending time with them and helping them learn how to build and experience a meaningful relationship with God and others, including a loving church community (relieves isolation)

You'll notice these all focus on helping the addict establish deep, meaningful relationships. Sanctification centers on relationships. Therefore, the sanctifying work of God is at the root of recovery.

This is often a long process. It takes time for the brain to heal and time for the addict to learn how to experience quality relationships. In the church, we must be patient and understanding. We must love as God loves and we will see the wondrous transforming sanctifying power of God at work in the lives of addicts.

Remember our sound man John? He now serves on our church board, no longer smokes, is completely sober, currently helps run our recovery group, and has been called to pastoral ministry. Through patient love, the support of a Christian community, and a deeper relationship with Christ, John has been truly transformed. His life is proof of God's sanctifying power at work—even in the life of an addict.

For the past nine years, RJ has served as the planting pastor of Living Waters Church of the Nazarene on the island of Oahu in Hawaii. He is the president of Kokua Compassion Group, a compassionate ministry that serves the underprivileged in our community. Prior to this, he spent nine years in skate park, surf, and youth ministry. He recently authored the book I've Never Told Anyone But... (Finding Hope in the Aftermath of Abuse).

Sanctification and Sustainable Sobriety:
Relational Spirituality in Addiction Recovery
Todd Bowman

Addiction is one of a variety of powerful manifestations of bondage in the modern world. For those seeking freedom from the addictive cycle, Paul's words from Romans 7:19-20 ring especially true, "For I do not do the good I want to do, but the evil I do not want to do—this I keep on doing. Now if I do what I do not want to do, it is no longer I who do it, but it is sin living in me that does it." This framework for bondage and addiction evidences an explicit duality—namely that bondage is reflected physically and psychologically in the addictive process, as well as spiritually in one's orientation toward God, self, others and creation.

At the core root of this addiction-based bondage is the psychosocial experience of shame. In its very essence, shame stands as antithetical to the notion of holiness. Specifically, shame serves as a manifestation of being psychologically cut-off from a primary attachment figure, namely maternal and paternal caregivers throughout childhood. Shame is behaviorally associated with covering and hiding, as manifested in the creation narrative (see Gen. 3); it should also be noted that shame operates identically in our spiritual formation, rendering us "cut-off" in our relationship with God, as seen in Colossians 1:21, "Once you were alienated from God and were enemies in your minds because of your evil behavior."

A sense of disconnection from God serves the primary indicator of sin in the Christian narrative. This rupture in the relationship is designed as a measure of proximity maintenance, similar to when a child returns to their caregiver as a secure base after becoming frightened or violating an established boundary, vis-à-vis a willful transgression against a known law. Sociologically speaking, our contemporary Western conceptualization of "shameless" does not indicate the absence of shame, so much as embody the idea that we have become desensitized to the separation that shame introduces into our relational experience.

From an addiction paradigm, this level of shame is experienced with a breadth and depth that transcends healthy affective functioning, such as feeling a twinge of shame in appropriate circumstances. With rampant individualism as a primary feature of many Western societies, little attention is paid to the impact of self upon others. In many respects, the sense of being cut-off from one another does not serve as feedback about a transgression between people, but rather serves as a mutually constructed state of being within the relationships created by people. This combination of shame and isolation serves as the soil from which objectification sprouts, rendering others not as individuals with a heart, mind, and soul, but rather as a means to a fundamentally egocentric end. This cultural paradigm cannot help but influence how we come to understand relationship with God, self, others and creation.

From a developmental perspective, shame is a very primitive construct that emerges in pre-verbal interpersonal contexts. As such, shame that is not mastered, per Erik Erikson's model, evidences itself in later developmental states as cognitive features such as the externalization of blame onto others and limited self-awareness, as well as affective features such as the limited capacity for empathy, unregulated anger and an aggressive interpersonal style.[302]

Bondage therefore, can be conceptualized as a state of perpetual shame-based isolation wherein are developed maladaptive coping habits intended to replace the foundational influence of relationship with primary attachment figures (i.e. caregivers, God). There are a variety of constructs in modern society that serve as agents of bondage; among them are sex, digital stimulation [Internet, video-gaming, etc.], gambling, shopping/spending, eating, exercise and, of course, a wide variety of substances (illegal drugs, prescription drugs, alcohol, nicotine, caffeine, etc.).

Over time, this experience of shame births a maladaptive coping style that centers on the experience of isolation, and our desperate attempts to fill the resultant relational void through the consumption of these self-regulating substances and/or experiences. In the addictive cycle, the short-lived escape and relief that is found through these means is quickly replaced by a combination of regret, remorse and despair, furthering the sense of shame and disconnection.

Many individuals struggling with the addictive cycle will eventually move into a façade, where their shame is veiled behind a mask of self-importance, self-coherence, or self-efficacy. From a distance, their attitude, behaviors, and spirituality appear congruent with how they desire to be perceived. However, over time or under scrutiny, the inherent flaws of the façade break down and expose the underlying intrapsychic conflict. This conflict between the parts of the self is reflected in Romans 7:21-23, "So I find this law at work: Although I want to do good, evil is right there with me. For in my inner being I delight in God's law;

---

302. Parker, S. & Thomas, R. "Psychological Differences in Shame Vs. Guilt: Implications for Mental Health Counselors," *Journal of Mental Health Counseling*, 31 (2009), 213-224.

but I see another law at work in me, waging war against the law of my mind and making me a prisoner of the law of sin at work within me."

This tension—between appetites and desires, bondage and freedom, sin and grace—creates a relational world defined by alleviating distress rather than deepening connections. The growing sense of detachment interpersonally culminates with a return to the previously identified state of isolation where shame and other affects (disappointment, sadness, fear, jealousy, etc.) grow in their influence, and this initiates the next cycle of addictive acting out. The more frequently this cycle operates, oftentimes on a preconscious level, the more familiar, and subsequently the more powerful, it becomes.

The desperation of Paul's plea in Romans 7:24 gives rise to the beauty of redemption offered through Christ in verse 25, "What a wretched man I am! Who will rescue me from this body that is subject to death? Thanks be to God, who delivers me through Jesus Christ our Lord!"

To understand sustainable sobriety in addiction recovery, one must first grasp the fullness of this process of being delivered "through Jesus Christ our Lord." In particular, the Body of Christ serves as the primary vehicle through which sobriety is sustained and holiness (a growing identification with the nature of Christ as equipped through the indwelling of the Holy Spirit) is truly experienced. As such, relational spirituality serves the critical function of transformational instrument on each account.

There are two main Scriptural narratives that orient us to the role of interpersonal relationship in sustained sobriety and deepened experience of holiness. The first is seen in chapter 12 of 2 Samuel in Nathan's confrontation of David. Inherent in this passage is David's growing sense of awareness of his guilt according to the law, and his experience of shame, as evidenced through the elaborate cover-up of his sinful deeds. Freedom from addictive processes and growth in grace are equally dependent on the process of increasing awareness and deepening insight. However, these processes are significantly informed by the relational context in which one exists. There is no objectivity with self in isolation. David, then, is dependent on Nathan to raise awareness of his need for transformation, and his ongoing relationship out of which a new capacity for being will emerge. Sobriety and holiness are context dependent: namely in our connection to community, the body of Christ, the church.

To understand the body and its role in spiritual transformation and sustainable recovery, one must explore a foundational premise of Christian community. Jesus states: "When Jesus saw his mother there, and the disciple whom he loved standing nearby, he said to her, 'Woman, here is your son,' and to the disciple, 'Here is your mother.'" (John 19:26-27)

In this revelation from the cross, Christ outlines the essentials of Christian community by redirecting us back to the simplicity, yet profundity, of the parent-child relationship. This unique relationship is considered a primary attachment and is designed to enable us to live with a greater sense of congruence in our personal identity. It is a place where we find a sense of connection, meaning, worship and self. It is created to be the source of comfort for our pain, presence in our sadness, acceptance in our shame and security in our fear. Here we find submission to a loving authority and freedom to explore the vastness and fullness of creation.

Unfortunately, there are many Christians who have yet to experience the security of this grace; instead, they persist in an experience of God that fosters fear, avoidance, or spiritual disorganization. Their attachment with God is more reflective of the disappointment of broken human relationship, rather than the expanse of restoration offered through Christ. In many ways, their addiction is to their fear.

Holiness, then, is as much a process of internal transformation spiritually, psychologically, and behaviorally, as it is a process of transformation relationally, communally, and societally. What happens internally must be lived out externally, and what is lived into externally reinforces those changes that take place internally. The two exist symbiotically; incapacitating one renders the other ineffectual, and vice versa. Much like the mystery of the Trinity, the concepts of holiness and sustainable sobriety can only be understood by their simultaneity, as evidenced in the larger context of a community of believers.

Todd Bowman, an Associate Professor of Counseling at Indiana Wesleyan University, earned his doctoral degree in Counseling Psychology from Oklahoma State University in 2008. He is the developer of the Sexual Addiction Treatment Provider (SATP) certificate curriculum and the director of the SATP Institute. He specializes in human sexuality, sexual addiction, and psychological assessment, and published his first book, Angry Birds and Killer Bees: Talking to Your Kids about Sex *(2013).*

Holiness as Identity

Roland Hearn

The crescendo has come and gone. The crowd pulsates as the music's final advance begins to wane. The energy flowing from the crowd borders on the tactile. The artist begins to wonder if any moment could be more real, or wonderful, than this. She utters a final phrase, "I love you all," and her status as a goddess is complete. The crowd can know no experience more utterly sublime. She holds her fingers to her lips and offers a sacrifice of her love as she blows to the multitude a kiss that is received as personal by each individual in the crowd. This, for those present, borders on a truly spiritual encounter.

"I love you all." Really? Is she even aware of the existence of a fraction of a percent of the people there? What might she really be saying? I suggest she is actually experiencing her own euphoria in the midst of the crowd's adulation. She is really saying, "As a recipient of your idolization, I'm feeling a lot of self-worth right now. Thank you very much."

While we are all familiar with the concept of self-worth, it may often escape our attention how deeply our sense of worth is tied into our very being. Allow me to illustrate. I am an Australian. That tells me something about who I am. In fact, it is loaded with cues as to why I do what I do and think the way I do. I don't think I can fully estimate how much of my existence is defined by the fact that I was born in the Land Down Under. While I enjoy most sports, I love cricket and Rugby League. Unless you are from one of a small handful of countries you probably think I mean "Rugby Union." You see, that distinction is important to me; it is a part of who I am. I am a father. I have four great kids. I have a wonderful wife. I am proud of what she has achieved with her life. I am a Christian. I am a member of the Church of the Nazarene. Each of these, and many more, says a little bit to me and to others about who I am. I draw a sense of worth from them all. I know I do because of how important they are to me.

We have some clues as to how much something is a part of our identity. When there is a threat—real or perceived—to an identity shaper, we generally experience a highly emotional response. This reaction indicates a deep link to our sense of identity. At our deepest level we make an unperceived connection between the sources of our identity and our worth as a human being. It is unavoidable and happens continuously. Not everyone is equally emotional, but everyone makes those links and has their own way of expressing it.

Consider this scene: A man is sitting at a crude desk in the corner of his dimly lit room. He is writing a letter to some friends. It is obvious that he is overwhelmed by his love for them. He tells them "I have you in my heart," and then he says, "I long for you with the deepest of affection." The people he writes to are a part of how he understands himself. He has been through some tough times in his life, and he is aware they are going through very similar things. His deepest concern for them is that they will learn a truth with a profoundly life altering impact. He looks back across his life, and recognizes it is filled with key identifiers. He has every reason to be proud of himself. His nationality and heritage are worth noting. He has had a great education, and he has lived a life of integrity and responsibility. His is the life others admire.

However, now his life perspective is revolutionary. He writes, "To me all of that is garbage. There is only one thing that counts." Something has transformed his source of identity. His identity is no longer rooted in the subjective and transient things that are common sources of identity. Instead, now he is rooted in something utterly objective and dependable.

He says, "But whatever were gains to me I now consider loss for the sake of Christ. What is more, I consider everything a loss because of the surpassing worth of knowing Christ" (Phil. 3:8). Knowing Christ is everything that is valuable. Christ has become how he knows himself. Christ is his worth. Paul is reflecting a profound connection that we may often miss, yet this connection is crucial for our understanding and articulation of holiness.

The other evening I watched another episode of the fascinating and informative television series *Cosmos: A Space Time Odyssey*. Hosted by Neil deGrasse Tyson, it gives a fascinating look into our understanding of the universe. In this particular episode, Tyson was considering the work of Michael Faraday, who tenaciously pursued an effective understanding of the relationship between electricity and magnetism. He ultimately postulated an additional connection with light. Eventually he proved it, and those understandings, Tyson suggests, have had perhaps the greatest role in shaping our contemporary world.

There is a connectedness in holiness that is equally mysterious, equally profound, and equally impacting. An intricate and intimate link exists between identity, worth, and our capacity to love. In fact, they are so closely linked that the defining boundaries are often blurred.

In the third chapter of Ephesians, Paul articulates his prayer for the Ephesians to embrace and comprehend love. He begins by stating he prays to "the Father from whom every family in heaven and on earth derives its name (Eph. 3:14, 15). That is an identity statement. Paul is suggesting that all of humanity derives identity from our eternal Father. The implication then is that the capacity to comprehend love comes directly from our relationship with the One who is the source of love, from the One from whom we ultimately derive our identity. Our identity can never be fully embraced until we have fully embraced Him, the One who is love, at the core of our being.

How does this connect with a sense of worth? Our sense of worth affects our perception of how loved we are. When we experience worth from another, we experience love. Conversely, when we feel worth-less before another, we do not experience love. When a crowd applauds, that is a lot of worth, received as a lot of love, and reflected in words, "I love you all."

The implication, then, is that in the embracing of the One who is love and in the establishment of His identity as the foundation of our own, we enter a relationship that affects our sense of worth. With identity, worth, and love all located in our relationship with God and in his gracious activity in our life, living out the life of holiness becomes truly possible.

Wesley conceived of holiness as love. Wesley's famous quote is worth noting here: "If you look for anything but more love, you are looking wide of the mark; you are getting out of the royal way."[303] Is that not what is reflected in Corinthians 13? To experience identity in Christ is to sense Him as our source of worth. To find our worth in Him is to experience His love. There is more, however; it becomes possible to love as He loves, by reflecting the worth of others to them.

As we seek to communicate to our contemporary cultures the central issues of holiness, we need to find constructs that are reasonable and effective. There is a wonder filled truth at the core of message of holiness that resonates with human need. God's grace means we are loved and empowered to love. We are valued and empowered to communicate value. It is important to unveil that truth for those not raised in the intricate, culturally influenced web of our historic terminology.

Many years ago it was common for preachers to talk of "death to self." That phrase is problematic now, however. An immediate question comes to mind, "Is the Christian message built on a premise of identity loss?"

I have become convinced that what this phrase was intending to communicate is not loss of identity, but a shift in the primary source of identity. If my self-identity and self-worth are products of my experience, perception, and relationships, then the goal is to shift the source of my identity from these things to Christ. This

---

303. John Wesley, *A Plain Account of Christian Perfection* (Kansas City: Beacon Hill Press, 1993, original work published 1872), 99.

brings increased clarity to Paul's words when he suggests that he counts his past achievements as garbage.

Thus, when I experience and live holiness, I allow the Holy Spirit to move to one side all my hurts, history, hopes and hurdles—all the things that have defined me without my necessarily even knowing it. The Spirit subverts them so that they no longer identify me as much as He does.

And how do I know this? Love! This is what John Wesley speaks of as "perfect love." Love becomes the defining principle of my life. I move from all that is temporal to the One that is eternal as my source of identity and worth. I embrace His love and live the life of love. Such a shift is an act of faith to which God responds with grace to bring us into more love.

Roland Hearn serves as the registrar and dean of students of Nazarene Theological College—Brisbane, Australia. He and his wife Emmy have been married for 29 years and have four grown children. Roland and Emmy have pastored four churches, in both Australia and the US, planting churches on both continents. They are currently planting a church on the north side of Brisbane. Roland serves on the district strategic missional board seeking to discern effective ways of advancing the church in a post-modern, pluralistic, multi-cultural environment.

Holiness and Identity in a Technological Age

Timothy R. Gaines

Contemporary formulations (and re-formulations) of what holiness entails cannot ignore the monumental advances in technology that have gripped the late modern world. If we are asking questions about the renovation of our understanding of holiness, we also ought to place those questions alongside the forces that are presently renovating the world around us, and technology stands out as one of the leading shapers of late modern society.

In this essay, I suggest that the use of technology is neither good nor evil, but that it has tinted our moral vision and understanding of self. A technological paradigm has affected our very sense of identity in such a way that leaves us longing for depth among sources of shallow identity formation. The use of technology is simply yet another aspect of the created order to be brought under the unifying authority of the exalted Christ. The pursuit of holiness is that process that furtively kindles a desire for something more than self-identity can grant, while simultaneously bestowing an identity upon the pursuer of holiness *in Christ*. The epistle to the Ephesians contains a "logic of holiness" which out-narrates the late modern technological paradigm, opening the possibility of identity-unto-holiness.

That we are frequent users of technology is not groundbreaking information, but we rarely stop to consider the ways that the technology we use deeply forms our understanding of ourselves in relation to the world (what theologians and ethicists call "moral vision").[304] For example, the use of digital technology has taught us that we can overcome the formidable forces of both time and space. While serving as a youth pastor outside Chicago, I had a conversation with one teenager about a middle school classmate of mine who wrote me letters every day. "Why didn't she just text you?" my bewildered student asked. That text messaging, let alone cellular technology, was in its infancy during my adolescence hadn't occurred to him. In his mind, formed by a technological paradigm, we ought to be capable of sending a message to a friend on a moment's whim, precisely because the technology at our disposal allows us to do so. Rather than waiting for an affectionate missive from a young admirer to arrive in my mailbox, sent from

---

304. See Brian Brock, *Christian Ethics in a Technological Age* (Grand Rapids: Eerdmans, 2010).

a house in the neighboring town, her message could arrive by text or email in an instant, overcoming both the time I would have to wait for the letter, and the space through which that letter would have to travel to reach me.[305]

Further, the use of agricultural technology has taught us that we should have affordable food during a drought. The use of transportation technology has taught us that a snowstorm shouldn't stop us from the trip we were hoping to take to see friends over Christmas. The use of medical technology has taught us that when an organ in our body fails, it ought not to mean certain death.[306] In short, our ubiquitous use of technology has taught us that we are not to be mastered by natural forces, but that we can overcome those forces, becoming the masters ourselves.

Friedrich Nietzsche, one of the leading philosophers of the modern era, was an acute observer of technological influences upon modern life. As he watched the proliferation of industrial technology take hold during the 19th century, he postulated that humans were poised finally to take hold of their own fate. Technology allows humans to overcome natural forces—to master their world and set their own course.[307] This, as Nietzsche understood it, is the fullest expression of human existence.

The technological ability to command our surroundings and to create the world of our desiring has also shaped the late modern sense of identity. Since the natural world will not have the last word over a people equipped with the technology to overcome it, neither will our identities be given to us from some source outside of our control. In the same way that we can construct a world free from the encumbrances of time and space, so too can we construct an identity for ourselves, one that suits our desires quite adequately. A people formed by a technological moral vision have been formed to think that they are the creators of their own worlds and therefore creators of their own identities. In short, we have been formed to believe that we can make ourselves be whatever we want to be; you and I are a constant construction project of our own desire.

This brand of thinking leads to a certain kind of *nihilism*, particularly because it begins within the self and it ends within the self.[308] There is nothing beyond or outside of our own desires that inform who we are forming ourselves to become. Like the circular logic of what philosophers call a tautology, it turns in upon itself

---

305. See George Grant, *Technology and Justice* (Notre Dame: University of Notre Dame Press, 1986).

306. See Allen Verhey, *Reading the Bible in the Strange World of Medicine* (Grand Rapids: Eerdmans, 2003).

307. See Friedrich Nietzsche, *The Will To Power*, ed. Walter Kaufmann (New York: Vintage, 1968).

308. See Conor Cunningham, *Genealogy of Nihilism* (New York: Routledge, 2002).

unto incoherence. Or, like a car in neutral, it exerts energy, but it cannot apply that energy to move beyond its present position.

Even more detrimental is the conclusion awaiting us at the end of this logic. Nietzsche saw it clearly: reconciliation among persons would not be a hallmark of societal life if our identities were the result of self-construction. Rather, those who were strongest and most driven toward their individual goals would be those who would ultimately prevail. Conflict, and perhaps even violence, would be an inevitable part of human association so long as we were all independently crafting our own identities and pursuing the horizons associated with those individual identities.

Self-constructed identity would have made little sense to the early Christians who first read the letter we know today as Ephesians. The ancient mind was far more attuned to look outside of and beyond itself for a source of identity than minds formed by a technological paradigm of mastery. The first Christians were more likely to want to *receive* their identity than *create* it. "For this reason I kneel before the Father," writes the apostle, "from whom every family in heaven and on earth derives its name" (Eph. 3:14, TNIV). This kind of language is usually far more passive than modern persons are comfortable with, yet it functions within the "logic of holiness" that undergirds the entire epistle of Ephesians.

The apostle establishes this "logic of holiness" upon the reality of the risen and exalted Christ who is over and above the world, "to bring unity to all things" (Eph. 1:10). It is Christ whom the apostle understands to be "far above all rule and authority, power and dominion," bringing unity to all things by virtue of his being exalted over all things (Eph. 1:21). It is "for this reason" that the apostle encourages his readers to kneel before the Father to receive their name, their identity. His pastoral concern for his people extends to his hope for what they might experience in kneeling before the Father, "that you may be filled to the measure of all the fullness of God" (Eph. 3:19).

John Wesley most likely held those words in mind as he crafted descriptions of the life of holiness. For Wesley, holiness was "love excluding sin; love filling the heart, taking up the whole capacity of the soul."[309] According to the "logic of holiness," the identity that comes to us as a gift of being filled with the fullness of God is a gift that comes to us from beyond ourselves, a gift given by One outside of ourselves.

Or, to follow the apostle's logic, we become something that we could not construct ourselves to become—a community marked by the absence of slander,

---

309. John Wesley, "The Scripture Way of Salvation" in *John Wesley's Sermons: An Anthology*, eds. Albert C. Outler and Richard P. Heitzenrater (Nashville: Abingdon, 1991), 374.

malice and bitterness, a community being "built together to become a dwelling in which God lives by his Spirit" (Eph. 2:22). Thus, the community of those who kneel before the Father, being filled with all the fullness of God are those who receive their identity from the sanctifying grace that allows them to live together in the absence of hostility and oppression. This is anything but a collection of self-identified individuals pursuing their own disparate ends.

While the technological paradigm teaches us that we are capable masters of our own identities, the "logic of holiness" would have us understand that the use of technology is yet another aspect of the created order that is being brought to unity as it is submitted to the authority of the resurrected and exalted Christ. The hope for life together in reconciliation, then, is not in furthering self-constructed identity, but in being brought to unity, as Ephesians states it so many times, *in Christ*.

Life according to the "logic of holiness" does not wish to master our world, or to construct our own identities. Instead, it seeks to be brought to unity under Christ and to live in reconciliation with others, precisely because we have been made capable of doing so by being filled with all the fullness of God. In this unity in Christ, we bear witness to the true fullness of human experience in charity, unity, mission, and reconciliation.

Tim Gaines (Ph.D., Garrett-Evangelical Theological Seminary) serves as co-lead pastor of the Bakersfield First Church of the Nazarene and as an affiliate faculty member of Nazarene Theological Seminary. His work in theology and ethics deals with the intersection of Christian doctrine and contemporary issues. He is co-author of A Seat at the Table: A Generation Re-imagining Its Place in the Church *and author of articles in* Wesleyan Theological Journal, Doxology: A Journal of Worship, *and* Didache: Faithful Teaching.

Holiness, Attachment Theory, and a Theology of Love:

It's Relationship

Janine M. King

A variety of terms and phrases has been used to define holiness and to describe the experience and meaning of holiness in the life of a believer. Here is a brief review of some of the terminology: Christian perfection, entire sanctification, full salvation, perfect love, the deeper life, the baptism of the Spirit, the fullness of the Spirit, radiant moral health, the victorious Christian life, spiritual health, a pure heart, having the mind of Christ, Christ-centeredness, full surrender, perfect integrity, living sacrifice, set apart for God, second work of grace, Christlikeness, the very life of God expressing itself in all its relationships.

Obviously, there are many ways to describe holiness because there are many people trying to describe their experience with God. Wesleyan theology allows for an abundance of ways to describe holiness because of "its emphasis on holiness as personal experience."[310]

Church of the Nazarene General Superintendent Emeritus Dr. Jim Bond described holiness as "The Relationship."[311] I believe that this synonym for holiness best reflects the truth that a believer's holiness or "spiritual health is absolutely dependent on a proper relationship to God."[312] We cannot be holy on our own; holiness requires a humble relationship with God. God wants us to be holy, but God will not manipulate our holiness or our love. We must choose to respond to His love for us. Only "a mutual agreeableness constitutes holiness. In essence it is a quality of relationship."[313] God created us with freedom to choose to live in loving relationship with God and with one another. "Freedom," Joseph Grizone explains, "is essential in the spiritual life if we are to respond to the Holy Spirit, and grow in God's grace."[314]

---

310. Mildred Bangs Wynkoop, *A Theology of Love* (Kansas City: Beacon Hill, 1972), 44.

311. Jim L. Bond, *Doctrine of Holiness Class Notes* (Nazarene Bible College, Colorado Springs, March-May, 2011).

312. Wynkoop, 360.

313. Ibid., 360.

314. Joseph F. Grizone, *Never Alone: A Personal Way to God* (New York: Doubleday, 1994), 60.

Bond's relational take on holiness directly relates to thoughts about love and attachment theory. Three books stand out in expounding these connections:

- A secular book, *Love Sense*, by Sue Johnson[315]
- A Wesleyan book, *A Theology of Love*, by Mildred Bangs Wynkoop
- A Catholic book, *Never Alone: A Personal Way to God*, by Joseph Grizone.

Dr. Bond works in parallel with these authors, looking deeply into the matrix of love and relationships. Through their experience and research, they have provided pieces of the map to the treasure of holiness and how to gain it.

One of my psychology professors often quoted the maxim, "All truth is God's truth." Truly, it is exciting to see the secular world discovering truth that God has revealed through the biblical text. For example, Dr. Sue Johnson, a respected clinical psychologist, research professor, and recognized leader in the science of love and relationships, claims that new research techniques using functional magnetic resonance imaging (fMRI) have enabled us to discover that the brain is hardwired to give and receive love.[316] This truth corresponds to the truth Jesus taught when he said that the most important way for humans to live is to "love God with all our heart . . .and love others . . ." (Mark 12:29-31); and again, "This is my command: Love each other" (John 15:17).

According to Johnson, the past thirty years of research reveal "that love is a basic survival code, that an essential task of our mammalian brain is to read and respond to others . . . that it is being able to depend on others that makes us strong . . . that a stable, loving relationship is the absolute cornerstone of human happiness and general well-being" and that "love is the lifeblood of our species and our world."[317]

Doesn't this sound like the truth presented in God's word? If "God created humans in God's image" (Genesis 1:27), and if "God is Love" (John 4:16), then it makes sense that love is the lifeblood of our species. If an essential task of our brain is to read and to respond to others, then we were created to fulfill the biblical instruction to "carry each other's burdens" (Galatians 6:2). If being able to depend on others is what makes us strong, then it makes sense that "God comforts us in all our troubles, so that we can comfort those in any trouble with the comfort we ourselves have received from God" (2 Corinthians 1:3-4). If loving relationship is the absolute cornerstone of human happiness and well-being, no wonder Jesus

315. Sue Johnson, *Love Sense* (New York: Hachette, 2013).

316. Johnson, 18.

317. Ibid, 6-7.

said that all the commandments are fulfilled by being in loving relationship with God and with others.

John Bowlby, the father of attachment theory, upon which Johnson builds her research, wanted to call his developmental perspective on personality, "A Theory of Love." However, he felt that he would be laughed out of the scientific psychiatric community if he gave "it its rightful name."[318] At the time when Bowlby was pursuing his research into attachment and emotions, the experts in developmental psychology opposed his ideas. They were in agreement with John B. Watson, who "was adamant that mother love was a 'dangerous instrument'; that women's sentimental natures were a defect which prevented them from pushing their children into independence."[319]

Thanks to attachment theorists, the psychological community is beginning to recognize that being in loving relationship is essential to healthy human development. We are discovering that "emotional dependency is not immature or pathological; it is our greatest strength."[320] Isn't this the essence of God's desire for our relationship with God? Dependence on God is a critical element of our relationship with God. Jesus said, "Abide in me and I in you . . .apart from me you can do nothing . . .as the Father has loved me, so have I loved you. Now remain in my love . . .that your joy may be complete" (John 15:4-11). Similarly, God expected dependence from Paul when He said, "My grace is sufficient for you, for my power is made perfect in weakness" (2 Corinthians 12:9). Paul responded in perfect "secure attachment" style by saying, "Therefore . . . I delight in weaknesses . . . for when I am weak, then I am strong" (vv. 9-10).

Grizone teaches that God did not create us to live in isolation. God "created each of us incomplete, so we would need one another, so we could help one another, so we could reach out and touch one another's lives. Holiness is growth in godliness . . . . Our holiness, then, is authentic when it is reaching out to others, sharing with others what God has poured so lavishly into our own lives."[321]

Bowlby and his associates discovered through their research that secure, loving, attached relationships are necessary for infants and children to develop into secure, loving human beings. Johnson's research reveals that secure loving attachment is necessary in the relationship between couples for them to "make, repair, and keep love."[322]

---

318. Ibid, 38.

319. Ibid, 33.

320. Ibid., 21.

321. Grizone, 80.

322. Johnson,19.

Along the same lines, Bond taught that an intimate relationship between a believer and God is necessary to make, repair, and keep Christlikeness. Bond stated that every human relationship pales in comparison to "The Relationship" between the Divine God and each human who has chosen to surrender everything to the love and Lordship of Jesus Christ. He implied that holiness is the result of secure, loving relationship with God when he explained that holiness is a relational word. God invites people to live in relationship with God through Jesus Christ by the Holy Spirit. Only through the healing relationship with Jesus Christ can relationship with God and others be restored. Bond suggested that holiness is synonymous with Christlikeness—living as Christ lived in humble, obedient love for God and sacrificial love for others.[323]

Bowlby's research refers to the relational love between parent and child. Johnson's research refers to the relational love between two people who are romantically involved. However, Bond, in his lectures on holiness, refers to the relational love between God and humans.

This divine love is described by Wynkoop as *agape* love. She explains that *agape* is first introduced in the New Testament in Matthew 5:48, "Be...perfect, as your Father . . . in heaven is perfect." This can seem like an impossible command. Yet, "it is in God's 'Fatherness' that *agape* love is revealed, not in the absolute perfection of God . . . *Agape* love is God's dimension of love which He wants to restore to all men. This is holiness."[324]

Grizone's ideas about *agape* love compliment Wynkoop. He says that when Jesus told his followers to love their enemies and do good to those who hate them—and when he followed it up with the seeming impossible command, "Be perfect, as your Father in heaven is perfect"—he was not referring to a perfection of keeping laws. He was referring, "to what is mentioned just before, perfection in expressing genuine love even of your enemies. . . . So, in enjoining us to be perfect like His Father, Jesus is challenging us to love as completely and as unselfishly as His Father."[325] This is holiness.

How can we live an *agape* relationship with God? It is "kept intact by a daily fellowship with God."[326] It involves humble prayers, such as these:

323. Bond, Doctrine of Holiness.

324. Wynkoop, 33-34.

325. Grizone, 93.

326. Wynkoop, 352.

Jim Bond's morning prayer, "Jesus, I love you. I want to think of you in everything I do today. Help me to bring you into everything of my life . . . May my every act, word, and thought—be love."[327]

Joseph Grizone's evening prayer, "God, I finished my job for you today. I may not have done a perfect job, Lord, but I tried. My life is to do your work, Lord. I am yours. Keep me in your love. Keep my soul at peace."[328]

Janine King earned her Bachelor of Ministry degree from Nazarene Bible College and her Master of Science in Clinical Counseling from Northwest Nazarene University. She is a counseling pastor at Springs First Church of the Nazarene in Colorado Springs. During her self-care time, she enjoys experiencing God while hiking in the mountains with her husband, visiting with her adult children, playing with her grandchildren, and training for triathlons.

---

327. Bond, Doctrine of Holiness.

328. Grizone, 100.

Holiness Weirdos
Jamie Gates

There was a particular time when I became aware that holiness Christians are weird. I was a young teen when it struck me that the most distinctive message of my church was that Jesus loves me and that this should most importantly lead to me not cussing, not dancing, not going to movies and not drinking (alongside the slightly more important not viewing/having sex or breaking the Ten Commandments). Generally, we were to not be like everybody else in "the world." I experienced the call to holiness as attending church as often as possible and as abstinence from a range of personal habits that were so ubiquitous in the lives of my friends and their families that just bringing up the subject made me sound weird.

I grew up in South Africa as the son of missionary parents, and missionaries make a vocation out of being weird. Heralded as icons of holiness vocation, missionaries are celebrated for their exotic presence in the country to which they are sent and valorized/humored for their peculiarity when they return to tell their stories. Missionaries are responsible for exporting our kind of weirdness and, with it, these particular holiness taboos no matter what the cultural context.

College is generally a time when young people investigate and challenge the traditions of their upbringing, often molting and leaving behind the dead skin of a faith that no longer fits. In college, I started paying attention to the broader social context of my very personal faith, the historical place that the holiness movement played in a much larger story of Christianity and the relatively narrow vision of holiness that I was living. While by this time I was good at abstaining from personal sins on the top ten list of holiness no-no's, my holiness theology at the time did not prepare me to understand let alone to resist the ways I was caught up in the social sins of our time.

When I came back from South Africa, American holiness Christians didn't seem to look very different from others around them. So many American Christians were caught up uncritically in consumer lifestyles that, compared to most of the lives I saw in South Africa, were excessive, even gluttonous. American Christians were blind to the exploitation of workers around the world that made that excessive lifestyle possible and blind to the nationalism/Americanism that idolatrously captured our loyalty.

In South Africa, many white Christians, my family included, worshipped in white enclaves. We were so focused on personal holiness that we were blind to the sins of apartheid that we participated in, sometimes actively and often with our silence

How were good holiness people with supposedly good intentions and clean consciences so easily complicit in these sins? Holiness of heart seemed little more than holiness of individual intent, and holiness of life seemed little more than holiness of my individual conscience or our individual choices. Maybe we weren't so weird after all.

As I tried to stretch my view of holiness around great social sins of our time, I became impatient with the smallness of the little list of holiness no-no's. In college, it became sort of a badge of honor for us good Christian kids to drop choice cuss words into private conversations to prove to ourselves that the Christian life was about way more than the little words that we say. While I had to carry around great guilt when I snuck off to a movie as a teenager, by the time I was in college, so many church people had VCRs that refusing to go to the cinema just seemed silly. In graduate school, having a beer with a side of deep intellectual conversation with professors and peers on Wednesday nights at Market Street Pub seemed a simple way to try to avoid missing the forest for the trees. I didn't mind being perceived as odd by the "weirdos" I had grown up with, since they tended to look like everyone else around them anyway, and I was well trained in the art of being weird.

But it slowly dawned on me that there was something deeper and more profound in my training to be weird than I had imagined. Being called to holiness at its core means being a called-out people, a people set aside for the purposes of God, called out to witness to the kingdom of God already at work in the world. If this is true, then being a certain kind of weird is in the DNA of what it means to be Christian. Being Christian means fundamentally being counter-cultural. But which aspects of culture should we counter? By what means do we discern this? What counter-culture should we create? From whom or what are we to be set apart? Toward what are we to be set apart?

I've written in other places about the calling of the church to "nurture the prophetic imagination." The holiness movement lies in the deeper roots of the prophetic traditions of scripture. The prophets were certainly weird. Even back then, it was weird to hang out in the desert wearing a homespun garment of hair and a leather belt, to chow on locust and honey and to declare that the Kingdom of God is at hand (Elijah in 2 Kings 1:8 and John the Baptist in Matt. 3:4).

Moses, Elijah, Elisha, Miriam, Deborah, Isaiah, Jeremiah, Amos, Ezekiel, John the Baptist . . . they were not so much diviners as they were reading their times through the lens of God's word and purposes, calling God's people to remain holy and set apart for God's directives, calling them to account for their compromises and idolatry, warning them of the consequences of their uncritical assimilation. They were astute students of their times while at the same time drawing on the deepest history of God's work in the world to understand their place in it.

A holy and prophetic people are weird because they have well trained memories. Holiness people learn what it means to be holy from the deep wisdom of our Scriptures, our tradition, divinely inspired reason, and the broad experience of a global church. A holy people remembers to keep the Sabbath wholly in worship, in remembrance and in acknowledgement that all time and industry and sustenance are gifts from God (Ex. 20). Holy people repent of their golden calves (Ex. 32) and won't bow to the idols of their time (Dan. 3). Holy people won't harvest all the way to the edges of their fields, refuse to oppress their workers, and release others from debt bondage (Lev. 19:25, Luke 4:16, James 5). Holy people do justice, love mercy and walk humbly with their God (Micah 6:8). Holy people find a place where truth and mercy meet, and justice and peace kiss one another (Ps. 85:10). Holy people know the plans God has for them, and— even in the midst of exile—live in such hope that they choose to plant gardens, build homes, marry, have children, and seek the welfare of their enemies (Jer. 29; Matt. 5:44-48).

Holiness people think about fear and death in weird ways. Holiness people ruminate on death and resurrection on a regular basis as food for the soul (Matt.26:17-30, Mark 14:12-26, Luke 22:7-23). Holy people sit in the midst of the violence and brokenness of the world and, like Rachel weeping for her children, learn to lament and refuse to be consoled (Jer. 31:15; Matt. 2:18). Holy people look squarely at the dangers of the world and the enormity of their calling and, rather than grow their defenses or crawl into a little debilitated ball, listen to the still small voice of God saying, "fear not, for I am with you" . . . even unto the end of time (Isaiah 41:10; Matt. 28:10; 2 Timothy 1:7).

Holy people look like the Good Samaritan who broke the barriers of social stigma to reach out to a stranger-cum-neighbor (Luke 10:25-37). When others around them fail, holy people refuse to be the ones to pick up the first stone (John 8:7). A holy people wash each other's feet, even the feet of those we know will betray us (John 13:1-17). Rather than being enamored by the powerful of their time and place, a holy people announce the upside-down Kingdom by following the One riding triumphantly into Jerusalem on a grey donkey instead of a white steed (Matt. 21:1-17). And a holy people are just weird enough to believe that death carries no real sting, no real victory and is not the final answer (1 Cor. 15).

These days I find myself a peculiar person among a peculiar people for reasons far broader and deeper than I ever thought possible. We choose to be a dry house and refrain from alcohol these days to remind us of our own addictions as a personal spiritual discipline, as a witness to living in an upside-down Kingdom, to welcome addicts and recovering addicts into our home with no hesitation, and to refuse to support an industry that preys on the poor and destitute.

I find my holiness commitments calling me to draw back from my overconsumption of entertainment and information overload. I struggle to be released from the unholy images of others and myself misshaped by millions of advertising images over the years, and so we keep the Sabbath in part by turning our TVs and other screens off on Sundays. We live in a world where sex-saturated images, music, conversations and relationships are so ubiquitous that we are numbed to the realities of sex trafficking in our midst, while many in our churches actively join in the "softer" side of the sex industry that fuels exploitation. Maybe those that called us to refrain from movies were onto something.

I'm thinking holiness Christians need to be weird. Being weird for the right reasons, for the sake of holiness of heart and life, for the sake of God's Kingdom come on earth as it is in heaven, for the sake of bringing release to the captive, sight to the blind, freedom for the oppressed, and declaring the age of Jubilee . . . if only we could be this peculiar a people.

Jamie serves as the Director of the Center for Justice and Reconciliation at Point Loma Nazarene University. His primary role is to motivate, mentor and disciple students to/ who get involved in contemporary social movements for the sake of the oppressed. He has co-authored Living Justice *(2007) and* Nurturing the Prophetic Imagination *(2012).*

Demonstrations of Holiness in the 21st Century
Jameel Lee

The Church, and especially those of us in the holiness tradition, have debated all aspects of holiness for centuries. It is imperative that every generation, culture, and demography contextualize this holiness message to our own circumstance. While there is a plethora of ideas of what holiness should look like, in essence holiness is the abandonment of selfish desires and the pursuit of the Christ-like lifestyle. It is to be Jesus to the world.

This leads me to explore further some demonstrations of holiness that seem to have been forgotten that we must force ourselves to reconsider; albeit, these considerations are not new but are easily overlooked if we focus primarily on a theological discussion. These aspects include **social justice**, **stewardship**, and **courtesy**. It certainly isn't my intent to suggest that these areas are the full extent of holiness. However, it is my hope to zoom in on some practical elements that are just as important as the syntax and pontifications of the doctrine itself.

When God chose the Israelite nation, it was not because of their military might. They had none. Neither was it for their numerical abundance. They were in fact the smallest of all nations. God, in His infinite wisdom, selected the "underdogs," as it were, to make them an example to the rest of the world. His intent was to show forth His power and splendor through them in unmistakable demonstrations of His glory. He said to them, "You will be for me a kingdom of priests and a holy nation" (Exodus 19:6). Note, God called them to be "holy," and he did not leave it to chance. Throughout the Old Testament God instructs and rebukes His people for their actions that He considered holy or unholy.

A consistent theme in the Old Testament is the discussion of **social justice**. And, while I say discussion, that is a very loose description of how it actually reads. Scripture presents a forceful demand on the "holy" people of Israel. Clearly, Jeremiah 22:3 posits, "This is what the Lord says: Do what is just and right. Rescue from the hand of the oppressor the one who has been robbed. Do no wrong or violence to the foreigner, the fatherless or the widow, and do not shed innocent blood in this place." God required that His people would be fair in how they interacted with each other. However, this passage takes it further. Israel should get involved if there were unjust acts being committed to another. The same sentiments are echoed again and again: Deuteronomy 1:16-17, 15:11, 16:20; Leviticus 19:15; Psalm 82:3; Proverbs 31: 8-9; Amos 5:11-24; Zechariah 7:9-10.

Let's look more closely at the discussion on fasting in Isaiah 58. The people were bewildered that they were engaging in a known and highly respected spiritual discipline but not receiving any results. They felt as if God was not hearing them. Finally, God responds to them and begs the question of the manner in which they were fasting. Israel had shut themselves away from the concerns of others and afflicted others for their own gain. However, God rebukes them and says that He expects that their fast should clothe the naked, feed the hungry, free the oppressed, loose the bands of wickedness, and break the yoke (vs. 6-7). He promised that when they do these things He will respond as soon as they call (vs. 9). This is the epitome of social justice.

Some argue that this is a solely Old Testament argument. But let's look at the New Testament as well. The shining illustration is John the Baptist. The Gospels indicate that he was beheaded because he spoke out against the unlawful marriage of King Herod. He told the crowds to share their food and clothes with the poor. All the accounts indicate that he was a holy man. There is a correlation in these passages between the holiness of John and his action in speaking out on behalf of the poor and against corruption in the government.

What does holiness look like in the 21st century? On this matter of social justice, the Church is rather quiet and timid. More specifically, the Church of the Nazarene has generally been "right-winged." We do not rock the boat too much and are very passive in our approach. We must give credit to Nazarene Compassionate Ministries that is a leading organization in the world—relieving the suffering of the hungry, naked, and sick. Alabaster and the other World Evangelism Fund Offerings make a significant contribution towards our social responsibility. However, scriptural holiness also requires actively fighting against the oppression of the weak and the injustice in our lands. This task rightly falls to the feet of the holy ones, who are of pure heart, clean conscience, and the mind of Christ. We of all people, should be able to judge what is fair and right, and then to take action. Holiness in our day should result in the united voice of the Church calling for justice and liberty as God intended.

Moving on to the question of **stewardship**, I have often questioned why we take such a strong stand as a church against gambling. Scripture is silent on the matter! I was mortified to find out that in other denominations many of our Christian brothers and sisters gamble. Please don't lose me here, I am not purporting that holiness in the 21st century embraces gambling. I believe that the principle of stewardship clearly hits the issue out of the park. God requires us to be good stewards of what we have received, to multiply it, and to use all of it for His glory. The parable of the talent is clear indication of this. One day we will give an account to God for all the resources that He has left us to manage (Luke 12:42-46). Therefore, squandering money through gambling cannot be considered good stewardship.

However, this principle must be applied to all our resources, and here is where the debate intensifies. Permit me to incite you a bit by asking a few questions.

- Is my fetish for shoes, in that I have so many they dry rot in my closet, a disregard for the principle of stewardship?
- Have I ignored the principle of stewardship when I purchase so much meat that sometimes it spoils in my freezer because I have forgotten it was there until it is cleaned?
- Can I still uphold the principle of stewardship when I spend most of my time watching television and neglect more beneficial or ambitious activities that I could pursue?
- Am I a good steward of this temple of the Holy Spirit when most of my diet is unhealthy, and I refuse to exercise?
- If all of these things constitute poor stewardship, then how am I any different from the gambler? Am I still "holy"?

"As each has received a gift, use it to serve one another, as good stewards of God's varied grace" (1 Peter 4:10).

Finally, we must consider **courtesy** an essential element of holiness. The world has increasingly grown selfish and cold. The first world nations are so developed and fast paced that every day is a mad-rush: a rush to get to work and meet deadlines, a rush to get the children to their appointments, a rush to lock in that next deal or big client. Jesus himself said of the last days, "because of the increase of wickedness, the love of most will grow cold" (Matthew 24:12).

It is, therefore, no surprise that many people do not know their neighbors. We have a lack of concern for our fellow man. Alarmingly, our society often shows more care and concern for the welfare of animals than divine image bearers do.

Paul instructs Titus in this manner: "Remind the people to be subject to rulers and authorities, to be obedient, to be ready to do whatever is good, to slander no one, to be peaceable and considerate, and always to be gentle toward everyone" (Titus 3:1-2). Peter takes up this argument and says, "Finally, all of you, be like-minded, be sympathetic, love one another, be compassionate and humble" (1 Peter 3:8).

The biblical expectation is that believers would be the most courteous people on earth. This can be as simple as extending a greeting when entering a room or passing someone. Courtesy can be further expressed by waiting patiently in line or even allowing someone else to go before you who may appear to be having an emergency. We may also show courtesy through kind acts to those who do not hide their displeasure for us.

In the 21st century, there is such an overwhelming focus on the "I" that this form of holiness certainly goes against the grain. Courtesy demands that I place focus on the other person, which is scripturally esteeming others better than me. It certainly is not complex, but it makes a significant difference. Our 21st century holiness people should not be like the Pharisee who passed the man on the Jericho Road. We should all be like the Samaritan who was looking beyond himself enough to see the hurt and distress of someone else. Sometimes, all it takes is a "Hello, how are you?" backed by a genuine smile!

Holiness begins as an internal work of the Holy Spirit but must have a powerful demonstration in my daily actions and activities. The book of Leviticus laid out detailed instructions of how the Israelites were to conduct themselves. It not only spoke to their ceremonies and beliefs or worship practices, but it extended to their clothing, diet, agricultural and hygienic practices. God gave them these laws because He expected them to be holy and He showed them how.

Certainly, Christ has redeemed us from the curse of the law and has written his law of love on our hearts rather than on tablets of stone. We do not need a list of rules to guide our behavior, but the principle remains. Holiness, even in the 21st Century, must affect every area of my life just as it did for the Israelites. If holiness is demonstrated before the world, we may not need to debate how and when heart purity occurs because we will see it lived out daily. Living makes a far stronger witness than talking!

Jameel Lee graduated from Caribbean Nazarene College in 2005. He is the grandson of Dr. Rosa E. Lee, who was the first female-elected District Superintendent in the Church of the Nazarene. Currently, he pastors the Beacon Light Church of the Nazarene Family Worship Centre, in Antigua & Barbuda—a church that his grandparents pioneered.

Sociology and Holiness

Marco A. Velasco Sosa

My discoveries in the field of sociology have helped me understand entire sanctification more broadly. Sociology has also improved my ecclesial and social practices. In this essay, I will relate entire sanctification and the concept of the "social construction of reality" to discern how they can be distinguished and how they work together. We will give special attention to how the concept of social construction may help us to a better understanding of the doctrine of holiness that goes beyond religious individualism and introspection and helps us to live the social holiness proclaimed by Wesley.

The doctrine of Christian holiness cannot be reduced to sociology, but a doctrine of holiness without sociological implications runs the risk of falling into spiritualism (trying to live a Christian life outside of this world as if it were in a dream). Sociology can make an important contribution to the implications of holiness in a fragmented world with a deep crisis of meaning.

From the start, the holiness movement was deeply concerned with society. It started in the midst of the British industrial revolution where extreme poverty and marginalization were seen on every side. Wesley said that the "world was his parish."

Sociology has different disciplines, each with a different approach to the analysis of society, and each with a valuable perspective for our understanding of holiness: Sociology of Knowledge, Phenomenological Sociology, Functionalist Sociology, Positivist Sociology, and Sociology of Conflict or Criticism.

In the *Sociology of Knowledge,* the basic emphasis is the social construction of reality. It reminds us of the enormous need for the doctrine of holiness to be expressed in an appropriate manner in our historic moment to transform society. The doctrine of holiness is not just a theoretical dogma. It is about transformation. We participate with God to make this world a more holy place, more suitable for human life in society—a place where respect and love of the neighbor and Creation will become a more palpable reality.

Many denominations without this emphasis on social holiness have lost legitimacy in this postmodern era. They are stuck in the modernist cultural mold of reason and technology. As a result, their voice becomes weaker as each day passes.

The social construction of reality can help us to remember that no system or institution arises from nothing, and that is necessary to build a proper understanding the historical moment in which we live. The institutions, as well as the theological systems, have not always existed as we know them. They are what they are because of the historical moment in which they are found. Both institutions and theology need to be renewed in the light of new knowledge and new developmental stages.

Phenomenological Sociology, on the other hand, discovers what is experiential, what is meaningful for everyday life. It points to the intersubjective experience or shared experiences as a signal to interpret the diversity of symbols. Each member of society develops a consciousness of his or her unique experience of God. It is not possible to reduce the Christian experience to a single template. Phenomenological sociology encourages us to accept differing Christian experiences of salvation and sanctification as valid and enriching for the whole community.

In *Functionalist Sociology*, society is conceived as a system of parts, interlinked and interdependent where each part plays a role in serving the needs of individuals. Functionalism assumes that the lack of balance or social dysfunction ("anomie") demands to re-establish a balance. Dysfunction is seen as something negative that needs to be fixed. The goal of functionalist sociology is to help recover social balance and minimize any possible dysfunction or anomie (lack of social standards or ethics).

Functionalist sociology also implies that we tend to accentuate the useful elements of our systems that help to maintain equilibrium. The status quo reigns. Power structures will naturally protect their own ideological interests and quiet the disrupting elements.

As Christians, we recognize the dangers inherent in maintaining the status quo. Wesley lived in an era of deep social chaos, and he did not close his eyes to this social and spiritual reality. Instead, he proclaimed the gospel in the midst of disequilibrium through compassion for the poor and the message of holiness.

In today's postmodern era, functionalism actually leads to dysfunction because our context and our individuals have radically changed. The context of a globalized world requires a new interpretation of the faith in which differences are accepted and valued. In this time of great disequilibrium, we must intentionally give space and value to the disruptive elements among us. These system-shakers will eventually enable us to find a new equilibrium together.

For the *Positivist Sociologist*, society is the sum of all its quantifiable elements. The greatest risk of this approach is the reification[329] of reality and human and even divine relationships. "Reification" is a sociological term that helps us to discern

---

329. *Reification* generally refers to "objectification" or making something real, bringing something into being, or making something concrete. "Reification," Wikipedia, http://en.wikipedia.org/wiki/Reification, accessed July 1, 2014.

how people and human relations are reduced to something purely observable, quantifiable, and predictable. The question is: "Can something like a relationship or a religious experience be measured or even be predicted by carrying out a series of steps?"

Unfortunately, something like this occurred in the teaching of the nineteenth century holiness leader Phoebe Palmer. She stipulated that whoever wanted to have the experience of heart holiness should go through a specific spiritual process that—if carried out in the correct way—would lead directly to entire sanctification. In our quest for quantifiable spiritual experiences, we created an overly structured formula for the experience of sanctification.

From the angle of the *Sociology of Conflict or Criticism*, societies are analyzed through a dialectical analysis. This work seeks to give a qualitative leap in social composition. This sociological approach accepts the differences, contradictions, and conflicts as a way forward to toward some more particular objective. This position has no problems with contradictions; it seeks rather to respond within a dialectical process. Thus social revolution could be a means to an end. One of the risks of this discipline is a materialist reductionism and a loss of all that is transcendent.

Each of these approaches represents different ways of understanding reality. We should not be surprised that the holiness movement has been influenced by some kind of social approach, unconsciously or inadvertently. For example, Wesley saw and sensed the implications of English empiricism of his time. He took out the best of it and applied it to the doctrine of holiness in the most creative way and avoided at the same time its negative implications for the Christian life.

One of the more surprising and controversial sociological approaches is the concept of social construction of reality of Peter Berger and Luckman. Such an approach reminds us that the holiness movement it is not an ideal or an abstract theory, but rather has been a historical force capable of transforming human relationships within society and where people are involved with God in the construction of a world where the holiness of God reigns.

The doctrine of holiness, as applied and understood in the nineteenth century by Phoebe Palmer and her followers, led to the objectification of the doctrine of holiness; it confused the end with the means. "Holiness" became an abstract doctrine independent of individual humans that then governed how those humans operated in real time and space. This conceptualization included an initial step called "whole consecration" or "a decision of faith" which became a mandatory process with an intrinsic independent power. To start the process, there was the altar as a special place to receive the experience of entire sanctification that was treated as if it were the only place where it was possible to receive entire sanctification. To receive the "Second Blessing," people had to follow a particular method with a controllable and predictable format to achieve a goal.

The process acquired its own life and power. What we have is a method, observable by cameras, which shows a predictable process and format to achieve a goal. While order is important, it confuses the source of the experience (God) with the method (Phoebe Palmer's guided process of placing your all on the altar). The formula takes on a power in itself independent of humans and even independent of God himself.

These various sociological models help us to have a better understanding and expression of our theological inheritance of holiness for the twenty-first century. Jesus used the metaphor of wineskins to illustrate what needed to change and what did not (Matt. 9:17). We need to express ourselves in such a way that the Christian life can be relevant to our times. The empiricist positivist sociological model has ceased to be the best way to express our concepts of faith and Christian life. It is our task in the twenty-first century to find new wineskins for the new wine to be enjoyed.

We must not forget that all theology is a construction of knowledge within a given historical situation. We have been heirs to western philosophy, especially the modern rationalist influence. Within that context, we built models that theologically responded to the questions of the past 250 years, but our theological work here often had little or no implication for daily life and social transformation. However, the historical situation and thinking have changed in our era.

These disciplines and sociological models can be companions that remind us not to forget that the world is the place where one must live the life of holiness. I have placed special emphasis on the principle of social construction because I believe that reminds us that God acts in our history and makes it together with us, working within the constructs of this world that belongs to Him.

As we find in the prayer of Jesus, "My prayer is not that you take them out of the world but that you protect them from the evil one" (John 17:15). We must live squarely in this world, speaking the message of holiness in terms that our world can understand, living holiness as authentic social transformation.

Marco is a pastor in Chiapas, Mexico and a professor at Seminario Nazareno Mexicano and Seminario Nazareno de las Américas (Costa Rica). He has two masters degrees and is currently pursuing his Doctor of Ministry at Nazarene Theological Seminary. He is married to Myrza, and they have two adult children: David and Ana.

The Role of Sociology in Understanding Sanctification

Catherine (Cathy) Lebese

My initial thought as I pondered this topic was, "What has sociology got to do with sanctification or holiness?" But as I thought more about what I understand sociology and holiness to be, the more I realized how intertwined they are.

John Wesley says it well when he says, "There is no holiness but social holiness." Sociology focuses on the social life of people and how they interact with their environment and each other. Sanctification brings God into that social life, affecting how as human beings we interact and respond to each other and to our environment in light of who God is.

What then is the role of sociology in understanding holiness? Does sociology even have a legitimate role to play in the understanding of holiness and sanctification? In response, I'd like to focus on several phenomena that are specifically affecting our youth: identity, culture, the socio-economic and political situation, and how all of this will influence their future and that of the generations after them.

My aim, then, is to focus on the relevance of sanctification to this generation, finding ways in which sanctification could respond to the social issues and challenges of our youth. I would like to find ways to interpret sanctification that would speak to postmodern youth without losing its true meaning. I am finding more and more young people, even Bible school students, who are struggling to understand the terminology that is used. Words such as sanctification and holiness are becoming scarce in the church. I believe it is partly because the pastors themselves do not understand them; therefore, they cannot make them relevant to their listeners.

Sanctification and Identity

Sociologists define identity as a distinctive characteristic of a person's (or group's) character that relate to who they are and what is meaningful to them. This will include one's name, gender, nationality, ethnicity, sexual orientation, and social class.

Sanctification gives us a new identity. We are no longer identified only in terms of our family and community, but we become identified with Christ. We become children of God (John 1:12). We assume the character and name of God Himself when we become His children with Jesus as our brother and Savior. A child of God is no longer just one of the many but is now one with the Creator in name and character. God's holiness becomes ours as we are set apart, made holy, purified and empowered.

We are given a new identity. We have hope, and we are no longer strangers and aliens to God but are God's family. Sanctification can thus be said to be God's stamp of acceptance on us. We are heirs of God and co-heirs with Christ (Romans 8:17). We are no longer condemned to hell but made one with Christ and heirs of the eternal life that is found in Him. Thus, our identity is no longer confined to our physical classification, but we have a heavenly identity as well.

Sanctification and Culture

Our culture determines whom we grow up to become, how we conduct ourselves in life's circumstances, as well as how we respond to others. It includes our belief systems, our identity, our language, and our outlook on life. When we become Christians, we do not cease to be part of a culture, but we adjust our culture to the culture of Christ.

As a result, sanctification also affects what we know as culture, discarding some of the things we say and do and adopting a new way of life. Culture by definition is characterized by common values, norms, ceremonies and a way of life of a particular group. Sanctification does not take away who I am, but molds and shapes me into a Christlike character. In other words, sanctification removes the negative aspects of my culture and add God's character to who I am so that I become fully who God had intended me to be.

Culture in itself is not evil, but there are some aspects of my culture as an African that are not Christ-like, such as the worship of ancestral spirits and consulting traditional healers instead of going directly to God through Christ. My African-ness shapes me to be the African woman that God created me to be, with the humility and dignity of an African woman. When I accept Christ and I am made holy through His Spirit, I do not cease to be African woman, I become an African Woman of God, set apart for Him and living the holy life I was created to live!

Sanctification and the Socio-economic and Political Environment

Socio-economic and political situations play a vital role in any individual's life, worldview, self-image, and even in their perception of who God is. Recently, many South Africans are turning from Christianity to Islam, and the main reason they cite is that Muslims are generous and kind. They provide food to the poor and needy using that as a way to introduce their religion. In a country like South Africa, where an average family gets one main meal a day and the destitute one or two meals a week, it is not difficult to woo people away from Christianity to Islam.

To explain a bit on what I am talking about, we have a situation in South Africa where most people do not get an education beyond high school, that is, if they are fortunate enough even to reach high school. The majority of the adults are unskilled laborers in the mines, factories or farms and earn next to nothing, yet often they must support not only their families but the extended family as well. Others are unemployed and depend on government support. Because many of our youth are unemployed, they often get involved in criminal activities or prostitution.

Sociologists would then argue that these young people have no other alternative but to live the way they do to meet their immediate needs, making this an economic problem. Or they may argue that society is not encouraging self-empowerment, and that is why the youth are disillusioned, making this a social problem. Or they may blame it on the corrupt politicians who do not care about the rest of the population but continue to enrich themselves.

Christians, on the other hand, will blame this on the devil and his evil schemes. The question is: can Christians respond effectively to these situations? Jesus' response is that we become the light and the salt of the earth (Matthew 5:13-16). As Deirdre Brower-Latz explains, if there is too much darkness, it means that the Christians are failing to shine their light to dispel the darkness. If there is too much rottenness, Christians are failing to be the salt.[330]

Sanctification draws the world toward a better life in Christ by providing the solutions to the problems. If Islam provides food parcels, Christianity should provide skills and education so that those affected may be able to support themselves and restore their dignity.

Conclusion

Holiness is as much a social phenomenon as it is a spiritual matter. There is no holiness but social holiness. God called us to be the light and the salt of the world, and our holiness cannot be seen unless it touches the lives of those around us. If our holiness cannot address the social issues of our society, then we are not a holiness people.

Cathy Lebese was born in 1964, the youngest of 6 children. She accepted Christ at the age of 17, and at the age of 19 God called her to serve Him. She is not married and has no children except the ones the Lord has brought her way in the ministry. In 2014, Rev. Lebese was elected principal of Nazarene Theological College—South Africa, after serving previously as facilitator, registrar, and dean.

---

330. Paraphrase from Deirdre Brower-Latz's chapel message at Nazarene Theological College—South Africa on May 15, 2014.

Wesleyan Social Theology in the Church Militant

Anthony Manswell

What is the practical implication of sanctification? How does it affect holiness? How does holiness affect social action? The Church must have a social theology in the world. This paper is an exploration of a Wesleyan perspective of a social theology in the Church Militant. The Wesleyan concept of love has implications for social obligation. Love assists and performs. These are vital aspects of sanctification and holiness. In this context, the word "militant" means to be intentional, radical, but not negatively warlike, or rebellious.

The social implication of the message of sanctification is radical, aggressive love. The Church can be healthily militant, but the root of its militant spirit is love. This love should be found in the midst of social ills, and it should permeate the intention of social activity. Sanctification must propel us to action!

Manfred Marquardt explains, "Using biblical passages and Augustine's words, Wesley solidified his view that ethical passivity and justifying grace are mutually exclusive. This theological dialectic ... made it possible for Wesley to emphasize equally the doctrines of justification by faith alone ... and the necessity of good works (against any mystical or pietistic quietism). It is through this synthesis that Wesley laid the foundation for his social ethics.[331]

Furthermore, Wesleyans maintain the tension between a scriptural position and practical endeavors in the Church Militant. The Church exists in specific context, and if it divorces itself from that society, the effectiveness of its existence becomes non-existent. Rattenburg argues, "Wesley's ... conscience was always alive to the needs of human beings ... [T]he early Methodists were [not] so immersed in introspection and raptures that they had no time to discharge their social duties."[332]

Kenneth Collins summarizes the crux of the argument:

> In light of this close connection that Wesley draws between inward and outward religion, two errors are possible: On the one hand, if the interior life is merely stressed, faith will not achieve

---

331. Manfred Marquardt, *John Wesley's Social Ethic* (Nashville: Abingdon, 1992) in John Lunn, "John Wesley's Social Ethic," Religion and Liberty, Vol. 3, No. 6, Nov-Dec 1993, http://www.acton.org/pub/religion-liberty/volume-3-number-6/john-wesleys-social-ethic, Accessed April 8, 2014.

332. J. Ernest Rattenburg, *Wesley's Legacy to the World* (London: Epworth Press, 1928), 234.

its proper end: namely, love. What will emerge, however, is a dead faith, the kind of spiritual narcissism that Wesley so rightly deplores in Discourse IV. But if, on the other hand, the life of the believer, the life of God in the soul, is not seen as the proper foundation for Christian activity in society, then the very heart, reason, and impetus for such activity will be obscured. Therefore, Wesley's social ethic should not be employed to repudiate or to undermine his emphasis on personal religion—that renewal of the believer's heart in righteousness and true holiness. His thought provides no warrant for this; in fact, it militates against it.[333]

The Church Militant must have a radical social theology that meets people where they live. This is where the doctrines of conversion, assurance, holiness, and perfection play a significant part.

The Social Implications of Conversion and Assurance

Conversion and assurance bring social equality as each person recognizes the worth of other persons. Socially it brings "dignity" and a new perspective on one's standing. Socially, the class structure of society can be broken down as all stand in Christ. Rattenburg elaborates, "The greatest social service of Wesley was after all not his teaching on social service, but his evangelical message. That message vitalized the dull soul of England, and in consequence the doors of a new era were flung open."[334]

What a profound insight! Basic to a Wesleyan perspective of a social theology is the conversion of souls. With the change of persons, there is hope for persons to recognize the worth of others.

The Social Implications of Holiness and Perfection

Bebb believes the love of God in the soul is the very essence of holiness. This experience is critical. According to Bebb, Wesley would have certainly denied that a person could be living a holy life and yet be anti-social because social actions are an outgrowth of the holy life.[335]

According to Wesley, every work of charity is an element of the holy life: feeding the hungry, giving clothes to the naked, assisting the stranger, visiting the sick and those in prison, giving comfort to those that are afflicted, attempting to instruct those that are ignorant, etc.[336]

---

333. Kenneth J. Collins, *Wesley on Salvation* (Grand Rapids, MI: Asbury, 1989), 101.

334. Rattenburg, 24.

335. E. Douglas Bebb, *A Man with a Concern* (London: Epworth Press, 1950), 35.

336. John Wesley's Sermons, vol. II: 426.

Robert Chiles explains that for Wesley, "Christian practice aimed at works of love, at a purity of intention, and quality of action that truly fit God's creatures to be His children. . . The 'social love' of the Christian entailed important social obligations"[337]

Similarly, Harper concurs that Wesley was demonstrating "that social holiness. . . must be and can be expressed in specific ways. For our purposes, this means that true spirituality is never made spiritual. Rather is expressed through concrete acts of daily living."[338]

The social importance of Wesley's appeal for Christian perfection is great because sin is not totally an individual question. The individual is always placed in a social setting, in which sin is wrong thoughts, evil desires, and impure actions towards others. Holiness affects one's social scope in thoughts, desires, and actions, and produces all things for the good, based on love working in the renewed heart. Hence, Bebb argues that all Wesley's "interest had a bearing upon salvation and as salvation was essentially social, that is, it had a social setting and social consequences, so religion and social life became coterminous."[339]

When one contemplates the essence of sanctification and its ability to bring social change, we find overwhelming hope. If every person is touched by God's power in sanctification, love will be at work. Love means the destruction of ill will and the inception of goodwill. This gives a meaningful paradigm for a social theology in the Church Militant.

The Church's Social Scope Within a Wesleyan Tradition

"One element in the strength of Wesleyanism as a social power," explains Francis McConnell, "lay in that it took any account at all of what we call the masses."[340] Taylor points out that the Wesleyan movement took action in the abolition of slavery and in improving the conditions of life for the poor and oppressed. The needs of people in the world are indicative of the need for the Church to be involved in social work. It was Wesley's theology and spiritual commitment that controlled his politics and social action. Involvement is the outgrowth of spiritual conversion that is based on new values. According to Taylor, activity in social life is a consequence of the experience and process of sanctification.[341]

While sanctification is personal, it has collective implications. Sanctification includes loving "the Lord . . . God with all your and with all your soul and with

337. Robert E. Chiles, *Scriptural Christianity: A Call to Wesley's Disciples* (Grand Rapids, MI: Asbury, 1984), 29.

338. Steve Harper, *Devotional Life in the Wesleyan Tradition* (Nashville: Upper Room, 1983), 66.

339. Bebb, 40.

340. Francis J. McConnell, *John Wesley* (New York: Abingdon-Cokesbury, 1984), 234.

341. Blaine Taylor, *John Wesley: A Blueprint for Church Renewal* (Illinois: Crouse, 1984), 165-166.

all your strength and with all your mind," and loving "your neighbor as yourself" (Luke 10:27). The sanctified heart can never rest at ease in any society where there is need for social improvement. Love compels one to act to alleviate problems.

Conclusion

In no way will the Church be fully able to put an end to social problems. However, this does not exempt the Church from its responsibilities. The Church is called to stand up, to speak out, and to act in its earthly context. The social implication of the message of sanctification focuses us. A Wesleyan perspective of a social theology is a theology of love. The Church can be militant, but the root of its militant spirit within the Wesleyan perspective is love. It is love in the midst of social ills and aggressive social action. Wesley exhorts us, "This love we believe to be the medicine of life, the never failing remedy for all the evils of a disordered world, for all the miseries and vices ... continually springing forth, not only in innocence ... but likewise in every kind of beneficence, spreading virtue and happiness all around it."[342]

A contemporary statement of the Church's social scope in a Wesleyan tradition can be as follows: The Church is called upon to be militant with a social theology, having love at its roots. Love is the pure unadulterated gift of God working itself out in goodwill towards all. The perspective calls for seeking the souls of persons and working towards social reform. This is a spiritually practical and physically practical scope. It is to be a practice of love applied in the whole range of human existence. In the Church Militant, we are called to affect and to infect our world with an aggressive theology of love that invites social involvement.

Anthony Manswell is a global missionary for God in the Church of the Nazarene, assigned to Caribbean Nazarene with his wife Barbara and four children. Anthony graduated with a Bachelor of Theology from Canadian Nazarene College (Caribbean Nazarene College campus) in 1990, a Master of Divinity from Nazarene Theological Seminary in 1994, and a Doctorate in Education from Trevecca Nazarene University in 2008.

---

342. John Wesley' Sermons, Vol. II:270.

Reclaiming Wesley's Class Meeting for Intentional Discipleship

Craig Drurey

There are a few things in life I absolutely dread doing. Moving is one of those things. I hate moving. When you move, you discover you have more stuff than you should. Moving is the process by which I sort out my stuff: stuff that is important, stuff I never really use, stuff that is broken and worn out. Moving should also be a social activity. It should never be done alone. So of course, I ask as many friends and family as I can to help me move. My closest friends and family help make my moving experience a lot easier. Moving into holiness can be viewed in much the same way.

John Wesley famously said that there is no holiness except social holiness.[343] What he meant was there was no living holiness by yourself. It was not a private, individual endeavor. Holiness can only be expressed in the context of relating to others rightly and never simply by how one privately lives life. John Wesley knew this very well when he required every Methodist to be active in class meetings.

The Church of the Nazarene's brand of Wesleyanism did not carry over John Wesley's emphasis on accountable discipleship through class meetings. Instead, the Church of the Nazarene, from its very beginning, has been heavily influenced by a revivalistic/camp-meeting emphasis. This emphasis has focused on crisis experiences of salvation and entire sanctification.

We have often seen growth in holiness as a cookie cutter experience of these two crisis experiences. A person could tell where she was at in the discipleship process by how many times she had been to the altar. We have viewed effective discipleship as convincing people to make the minimum required two trips to the altar.

With this emphasis on crisis experiences, discipleship in the Church of the Nazarene has been carried out mostly by: counseling at an altar (while one sought or solidified one of the crisis experiences, preaching, Sunday School, and private Bible study and prayer. Spiritual formation did occur in people as the Church

---

343. Wesley, J., *The Works of John Wesley*, Third Edition, Vol. 14 (London: Wesleyan Methodist Book Room, 1872) 321.

of the Nazarene grew, but now we must face how times have changed. We have to ask if we are not overemphasizing crisis experiences, private discipleship, and the transfer of knowledge. Has the authentic living and spreading of scriptural holiness been impacted by a lack of accountable discipleship?

John Wesley had a relational view of discipleship. He referred to the way of salvation as moving into the house of God. The porch, door, and rooms of the house equated to prevenient, justifying, and sanctifying grace.[344] Scriptural holiness was nothing less than moving back home and living with God and God's family.

This moving back home with God was best accomplished through the class meeting. Wesley recognized that any response on our part always begins with grace—God's love enabling us to recognize and respond to God. However, he considered the class meeting a means of grace whereby God was able to work grace more effectually in and through people. The class meeting was essentially family and friends helping each other move back home and live with God and others.

There is a process by which people move and help others move back into the house of God. This process consists of three doctrines Wesley thought to be essential—*holiness, repentance, and faith*.[345] When we recognize holiness in God or in others, we are brought to awareness in ourselves where we are lacking. We are magnetized, compelled, and drawn to want to exhibit this perfect love we call holiness. This awareness helps us to admit to our lacking and creates a desire for growth to occur. This process is what repentance entails. With this awareness, confession, and desire, God enables faith in God's grace to bring about transformation. We then grow in holiness to be more like this perfect love we have experienced in God and others. Then the process begins again: holiness experienced, repentance, faith, and then holiness lived out. This process is how we move into God's house and explore the rooms of holiness in God's house.

Besides displaying perfect love to other class members, helping others remove *blockages to God's grace* will effectively enable others to be able to respond and move forward in God's grace. Blockages to God's grace take many shapes and are caused by various people, situations, and factors.

One of the first common blockages to God's grace are barriers that the church erects around God's house. These barriers act as fences which determine who can experience God's grace. God's grace is abundant and free, yet the church often likes to control how God's grace is measured out and to whom. An effective class

344. Ibid., Vol. 8, 472.

345. Ibid.

meeting breaks down the artificial barriers the church has erected to limit God's free flowing grace.

These fences take on many different appearances. For example, the church often overloads justifying grace by making justification about adopting beliefs and practices in order to be "properly" justified.[346] Justifying grace needs to be restored to the proclamation that God's atoning work has already been completed by Jesus. People simply need to accept the salvation God has already provided.[347]

Another example is when the church wants everyone to fit into the cookie cutter milestones of grace. Yes, justifying grace and sanctifying grace are available and true. However, each person has unique experiences of God's grace. The timing and how God extends grace varies from person to person. A class meeting will have complete confidence in God's grace and God's time with how each person responds to God's grace.

Another artificial fence results when the church does not extend biblical hospitality to the stranger. In our current modes of discipleship that seek to protect right morality and right beliefs, we actually cease being hospitable to the biblical stranger we are instructed to love. Strangers need to be seen as people loved by God, not as objects of our spiritual, moral, and political warfare. True hospitality allows people to enter our community without expectations.

For this reason, accountable discipleship should begin at the moment one begins to recognize her need for God. John Wesley would admit a person into a class meeting at the moment one was "awakened."[348] For Wesley, someone simply needed to have the beginning awareness of God and a desire for something more to enter accountable discipleship.

The stranger is often tired and wounded from the journey. The church community, properly relating through class meetings, will offer a sanctuary and a safe place for this stranger to enter and find healing and rest. This does not imply that the stranger will not change and find healing. It does imply that the healing and rest is up to God and placing confidence in God's amazing, always at work, grace. The church blocks grace when the church fails to begin accountable discipleship with a person prior to justification.

Another type of blockage to God's grace takes the form of *baggage*. The class meeting will help fellow members sort through, carry, get rid of, and minimize baggage that blocks the free flow of God's grace. Baggage takes the shape of

---

346. Watson, David L., *God Does Not Foreclose: The Universal Promise of Salvation* (Nashville: Abingdon Press, 1990) 108.

347. Ibid., 107.

348. Wesley, J., & Wesley, C., "The Nature, Design, and General Rules of the United Societies," *The Works of John Wesley Third Edition*, Vol. 8 (London: Wesleyan Methodist Book Room, 1872) 270.

heredity, addictions, peer pressure, past choices, illnesses, abuse and many other factors. This baggage can limit or interfere with our ability to respond to God's grace.

Much of this baggage takes time to work through. It should be acknowledged that some of this baggage may never be thoroughly overcome this side of God's glorifying grace. Yet, no one should ever despair of God's sustaining and delivering grace in this life. Accountable discipleship through class meetings is an intentional way to help each other sort through, get rid of, and overcome baggage that blocks God's grace. Class members, in perfect love, will provide the support, encouragement, and care to help fellow class members move and minimize the baggage in order to move into God's house.

I would like to share the story of my experience moving into God's house from within my Church of the Nazarene upbringing. I was saved at the age of seven in a Sunday morning revival service. After being saved, I began hearing testimonies of entire sanctification. I heard it preached often at camp meetings and revivals. I read of our denomination's early history. With all this exposure to our teaching on entire sanctification, I earnestly sought this experience.

I cannot say how many trips I made to the altar seeking the experience. I thought I "got it." Then, I would go home, and—in my living or failure to live out what I considered to be holiness—I would determine I must not have gotten it.

The church provided me the discipleship model I described earlier. Even though I did not realize it, deep in my heart, I was yearning for family and friends to help me move back home to God's house of holiness. It was not until very recently that I got that help. It took almost 40 years to have assurance of the ability and reality of living in God's house of holiness.

Today's culture is ripe for our optimistic holiness message. We must be willing and ready to help people move home with God by reclaiming Wesley's class meeting.

Craig Drurey is a life-long member of the Church of the Nazarene residing in Ohio. He is currently a Doctor of Ministry Student at Ashland Theological Seminary. His Doctor of Ministry emphasis is in Wesleyan practices with a particular focus on relational discipleship. He currently leads the educational and discipleship ministries at Wadsworth Church of the Nazarene.

Covenant Discipleship:

Recovering the Class Meeting for Today

Jay Sunberg

Hebrews 10:24 calls believers to consider how they can spur one another on toward love and good deeds. In every generation, the church has the responsibility of discipling those who have chosen to follow Christ. However, this spurring on and being spurred on toward better discipleship practice is challenging for our generation. How do we find a way to open ourselves up to be transformed and live transformationally in our world?

The early Methodists of the 18th century certainly took seriously the task of discipling their generation. Part of John Wesley's genius was his ability to combine effective evangelism with fruitful discipleship. When people responded in mass to the preaching of the Gospel, they were invited to enter the Methodist discipleship system of society, classes, and bands.

As the Methodist system evolved, the class meeting became the entry point to their discipleship system. It became an accountability group that helped the participants watch over the development of everyone in the group. Sondra Higgins Matthaei summarized what took place in the class meeting: "Each member . . . received instruction in the faith and nurture for holy living in a system whose purpose was behavior change, spiritual growth, personal interaction, and community transformation."[349] The intent of the class meeting was to ask each participant to give a straightforward accounting of what had taken place the previous week according to the general rules of the Methodists.

The participants of the class meetings were asked to live out discipleship in two forms. *Works of mercy* included those practices that responded to God's grace by serving Christ in the world.[350] These were defined as feeding the hungry, clothing the naked, visiting the prisons and the hospitals, and seeking out those in need (Matt. 25:35-36 and James 2:14-17). *Works of piety* included the basic spiritual disciplines through which a person could further open themselves to God's grace. These encompassed prayer (private, family, and public), searching

---

349. Sondra Higgins Matthaei, *Making Disciples: Faith Formation in the Wesleyan Tradition* (Nashville: Abingdon, 2000), 131.

350. See *The Works of John Wesley*, 14 vols., ed. Thomas Jackson (Grand Rapids, MI: Baker, 1979), 8:322-23.

the Scriptures, the Lord's Supper, fasting, and Christian conference. Works of piety also incorporated forms of personal disciplines and fellowship including the class meeting itself.

Watson explains the results of the class meetings:

> The priority of the early Methodists was not to seek a particular religious experience, but to pursue an obedient discipleship. Their commitment to the class meeting expressed belief in a salvation which gave them freedom *and* responsibility under God's grace. It was a supportive structure for discipleship, grounded in the realities and the common sense of worldly living; and . . . it was the muscle of the Methodist movement.[351]

Wesley also noted the effectiveness of the class meetings:

> Great and many are the advantages that have ever since flowed from this closer union of the believers with each other. They prayed for one another, that they might be healed of the faults they confessed—and it was so. The chains were broken, the bands were burst asunder, and sin had no more dominion over them. Many were delivered from the temptations out of which till then they found no way of escape. They were built up in our most holy faith. They rejoiced in the Lord more abundantly. They were strengthened in love, and more effectively provoked to abound in every good work.[352]

By opening themselves up to be accountable to each other for spiritual growth and by turning their discipleship outward toward the hurting world, not only were the Methodists transformed, but they also became agents of transformation in their society.

In our generation, instead of cutting and pasting the 18th century Methodist class meeting into our setting, David Lowes Watson sought to recover valuable aspects of the class meeting through Covenant Discipleship. Watson defined Covenant Discipleship simply as "Christian formation through mutual accountability." He later expanded that definition, "A covenant discipleship group

351. David Lowes Watson, *Accountable Discipleship: Handbook for Covenant Discipleship Groups in the Congregation* (Nashville: Discipleship Resources, 1984), 35.

352. Rupert E. Davies (Ed.), *The Works of John Wesley*, Volume 9: The Methodist Societies: History, Nature, and Design (Nashville: Abingdon, 1989), 268.

consists of two to seven people who agree to meet together for one hour per week in order to hold themselves mutually accountable for their discipleship. They do this by affirming a written covenant on which they themselves have agreed."[353]

It is a group of people who come together to help each other be consistent and faithful in the essential practices which spur on the life of discipleship. In doing so, the responsibility for discipleship is not left in the hands of each individual disciple, but discipleship rather becomes a group project. No longer do individuals say, "*I* am responsible for *my* discipleship, but instead covenant group members now say, "*We* are responsible for *our* discipleship. I for you, you for me, and we for each other."

At minimum Covenant Discipleship establishes a small group of people who decide to hold each other accountable for being consistent in the essential discipleship practices that will help each person grow in their Christian lives. Beyond that, covenant groups become a place where a group of people *together* are transformed as they open themselves up to each other to the transforming power of a consistent and balanced life of discipleship. And in the process, they offer themselves *together* to be ministers of transformation in their society. They shape their lives after Jesus to effectively live in and transform the contemporary world.

Permission to spur one another on in the area of discipleship, however, is not automatically given in our generation. Arriving at this level of openness to others is not easy to achieve. Covenant Discipleship, then, requires a re-wiring of how we think of discipleship. It requires opening ourselves to others for the sake of growing deeper in Christ than we could have or would have on our own. Covenant Discipleship participants must be willing to join with others of like purpose in living out an obedient discipleship in the world by making discipleship more accountable and effective.

David Lowes Watson claims that by failing to help one another to be open to God's grace, we are deliberately opting for self-sufficiency in our discipleship.[354] Opening ourselves up to each other relies instead on the covenant relationship of the group.

So how does Covenant Discipleship work? Generally, the best way to kick off a Covenant Discipleship group is with a weekend seminar. The content of the weekend seminar begins with an examination of the biblical meaning and historical practice of discipleship. The concept of Covenant Discipleship is also explored, including the details of how Covenant Discipleship groups function. The

---

353. David Lowes Watson, *Covenant Discipleship: Christian Formation Through Mutual Accountability* (Nashville: Discipleship Resources, 1991), 97.

354. Ibid, 17.

seminar concludes by forming the participants into covenant groups. Each group crafts a covenant statement containing six to ten discipleship practices which each participants agrees to keep on a weekly basis. The participants acknowledge their commitment to the covenant statement by signing their signature to it.

Wesley provides the structure on which discipleship covenants are built. Watson reworked Wesley's two discipleship categories (works of piety and works of mercy) into four new categories. Works of piety become *acts of devotion* and *acts of worship*; and works of piety become *acts of compassion* and *acts of justice.*[355]

After the weekend seminar, the participants agree on a time and a place for the group to meet. As they gather weekly, the group begins each session by reading the discipleship covenant to which they have committed. Each member then gives an account of how they have met the discipleship commitments in the previous week. The other participants then speak words of encouragement or exhortation to each other as needed. The meeting then closes in prayer, and the participants begin fulfilling their discipleship commitments for the following week.

A record is maintained each week of each participant's assessment of how well they kept each discipleship commitment. Over time, the group begins to see patterns for each participant of which discipleship practices are more easily kept and which are more difficult. The members then explore ways to help each other improve where improvement is needed.

I have had the privilege of helping to establish several successful Covenant Discipleship groups in Eastern Europe. The good news is that even the simple effort to focus intentionally on discipleship begins to yield positive results in the lives of those who agree to be a part of a Covenant Discipleship group. Furthermore, if participants are willing to take the risk of opening themselves up to the care of others as well as to take on the responsibility for the discipleship of others in their group, some level of transformation will happen in their lives. Over time, as the group gets beyond acts of compassion and progresses with acts of justice, transformation of society moves from a theory to a real possibility. In Covenant Discipleship, David Lowes Watson has gifted the contemporary church with a powerful tool for transformation, both for disciples as well as for their communities.

Jay lives in Budapest, Hungary and serves as the Field Strategy Coordinator for the Central Europe Field. He oversees the development of the Church of the Nazarene in two pioneer areas and 5 new (Phase 1) districts spanning 11 countries. He loves his jobs and the people of Central Europe. He and his wife Teanna have four daughters.

355. Ibid, 68.

Functional Holiness
Douglas R. Milne

Believers can only function in the life of holiness because God is the author of holiness and the very nature of what it means to be holy. While living a moral and ethical life dedicated to Christ is part of holy living, making holiness about something believers do negates the fact that living holiness in this life is possible because of what God does. God enables believers to be functional human beings.

This term "functional" is essential for understanding the lifestyle of holiness. Those things believers say, the love they offer, the blessings they extend, the mercy they grant, and the compassion they bestow are available because God empowers them to live holy. Furthermore, as a key proponent of biblical and practical holiness, John Wesley helps us understand functional holiness.

Being an authentic "believer" means more than just making an initial commitment to Jesus Christ. Authentic believers are also dedicated followers of Jesus—in belief, ethic, character, and affinity. Being a follower indicates a reliance on the leader that can only be developed by a continuous, growing relationship. Wesley preached a livable, practical holiness in a broken world; thus, holiness was functional and not some obscure, unattainable biblical concept.

The major issues within the holiness theology conversation are two-fold. First, holiness remains a complex topic because it has proven to be difficult to define and explain. Either "holiness" results in a rigid, legalistic lifestyle, or "holiness" is assumed to be unattainable and therefore lacks practical application. Second, scholars from various theological backgrounds begin the conversation from different perspectives—e.g. sin, love, judgment. Therefore, the value of Wesley's message lies in his biblical and theological explanations of holiness as a functional part of the Christian life.

God is holy; therefore, holiness is rooted in a loving, Trinitarian God. Believers can be holy because God loves them. Thomas Oord offers an excellent definition of love that provides a solid foundation for this idea of functional holiness, "To love is to act intentionally, in sympathetic/emphatic response to God and others, to promote overall well-being."[356] Theodore Runyon adds, "Love cannot be appropriated as an abstract idea; it must be encountered, it must be participated

---

356. Thomas J. Oord, *The Nature of Love: A Theology* (St. Louis: Chalice, 2010), 17.

in. It must be allowed to work its transforming power in our hearts, at the center of our identity, where its affirmation is received and responded to. And precisely through this love God continues to be our Creator!"[357] Thus, our Trinitarian God, through love and grace, empowers believers to live functional holiness unto God and in to the world.

Defining Terms

Functionality is the ability to fulfill those useful, specific actions given by God and offered to the church and the world as an extension of the Christian faith. God has blessed humanity with specific giftedness, and humanity, in turn, shares that giftedness as an extension of faith in God—the Creator of humanity, individuality, and holiness. Arguably, using the term "functional" allows God's holiness to be more accessible. The term does not devalue holiness, but it assists in strengthening the relationship between God and believer. Additionally, functional holiness combines faith, Christian maturity, and action.

Holiness is a theological concept that creates freedom for some and burden for others solely based on its definition. Holiness does not and cannot begin with human beings because it is a reflection and response to an initiating, empowering God. For those who consider it unattainable, the command to be holy becomes a burden. However, for those who recognize that God's holiness is meant for hope, it becomes freedom in the Christian life. For our purposes, *holiness* is the gracious, loving gift of God for humanity to live out the biblical mandate to "be holy as God is holy.'

Inherent to functional holiness is mission. Believers who act on their faith and live the life of holiness become missional. They have the ability to function in this world. Michael Goheen suggests that believers who enact their faith follow God's intention for them to be people who are blessed by God so that they can minister to the world [358]

Within his sermons, Wesley developed a theology of holiness that urged hearers and readers to accept God's holiness as a livable aspect of the Christian life. His theological convictions led him to become a proponent of a lifestyle of holiness and sanctification. Although Wesley preached these sermons in the eighteenth-century, the sermons present contemporary implications for the twenty-first-century church. Wesley's understanding of a loving and gracious God remain relevant in our contemporary church culture and in our efforts of sharing love and grace with the world.

357. Theodore H. Runyon, The New Creation: John Wesley's Theology Today (Nashville: Abingdon, 1998), 226.

358. Michael W. Goheen, *A Light to the Nations: The Missional Church and the Biblical Story* (Grand Rapids: Baker Academic, 2011), 32-2, 100.

The Holy Spirit

For Wesley, the Holy Spirit made the Christian life livable; it empowered, enabled, enriched, encouraged, and educated. Wesley wrote that, apart from the Spirit, believers would not last, left to our own human devices.[359] Therefore, reliance on the Spirit brought dependence, allowing humanity to respond in a proper way to sin and corruption.[360] Wesley claimed that the Spirit enriched the life of Christians by cleansing their minds and bringing them to understanding through enlightenment.[361] The Holy Spirit encouraged every believer, "Indeed it is the same Spirit who works in them that clear and cheerful confidence that their heart is upright toward God; that good assurance that they now do, through his grace, the things which are acceptable in his sight; that they are now in the path which leadeth to life, and shall, by the mercy of God, endure therein to the end."[362] Total reliance on the Spirit of God brought new life on earth and for eternity. Finally, Wesley contended that the Holy Spirit educated humanity by continually renewing our minds, so believers would understand important truths through the gift of discernment.[363] Through all this, Wesley summarized the glorious optimism of a Christian life dependent on the Holy Spirit.

Inward and Outward Holiness

The message of inward and outward holiness changed very little from sermon to sermon for Wesley. Inward holiness was the work of God within the hearts of humanity.[364] God cleansed the very soul of creation. Inward holiness also demonstrated God's desire for humanity to respond to the invitation for cleansing. If an individual possessed inward holiness, then it was natural for him or her to show fruits of that spiritual growth.

Outward signs of inward holiness were part of the Christian religion. Wesley believed that Christianity was a social religion. If this was the case, then holy individuals practiced visible ministry through the Spirit of God.[365] Individuals formed the church body. Therefore, Christ used the populace of believers to perform outward acts for the betterment of the world. Wesley saw the church as a collective body functioning to advance the present reality of the Kingdom of God. A believer could not remain an inward Christian only: "So impossible

359. Wesley, "The Circumcision of the Heart," 1:401–14.

360. Ibid, 402–3.

361. Ibid, 405.

362. Ibid, 406–7.

363. Wesley, "The Circumcision of the Heart," 1:402.

364. Wesley, "Upon our Lord's Sermon on the Mount, Discourse IV," 1:531–2.

365. Ibid, 540–1.

it is to keep our religion from being seen, unless we cast it away; so vain is the thought of hiding the light, unless by putting it out. Sure, it is that a secret, unobserved religion cannot be the religion of Jesus Christ. Whatever religion can be concealed is not Christianity."[366]

Because humanity, sin, grace, God, and holiness all worked together, Wesley applied many concepts from Scripture to the eighteenth-century Christian life. Faith was the all-encompassing catalyst. Through faith, Christ strengthened and empowered humanity to live spiritually.[367] God made sinners new, bringing them from darkness into light.[368] Christ offered full deliverance, atonement, and fulfillment.[369] God, particularly through Christ, served as the model of love. Wesley believed that love made the Christian life work properly, "When we love one another, there is no need of either disguise or reserve."[370]

The lifestyle of holiness is a life filled with love, grace, freedom, purpose, and mission. The very nature of holiness brings function to humanity. God continues to bless human beings with a loving purpose and allows them to participate in building the church and building the Kingdom. It is here that Wesley's sermons serve as a guide. Even his eighteenth-century preaching speaks a clear and relevant message to our context today: holiness is a social, active, and functional.

Doug Milne has served in six churches in the areas of music, worship, and youth and families, and he is currently Lead Pastor at Grace Church of the Nazarene in Rochester, NY. He is a graduate of Eastern Nazarene College and Northeastern Seminary. In addition, he is an adjunct professor of religion at Roberts Wesleyan College and is a second year Ph.D. student at McMaster Divinity College in Hamilton, Ontario, Canada.

---

366. Ibid, 540.

367. Wesley, "The Repentance of Believers," 1:350.

368. Ibid, 350.

369. Ibid, 351–2.

370. John Wesley, "Letter to Mrs. Bennis," in *John and Charles Wesley: Selected Prayers, Hymns, and Journal Notes, Sermons, Letters and Treatises*, ed. Frank Whaling (New York: Paulist, 1981), 162.

Ordinary Holiness and the Recovery of Practical Moral Reasoning

Joshua R. Sweeden

I grew up in an age of holiness polarities. Like many Nazarenes of my generation, holiness was often presented through abstinence on the one hand, and pursuit on the other. The forms and practices of holiness were interpreted as abstaining from worldly pleasures, temptations, and indulgences—while pursuing devotion, discipline, and spiritual experience. For many Christians who are part of the Wesleyan-Holiness tradition, church experience was a balancing act between two ends of this spectrum.

The polarities were fleshed out in tangible forms. There was a clear imperative to abstain from personal extravagance in clothing and jewelry, to avoid expensive or unnecessary things like luxury vehicles and tattoos, and to refrain from those activities relating to "desires of the flesh." This modern truncated version of Christian asceticism bore an equally strong imperative to embrace the excesses of the holy life. The importance of "assurance" and the experience of God took center stage. Alongside devotion to prayer and scripture reading, revivals, camp meetings, and altar calls exemplified the requisites for a complete change of heart. Sunday school and Caravans (a.k.a. Nazarene Boy Scouts for any uninitiated readers) provided the backbone of discipleship and formation in our way of life.

At the time, the beauty of the culture in which I was being formed was less apparent to me than its oddity or strangeness. The holiness worldview seemed to be constructed of binaries: Christian and unchristian, holy and unholy, *dos* and *don'ts*, all out or all in. As I got older, I began to wonder just what my church thought they were holding in balance when teaching detachment from the world alongside attachment to God, or insecurity of material things in contrast with certainty in faith, or thriftiness and simplicity next to an overabundance in joy. Just how did abstaining from drinking spirits relate to a desire to get drunk on the Spirit?

I have discovered that such questions are common for members of the Wesleyan-Holiness tradition. Embodying what John Wesley called "holiness of heart and life" requires a difficult and on-going process for the church. The

Church of the Nazarene has excelled at extending various holiness emphases or expectations taken up by preceding generations. Indeed, the church's structures of discipleship and formation enable it to pass on its traditions very effectively, and my own experience of inculturation into this odd way of life is testimony to the church's formative strength.

However, we are still left with the difficult task of connecting first-order mores and ethics to their second-order frameworks, narratives, and presumptions. Behind each explicit imperative, directive, or expectation lie implicit suppositions of their value and purpose. Identifying and wrestling with the latter is an ever-present challenge for the church, especially the Church of the Nazarene as it emerges from the 20th century that largely underscored and reiterated past mores and ethics.

Many of the holiness binaries I experienced are appropriately rooted in the ministry of the Wesleys and the early Methodist movement. John Wesley continually asserted that "inward change" should be accompanied by "outward righteousness." His own desire for assurance and deeper relationship with God was coupled with a commitment to Christian action. John Wesley's dual emphasis on "works of piety" and "works of mercy" also attests to the interdependence of inward change and outward righteousness. In this regard, Wesley did not reinforce binaries, but instead assumed overlapping and mutually dependent practices of Christian faithfulness.

Not surprisingly, John Wesley's own ethical admonishments to the people called Methodists can read like a mid-twentieth century list of holiness rules. He had no hesitation to declare a set of *dos* and *don'ts* in various situations and contexts. Later in his life, in fact, Wesley became more vocal about the Methodists' specific ethical practices. In his sermons "Scriptural Christianity," "The More Excellent Way," and "Causes of the Inefficacy of Christianity," Wesley urged the people called Methodists to attend to ordinary matters such as sleep, prayer, work, food, conversation, diversions, and money.[371] On the appropriate use of money Wesley was particularly adamant, and in his sermon "The Danger of Riches," he chastisedthe people called Methodists for their lack of attention to this "precious talent."[372]

---

371. See John Wesley, "The More Excellent Way," in John Wesley's Sermons: An Anthology, eds. Albert Outler & Richard Heitzenrater (Nashville: Abingdon Press, 1991), 520.

372. At times, Wesley refers to money as the most "precious" or "comprehensive" talent to be employed faithfully for God's purposes. For Wesley, money was a danger or temptation, but could also be used for good. See "The Good Steward," in John Wesley's Sermons: An Anthology, eds. Albert Outler and Richard Heitzenrater (Nashville: Abingdon Press, 1991).

Wesley's admonishments to the Methodists on ordinary matters were surprisingly specific. He had instructions on how to work, use money, and dress; he freely offered advice for how to eat, sleep, and remain healthy. Wesley referred to these early Methodist daily practices as "ordinary fruits" or "gifts" with the purpose of exemplifying for the broader church and world the faithful embodiment of the holy life.[373] Subsequently, Wesley's ethical admonishments and the practices of early Methodists provided the impetus for the later Holiness Movement's convictions regarding similar matters.

Analogous to the extension of Wesley's ethical admonishments is a lineage of social concern in the Wesleyan-Holiness tradition. Wesleyan-Holiness churches embrace their heritage of social reform and involvement in abolition, the purity crusade, women's suffrage, temperance, and alleviation of poverty. But by the mid-twentieth century many of these reform movements moved to the backdrop of ecclesial identity. Had they been "successful," run their course, or simply diminished in light of other holiness distinctives? Regardless, what remained were ethical maxims and imperatives without the theological rationale needed to sustain them. In other words, Nazarenes like me were often receiving first-order ethics and mores with little connection to the second-order framework and purpose.

Wesley had constructed his ethical admonishments alongside larger social concerns, which, it so happens, were constructed in response to outward righteousness and holiness of life, and which, again, were constructed in tandem with inward change and holiness of heart. Of course, such connections were not always clear in his lifetime, which may explain why, for example, the early Methodists struggled with Wesley's teachings on money and wealth.[374] Furthermore, what connections may have been clear in Wesley's mind, or the connections scholars have pieced together from his writings, cannot presuppose that they were clear to the people called Methodists.

Even still, many of Wesley's ethical assertions had significant traction, enough, in fact, to stretch beyond the social concerns in which they were rooted. A primary example being Wesley's opposition, on behalf of the poor, to spirited

---

373. Wesley believed addressing the ordinary fruits to be "more useful [for his] generation," arguing it could "'sound the unbelieving heart'; and [be] the gift of persuasion to move the affections, as well as enlighten the understanding." In other words, attending to the ordinary fruits was both Christian witness and formation. John Wesley, "The More Excellent Way," in John Wesley's Sermons: An Anthology, eds. Albert Outler & Richard Heitzenrater (Nashville: Abingdon Press, 1991), 512.

374. Wesley's sermon, "The Danger of Riches" is testimony of the Methodist hesitance to follow Wesley's economic exhortations. As Outler and Heitzenrater note, "Many, if not most, of the newly rich Methodists were stubbornly unconvinced that their affluence was a fatal inlet to sin. Therefore, they simply ignored Wesley's insistence that they part will all but their 'necessaries and conveniences'." See "An Introductory Comment" to "The Danger of Riches," in John Wesley's Sermons: An Anthology, eds. Albert Outler and Richard Heitzenrater (Nashville: Abingdon Press, 1991), 451.

(distilled) liquors. Wesley's concern was not alcohol *per se*, but the industry that preyed on the underclass and the wastefulness of grains that drove up food prices for the poor.[375]

The challenge for the Church of the Nazarene is to recover holiness beyond the polarities. Our Nazarene forebears shared Wesley's impetus to connect holiness to matters of dress, drink, and excess. Today, however, those holiness codes are widely viewed as static and outdated. In some cases, the practices no longer fit contextually, and it is appropriate to leave those first-order ethics behind. Gone are the days of pantyhose and the removal of wedding bands. In other cases, it is a lack of understanding the second-order ethics—the deeper purpose and theological rationale -that has caused many to throw the proverbial baby out with the bath water. We need to recover the interdependence of inward change and outward righteousness, so the binaries—including those of "heart" and "life" and "personal" and "social"—are intertwined in our daily practices of holiness.

Education and reeducation is a first task for the Church of the Nazarene to reclaim the relationship between inward change and outward righteousness. As part of discipleship and formation, the connections between the first-order and second-order ethics must named, discussed, and—when necessary—reconsidered.

A second task, which flows out of the first, is to recover processes of practical moral reasoning in the life of the church. Such processes would entail communal deliberation and discernment of embodied holiness in its tangible and daily forms. In place of simplified presentations of holiness practice, often relegated to binary constructions, practical moral reasoning demands patience and persistence— the ability to sit amongst the complexities of Christian convictions and ethical embodiment without needing to resolve the ambiguity too quickly.

Undergirding processes of practical moral reasoning is recognition of the communal and contextual nature of ethics. In place of the extremes of ethical *formalism* or *situationalism*, where ethics either transcends all time and space or remains entirely subject to time and space, the contextuality of ethics is recognition that faithful Christian action does not exist in a vacuum. As the church today engages in practical moral reasoning, new possibilities for holiness in the "ordinary fruits" and "gifts" can become apparent. Considering the relationship between Wesley's ethical admonishments, his broader social concerns, and theological convictions, Nazarenes today can discover how our theological convictions shape holiness practice. Such discovery might propose, for example, a commitment to holiness that addresses issues such as global poverty, environmental degradation,

---

375. See John Wesley's, "Thoughts on the Present Scarcity of Provisions" and Richard Heitzenrater's *The Poor and the People Called Methodist* (Nashville, TN: Kingswood Books, 2002).

human trafficking, and racism. Furthermore, like Wesley's 18th century everyday directives, we can identify how the ways we eat, drink, sleep, work, converse, relax, and spend money are still matters of ordinary holiness.

Ultimately, engaging in processes of practical moral reasoning might mean we give our Nazarene forebears more credit. Once provided the opportunity to uncover and wrestle with the theological assumptions and rationalities of past generations, Nazarenes today are better equipped to understand and embrace a rich heritage of holiness practice. Accordingly, ordinary practices of holiness can be engendered that are neither the simple reiteration nor rejection of past mores and ethics. Instead, we can develop fresh and dynamic expressions of the holiness commitments that remain central to the Wesleyan-Holiness tradition.

Joshua R. Sweeden is Assistant Professor of Theology and Richard B. Parker Co-Chair in Wesleyan Theology at George Fox Evangelical Seminary. He is appreciative of various Nazarene communities and their commitment to his Christian formation.

The Duty of Constant Confession:

The Wesleyan Way of Holiness

Jason T. Rowinski

Means of Grace

Imagine you're an eleven-year-old Roman Catholic schoolboy. It's Tuesday morning, and you're sitting quietly in a church with wooden pews, stone floors and marble walls. You're in church preparing for confession. You enter the confessional booth. On the other side of a screened wall, a priest sits waiting for you to speak. You proceed to tell him your sins, which at eleven sound something like, "I've said some cuss words. I punched my sister in the stomach when she took my Legos. I lied to my mom about watching HBO movies after 11pm." The priest listens intently and asks a few questions to probe the sincerity of your repentance. He assigns you some prayers to say, then proclaims, "God the Father of mercies, through the death and resurrection of your son, you have reconciled the world to yourself and sent the Holy Spirit among us for the forgiveness of sins. Through the ministry of the church, may God grant you pardon and peace. And I absolve you of your sins, in the name of the Father, and of the Son and of the Holy Spirit. Amen." You leave the confessional booth, go to a place of prayer in the sanctuary and begin your prayers. *You rise from your place of prayer and you leave the sanctuary. You feel something in your spirit. You feel clean. You feel free. You feel forgiven. You feel new.*

Imagine you're a fifteen year old at a Church of the Nazarene camp meeting. You're sitting in a tabernacle with a few thousand worshippers. If there's air conditioning in the room, you can't feel it—because it's a hot, humid July summer night, and the room is packed. The evangelist is talking about the need not only to be saved but to be sanctified, to have victory over the sinful nature through heart cleansing and Spirit-filling. He invites the congregation to stand, to sing, and to come to the altar to confess the need for sanctification. The song leader sings, "All to Jesus, I surrender, all to him I freely give. I will ever love and trust him, in his presence daily live. I surrender all." Dozens of people are already at the altar, yet the evangelist continues to call others to come and take these public steps forward in the presence of God and others. You feel the conviction to move forward, kneel and pray. You're surrounded by friends and strangers who lay their hands on you and pray over you to be cleansed from sin and filled with the Spirit. *You rise from your place of prayer and you leave the tabernacle. You feel something in your spirit. You feel clean. You feel free. You feel forgiven. You feel new.*

Imagine you're a twenty-year-old college sophomore. You're a part of an accountability group with your friends. By this point, you've been a Christian long enough to hear good and bad preachers, to see healthy and unhealthy churches, and to discern successful and unsuccessful patterns of Christian living in your own journey. You believe in the holy life, but experience tells you that it's not as simple as it was often portrayed. The old adage, "Don't drink, smoke, cuss, chew or run with girls who do," is the ideal you've complied with, yet you don't feel more Christlike. In fact, you've witnessed the failure of legalism in your life and in the church. Many of the people you know who claim to be holy and sanctified actually lack severely the fruit of the Holy Spirit, which leads you into spiritual cognitive dissonance. You and your friends gather together for encouragement, accountability, and prayer to become more like Jesus. Sitting on an old couch that you brought to college from your grandmother's basement, you wait your turn as the guys in the group honestly share their temptations and failures. Encouragement is offered through scripture and wisdom. The young men bow their heads together and pray for one another. *You rise from your place of prayer and you leave the apartment. You feel something in your spirit. You feel clean. You feel free. You feel forgiven. You feel new.*

These vignettes describe scenes from my encounters with Christian confession, but these experiences are not unique to me. We humans know we are sinners—sinners that need forgiveness and hope. We need cleansing and new life.

Scripture recognizes this and portrays confession as a positive and regular spiritual discipline. Jesus included confession in the Lord's Prayer, "Forgive us our sins as we forgive those who sin against us" (Luke 11:4). James 5:16 instructs, "Confess your sins to each other and pray for each other that you might be healed." In John's gospel, Jesus tells his disciples, "If you forgive anyone's sins, they are forgiven. If you do not forgive them, they are not forgiven" (20:23).

Despite its scriptural and practical importance, not all Christians fully understand or willingly practice confession regularly. Some proclaim they have no need to confess, nothing to reconcile with God or others. The truest Christian view is that confession is meant to be practiced as a spiritual discipline that becomes a means of grace, faith, and holiness.

Via Media
John Wesley is the theological father of the Wesleyan-Holiness strand that runs through Protestantism, evangelicalism, and revivalism. Yet his understanding

of the Christian life has a different flavor compared to that of his Reformed and Calvinistic contemporaries. Wesley's theology draws on such influences as Eastern Orthodoxy and Roman Catholicism, just as he pulls forward his Anglican heritage and experience with the pietism of the Moravians.

Wesley seemed always to search for the *via media*—the middle way. He synthesized theology toward a common goal that he observed in both scripture and tradition—the renewal of the *Imago Dei*.

Wesley understood that the grace of a holy life would not be the normative Christian experience without a system of discipleship developed specifically for that goal. He set out to discover and implement discipleship practices that would enable even the poorest of the poor to progress in the holy life. It is for this reason, he and his friends were called (derogatorily) "Methodists."

Appropriating the scriptural, sacramental discipline of confession, Wesley combined it with the Reformer's understanding of the "priesthood of believers" and placed it within the context of highly relational, confessional discipleship. His goal was the renewal of the *Imago Dei* in the head, habits, and heart of each Christian. His middle way of confessional community lead to spiritual revival and societal change.

The Medium Is the Message

Twentieth century communication theorist Marshall McLuhan coined the phrase, "The medium is the message." This is a clever way of saying that the way we do things (medium) is not just arbitrary or inconsequential; rather, it shapes the message itself. Form communicates content. Separating form from content alters the message.

Wesley's maxim "There is no holiness but social holiness" is oft quoted by (post)modern Christians reminding us that the faith is not first and foremost about me, my experiences, and my salvation from damnation. Christianity is more: participation in the reign of God and the fellowship of believers. Wesley applied social holiness through a multi-level relational discipleship.

In *John Wesley's Class Meeting—A Model for Making Disciples*, D. Michael Henderson describes Wesley's discipleship as a series of interlocking groups:[376]

1. *Society Meeting* (50-70 people, mixed gender, weekly)—aimed at COGNITIVE renewal (*mind change*) through instruction toward holiness by singing, teaching and/or preaching.

---

376. Michael D. Henderson, John Wesley's Class Meeting: A Model for Making Disciples (Nappanee, IN: Evangel, 1997), 83.

2. *Class Meeting* (10-12 people, mixed gender, weekly)—aimed at BEHAVIORAL renewal (*habit change*) through the fellowship of believers helping one another through guided discussion and personal inquiry examining their love for God & others, talking about their trials and how to overcome them, helping new Christians learn how to mature, and to reinforce & explain what was taught in the societies. The class meeting was Wesley's most innovative and effective instrument of discipleship, according to Henderson.

3. *Band Meeting* (3-6 people, same gender, same marital status, weekly)—aimed at AFFECTIVE renewal (*heart change*) through ruthless honesty & frank openness for those committed to the desire to grow in love, holiness, and purity of intention. Serious questions were asked, such as:
   - "What known sins have you committed since our last meeting?"
   - "What temptations have you met with?"
   - "Is the love of God shed abroad in your heart?"
   - "Has no sin, inward or outward, dominion over you?"

This cursory examination of Wesley's system of discipleship clarifies that the goal of the renewal of the *Imago Dei*—and the holy life—is possible only in the context of community, through the regular practice of an examined life. It shouldn't come as a surprise to us that many today feel that the holiness message has lost its power and purpose. This felt experience is a natural result of forsaking the scriptural call and Wesley's practices. *There is no holiness without regular confessional holiness.*

Called Unto Holiness

Imagine what the holiness movement would look like if we practiced confession as a spiritual discipline and regular means of grace. Imagine churches setting aside regular time each month for parishioners to come and speak honestly with pastors about their lives. Imagine people honestly responding to God's grace at an open communion table and open altars—embraced by a reconciling Savior and enveloped in a reconciling community. Imagine the personal and societal transformation resulting from participation in class-meeting-like community groups and band-type accountable relationships.

The holy life is promised and possible, but only through practicing the means of grace, including confession. The call to renovate holiness often originates from the approach of message clarification or special rule observation. The problem is not so much our message but our methods. For too long, we've neglected the practices that give power and purpose to the message. If we desire a true renovation of Christian holiness, we need to turn to the deeper scriptural and Wesleyan disciple-making practices.

Jason Rowinski resides in the Kansas City metro area with his wife Stefanie (also an ordained elder) where he serves as the Lead Pastor of Shawnee Church of the Nazarene. He served previously on the pastoral teams at Bethany First (Discipleship), Overland Park (Outreach & Youth), and West Broad (Youth). He is a graduate of Mount Vernon Nazarene (B.A., 1996), Nazarene Theological Seminary (M.Div., 2000), and Gonzaga (M.A., 2010). His deep desire is to see a renewal of Wesleyan practices within the Church.

Helena the Hedgehog and Holiness

Janel Apps Ramsey

The community where I serve expresses its vision as "cultivating gardens of resurrection." To explore this idea more fully, I'd like you to meet Helena the Hedgehog. A hedgehog is a softball-sized insectivore with short sharp spines on her back and sides. They have a soft furry underbelly and an expressive face with a cute button nose that wiggles from side to side. Hedgehogs, in their native habitat, live in gardens and hedgerows in several parts of the world.

Helena lives in a cage in the corner of my living room. In a perfect world, I could train Helena to live in my garden during the summer and then bring her inside to protect her during the winter and spring. (They hibernate and often die in the cold.) But unfortunately, when she does what she was created to do, she isn't really thinking about the fact that I want her to stay only in my patch of garden. Helena was created to tend the garden at large to help make all things new.

Stewardship is in her DNA. Eating bugs, stirring up the soil, and protecting the garden are all things she does naturally. She is a kingdom creature, cultivating what is given to her. However, when my cats want to play with her, or when she sees an arm come over her like the shadow of a bird, she takes a defensive posture. She immediately curls up into a ball and puffs out her quills. In this defensive posture, safety means keeping everything else out.

For Helena, vulnerability comes when she is doing what she was made to do. Moving around in the garden means that her belly is exposed and her defenses are down. A few weeks ago, I let her out to roam the yard. She was SO excited. She walked the entire fence line, rambled through the raspberry bush, and foraged through the grass. In her excitement, she got a little cut on one of her legs, which she barely even noticed. I had to keep an eye on it the next few days and make sure she was okay.

If I just put her in a cage with food, water, clean bedding, and a wheel to run on, she would be well taken care of. But if I never picked her up and played with her, or let her run around outside, she would get bored, which would lead to several negative behaviors. When bored with the world, hedgehogs will self-harm.

To release their energy and frustration, they will gnaw on their feet, sometimes until they can't walk. Second, if they get suspicious and paranoid, they will stop allowing you to tend to their needs. From rolling into an indistinguishable ball of prickles to head butting you when you are trying to care for them, they can become extremely difficult to interact with. Even though I am trying to help her, to trim her nails so she can move around better, she butts me out.

Sometimes, when she is in this mood, I have to put her down and walk away. Luckily for her, I'll come back and try again. But if Helena started taking this posture every time I went to tend her, it would lead to estrangement and death. If she wouldn't let me feed or water her or clean her cage, eventually the buildup would kill her, and she would never even know it was her fault.

At her best, Helena tends to the world. She brings life to the garden, much like we are called to cultivate the kingdom of God on earth. In our spaces, the places we inhabit, the people we intersect with, we are to bring the kingdom. To do this successfully, we have to be vulnerable.

Like Helena, to do our work, we have to take a posture that lets the world near us in uncomfortable ways. This is when the church is at its best. Pouring our being into our work when everyone else is slacking. Reaching out to people groups that don't have any other help: children, adults, addicts, the abused, the disabled, or the homeless. Taking care of our homes. Reaching out to neighbors that might reject us. Walking with our friends through hardship, turmoil, and doubt. Giving a hug. These are things we do to posture ourselves in service to the world. They open our hearts, and while we may get hurt, they are things that God desires for us.

Like Helena, we can turn inward. When we stop building the kingdom and tending to the world that we have been given to steward, we can start to harm ourselves in serious ways. We become obsessed with preserving and protecting instead of engaging with creation. Our world becomes one that is closed to newness, bounded by rules, and well-rehearsed in head butting.

The desire to insulate, burrow down, become lethargic, and react violently to threats is normal. But, when this happens, growth is stunted and the garden of the Kingdom goes untended. Specifically, when one has to be more worried about continued admittance to the garden than living out who they were created to be while tending the garden, one loses the opportunity for growth and development. When we emphasize behavioral norms above relationships with real human beings, we all end up chewing our feet off.

To have a relationship with Helena, I have to accept that sometimes I will get poked. Sometimes she will pee on my lap, and sometimes I have to clean up her mess. Authentic relationship with people is even harder. Sometimes we will fail, be disappointed, or hurt. But authentic relationship means that we love more deeply, embrace the failure with love and forgiveness, and work toward a future filled with love and meaning. "We are biologically, cognitively, physically and spiritually wired to love, to be loved, and to belong. When those needs are not met, we don't function as we were meant to. We break. We fall apart. We numb. We ache. We hurt others. We get sick. . . . the absence of love and belonging will always lead to suffering."[377]

When we create a garden Kingdom that lets people grow as they pursue living out the new creation, the essence of post resurrection sanctified living comes to fruition. When we live out the new creation, then the "Kingdom of God on earth" steps beyond the bounds of a prayer and becomes reality.

This is a kingdom that has space for all people and empowers its people to bring the kingdom with them in whatever they do. Whether teacher or mechanic, pastor or tech worker, the church becomes the resource that gives the support they need to build gardens of resurrection in the world around them. As people live out their vocation and purpose, as they are continually being transformed, it brings holiness and wholeness into the world. Dr. David Benner says, "Communities that support transformation in their members and adherents are communities that are themselves open to transformation."[378]

As holiness is expressed as wholeness, not only do the people grow and become more like Christ, but the church also lives out its mission more fully. Instead of sitting in the fellowship hall biting our feet and polishing our quills like a frustrated and restrained hedgehog, we go out into the garden of the world and make things new. We pull up weeds, fertilize the soil, and make gardens of resurrection that people can see from afar. This holiness—one that is green, growing, vibrant and captivating—draws people into the life of the church and into the life of resurrection and holiness.

As we live out this call of wholeness, whether in a Church of the Nazarene community or outside of it, we are agents of transformation. We take our daily tasks, our vocations, and our purpose, and share them with a world that needs to be made whole. May we more fully embrace people as they grow so that the world can partake in our mission, that the new creation of the kingdom will spread, bearing fruit in ways we never expected.

377. Brown, Brené. *The Gifts of Imperfection* (Center City, MN: Hazeldon, 2010), 26.

378. Benner, David G. *Spirituality and the Awakening Self: The Sacred Journey of Transformation* (Grand Rapids, MI: Brazos Press, 2012), 185.

Come join Helena in the garden. She is waiting for you. She can't wait to help you build the Kingdom for her Creator God. May you tend it well, with grace, love, and vulnerability.

Thy Kingdom come, Thy will be done, on earth as it is in heaven.

Janel Apps Ramsey is a staff member at Bloom Church Denver. She graduated from NTS with an M.A. in Theological Studies. She loves exploring topics of women and church, wholeness and healing, and techno music. She lives with her husband Baird, cats Yao and Ty, and Helena the Hedgehog. She loves waking up and seeing mountains every single day.

Those Walking Among You

Hannah R. Beers

Each corner of the room was filled with energy. A gentle hum of conversation was laced with expectation of future events. Every individual was being pulled by social connection. Throughout the room were stations where people could stop to refresh their beverages and renew their plate with artisanal food. The lights cast a glow over the entire gathering despite the gloomy weather outside.

Nothing could deter the events of the day for today was a cause for celebration. History was being made in this very room. As I walked over to where the food was being served, I noticed those wearing simple black and white attire ready at attention to attend to even the smallest need of those in attendance of the event. From far away, I had not noticed the attention to detail that went into the preparation of such fine food. Up close, the table was truly a sight to behold.

I turned to the young woman attired in black and white to remark on the elegant assembly of food. "Thank you for your words, ma'am. I'm surprised you noticed. Normally, people don't even acknowledge us. It is as though we don't exist."

Suddenly, the room seemed suffocating and felt constricting as if all the energy had been extinguished. My heart grew gloomy as if to match the weather outside. My thoughts raced to all of those gathered within this room for such an auspicious occasion, and yet this young woman, called Sarah, barely felt human among them. On so many similar occasions, she had been made to feel as if she belonged only in the background. The very people she was here to serve robbed her humanness from her. At that moment, I felt ashamed that I myself am a participant in making others feel as part of the scenery.

I looked into Sarah's eyes and said, "I see you."

Her whole countenance changed, and she smiled, "Thank you."

Society hustles and bustles at an ever-increasing speed. People late for work, busy with an ever-growing need to check off the to-do list, picking up kids from school, running errands, attending weekly social events with friends, and concerning ourselves with a limited focus of the things in front of us. Blinders are created for those busy with only their personal agendas. Our society has grown individualistic, and we are further dividing the very essence of who we are as relational beings.

In Robert Putnam's book *Bowling Alone*, he shows how society has become increasingly disconnected from those around us. He warns that our stock of social capital—the very fabric of our connections with each other—has plummeted, impoverishing our lives and communities.[379]

God desired covenant relationship with his creation from the very beginning of time. "Then the Lord God said, 'It is not good for the man to be alone'" (Gen. 2:18). Humanity was not created for solitude. We were created as relational beings to fellowship and to dwell with all created order. God wanted to dwell with Adam and Eve in fellowship, but our humanness took hold of our desire to know. Our innate desire to know and to be known is also our greatest weakness.

God did not simply cut himself off from this covenantal relationship with his created order; rather, God has been pursuing his creation ever since The Fall. In the Shema passage of Deuteronomy 6:4-9, we read of God's desire for Israel to turn away and to acknowledge the Lord as God with all heart, soul, mind and strength. God's standard for the Hebrew people is an expectation that they attempt to live back into the covenantal relationship that He wishes for them. Throughout the Bible, God directs his people towards reflecting the *Imago Dei* in a holistic way in relationship with God and people.

The *Imago Dei* is central to biblical teachings and is seen in the incarnation. Jesus Christ enters as a new covenant to the people of God. He brings with him the understanding that the Father desperately desires relationship with the created order. Jesus came willingly to a world that would both love and reject him. As the incarnate king, he would have known the purpose and potential found in the Shema, and this would have been central to His conceptual picture of the Father. Jesus came to dwell with people and provide an earthly example of the love our Father has for his created ones.

As a student of theological education, I have had the opportunity to learn from some of the most influential people in our denomination. In one of my classes, I was introduced to the concept of missional holiness. At first, the concept seemed to apply only to those studying to participate in God's mission overseas or in a context other than their own. For me, I was simply a student of theology, so how did the concept of missional holiness apply to my life? My professor challenged me by saying, "Missional holiness is not what you do but who you are."

My entire perception of holiness changed. It was not simply something I was individually participating in, but rather it was something we were participating

---

379. Robert Putnam, *Bowling Alone: The Collapse and Revival of American Community* (New York: Touchstone, 2001).

in together. As a body of believers, we were to respond to the needs around us. Holistic mission is an attempt to define the relationship between evangelism and social responsibility and transformation.

When we acknowledge the needs around us through active participation, we are engaged in covenant relationship. We realize that God is the one who has called us to himself, only to send us back out again as representatives of his message to all people.

As our busy lives pick up and we hurry through life, we are missing sacred opportunities to interact with people on the sidelines of our lives. Instead of going through life with a me-myself-and-I complex, why not include those around us to participate in daily relationship with us? Each interaction we have with people leaves us distinctly changed, and we cannot help but also change those with whom we have interacted. The key question is whether we leave them changed in a positive or negative way. Better yet, are they able to see Christ in our actions?

I think back to my interaction with Sarah just a few days ago. If I had not taken the time to meet her truly and to admire all the hard work she had been doing, then I would have been treating her as simply an object. Sarah is a child of God, and I am blessed that she took the time to challenge me in how I see those around me.

Am I living the example of missional holiness in my day-to-day life? Am I acknowledging those around me, or am I simply too busy with my own affairs that I miss how God is working all around me?

Those living by the Shema live covenant and thus participate in holiness as a means of living into the restoration of the *Imago Dei* in creation. Living Shema is connected to the works of Jesus and those faith pillars of our faith, yet truly living Shema is one of the most difficult things any Christian can do. Living Shema takes sacrifice and means that we are removed from the situation as an individual to be placed within a holy fellowship, a dynamic story of God deeply invested in the life of his creation through our willingness to turn to others saying, "I see you."

Jesus living in close understanding of Shema said, "Love the Lord your God with all your heart and with all your soul and with all your mind. This is the first and greatest commandment. And the second is like it: 'Love your neighbor as yourself'" (Matt. 22:3740). As we live in Christlikeness, learning daily what it means to be more like him, may we not forget to practice the second greatest commandment of loving our neighbor as we love ourselves. Then, are we truly practicing Shema.

Hannah earned her M.Div. from NTS as well as a diploma in Cross-Cultural Studies through the 365m program. As a youth pastor, she constantly seeks to empower her students to engage with the world around them in love and grace. As an avid outdoors-woman, she finds solace in spending time in God's creation. One day she hopes to establish a non-profit that combines outdoor hobbies with holistic ministry for at-risk students and individuals rescued from violent backgrounds.

Holiness and Small Groups

Janary Suyat de Godoy

The Checklist

I grew up in a church that led me to place my faith in Jesus Christ. At age 9, I was taught that a good Christian ought to go to church regularly, be present in all the activities and programs of the church, attend the Sunday School classes, and have a regular quiet time. The list grew as I grew. A good Christian ought to give his or her tithes and offerings regularly, pray and fast often, live a life of purity, and do many other spiritual disciplines.

I do not have anything against spiritual disciplines. They are a means of grace, which usher us to an encounter with God. In my experience, though, these can easily become a checklist, or a burden. The guilt can pile up when life becomes busy.

When I graduated from Bible School, I worked for 5 months at a call center. I had to earn some money, and I just wanted to experience what it was like to work in a different environment before I started working full-time at the church. I tried my best to make friends with my team, and when one of my co-workers knew that I was a Christian, I remember vividly how she reached out her hand to me, touched me and made the sign of the cross. In a sarcastic tone, she said, "You are holy," and then she invited everyone for drinking sessions except me.

After that encounter, my mind started thinking of the people in the church. I realized that I lived in a bubble, which was not entirely bad, but in that setting people only talked about God, the church, and the Bible. I do not remember people sharing much about their struggles. People tend to go to the church and hurry out. People do not have time to sit down and share life. The church has become a place where people sit down to listen to the Word, worship for an hour or so, so that they can mark off one of the things on their list, and the week can go on again.

My experience at the call center led me two parallel observations. First, most Christians spend six days a week surround by non-believers in their neighborhoods, school and workplaces. They face the challenges of temptation, subtle ridicule, and the call to make a difference in the midst of people walking to the beat of this world. Second, church people tend to talk about holiness as a set of disciplines that a believer has to follow. When the checklist becomes the goal, then it creates feelings of inadequacy. Holiness becomes a tiring pursuit, and people inside the church tend to judge each other according to how they have fulfilled the checklist.

With real struggles in the world and the church's emphasis on a list of disciplines, many our people are honestly asking, "Is holiness possible for me?"

The Masquerade

When Christians realize that the temptations do not go away after placing their faith in Christ, the torment begins. When people do not meet the standard that the church shows us, then the masquerade party happens. I have seen many times how we try to put our best foot forward, but we do not have the chance to talk about our real struggles. Through the years, I have seen fear among God's people, fear that they cannot keep up with the rules or the requirements imposed on them. The journey towards holiness becomes a lonely pursuit, and many times I have seen people choose the other way.

I have heard some of our brothers and sisters say, "Pastor, I would only come back to the church when I have the strength to do what is required from me." "Pastor, I will not be attending church until I am able to get my act together. I know that I am a failure, and I am not worthy to be inside the church."

Jesus' words started ringing in my head, "Come to me, all who labor and are heavy laden, and I will give you rest. Take my yoke upon you, and learn from me, for I am gentle and lowly in heart, and you will find rest for your souls. For my yoke is easy, and my burden is light."

The Journey

When Jesus told his disciples, "Come, follow me," it was an invitation to a journey of sharing life. This invitation is loaded with relational implications. During the time of Jesus, the disciples' goal was to become like the teacher, following him and watching how he lived his life so that they would move and talk and be like the teacher. As we follow Jesus today, he is indeed the perfect example of what holiness looks like.

1 Peter 1:13-16 says, "Therefore, preparing your minds for action, and being sober-minded, set your hope fully on the *grace* that will be brought to you at the revelation of Jesus Christ. As obedient children, do not be conformed to the passions of your former ignorance, but as he who called you is holy, you also be holy in all your conduct, since it is written, 'You shall be holy, for I am holy.'"

It is true that we have received an upward call, a holiness that is required of us, but we can't get there in our own strength, but through the grace that our faith in Jesus brings. We want to make Christlike disciples in the nations, but as ministers and the body of Christ, we have to remember that making disciples does not mean we ought to treat everyone as the same. In his book *Transforming Discipleship*, Greg Ogden talks about how programs in the church can contribute to discipleship development, but he also notes the dangerous side of church programing: "the concept of making disciples becomes mechanical and similar to a serialized production line in which training and expectations are the same for everyone; this is in direct opposition to a God who has revealed himself to human beings as 'unpredictable, not smooth, and asymmetrical.'"[380]

When people fail these programmatic expectations, we look at them as bad disciples, as not worthy of our time. I have seen many of my beloved youth group members in the Philippines feel pressured into conforming to the demands of discipleship programs. But I wonder if we missed the point. When I got deeper into knowing these young people, I started hearing of their great struggles with relationships, pre-marital sex, homosexuality, addiction, and many issues of morality. However, revealing these struggles is a "no-no" in the church, lest they would be looked down on inside the church. Conversations have been limited to prayer requests, how God is faithful, questions of how people are doing, and the automatic answer is "I am doing well."

Small Groups: A Holy Community

However, in the last five years, I have enjoyed the richness of small groups, and I see that many of our churches today still have not been able to enjoy true community: sharing life, feeling supported and accepted, and learning together and from each other.

While our people "go to church" regularly, only a few of them attend Bible studies, and most of the time, in these settings, the main activities tend to be one-way teaching and shallow conversation. Every once in a while, we get a brave soul who confesses their struggles in light of what was discussed in Scripture, but these do not intentionally happen most of the time.

The pursuit for holiness is not meant to be travelled alone. That is why we are called the body of Christ as we live together and walk on this journey together. Yet, we are all different. A small group that intentionally asks questions about life and provides avenues for accountability is a place where one can realize that the family of God cares for them, accepts them despite their failures, and wants to help them overcome the struggles and temptations that they face every day. John Wesley had the Methodist Class Meetings during his time where members were

---

380. Greg Ogden, *Transforming Discipleship: Making Disciples a Few at a Time* (Downers Grove, Ill: InterVarsity, 2003), 37.

accountable to each other and the word of God was examined in light of people's actual personal experiences. However many of our churches have forgotten the intentionality of these relationships.

When James calls us to "confess your sins one to another, and pray for one another so that you may be healed," (James 5:16), he is not referring primarily to the diseased or bedridden, but those who have grown weary and spiritually and morally weak because of sufferings and struggles. If we would remove the masks that we wear on Sundays and admit our temptations, suffering, and struggles, then our mutual concern and accountability can build us into a holy community. As Christ calls us to find rest and healing in Him, we all usher each other to Him for that rest and healing.

The biggest hindrances to becoming a holy community are pride or shame. In small groups, one has to be humble and honest, so that the community would be able to provide support. The struggle is real, and one cannot do it alone. The spiritual disciplines are not the end in themselves. The point is how we love and accept each other so that we can shine brightly in this dark world. We are all in this journey together.

Janary Suyat de Godoy was born in the Philippines and is an ordained minister on the Metro-Manila District. She is serving as the Asia-Pacific NYI Coordinator and is also a missionary teacher in Okinawa, Japan. She finished her Master of Divinity at APNTS. Her passion is discipling the youth, preaching, and teaching God's word. She is married to Anderson Godoy.

Whole-i-ness through Togetherness

Ryan Scott

There is an episode of the television show "Louie," comedian Louis C.K.'s quixotic, often profane tragi-comedy, in which Louie's pregnant sister is visiting. She wakes up in the middle of the night in searing pain, screaming to be taken to the hospital. Louie is overwhelmed by the situation, which includes what to do with his two young daughters sleeping in the next room. Crippled with panic, Louie's chaos is compounded by an increasingly ferocious knock at the door. Louie finally opens the door apologetically, trying to explain that the noise is an emergency and not inconsiderate. The couple at the door, clearly strangers to Louie, introduce themselves as his neighbors and say, "We're not here to complain; we're here to help."

The neighbor steps through the door and calmly walks Louie through the stress, helps him make sound decisions, and accompanies Louie and his sister to the hospital, while his spouse stays behind in case the kids wake up.

Once the ordeal is over and they're back in the hallway of their apartment building, Louie tells the man, "I couldn't have gotten through that without you." The neighbor responds, "That's why you need neighbors—people who are not in your family to help you when you need it. Now you know who your neighbors are; don't forget it."

I have always been told that holiness is not something you get by trying. We are incapable of being the kind of holy people we're called to be on our own. However, through most of my life, the inherent implication has been that God supplies the lack directly to us. We can be holy because God makes us holy (presuming we're willing to submit to God's direction and be obedient).

My experience, however, is that this plan still ends up in failure, and increasingly it seems more and more of us are willing to admit similar frustrations. We often find ourselves struggling—not to be holy—but to be whatever it is we're supposed to be in order for God to make us holy.

I had a pretty profound sanctification experience. I was at a crossroads in my life, with no clear direction forward, likely on the verge (if not in the midst) of a nervous breakdown. I laid on the floor in tears of desperation, and I truly gave myself to God. I rose up a different person. I felt different. I acted different.

I was different. This was the culmination of everything I'd been taught about holiness growing up. It was proof of a reality I'd begun to doubt. It was perhaps the greatest moment of my life.

It lasted about eighteen months.

While I did have a new direction and had been irrevocably changed, I soon found myself struggling in the same way I'd struggled before. I might have progressed to the next level of spiritual maturity, but my holiness was not complete. It was not as it had been a few months before and not as it had always been described to me.

I'm pretty sure I don't have it all figured out. Scratch that—I am absolutely sure I don't have it all figured out. But I have begun to realize the missing factor in the traditional understanding of holiness as it had been taught to me: God is not here to solve all your problems—at least not directly for us as individuals.

God did not design us to operate individually—not when it comes to salvation and not when it comes to lifelong holiness. When John Wesley said, "there is no holiness but social holiness," he meant, I think, individual holiness expressed socially, in relation to other people. Our individual holiness only has meaning as it participates in communal (or social) holiness.

God's relationship to humanity is a social relationship. We, as a people, were created to superintend God's good creation; we, collectively, have a responsibility to live rightly within that call. Holiness is the means by which we, collectively, embody the task for which we were created. It can only happen together.

Previously, our congregational holiness component has been as a support group, cheerleaders, willing and praying and pushing each individual towards individual holiness. We need to alter that perspective radically. God has called the Church to be holy, an example, an outpost of heaven in the midst of the world. Our individual holiness really only has meaning as we participate in that collective calling.

A motto I've picked up and tried to share is: *Wherever this life is heading, wherever we're going, whatever the point, we're going to get there together or we won't get there at all.*

True communion with our fellow humans cannot make us whole, of course. Only God can do that, but it does give us a sense of whole-i-ness without which, I suspect, we can neither be holy nor whole.

In terms of our understanding of holiness, the primary difference between my generation and previous generations is simply that we're more comfortable abandoning the individualism of the enlightenment. We're more receptive to the notion that the world is necessarily interconnected and that our necessary individuality is part of a larger whole. We can't fully handle our "stuff" by ourselves. We need other people—not just for our own individual success, but for the very fulfillment of our universal creative purpose. This is not just a practical concession, but a powerful underlying principle for theology and faith.

I support a group in my state (Delaware) working to ban the death penalty. Obviously many different arguments play into this complex issue. One I hear often is the appeal to emotion, "If your wife or daughter were killed, wouldn't you want that killer to die?"

I hope not, but I expect the answer is probably, "Yes." That is all the more reason for me to support a death penalty ban. I've seen the effects revenge can have on both victim and perpetrator; it is not healthy and not something I want for my life or the world in which I live. I need my various communities (family, congregation, denomination, nation, etc.) to hold me to an ethical standard I believe in—especially at times when my emotion or circumstance would lead me in another direction. I gladly and willingly give power over to the community in order to safeguard those things I hold dear. That is the essence of social holiness—not just voluntary participation in community, but inextricable participation.

I live in a culture that upholds liberty and freedom as ultimate good. Above all else, we celebrate the ability to make unencumbered choices. While I believe wholeheartedly in the ability for individuals to make their own choices, I don't believe it is always beneficial to do so. Furthermore, I do not believe unfettered freedom is consistent with a Christian understanding of the world in which we live. We struggle against the submission of our individual will to make decisions, but in the end—as difficult as it is—this submission is completely in line with how God created us to function.

God created the world and is working to redeem the world. God created humanity, tasked us with powerful responsibility, saved and empowered us through the life, death, and resurrection of Jesus Christ, and will ultimately redeem humanity as a whole (or at the very least, the whole of those participating in humanity as God intends). Rarely do we see scripture address salvation in individual, personal terms. In the life and teachings of evangelicals, we rarely see it expressed in any other way.

There is vital importance to our individual decisions, to holiness ethics on a personal level. But it is just as vital for us to move beyond individual participation and to embrace a communal holiness of heart and life. Without both elements, we are missing a key piece of the gospel.

This notion is downright terrifying. We often don't trust each other enough to give someone else a real, irrevocable say in our lives. We're shaped and formed by society to think independently and self-sufficiently. Even our faith tradition tends to emphasize individuality over corporate responsibility. We struggle mightily with the reality of people suffering because of factors outside their own control.

But ultimately, this is the way the world works. Our unease with interdependency does not negate its reality. The progress of Western civilization has been a move from the communal to the individual—a move towards freedom. This is a good and righteous move away from coercion and suffering. However, this must not be the final move.

Our gospel has long taught us the best exercise for freedom—and for power—is to submit it to God and to the Church. This voluntary subjugation is not a step back but a move forward, in which our individuality finds true fulfillment in participation with the whole. In Philippians 2:12, Paul calls each individual Christian to work out a collective salvation "with fear and trembling." We cannot be holy on our own. We need God. We also need each other—the community God provided to safeguard and to nurture holiness until it finds fulfillment at the end of all things.

Wherever we're going, wherever this life is headed, we're going to get there together or we won't get there at all.

Ryan Scott lives with his wife, daughter, and two cats in Middletown, Delaware, where he is incredibly grateful for a unique, diverse group of neighbors and friends with whom he's privileged to do life. He is a graduate of Eastern Nazarene College and Nazarene Theological Seminary, and the author of The Sinai Experiment. *Ryan loves writing at onemorethingblog.blogspot.com, watching sports, and overanalyzing movies.*

Holiness in Community
Richard Giesken

All is not well with the world. We have greater wealth than ever before, greater freedom than ever before, greater knowledge and education than ever before. Despite all these human advancements, there is an insecurity and crisis of self-identity that eats at the soul of our world.

In a material world where the individual is increasingly celebrated, it is becoming obvious that happiness is not found in the possession of wealth or knowledge or individual achievements. While the Enlightenment gave rise to the celebration and elevation of the so-called individual, people around the globe are recognizing their social and spiritual poverty—their lack of genuine community.

The Bible presents an account of the development of a particular community. It is not a utopian community devoid of struggles, but it presents a model of being which holds the salvation of the world. The record of the formation of this people reflects their understanding of being established in covenant with the Divine. Old Testament narrative reflects that God's goal for humanity is solidarity with God through understanding and incarnating God's essential character—holiness. In the story of the birth of the community of Israel, we can discover principles that transcend time and culture that might be applied to community building today.

The account of the biblical community describes the vitality and formative power of community. It also explores obligations and responsibilities that exist to form and to maintain such community. It is a view of holiness that is not individual, but holiness in community.

Romanticized ideals of what "community" means may abound, but the hard reality of living in community remains a shaping factor in people's personal lives. From the tight knit support group, to the broader subtle (or not so subtle) cultural gravitational pull, our communities regulate who we are. Within these groups, we experience a complex, dynamic matrix of relationships, which contributes to our sense of belonging.

Every community needs a cohesive center to create a sense of belonging. This center draws people into relationship and tends to characterize the community. It distinguishes one community from another. The cohesive center gives expression to the community's core values.

Incarnation of the group's core values is essential to cultivating community. Without such common values, ideals and norms, there would be little cohesion within the group, to the point that it may be a collection of people, but not necessarily a community. Commitment to shared core values serves as a motivating and sustaining force among members of a community. A statement of shared values on its own is insufficient to shape or transform a community. The community is only transformed as members align their personal values to their community's stated core values.

Social capital has been used to refer to the relationships existing between individuals that can result in economic gain. The concept of resultant gain may also be expanded to include especially the increase in community well-being. This sometimes necessitates individuals to look beyond their own personal agendas, in order to realize a benefit for community as a whole. Social capital resides in the constituents of the community. Robert D. Putnam defines social capital as "networks, norms, and trust, which facilitate coordination and cooperation for mutual benefit."[381]

The Biblical perspective of healthy community is rooted in the quality of interpersonal relationships. The Biblical story is about living in "right" relationship with God and with neighbor. It is the story about the movement between what is and what will be. The biblical text outlines the rules of personal engagement. With careful exegesis, these rules—or their underlying principles—can help us develop healthy functional communities today.

The inception of the community of Israel is linked to God's self-identification in the formula "I am YHWH" or "I am the LORD." Canonically, the formula has its origin in the call of Abram (Gen. 15:7), and it is directly associated with the Exodus mission of Moses (Ex. 6:2-9). It is subsequently used to preface the issuing of the Decalogue, and it finds prominence in the so-called Holiness Code of Leviticus 17-26, where is appears 50 times. Similarly, the use in Leviticus 17-26 envisions the social health of the community and is expressed as holiness that is derived from the presence and holiness of YHWH.

This expression of holiness is epitomized by the call of YHWH in Leviticus 19:1-2, "The LORD spoke to Moses, saying: Speak to all the congregation of the people of Israel and say to them: You shall be holy, for I the LORD your God am holy." This social vision of holiness is based on the observation that many of the laws in Leviticus associated with YHWH's self-identification involve interpersonal responsibilities within the community. J. David Pleins writes, "Law-

---

381. Robert D. Putnam, "The Prosperous Community: Social Capital and Public Life," *The American Prospect* 4 no. 13 (1993). Retrieved on July 25th 2014 from http://prospect.org/article/prosperous-community-social-capital-and-public-life

making tradition was clearly taken up with matters of social obligation, justice, and the treatment of the disenfranchised."[382] These laws offer a foundation for building communities of justice and compassion, reflecting the holiness of God.

YHWH is the cohesive bond for the Exodus community. Their identity is established, not in their own ability, but in their redemptive relationship with YHWH. Leviticus 19, as representative of the implications of this relationship, provides a supportive framework for Israel to develop community wholeness. By establishing order and cooperation, they were able to develop the social capital essential to ensuring their continued existence as a people.

From beginning to end, the community building process of the biblical community is wrapped up in the identity of YHWH, to whom the people belong, and through whom the people belong to each other. The account of the establishment of the biblical community is an insight into the development of an enduring community, which has holiness at its heart.

The Old Testament presents YHWH as a holy God who calls people to be holy. Baruch Levine interprets the call to holiness as follows: "The central idea of the Holiness Code is that the people of Israel bear the collective responsibility to seek to achieve holiness . . ."[383] It is this idea of a "collective responsibility" which I think is missing in much of our tradition's emphasis on holiness. Too often holiness has been promoted as a personal or individual matter. The reality is that we need to talk to each other about our experiences of the pursuit of holiness. We need to support one another, correcting and encouraging, modeling and observing, praying and worshiping together. Through this dialogue, we may discover that holiness is multifaceted. We may discover that there is no monolithic understanding of holiness within the Biblical witness.

Biblical holiness can be conceived as three-dimensional: as "being," "doing," and "thinking." These three dimensions reflect elements of the mystical, ritual and ethical. One without the others decays respectively into esotericism, legalism or relativism. Mystical holiness ("being") alerts us to the notion that there is more to the universe than meets the eye and develops in the individual an identity that is connected to the Divine. Ritualistic holiness ("doing"), grounded in the mystical experience of God, expresses the sanctity of life recognizing sacred time, space and people, and establishes a framework of support. Ethical holiness ("thinking") is then a response to the mystical, guided by ritual that recognizes and builds social capital as it enriches life and relationship. This three dimensional model

---

382. J. David Pleins, "The Social Visions of the Hebrew Bible." Retrieved on July 25th 2014 from http://www.bibleinterp.com/articles/hebrewbible2.shtml.

383. Baruch A. Levine, *Leviticus, JPS Torah and Commentary* (New York: The Jewish Publication Society, 1989), 11.

of holiness provides a paradigm for understanding God's call to holiness given to the Exodus community. The call to holiness, while given in the context of the community's mystical experience of God, encompassed ritualistic holiness and addressed social holiness. People are not isolated individuals, but interconnected beings who have the potential to inflict suffering on others, or to bring relief for those who are afflicted.

Holiness is not simply an individual preference, but a universal call for relational responsibility. Holiness is not simply a religious relic. It speaks to the essence of what it means to live as a human being with other human beings. Holiness is not simply a list of rules and regulations, but an understanding relationship with others that flows out of a dynamic relational encounter with God.

Holiness is a vision of God not as judgmental, but as a healing presence in both personal and communal lives, reshaping how we think about being human, affecting how we treat people and the environment around us, and calling us to contribute to the well-being of both. Holiness is a call to participate in the life of God, and to root our participation in the community of God's people.

Richard is originally from South Africa and moved to Australia in 1996 to pursue Theological Studies. That journey also led him and his family to further studies at APNTS in Manila, Philippines. Richard currently lives near Brisbane, Australia with his wife, Judy and their four sons. He teaches Old Testament studies and missiology at NTC, Australia—New Zealand. He also co-pastors the Redlands Church of the Nazarene.

Holy Hospitality

Lori A. Ward

Every Sunday morning, the scene is the same in my home. I, ever the last-minute gal, awaken leisurely and fumble around my favorite foodie blogs to choose a treat to share with those who will gather in our home for worship. I avoid nuts for the little one among us with allergies, and I look for vegan options to accommodate the food choices of others. While I measure and pour and beat and bake, my brood of boys joins in the preparations with varying levels of helpfulness. The floors must be swept, the tabletops cleared and washed, and the bathrooms tended. A selection of tea is arranged on the dining room table. Hot cinnamon spice is a favorite in the fall, and peppermint is a winner at Christmas. Inevitably, someone makes a run to the little store on the first floor of our apartment building to grab eggs for my batter or grape juice for communion. The furniture is rearranged to prepare a space for worship while we wait for the warm treat to emerge from the oven for our after-service fellowship.

I'd like to report that after years of hosting a house church our routines are seamless and our family interactions are a model of harmony and peace deserving of the worship space, but it is really rather ordinary. Our family rushes around to get ready for guests. Sometimes, we don't really feel like doing the work. It is taxing. There is often a raised voice (or five), and occasionally there are tears of anger or frustration. And when the first guests arrive, we are often running around finishing the final details.

The fact is, having people in our space—our home—week after week is exposing. I simply cannot guarantee that the vacuum will be pushed *under* the chairs, or that the cake will always rise, or that my kids or the cat or the phone will not distract or interrupt the worship gathering. But the practice of welcoming others regularly into our home has forced me to let down my pretenses and simply be who I really am.

And in so doing, I am finding the words of Jesus in the Sermon on the Mount to be true, "Keep open house; be generous with your lives. By opening up to others, you'll prompt people to open up with God, this generous Father in heaven" (Matthew 5:16 *The Message).* Our shared experiences over time allow me to love these people. And because I love them, I give space for their quirks and edges—just as they do for me. We are more open-minded toward one another and gracious in our dealings with each other. Hospitality makes room for this. If we choose not to play the distant host but instead to offer an authentic, vulnerable gift, then we open ourselves to others. Others, then, shape who we are and who we are becoming. Christ-in-us sees Christ-in-the-other, and we experience holy love.

We see examples of hospitality throughout the Scriptures. When strangers arrived at Abraham's home in the heat of the day, he ran out to meet them. He pleaded with them to stay so he could refresh them with a foot washing and strengthen them with a hearty meal. Bread was baked. The fatted calf was prepared. Strangers were welcomed with great care. Abraham's openness to the visitors made room for him to receive their blessing—and what a blessing it was! Finally the promised child was coming! "I will surely return to you about this time next year, and Sarah your wife will have a son" (Genesis 18:10 NIV). The guest brought a message of God's faithfulness. A life marked by mistrust and mistakes was redeemed. Abraham would indeed father God's people, a role God designed for him to play. By extending his hand in hospitality, Abraham engaged the God-sent ones and experienced the gracious gift of God.

King David asked, "Is there anyone still left of the house of Saul to whom I can show kindness for Jonathan's sake?" (2 Samuel 8:1, NIV). Jonathan's son Mephibosheth was the only living heir in Saul's family. With two lame feet, there was little hope of him amounting to anything. When the king encountered him, he opened his royal home in hospitality. He gave to Mephibosheth all the wealth that had belonged to his grandfather Saul. What is more, David welcomed Mephibosheth to his dinner table as a son from that time forward. David's hospitality emerged from the deep, holy love he had for Jonathan and resulted in the complete transformation of Mephibosheth's life.

Having just heard the news of John the Baptist's beheading, Jesus wanted to retreat and grieve. He was exhausted. But the crowds would not leave him alone. They followed him, longing to be with him. Jesus welcomed them, all 5000 of them. He talked with them about the kingdom of God. Even in the grief of his own loss, he reached out with healing to those who needed it. And at the end of the day, when the people were hungry, he provided them a meal: bread and fish. He broke it, thanked the Father for it, and served it up to the uninvited-yet-welcomed guests. The apprenticing Twelve encountered the loving and transforming grace of God through the actions of welcoming, feeding, and tending to guests. Following this act of hospitality, Peter confessed to Jesus, "You are God's messiah!" (Luke 9:20).

In all of these examples, we find that there is something powerful in sharing a meal together. I hear echoes of the Israelites about to flee Egypt, cooking their unleavened bread behind bloodstained doors. "It's not proper to eat with our shoes on, and it won't taste as good as it would if we could let the yeast work, but we don't have time to lose. We must be ready together for God's redemption."

I see Jesus, gathered with The Twelve in the upper room. He has taught. He has healed. He has fed. And now he tears open the loaf in anticipation of the brokenness he will embody for us. He gives himself as host—the bread and the wine. Jesus gives himself fully to those welcomed at his table, even to those who will betray and deny him. And when we share a meal together in Christian hospitality, Christ is revealed among us.

The truth is hospitality is taxing. It's messy. It is exhausting. But, somehow, by opening our lives and homes with all their limitations and imperfections, we live into our identity as the Church of Jesus Christ. Our hearts connect with others. Together we experience the loving, grace-giving, redeeming, healing presence of God in our midst. In these sacred moments, we are nourished and strengthened. When we offer true hospitality to others, we come to recognize that what used to seem like good deeds done for strangers have become acts of love toward new friends.

Holy love necessitates action. It is more than a mental ascent or an emotional attachment. It is living Christlikeness. When we open ourselves in hospitality, we extend the welcome of God's love. Engaging the hurting, joyful, or mundane lives of others allows us to receive Christ among us. It's graced.

The more I experience of the Christian life, the more I am coming to see that it is not the mountaintop experiences that truly evidence the presence of a Holy God within us. Instead, the evidence of holy living is revealed in the ordinary, routine living we do between our mountaintop mile-markers: making room, preparing a space, tending to guests, and breaking bread. Whenever we encounter others in holy love, our lives together evidence the presence of Christ in the world.

Lori Ward lives with her husband and five sons in South Korea, where she teaches at a Christian international school and pastors a house church. She has also ministered in Oregon, Nevada, Idaho, Missouri, and Wisconsin. She enjoys sharing meals with guests, especially when she can experiment with a new recipe. She has a M.Div. from NTS and a B.A. in Elementary Education from Northwest Nazarene University.

Corporate Worship:
More Than Icing on the Cake
Brannon Hancock

Let's get this part out of the way. I'm a Church of the Nazarene pastor's kid, like my father before me—in fact, *his* dad (my grandpa) was even a District Superintendent! "Nazarene" is in my blood. So naturally, I've been hearing words like *holiness* and *sanctification* my entire life.

One of my earliest memories—although it's hard to say whether it's an actual memory or something I've (re)constructed from the story my parents tell—is standing next to my mom at Brunswick (Ohio) First Church of the Nazarene during a revival as the congregation sang Johnson and Miriam Oatman's 1905 holiness hymn "Oh I never shall forget how the fire fell / when the Lord sanctified me." The selection is probably a giveaway that we were in revival services. Nelson Perdue was the evangelist. Something about the imagery of this song, particularly the repeated line "how the fire fell, how the fire fell," captured my 3-year-old imagination. And not in an uplifting way. I turned to my mom and nervously asked, "Where the fire fall, mommy? Where the fire fall?" (I doubt it was the hymn writer's intention to scare the hell out of anyone, but it seems to have worked on me.)

This serves as a good marker of the beginning of a lifelong process by which God, through the Church, has shaped me, formed my imagination, saved me, sanctified me, and given me an identity that I could not and would not have ever come up with on my own. This formation occurred and continues to occur in the context of the communal life of the Body of Christ called Church—for me, the Church of the Nazarene.

Early on, I didn't have much choice but to submit to the life-rhythms of the local church. The pastor's family is there every time the doors are open, and they are typically the last ones to leave. But when it came time that I felt the need to choose for myself, I came to the conclusion that it wasn't my place to unchoose what God had chosen for me. Indeed, long before I claimed the Church of the Nazarene, the Nazarenes had already laid claim to me. As one of my Trevecca professors once professed, most of the important things in life, you don't choose—they choose you.

So it is not an exaggeration to say that I only know how to be a Christian because of the Church—because God, through the Church, has adopted and incorporated me into His family. I only know how to pray because I've had the privilege to eavesdrop on the prayers of the saints and sinners with whom I've shared a pew. I only know how to read the Bible because Sunday School teachers and Bible quizzing coaches taught me the stories that declare God's redemptive work in the world. I only know how to worship because the Church has shown me how to sing the faith, give my offering, receive the Word in sermon and sacrament. I am only a pastor today because, even during times when I questioned whether I wanted anything to do with the Church, the Church seemed to repeatedly say, "We need you . . . there's room for you . . . you belong to us."

God forms us, individually and collectively, into a holy people through the communal life of the Body of Christ called church. At the center of this communal life is our worship. Worship is the action by which we are made into the Body of Christ.

But as a worship leader for the better part of two decades, I struggle with some of the ways we talk about worship. I've heard sincere and thoughtful Christian leaders say things like: *Going to church on Sundays doesn't make you a Christian any more than sleeping in the garage makes you a car.*[384] *We worship from the overflow of lives of worship. You should be worshipping Monday through Saturday, and then when we come together on Sunday. Worshipping together is the icing on the cake.*

At first glance, this may sound good, but the implication is that "individual" or "non-corporate" forms of worship precede and are superior to the gathered experience. Thus, we often make a distinction between *personal* worship and *corporate* worship. This differentiation may be useful, as worship when I am (seemingly) alone is expressed and experienced differently than when I am with the gathered community. However, at times I fear we get the cart before the horse when we begin parse worship in such a manner. As such, anything may be construed as worship. And if everything is worship, then nothing is worship.

But not everything is worship—at least not *Christian* worship. At their root, shopping at the mall or attending a sporting event or viewing pornography may be acts of "worship." But the object of such worship is not the God revealed in Jesus of Nazareth. Precisely because of our inclination toward idolatry and the allure of such false gods, I've encountered pastors who make valiant efforts to

---

384. No, sleeping in the garage doesn't make me a car. But if I really want to learn how cars work, the first thing I should probably do is head out to the garage—or better yet, head to the garage of a friend who knows a lot about cars, and who can lend me the tools, show me the methods, teach me the terminology, etc.

convince their congregations that everything they do can, and should, be an act of worship. Their hearts are in the right place, but let's get real. Picking up a piece of trash is not worship; it's just a good deed. Letting someone go ahead of you in line at the grocery store checkout is not worship; it's just being kind. I fear that this understanding, at least as a starting point, devalues and diminishes worship from a set of concrete practices performed at the personal and corporate level into worship as "whatever I want it to be."

At the same time, I affirm Brother Lawrence's teaching in *Practice of the Presence of God* that we can achieve communion with God in even the tedium of daily life. It is possible to pick up litter with the intention of bringing glory to God and caring for creation or to experience His presence in acts of compassion toward others. In my better moments, I strive to encounter God even in such mundane chores as bathing my children, which is an opportunity for me to help them remember their baptisms, and my own.

But while worship is a matter of the orientation of the heart, *Christian* worship is also a set of concrete, corporate practices—singing praises, reading Scripture, confessing sins, interceding in prayer, giving thanks (Eucharist), passing the peace, giving alms, breaking bread, initiating new members (baptism), being sent forth for mission. Without these essential embodied elements, it's difficult to ascertain whether we are even being Christian, much less faithful.

Corporate worship is foundational and primary in the Christian life. Worship may be personal, but it is never private. Personal expressions of worship, while vital, are secondary at best. Their significance and intelligibility flows out of the corporate experience—not the other way around.

Corporate worship is not merely the "icing on the cake." It's more like the cake pan. If you try to make a cake without a cake pan, you end up with a giant mess of batter that doesn't even remotely resemble a cake. Like the cake pan, corporate worship gives form and shape to what goes into it (our whole life, our entire person), so that what comes out is recognizably "Christian" and reflects and brings glory to God. Is "Sunday morning Christianity" sufficient? Absolutely not. But we cannot possibly know or experience personal worship without our person first being formed into Christlikeness through His Body called Church.

This is why it is so important that we do not neglect the doctrine of the Trinity. The God we worship exists eternally as the intercommunion of three persons: the Father, the Son, and the Spirit. *Father* and *Son* are relational terms; each derives His personhood from the interrelationship with the others.

Being created in God's image, we share this inherent relationality. The sinful condition into which we are born is fragmentary, selfish individualism. But God has redeemed us from our individualism into authentic personhood by the Christ event.[385] Thus we may be adopted into the family of God and made (as the old song says) "joint-heirs with Jesus." We receive our true personhood in relation to the Trinity, into whose life we are engrafted because of what Christ has done. Made one with Him, we offer our worship and ourselves to God as a single, holy, living sacrifice.[386]

Therefore, although we may enter worship as individuals, worship must never be conceived as individualistic. God uses worship to draw us into community and to transform us not only into holy persons but also into *a Holy People*.

Brannon Hancock is Assistant Professor of Practical Theology and Christian Ministry in Wesley Seminary at Indiana Wesleyan University. He a pastor, a worship leader, and the author of The Scandal of Sacramentality: The Eucharist in Literary and Theological Perspectives.

---

385. Cf. John D. Zizioulas, *Being as Communion: Studies in Personhood and the Church* (Crestwood, NY: St. Vladimir's Seminary Press, 1985); James B. Torrance, *Worship, Community, and the Triune God of Grace* (Toronto: University of Toronto Press, 1996).

386. This is a paraphrase of the 1982 eucharistic liturgy of the Scottish Episcopal Church.

The Altar: Presence and Dialogue

Ataulfo Lopez

> *"If you are presenting your offering at the altar, and while there you remember that your brother has something against you, leave your offering there before the altar and go, reconcile first with your brother.... Reconcile quickly with your adversary while you are still on the road with him ..."* *(Matthew 5:23-25).*

In churches on the border between Mexico and California, including the Nazarene churches, the altar is transforming into a scene similar to musical concerts, and there are few icons from church history still in use. In this context, there is no defined liturgy to unite our altar practices, no common understanding that the altar is essentially an encounter with the presence of God, instead of just a specific place in a church building. In this essay, then, I propose the possibility of re-engaging with the symbols of the altar, so that new generations can recognize them.

First, we will look at the figure of the altar in one moment in the history of God's people. Here we find Jacob: a nomad with a limited knowledge of God, but building altars as a marker in every significant moment of his life (Genesis 28:10-22; 35:1-7). Second, in the New Testament, we will look at the dialogue between Jesus and the Samaritan woman regarding where one should worship (John 4).

First, we see the example of Jacob: a young man in a context where there are a variety of religious beliefs. In the story of his dream, in which he had the vision of the stairway to heaven, he exclaimed that he did not know that the Lord was there. Before this, his brother Esau had been seduced by the neighboring religious practices, in "competition" with the God of Israel. This parallels the religious syncretism that we find in our society, in which many are seduced by religious practices of questionable origin that have been introduced to our congregations. However, like Jacob, others have had the opportunity along their pilgrimage to encounter the truth of God's presence through a sign or an "altar, and its power causes their behavior to truly begin changing.

So this text gives us a sense of how the altar is a point of encounter with God's presence. Jacob sets out with his family and returns to the same place to rebuild the altar, even though he had just left a house in which there were household idols (Genesis 31:17 etc.). The altar is an important point in the formation of a community, but it is also definitive in the individual's experience with the real presence of God. It transforms a person's behavior and capacity to take hold of his life direction. And as for us, in the midst of diversity, we find the opportunity to take back the altar's use as an instrument to abandon falsehood.

The other text we'll examine is the conversation between Jesus and the Samaritan woman, in the context of the Roman world's multiplicity of religions. Here we see the context in which our Lord lived: religious pluralism and dialogue with other nationalities.

The interesting point is the religious confrontation between the Samaritans and the Jews about where one should worship. Jesus set the tone for the liturgical dialogue with someone who would seem to be unworthy. He tolerated it for the goal of defining what is essential. Yes, where to worship is important, but in the end, true worship comes from the those who worship "in spirit and in truth." Here, Jesus defined the essence of worship.

The encounter between Jesus and the Samaritan woman is a model for the dialogue among today's pastors, to redefine the models of altar use and discover its essence. Our goal is to transform lives and to make of the altar not an object of religious infighting, but an opportunity for spiritual unity.

In our two scriptures, from both Testaments, importance is placed on special places to worship God. In both places, we catch a glimpse of Christ on the altar, a point of encounter with the God's presence, with Christ as the minister. Although both of these scriptures were about God touching the individual, they also speak about the community. Jacob as an individual builds an altar, and Jesus and the Samaritan woman represent two communities worshipping only one God, with different perspectives about place and form. Both passages also have the figure of Christ either as a symbol or as a real presence, and so it is with us. We see that despite our differences in tradition, Christ present at the altar becomes our point of convergence, and more so when we are united in theology. If Jesus' intent was that each member of the various communities become true worshippers, that is our intent as well.

What can be seen in the history of our churches, in the function of the altar, is that sometimes the emphasis is placed on the community and other times on the individual. However, it appears that in our context, it has been focused inside the church, so that at some point the altar and its icons lost their transcendence in the life of the believer.

In our environment today, we have a "spiritual market" and maybe even a fierce "competition" with the different religious groups to "win souls." It is a reality in which the Nazarene Church in border communities is immersed, with mixed influences from North American and Mexican practices. Here, we are confronted by the challenge to find a practical way to use our altars in encountering God.

For this to take place, our duty is to encourage sacramental values in our altars, and to emphasize and relearn how to use them, instead of simply constructing artistic scenes in which there are no meaningful symbols. On the other hand, we have the duty to abandon our prejudices. The Latin American Roman Catholic heritage, for a period of history, oppressed the people with religiosity and empty ritual. As a result, our ministers stirred up great prejudice toward the sacraments, confessions, and symbols, and abandoned them. As the famous expression goes, "We have no religion, only Christ," but this leads us to minimize the use of the altar. Now, in the architectural arena of our newer church buildings, we can take back the realm in which these icons—like the table, the cross, or the baptistery—are a reality. In addition, we can encourage families to use these symbols to help the new generation understand their Christian significance, creating, just like Jacob did, a family altar.

Taking our cue from the biblical stories mentioned, in which the use of the altar was so important, we the ministers can take up teaching the tradition of the altar, where the body of Christ can be edified. We can also open ourselves to its use by the individual, a practice by which the believer can experience the meaning of the altar as a way of receiving grace even outside of the church building. Then, each believer with his/her family can discover that, with God's presence, amazing strides can be made in life change. This allows believers, little by little, to let go of the idea that the only way to receive grace is at the altar of a church building. Instead, they can bring the altar environment also to the intimacy of Christian homes, where new generations can learn to practice it.

Today more than ever, we can enter into the territory of liturgical discussion and dialogue about how or where to use the altar, whether it be in our church buildings, in the home, or some individual space. We can take hold of the important symbols of the altar, enriched by the experience of every believer, opening ourselves up also to different ways of offering the sacraments without taking away the transcendent meaning of the altar. That is not to make it superficial because our goal is that it can be transcendent also for future generations, just as we place ourselves on the altar to be sanctified with Christ as our minister.

We are also in a time in which we can return the dialogue to a balance. We can encourage the altar to be used in our church buildings and programs as means of engaging other Christian symbols and engaging in the Christian discipline of confession. We want our altars to leave a mark on the minds and experiences of young believers, without allowing it to dissolve into a meaningless pluralistic blur in which the meanings of the traditions would change.

If God gave someone who "did not deserve it" the opportunity to dialogue with him, then now it is time to talk about place and form, first, with those who truly need the altar as a place of spiritual encounter (the individual), to find there truth for living, that is, Christ. We also must open ourselves to new ways and places. This is not to discover the yet-unfound "true" form or place, but in order to find that important point convergence where the essential is revealed. In this way, we can strip away both the superficiality of the altar as entertainment and the emptiness of boring ritualism, and instead reach our goal that new generations be the ones to continue building the kingdom and regaining life wholeness, just like Jacob and the Samaritan woman.

If we consciously see God intervening in the story of His people, and if the altar has formed part of that individual or corporate encounter with God's presence, then we can also see His intervention for us now to seek out that encounter with Him at an altar that is not found exclusively in a church building. If that is the case, then let us dialogue, and travel the road together. Let us discover that the altar is not just a place, but a moment of encounter on the road of the Christian life and a deepening of our liturgical practices.

Our altars should be places of transcendence for the believer and a way to bring him to a transforming experience in his life through the action of the Holy Spirit, causing the conversion and sanctification of his life. Let us then come to a convergence in which, in our church buildings, families, and individual lives, we can value the use of the altar as our encounter with God's presence, where we come to be a pleasing offering to Him.

Ataulfo (Fito) Lopez is pastor of Tijuana First Church of the Nazarene and professor at Tecate Nazarene Seminary. He is frequently involved in discussions and conferences regarding immigration and ministry on both sides of the USA-Mexico border. He ministers together with his wife, Laura, in northern Mexico.

Holiness Through Water and the Word

G. Michael Scarlett

Who is calling us, and to what are we called? Answering this two-pronged question will give us a perspective on holiness and sanctification that might surprise us.

We understand that it is God who calls us—the God and father of our Lord Jesus Christ. We, in the holiness tradition, have heard God's clarion call to be holy as God is holy and understand that the holy life is dedicated to God in Jesus through the Holy Spirit.

We read in the Hebrew Scriptures how, when Yahweh called a people out of Egypt and gave them a new name (Israel), God set them apart. They were to be God's people--a holy priesthood, a holy nation, modeling for the world what relationship with Yahweh looked like. They were to point the nations of the world to this great God who created heaven and earth—the one true God whose name is I AM. What is interesting is how God saved this Hebrew people. In the exodus, Yahweh rescued his people and set them free *through* water. God washed them through the way of the sea and set them apart to be his people, "I will be your God and you will be my people."

St. Paul, in 1 Corinthians 10, makes the connection that the people of Israel were baptized into Moses; they were set apart for God with Moses as their leader. St. Peter, in his first epistle connects another people who were redeemed through water. Noah and his family were saved through water by God in the ark. St. Peter goes on to say, "And baptism, which this prefigured, now saves you—not as a removal of dirt from the body, but as an appeal to God for a good conscience, through the resurrection of Jesus Christ . . ." (1 Peter 3:21).

When the Israelites turned away from Yahweh, defiling themselves and their land, the result was exile. God, through Ezekiel, said that because of his great name and his own reputation, God was going to purify his people, "I will sprinkle clean water upon you, and you shall be clean from all your uncleanness, and from all your idols I will cleanse you. A new heart I will give you, and a new spirit I will put within you; and I will remove from your body the heart of stone and give you a heart of flesh. I will put my spirit within you, and make you follow my statutes and be careful to observe my ordinances" (Ezekiel 36:25-27, NRSV).

413

God saves through water. Jesus told Nicodemus, "Very truly, I tell you, no one can enter the kingdom of God without being born of water and Spirit" (John 3.5, NRSV). God's people are set apart through baptism. God's people are saved, redeemed through baptism. "Therefore, we have been buried with him by baptism into death, so that, just as Christ was raised from the dead by the glory of the Father, so we too might walk in newness of life" (Romans 6:4, NRSV).

"In him also you were circumcised with a spiritual circumcision, by putting off the body of the flesh in the circumcision of Christ; when you were buried with him in baptism, you were also raised with him through faith in the power of God, who raised him from the dead. And when you were dead in trespasses and the uncircumcision of your flesh, God made you alive together with him, when he forgave us all our trespasses, erasing the record that stood against us with its legal demands. He set this aside, nailing it to the cross" (Colossians 2:11-14, NRSV).

Throughout the centuries, the Church has understood baptism as the mark of entrance into the life of Christ and the mark of initiation into the Church. Notice St. Peter's language in his great sermon on Pentecost in Acts, "*Repent*, and *be baptized* every one of you in the name of Jesus Christ *so that your sins may be forgiven*; and *you will receive* the gift of *the Holy Spirit*" (Acts 2:38, NRSV, italics added). The Church has said through the centuries that it is in our baptism that we receive the Holy Spirit. We enter into life with God through our baptism. The "Sinner's Prayer" is a rather recent evangelism tool that was developed in the mid-1800s in America. There wasn't anything like it until that point. Baptism was the evangelism tool. In the ancient liturgy, the baptism candidate was asked, "Do you renounce sin, the devil and evil? Do you turn from your wickedness? Do you turn to Jesus Christ and accept him as your Savior? Do you put your whole trust in his grace and love? Do you promise to follow and obey him as your Lord?"

The author of Titus says, "For we ourselves were once foolish, disobedient, led astray, slaves to various passions and pleasures, passing our days in malice and envy, despicable, hating one another. But when the goodness and loving kindness of God our Savior appeared, he saved us, not because of any works of righteousness that we had done, but according to his mercy, through the water of rebirth and renewal by the Holy Spirit. This Spirit he poured out on us richly through Jesus Christ our Savior, so that, having been justified by his grace, we might become heirs according to the hope of eternal life" (Titus 3:3-7).

Before we came to Christ, our lives were profane. But, through our confession in Jesus Christ, through our faith in him, through the washing of water through the word (Ephesians 5:26), through the reception of the Holy Spirit in our baptism, we are made holy, we are purified, we are cleansed for the Lord's use. We are sanctified for service in the God's kingdom.

But it's not static, like the tools and instruments used in the tabernacle or the temple. Paul says that we are brought to life in Christ and empowered to live not for ourselves but for the one who died and was raised for us (2 Cor 5:14f). Then he says it, that explosively powerful good news:

> "So if anyone is in Christ, there is a new creation: everything old has passed away; see, everything has become new! All this is from God, who reconciled us to himself through Christ, and has given us the ministry of reconciliation; that is, in Christ God was reconciling the world to himself, not counting their trespasses against them, and entrusting the message of reconciliation to us. So we are ambassadors for Christ, since God is making his appeal through us; we entreat you on behalf of Christ, be reconciled to God. For our sake he made him to be sin who knew no sin, so that in him we might become the righteousness of God." (2 Corinthians 5:17-19, NRSV)

Baptism isn't something that we just check off the list of "Things Christians Do." It's not just something that we do once and then tuck into the memory files with other fond moments of our past. Because Baptism is a sacrament, *GOD* is doing something in and through it. Through faith, God is washing our sins away.

Baptism is a lens through which we can see and understand holiness and sanctification. We are not made holy so that we can feel good about ourselves or so that God can feel good about us. We are made holy, we are brought up into life with God in Jesus through the Holy Spirit, so that we can become not *just* partakers of the divine nature (2 Peter 1:4) but can also become partners with the Lord in his redeeming work of restoring his creation that he named "good" (Genesis 1). Our holiness has less and less to do with us, and everything to do with God: Father, Son, and Holy Spirit.

When we live our Christian life from our baptism, we bring a completely new perspective to the holy life. We hear Paul's words to the Galatians in a completely new way, "I have been crucified with Christ and I no longer live, but Christ lives in me. And the life that I now live in my body, I live by faith, indeed, by the faithfulness of God's Son, who loved me and gave himself for me" (Galatians 2:20, CEB).

God washes us with his Word, Jesus Christ (Ephesians 5:25-27) and purifies us from all our unrighteousness (1 John 1:9). We live out our confession that we made when we entered those cold waters of our baptism and live deeper into God's holiness. Every day we enter new space that needs to be marked by our baptism. And so with baptism as our lens for the Christian (holy) life, we intentionally choose to live out, live by, live from, and live deeper into the death and resurrection of Christ that we participate in by passing through water. God saves his people through water. God makes his people holy through water. God distinguishes his people by water.

God—Father, Son, and Holy Spirit—is calling us to communion to be brought up into life with our triune God. He calls us to a holy participation in the ministry of reconciliation. We are his holy priests. We are his holy hands in the world, reaching out and pulling up others from their desolation and bringing them into life with God. Baptism opens for us a new life with God, and a way for us to continually offer ourselves as a living sacrifice to God (Romans 12:1-2).

It's said that we come by our theology of holiness through life and learning. We try to understand holiness through words, but words fall short. This is exactly why we need more than words. We need symbol and sign. We need the tangible, touchable water that is sprinkled on, poured over, or in which we are immersed. We need the liturgy of baptism to help us visualize holiness, and to remind us repeatedly, that we are no longer our own. We joined Christ in his death and resurrection.

Now, we don't get rebaptized, as the Nicene Creed reminds us that we acknowledge one baptism for the forgiveness of sin. When new converts are baptized, we remember our own baptism (even for those who were baptized as infants) and renew our commitment to God when we were grafted to Christ through those holy waters. We remember that God—Father, Son, and Holy Spirit—makes us holy, and he is continuing that good work in us.

May we swim in the waters of our home. May we find our holy life in Christ's death and resurrection. May we live out our baptism and find that Christ is being fully formed in us through the power and presence of the Holy Spirit. Thanks be to God!

Michael met his wife, Amy, while they were at NTS. They married in 2004 and have two boys—Avyn and Brynnan. Michael and Amy are currently serving as co-pastors at First Church of the Nazarene in Mansfield, TX, a suburb of Fort Worth. Michael studied Religion at SNU (1998) and received a M.Div. from NTS (2006).

An Altar Call Every Week:

Holiness in the Eucharist

Matt Rundio

As the pastor of an established congregation in the Church of the Nazarene, some of the parishioners in my congregation have ideas and expectations regarding holiness that differ significantly from mine. One man, for example, came into my office with some concerns about the lack of "moments of crisis and decision" in our gatherings. He wanted camp meeting style sermons and altar calls like those that he remembered from years gone by. We had a lengthy discussion about why we do what we do. At one point, I said to him, "Don't you realize that we have an altar call every week?"

The table on which the elements of communion rest has another name: the altar. Each week, therefore, we have an altar call as people receive an invitation to come forward and receive. I firmly believe that, through this weekly altar call, God forms Christlike disciples and that people's hearts are formed in holiness.

Holiness is at the heart of the Eucharist, which Church of the Nazarene theologian Rob Staples calls "the sacrament of sanctification."[387] Several aspects of the Lord's Supper inform a theology of holiness. We celebrate communion as a community, not as individuals. At the table, we offer ourselves to God in thanksgiving. At the table we are unified, healed, graced, and filled. To the table we continually come. From the table we are sent. These aspects of Holy Communion give shape to a sacramental understanding of sanctification.

Community

The Eucharist reminds us that we "do" holiness together. *We* are gathered. *We* lift up *our* hearts. *We* give thanks. *We* are filled. *We* are sent. Most of the *you's* in scripture are actually plural *y'all's*. For example, "*Y'all* are a royal priesthood, a holy nation, God's own people." Important scriptures like that apply to a group of people together, a congregation, a community. This speaks to the fact that we cannot live out holiness alone or disconnected and that our holiness goes on display as a people, not as individuals. By celebrating the Lord's Supper together,

---

387. Rob Staples, Outward Sign and Inward Grace: The place of Sacraments in Wesleyan Spirituality (Kansas City: Beacon Hill Press of Kansas City, 1991), 201ff.

in community, with all the plural pronouns involved, we find grounding in our common life, in our life together, in the communal nature of holiness.

Sacrifice

Some people find the concept of offering (or "sacrifice" or "oblation") in the Eucharist difficult to grasp or even offensive. Yet sacrificial language and symbolism drip from the elements. Such language facilitates our understanding and our entering into holiness. Each week, after the words of institution, we pray, "And so, in remembrance of your mighty acts in Jesus Christ, we offer ourselves in praise and thanksgiving as a holy and living sacrifice in union with the sacrifice of Christ for us . . . ." True, the elements are Christ's body and blood, broken and shed, offered to and for us all. But remember what Paul taught us, "Y'all are the body of Christ." So there on the Table rests the body of Christ, which means that the church lays there as well. He is there, and we are there. "We feed on Christ and Christ feeds on us."[388] As we walk to the altar to offer ourselves, to die to the self, holiness takes root. (The importance of that last sentence cannot be overstated.) If ever a Christian action embodied holiness, coming to the altar at the Eucharist certainly does.

Unified, Healed, Graced, and Filled

If we come to the table in sacrifice, having emptied ourselves of our own intention and will, then at the table God fills us up with grace, heals us, and unifies us.

Celebrating Eucharist leads us to unity and healing. Typical aspects of preparing to receive the elements include confession, forgiveness, and the "passing of the peace," a time when we offer forgiveness and peace to one another. Thus, Eucharist helps restore right relationship, a hallmark of holiness.

Every week at the table I say, "There is one bread and one cup, for we, though we are many, are one." Sometimes I elaborate, "Be you Nazarene or Baptist, Roman Catholic or Eastern Orthodox, Presbyterian or Methodist or whatever, there is one table, one supper, one church. We are one, and all are welcome here." Other times I might add, "Be you rich or poor, English speaking or Spanish speaking, of any race or gender or whatever, we are brought into unity at this table." The proclamation of truth brings about change. I have seen God bring unity to Scottsdale First, where I serve. Discord once marked this church. Quickly, having come to the table week after week, God has brought healing and unity to our church. This is not mere theory; God truly uses this means of grace to bring about holiness.

---

388. I first heard this marvelous phrase from two professors at NTS: Steve McCormick and Dean Blevins.

Speaking of means of grace, the Lord's Super fills us with grace. As we come to the altar as broken and imperfect people, God fills us with God's very Self. As stalagmites are formed drip by drip over eons, so God forms a holy church and holy people, drip by drip over time. As we open ourselves to God, the Lord fills us. And that filling up adds up. It increases. It ultimately results in noticeable change.

Constant

I remember being taught that heart holiness happens in an instant. But I have come to understand holiness as a process, a long slog of growth in grace. While defining moments certainly occur, the maturity of a holy character takes a lifetime of God's work in us. The weekly habit of coming to the table helps us live into the ongoing and progressive nature of holiness. At least weekly, in communion with my sisters and brothers, we renew our sacrifice and commitment while God renews our unity, healing, and fills us anew.

A once-and-for-all approach to a holy life simply does not work. Right relationship defines holiness. Relationship, by definition, implies constancy. The supreme act of right relationship in the church happens as we celebrate the Lord's Supper together each time we gather for worship. The importance of regular attendance at the Lord's Supper for growth in holiness explains why John Wesley taught us, "It is the duty of every Christian to receive the Lord's Supper as often as he [or she] can."[389]

Sent

The Eucharist week by week contains beautiful rhythm: we are gathered, unified, healed, graced, filled, then broken and sent back into the world (from which we are gathered, unified, graced, filled, and sent). The sending prayer we use at Scottsdale First comes from the *Book of Common Prayer* and reads, "And now, Father, send us out to do the work you have given us to do, to love and serve you as faithful witnesses of Christ our Lord. To him, to you, and to the Holy Spirit, be honor and glory, now and forever. Amen."

We live holiness out in our everyday lives. We are sent out into those lives from the altar, from the table. Thus, the table forms the footing for our life and mission in the world. We are sent by God to join in God's work. To live obedient lives. To embody Christ's presence to those we encounter. To be a holiness people. We live this holy life from the table, from the Altar call every week.

---

389. John Wesley, "On Constant Communion" in *The Works of John Wesley*, Volume 7 (Third Edition; London: Wesleyan Methodist Book Room, 1872), 147. Gender inclusive language added.

A theology and practice of holiness informed by the Eucharist resonates with me and with many I know. Nothing in this essay originates with me. The church has had at its fingertips, throughout its history, a good "Wesleyan" theology of holiness built right into the Church's practice of the Lord's Supper. It is time we reclaim that heritage and make it our own once more. As I say at our altar call every week, "The Table is prepared. All who are hungry and thirsty are invited to come forward and receive these gifts of grace; may Christ be fully formed in you."

Matt lives in Arizona with his wife Shar and their daughters Courtney and Kiersten. He serves as lead pastor at Scottsdale First Church of the Nazarene, teaches from time to time, and stays deeply involved with the discipleship ministries department on his district. Also, he makes fabulous pot roast.

The Eucharist, Suffering, and Holiness

Elizabeth Palmer

> *Eucharist (thanksgiving) is the state of the perfect man. Eucharist is*
> *the life of paradise. Eucharist is the only full and real response of man to*
> *God's creation, redemption, and gift of heaven.*[390]

Eucharist refers to the Lord's Supper and means *thanksgiving*. In the New
Testament passages of the Lord's Supper, "he gave thanks" is our translation
of the original Greek word "eucharisteo." The meal the Lord shared with his
disciples, that meal that preceded the cross, *is* thanksgiving.

It was Passover, a time to remember and be grateful for God's rescuing grace
in Egypt. It was a time to remember that when God's people were suffering
slavery in Egypt they came to a point of life or death. Death was the plague,
but the blood of a slaughtered spring lamb was the rescue. The symbolic blood
was to bring life because it showed that the lamb died in the stead of a man.
Henceforth, a meal was the appropriate ritual of remembrance and gratitude for
the liberating bloodshed of a lamb. And so, before the agony and affliction of the
cross, Jesus joined with his disciples, washed their feet, and served them that meal
of thanksgiving and remembrance.

> *While they were eating, Jesus took some bread and thanked God for it*
> *and broke it. Then he gave it to his followers and said, "Take this bread*
> *and eat it; this is my body." Then Jesus took a cup and thanked God for it*
> *and gave it to the followers. He said, "Every one of you drink this. This*
> *is my blood which is the new agreement that God makes with his people.*
> *This blood is poured out for many to forgive their sins."*
>
> Matthew 26:26-28, NCV

With the daunting darkness of the cross approaching, Jesus took some bread
and wine and gave thanks. He shared with his loved ones. He broke the bread
and asked his disciples to remember his body and the suffering he would bear

---

390. Alexander Schmemann, *For the Life of the World: Sacraments and Orthodoxy* (Crestwood, NY: St. Vladimir's Seminary Press, 1973), 37.

for them. He poured them a drink and explained that this new agreement God makes with his people would begin with his own blood.

New life—transformation—begins with suffering.

Jesus equated bread and wine (the provisions of God, the sustenance of life, the manna) with his own body that was to be broken and his own blood that would be spilled out. He gave thanks for the elements, those symbols of suffering, and he offered the opportunity to partake—to join together in a new level of intimacy.

As he called his disciples to partake of the body and blood—to join in his suffering—he offered the hope of life.

> *Because I live, you will live, too. On that day you will know that I am in my Father and that you are in me and I am in you . . . Remain in me, and I will remain in you.* John 14:19-20,15:4, NCV

"Remain in me and I in you." Remain in the suffering of the cross that leads to the joy of resurrection. Remain in the gift of weakness that draws us to the strength of Omnipotent God. Remain in the intimacy that grows from our constant need for him. Dwell in the mystery of God taking all of our ugly pain, suffering and brokenness and transfiguring it into something new and beautiful and holy. For this is communion—circular, unbroken communion with God.

Our communion with God is a reminder that this depth of intimacy comes from the depth of sacrifice he has given to free his people—no longer by blood of a lamb, but by the blood of his own Son. This is the life-giving death that draws us into the presence of God where true life dwells.

And so the Eucharist is a reminder that death brings life. True life comes when we come to the end of ourselves, and there die. Die to the chaos and struggle of trying to live in our own strength, so to remain in the peace and surrender of life in God's strength. Die to the straining reach for independence, so to remain in the freeing rest of total dependence on Christ. And there, at the end of ourselves, live in the beauty and joy and gratitude of life born from death.

For there are two ways to live in this pain and suffering drenched world, the way of life or the way of death. Life that leads to death or death that leads to life. The first of these begins with clenched fists, gripping tightly to our own security as if to control. This grip moves up the arms and they draw in close, as if to protect or hide. But this is not to live, for this is the posture of death.

The posture of life, the other of the two, is a response to this death—death to self. It begins by un-clenching tight grips, loosening closed arms until wide spread open in the posture of the cross. This is a posture of life and freedom—

though a vulnerable one, indeed. So as suffering in this cruciform posture strips us of control, self-reliance, fear, hurt, disappointment, shame . . . we are left in a beautiful state of having nothing, yet possessing everything. Having nothing, but possessing *all* of God's gifts. Thus, we are thankful at all times, for to know God's gifts is to give thanks.

In Ephesians we read Paul's prayer that all the holy people will have, "greater understanding in [their hearts] so [they] will know the hope to which he has called [them]. And know how rich and glorious are the blessings God promised his holy people" (1:17-18).

Paul was a man who knew suffering. He understood the communion of suffering with Christ. When Paul was weak in his suffering, stripped of all and having nothing, he was then filled with God's sufficient grace. He knew how to live with nothing because he possessed all of the glorious gifts of God, and his response was thanksgiving, for there was great joy in the hope of Christ.

Thanksgiving is the only true response to God's redemptive acts. Joy and gratitude are at the center of a life lived reflecting the image of Christ—arms spread open wide.

And this cross-like death-to-life sort of posture, it is the natural form of receiving. We cannot receive a gift with clenched fists and folded arms. We must open wide. Release all to gain all. Die to live.

When Christ took this posture, he suffered the pain, agony, and death that bore the free gift of life and hope and joy. And this is how God redeems the world and brings new life. He invites us to participate in the pain and suffering of this world, with thanksgiving, to awaken us to his presence. "Christ's death [was the new agreement that] brought us into God's presence as people who are holy" (Colossians 1:22). In his presence we are on holy ground—right where he wants us to be.

To partake in the body and blood (suffering) of Christ is to partake in the holy divine life. Suffering bears holy. So, "rejoice that you participate in the suffering of Christ" (1 Peter 4:13).

Yes, rejoice and give thanks! Because this death-to-self, in order to take on the life of Christ, this is Eucharisteo. This is communion with God. This opening our arms wide to remain in the knowledge of our weakness, allowing the strength of God to remain in us—this is how we were brought into God's presence, giving thanks always. And this, this is holiness.

Pray for great wisdom and understanding so that we have God's strength, perseverance, patience, joy and thankfulness. We are free and forgiven. Colossians 1:9-14

423

Elizabeth Palmer earned her B.A. in Ministry from MNU (2006). She has served the denomination in Iowa, Kansas, Switzerland, Missouri, and South Korea. Elizabeth currently serves alongside her husband, Michael Palmer, at Living Vine Church in Napa, California. Elizabeth is also a full-time mother to Ella and Henry.

What the Joker Taught Me about Holiness

Jon Middendorf

Reasonable adults agree. Batman is the greatest superhero in the universe. Spare me your "but he doesn't have superpowers" protests. If anything, that makes Batman all the more impressive. No, he wasn't bitten by a radioactive bat. No, he isn't from another planet. No, he isn't the result of a failed science experiment. He's just a guy—a dark, driven, mysterious, dangerous, guy of phenomenal personal ability.

When you have to do business with the list of super-villains always on the prowl in Gotham City, you better be way above average. Penguin, Catwoman, Bane, Mr. Freeze, the Riddler, Poison Ivy ... the list goes on and on and on. Does Batman ever sleep?

But there's one more criminal that tops this and all other lists of the worst villains of all time—Batman's greatest headache—the Joker. Listen to his list of "accolades":

- *Wired* named the Joker "Comics' Greatest Supervillain."[391]
- *IGN* (an entertainment industry website) listed him the top DC Comics villain and the second greatest comic villain of all time.[392]
- *Total Film* rated the Joker as the greatest (or baddest) movie villain of all time.[393]

The Joker is, and always has been, different by design. The writers and storytellers who construct the Joker's character intend the "Clown Prince of Crime" to be evil, maniacal, disturbed, and disturbing. Jerry Robinson, Bill Finger, and Bob Kane (the original architects of the Joker's persona) wanted readers to be shocked and appalled. Those who continue to craft the Joker's mythology still want readers to

391. Scott Thill, "Comics' Greatest Supervillan? No Joke, It's the Joker," *Wired*, Oct. 27, 2011, http://www.wired.com/2011/10/joker/?viewall=true%5D, accessed June 18, 2014.

392. "Top Comic Book Villains," IGN, http://www.ign.com/top/comic-book-villains/, accessed June 18, 2014.

393. "100 Greatest Movie Villains," *Total Film*, http://www.totalfilm.com/features/100-greatest-movie-villains/the-joker, accessed June 18, 2014.

be frightened by the depth of his insanity, his complete insensitivity, his ruthless sense of humor, even his laugh.

But there's more. The Joker, from the beginning, has been written/created with the ability to pierce the "fourth wall." Where dramatic presentations are concerned, the fourth wall separates the world of the audience from the world of the characters on the stage or the screen or in the pages of the book. The Joker, magically and mysteriously, has always demonstrated the uncanny ability to recognize his own fictionality; he seems aware both of his predicament and of the presence of the audience.

In the old TV shows, Caesar Romero, playing the Joker, would at times look into the camera to access his audience. The cartoon versions of the Joker would do the same. The comic book versions of the Joker go even farther. Sometimes, the "Ace of Knaves" tells the reader when and how to turn the pages of the comic book.

You get the sense that the Joker is present (and genuinely dangerous) in ways that other two-dimensional, flat villains aren't. Creepy.

The Joker is evil in every sense of the word.

That's a problem for a method actor.

When a method actor agree to play a particular role or character, he tries, as best he can, to learn the character, to immerse himself into his chosen role, to blur or even eliminate the line between the actor and the character he is portraying.

When Jack Nicholson, a method actor, agreed to play the Joker in the 1989 *Batman* movie, Nicholson immersed himself into the character and nature of the Joker. By the time he reached the set, Nicholson had so identified with his role that he was no longer acting like the Joker; he was thinking and behaving *as* the Joker. And to hear Nicholson tell it, method acting the Clown Prince of Crime was costly. In fact, after hearing that Heath Ledger, another method actor, had agreed to play the Joker in *The Dark Knight*, Nicholson warned Ledger to proceed with caution. After learning of Ledger's death, two weeks before the final wrap of *The Dark Knight*, Nicholson's quote was short and to the point, "Well, I warned him."[394]

What happened?

Like all good method actors, Ledger sank himself into the role, working intently to identify himself with this character, all in the hopes of blurring the lines and becoming the Joker. He isolated himself from friends and family, consumed

---

394. Joe Neumaier, "Jack Nicholson Warned Heath Ledger on 'Joker' Role," *Daily News*, Jan. 24, 2008, http://www.nydailynews.com/news/jack-nicholson-warned-heath-ledger-joker-role-article-1.340786, accessed June 18, 2014.

every piece of literature he could, logged his findings in a journal, and slowly but surely blurred the line between himself and this dark character.[395]

By the time Heath Ledger reached the set, he was no longer acting. Before the cameras rolled, he was the Joker. When the cameras were shut down for the day, he was still the Joker. Method acting makes for remarkable performances, but, as Nicholson warned, there is a significant price to pay when the character is this dark, this disturbed.

The story of Ledger's insomnia while playing the Joker is well chronicled by now. There were rumors of nightmares and extreme anxiety. Ledger sought medication to calm his nerves to allow for sleep. Ledger died on January 22, 2008, from a lethal combination of painkillers, anti-anxiety medication and sleeping pills, all prescribed by doctors who'd worked to bring Ledger some sense of relief and comfort.[396]

It seems Ledger had achieved his goal. The line between the actor named Ledger and the character named Joker had been blurred—if not completely eliminated. The doctors, in so many ways, found themselves treating the Joker's illnesses. Ledger was lost somewhere inside of the Joker. It was as if Ledger had died and the Joker was now occupying Ledger's body. On the last page of his Joker diary, an already-gone Heath Ledger wrote "Bye Bye"- a chilling final indication of Ledger's abduction at the hands of the evil mastermind.

It's a tragic story and a cautionary tale. Be careful when blurring the lines. You never know where you'll be taken.

As awful as this is, is it possible to find something helpful here? Our instincts are to run and hide from stories and situations like this one, but might there be insight here to help us consider (or reconsider) what we mean when we use a word like holiness?

Years ago, Christians everywhere were asking an important question, "What would Jesus do?" Drawn from the pages of Charles Sheldon's book, *In His Steps*, well-intentioned believers tried as best they could to follow and imitate the Savior. In any and every situation, they employed the question—"What would Jesus do?"—to try to act more like Jesus.

But Jesus isn't seeking actors. Jesus wants to blur the lines.

Acting like Jesus doesn't change the spiritual DNA of the believer. I'm not saying it was all wasted effort. I'm sure many wonderful things have been done

395. White, "Inside Heath Ledger's Private Diary," *Daily Mail*, May 31, 2013, http://www.dailymail.co.uk/tvshowbiz/article-2334159/Inside-Heath-Ledgers-private-diary-Batman-stars-heartbroken-father-shares-personal-notes-dark-Joker-role.html, accessed June 18, 2014.

396. James Barron, "Medical Examiner Rules Ledger's Death Accidental," *New York Times*, Feb. 7, 2008, www.nytimes.com/2008/02/07/nyregion/07ledger.html?_r=1&, accessed June 18, 2014.

as people have "self-controlled" themselves to acts of piety and service, and God honors and can use these types of people and behaviors to further God's name and purposes.

But I'm not sure these actions rise to the level of what is intended by a word as "dangerous" as holiness. Perhaps it's a positive step along the way, but it's not the destination Paul had in mind. The Apostle Paul wanted and got something more, something so deep and transformative that it sounded much more like method acting, "I have been crucified with Christ; and it is no longer I who live, but it is Christ who lives in me. And the life I now live in the flesh I live by faith in the Son of God, who loved me and gave himself for me" (Galatians 2:19-20, NRSV).

Paul immersed himself in Christ. In fact, Paul seems to have submerged himself so deeply that the lines were blurred and perhaps eliminated. Paul's life was no longer his own. Paul was no longer acting like Christ. Paul was living *as* Christ, having died out to his own story and plot line. When the cameras were off, Paul's life demonstrated his new nature and character.

Paul wasn't acting.

Christians, good people who want to do the right things, are often guilty of acting like or mimicking Jesus. The planet needs less acting and more character transformations like those that we see in Paul or even Heath Ledger.

What would happen if I were to immerse myself into Christ? What if I tried to live the character of Jesus in my world? What would happen to me if I pursued this Jesus with the passion and desire I see reflected in Heath Ledger's relentless pursuit of the Joker? What if my pursuit were to result in my being lost in the person of Christ? What if I was no longer just acting like Jesus?

Paul's words in Galatians measure me, measure us. Holiness is something more than acting.

Less acting like Jesus. More living as Jesus. God, help us to blur and eliminate the lines. God, take us and make us holy.

Jon is now serving in his third decade at Oklahoma City First Church of the Nazarene. He has been Senior Pastor since 2007, but previously he served as Youth Pastor, Sr. Associate, and Pastor of Student Ministries. Jon's best days are spent living life with his family he loves so much: wife Kelly, and children Taylor & Drew.

On Sanctification and Marriage

Michael R. Palmer

Sanctification nearly pushed me out of the church.

Being a child of the church, I had from an early age experienced the beauty of the community of believers. I had witnessed God's provision, seen miracles and the power of Spirit-drenched corporate worship. Church and the church life came easy to me. Sanctification, however, did not.

Sanctification was this little voice inside my head reminding me of all the ways I fall short. I was supposed to be "perfect," but my lack of success at being sanctified proved something much different; it was the tangible proof of my inadequacy.

Hearing story after story, I began to believe others had it all together, and as a result, were happy. I, however, didn't have "it" together and, as a result, had a growing dissatisfaction with my own spiritual life.

About Marriage and a Lamb

Through the Gospels, Jesus often refers to a coming wedding. A unification of heaven and earth. A reestablishing of shalom and a complete reparation of the deep wounds that afflict our world.

Having been married for 5 years, I am relatively new to married life. I am daily realizing more and more what it means to commit myself fully to someone. This awareness began on a (seemingly) unremarkable spring afternoon in the lobby of the Smith Building at MidAmerica Nazarene University when I crossed paths with an impossibly bright and beautiful fellow religion major. I didn't know much about her, but what I did know was that she was beautiful, talented, and universally loved by everyone who knew her.

Our relationship began with dinner and grew. It grew over the course of the following weeks and months as we shared hopes, dreams, fears, preferences, and often hidden personality quirks. Hundreds of conversations paved the pathway over which we slowly walked towards our becoming one.

As great as our conversations were, there was a day I realized that, without hesitation, I could be offered anyone of my choosing and the only person I would choose was Elizabeth. It was in this moment I realized the depth to which I had trusted her with my heart, and so I knew the only logical next step was for me to invite her to join me in a life-long journey together.

Brimming with hope, I invited, and she said yes!

Over the next six months, we called churches and made reservations. Dresses were chosen and flowers were selected. The cake was designed and invitations made, folded and stuffed into envelopes.

I blinked, and six months later I arrived at a church in St. Louis, Missouri. In front of our closest family and friends, I found myself standing hand in hand with a stunning woman in a white dress. Catching myself in wonder at the magnitude and depth of the situation, I was brought back to reality by a simple question—a question that would forever alter my life and the life of this beautiful woman whose hands I held. The question? "Do you take this woman, to be your wife . . . till death do you part?"

Of course, I said, "I do."

On Clipboards and Greek Tragedies

Early in my spiritual journey, I saw my relationship and sanctification as God holding a clipboard with a long list. This list included all of the possible sins, and each sin had a box on the left side of it. This box would be checked every time I failed. God was keeping score, and the story my score closely resembled a Greek tragedy.

With the weight of my inadequacies hanging around my neck, a spiritual night surrounded me. My world became darker and darker. When I had nearly abandoned hope, God began to tear down many of the "realities" which had become millstones around my neck.

If I really search back to the beginning, as far back as I can remember, God has always been part of my thoughts. I always wanted to learn about who Jesus was and what he meant for me. There was a point, though, when I realized other people's conversations about God no longer were enough. Another person's story and experience can only be enough for so long before one must live their own story.

God wooed, I responded, and a relationship was formed.

Somewhere along the way I realized that doing the acts of following God—devotions, attending church, etc.—weren't enough. I realized the love and affection I felt for God ran deep, and I knew these were feelings no human could fulfill. It was this moment, a moment that happens at one point or another in every relationship, in which an unavoidable decision had been thrust upon me. Either I had to go all in, or I had to fold and walk away.

There was no third option.

God would have either all of me, or none of me. Was this a marriage or a fling? Was I willing to give up all of my power and leverage to follow the One to whom I had trusted my heart? In this moment, I chose to go all in, and I was now no longer the master of my own domain.

At the Altar

All who have said "I do" know the story doesn't end with those two words. With our vows spoken, the cake consumed, and hugs of family exchanged, we drove into the night and towards a new reality. This was a new reality where "wise words" came up short and pre-marital counseling was inadequate in preparing me for what was ahead. It is a new world in which I am no longer my own.

I wish I could say it came together easily for me. However, in those early marital moments, I quickly learned the depth of my selfishness and incompetence as a husband. Sure, I occasionally did a few things right, but more times than I want to admit, I did things completely wrong.

This marriage could have ended in disaster, and had this been a casual relationship, Elizabeth and I almost certainly would have parted ways. What made this different was the deep understanding and agreement that our mutual commitment trumped all. It was commitment that drove me to own my failures and pressed me to strive to become more than I once was. When I messed up, I fought to do things better the next time. I still failed, often miserably. However, I had a deep desire to do it right the next time . . . or the time after.

For me, the old cliché rang true. I was a work in progress.

Our Desire for Restoration Proves our Loyalty

In our marriage, Elizabeth and I both fall short. However, it is in our failures where we learn to offer and receive forgiveness. Nothing drives us towards forgiveness like our own overwhelming need for forgiveness.

To be married means to be known, and it's this being completely and wholly known which accomplishes something guilt and manipulation can never dream of accomplishing: a deepening trust and the desire to give even more of oneself no matter the cost.

Love propels us to become more, and it encourages us towards becoming what we are not in this moment. In a healthy marriage, there is no list of past faults and failures (1 Cor. 13:5). Being known would never stand for such a list. When a person is known and accepted, there is no mask to hide behind, and it is in having our masks stripped away, that we no longer feel the right or the desire to keep a list against another. To be known is to be humbled.

A Slow Transformation

Early on in my spiritual journey, my relationship with God was defined by a broken system of sin lists and petty nitpicking. However, through a dark and painful time of spiritual reflection, I was forced to acknowledge my actions as nothing more than man-made attempts at holiness.

Admitting the problem was, to borrow the language of addicts, truly the first step towards recovery, and it was the admission of guilt that began a new journey—a journey towards wholeness. This journey will wind its way through amazing victories and crushing defeats. I will have to re-surrender myself to God hundreds and thousands of times. However, over the course of this journey, I will continue to learn that my strength comes, not from my own ability to stay the course with God, but from God's commitment to stay the course with me.

Pierre Teilhard de Chardin, a Jesuit priest and philosopher, wrote one of my favorite poems in which he implores us to, "Above all, trust in the slow work of God."[397]

In its purest form, sanctification is, like marriage, about hope. Hope that God is not done with us, and hope that He will finish what he started. And we can trust that this hope in God is hope well placed. Each step we take is propelled by hope, and as the poem so beautifully says, we "Give our Lord the benefit of believing that His hand is leading [us]."[398] We are on a journey that will take a lifetime, but we have started that journey with the Love of our lives.

In my story, it was sanctification that nearly pushed me out of the church, and ironically, it was sanctification that kept me here.

Michael Palmer is a pastor, with his wife Elizabeth, in Napa, California. He is a graduate of MidAmerica Nazarene University. Michael is a proud father to Henry and Ella, avid St. Louis Cardinals fan, lover of cultures, travel, food, and theology. He's been published in Holiness Today, Standard, Reflecting God, Barefoot: Faith and Film, *and is an "Off the Shelf Blogger" for Beacon Hill. You can find his thoughts on faith, culture and life at michaelrpalmer.com.*

---

397. Pierre Teilhard de Chardin, "Patient Trust," Ed. Michael Harter (Chicago: Loyola, 2005), 102-103.

398. Ibid.

Created to Love, Created to Dance:

A Glimpse of God's Holiness

Philip J. Rodebush

There is a strange step in my feet lately. The sky is bluer than I remember. Flowers that I would have never noticed before suddenly beam bright with colors and loudly whisper, "Look over here. God made me!" Birds don't just chirp; they sing sonnets and Nat King Cole love songs. And my feet betray my Church of the Nazarene upbringing; they want to dance—at least dance as much as a Nazarene with two left feet can feel like dancing. No, I am not crazy, at least not completely. I am in love!

I recently became engaged to a beautiful girl named Katy and now have this strong desire to bring my dancing shoes out of retirement. (Side note for my grandma and the denomination's old-timers: this is just an analogy. I don't really have dancing shoes, just *New Balance* running shoes). It's embarrassing to admit, but if I didn't control myself, there are moments that I could almost break out in a song and dance routine among unexpected strangers in the street, like a silly scene in an old Elvis movie. No place is safe or off limits. Love has this way of infecting us and seeping into our thoughts and all the corners of our lives.

John Wesley got it right. "Love is the end of every commandment of God."[399] The aim of our faith is nothing more or less than the "pure love of God and man."[400] Holiness is ultimately about love. This is the type of relationship God intends for each of us to have with Him—a love relationship that affects every part of who we are and all that we do. Of course by "love," Wesley meant much more than the way we typically use it to describe couples who have gone off the deep end for each other. However, I am convinced that the best expressions of love between people can give us a glimpse of God's heart and design for us.

This isn't the first time I've experienced love. I first met a teenaged Amy Porter at a General Assembly when I was seventeen. A few years later, we fell in love and were engaged. In December of 1995, shortly before we were to be married, she died after a courageous battle with cancer.

---

399. John Wesley, *Works* XI, p. 416.

400. John Wesley, *A Plain Account of Christian Perfection* (Kansas City: Beacon Hill, 1966), 55.

For almost two decades, I've intended to write a book telling pieces of our love story and my journey grief, interweaving it with analogies gleaned from that period which help shape my view of God, sin, and holiness. I've had many false starts and stops and always assumed that if I ever found love again prior to writing the book that it would never stand a chance of being completed. Quite surprisingly, however, my amazing fiancée Katy, has me not only attempting to dance again but is also encouraging me to write and finish this long overdue project. The following is an excerpt from that upcoming book, portraying a God-encounter that is forever seared on my mind.

About a year after my fiancée Amy died, I was reading a book that talked about the fear of the Lord, called *Intimate Friendship with God*.[401] One of the key concepts of the book was that we should hate sin as God hates sin. Still, in the grieving process and pondering that idea, I asked the Lord a question that went something like this, "Lord, why do you hate sin—because we all seem to like it down here?"

I seemed to sense Him saying, "Philip, why do you hate cancer?" That was an easy answer. I hated cancer because it robbed me of Amy. It not only stole our future as a couple, but its very presence also handicapped the time we did have together. Amy's life had been drastically changed and limited because of this disease. She was no longer free just to go out. She lost control of many things. Her life was controlled by medical tests, treatments and white blood cell counts. Although she tried with her utmost effort, she couldn't live the full life that most college students are able to live effortlessly. Amy, one of the most joyful and fully alive persons that I ever knew, now had to struggle just to make it through the day.

And the more the cancer took over her body and her condition worsened, the more it limited both our freedom and choices. We couldn't go out on a date anymore. Our time together was often just sitting together watching a movie in a hospital room. We couldn't go out with friends or go dancing. (Not that we could really dance, but even if we had wanted to go, she physically wasn't able.) The cancer took more and more away from our lists of things we could do together. Sometimes, all I could do was just sit by her side and hold her hand. We could talk but not much else. When she lost consciousness, we couldn't even do that. As the cancer continued to spread, the cancer not only limited our relationship but also ultimately destroyed it.

---

401. Jay Dawson, *Intimate Friendship With God: Through Understanding the Fear of the Lord* (Grand Rapids, Michigan: Chosen Books, 1986).

God seemed to say to me, "See. That is why I hate sin, because I love relationship. Sin limits my relationship with my people. Sin keeps me from dancing with them. When sin enters their lives, there are things that we can no longer do together, things that I love doing with them. I didn't create them for sin, and sin begins to destroy my creation and my beloved. When sin increases, I can sometimes only hold their hand. There is nothing constructive that we can do together. And worst of all, when sin is left unchecked, it wreaks havoc on the bodies of my people and can eventually destroy my relationship with them altogether. I long for people to be fully alive through relationship with me, and that is impossible when their lives are captivated by sin. That is why I hate sin! I hate sin for the same reason you hate cancer—because I love people and love relationship with them."

It may sound incredible, but I honestly believe we were created to love and created to dance! So many times, I have found myself limping, just barely holding onto God. I'm thankful that He upheld me during those critical times. Yet, God never intended that to be my natural state. You and I were created to dance, to jump, and to leap—to spend eternity learning to follow the lead of our Dance Partner who is the Creator of the Universe. However, if you are like me, your own fears, failures and sins have often kept you from dancing.

Despite the awkwardness with which the Holiness tradition may have at times described sanctification (the surrendered life, Spirit-filled life or whatever term you choose to call it), in the past and despite its occasional tendencies towards legalism, there is a beauty in its essential teaching. The beauty is found in the understanding that the saving work of Christ on the cross is not just about eternal life and heaven. The essential beauty of our teaching is that Christ also restores us to a relationship with God so that we can once again begin to dance with Him on this side of heaven and learn to know Him and walk with Him as Adam and Eve did in the Garden.

We were created to love and dance with our Creator! As John Wesley himself understood, the end goal of holiness isn't a life without sin, but love, and a radical love at that. Full love of God and neighbors causes sin to lose its grip and even its attraction for us. This is a love that colors all of life and overflows into all we are and everything we touch and do. We have been called to love and to live in such an inviting way that those all around us who are also poor in spirit, who have been beaten up by life, who have been blinded, crippled, and devastated are **all** welcomed to throw away the crutches of sin and join the dance party as they too become captivated by God's love.

My prayer for myself and for those of our tradition is that the beauty of holiness may once again be known for the incredibly attractive all-out love relationship it is meant to be and that God might rekindle the flame of our first love (Rev. 2:4). May we learn the joy of dancing and keeping in step with the Spirit of the One who first loved us (Gal. 5:25; 1 John 4:19), and may many in our desperate, lonely, broken world be drawn to join in the dance.

Philip Rodebush loves laughter, all kinds of food and people. He has been involved in some sort of cross-cultural ministry most of his life, has worked with youth and college students, and has served the Church of the Nazarene for ten years in the Middle East. He is currently the director of the Creative Leadership Institute, training pastors and leaders in the Horn of Africa. In 2011, he ran his first marathon and lived to tell about it.

Holiness and a Kiss

Ryan Patrick McLaughlin

Holiness is not a quality that someone possesses in and of herself. It's a *relative* or *relational* quality. It can only exist in proximity to something else. Holiness denotes being "other" or "set apart." Being "other" requires something from which to be other—something that is different. Even God's holiness is like this—at least with reference to creation. God cannot be "wholly other" than the creation if there is no creation from which to be other.

However, from a Trinitarian perspective God is eternally (and internally) holy inasmuch as the persons of the Trinity are genuine others in relation. Significantly, though, otherness is qualified in the Trinitarian life. The persons are others in perfect communion. They are others for each other. This point is significant in that it suggests that the "otherness" of holiness is meant for communion. We should thus not think of holiness as *simply* distance or otherness. The Trinity reveals that holiness is a *directional* otherness, an otherness *toward* that which is other, otherness for communion.

The directional quality of Trinitarian holiness is also evident in God's holiness in relation to the creation. God is not merely wholly other than the creation; God is wholly for the creation. God desires communion with the creation. It is indeed otherness from the creation that makes this communion with creation possible.

Thus, the Trinity—both in terms of the internal relations of the divine persons and in terms of God's relation to the world—reveals the heart of holiness. Simply put: holiness is distance *from* an other (which allows them to be an other) for the sake of relationship *with* the other.

The divine call for humans to be holy reflects the directional holiness of God. God commissions Israel to be a nation set apart from the world for the sake of the world (Genesis 12:1–3, Exodus 19:3–6). The holy priests within Israel bear the responsibility of mediating between God and the rest of the community. Demons recognize Jesus's identity as "the Holy One of God" when he works toward the wellbeing of those they have victimized (Mark 1:24; Luke 4:34). Those who have received the Holy Spirit form an identity conducive to the wellbeing of others, whether through the fruit of the Spirit or through the gifts of the Spirit, all of which tend to aid others in the community.

437

Holiness implies two inseparable dimensions: distance and direction. By "distance" I mean one thing is set apart from other things. By "direction" I mean the otherness of that which is set apart is directed toward the wellbeing of that from which it is set apart. Said differently, holiness is both identity and vocation. As identity, holiness is the call *to be different from others*. As vocation, it is the call *to make a difference for others*. The vocation of holiness, if it is modeled after the relationships of the persons of the Trinity, is love. In this sense, there is no holiness without God, who *is* love (1 John 4:8).

Holy distance, then, is radically different from other kinds of distance, for example when we try to create separation between some unwanted intruder and ourselves. This distance exists for the sake of isolation, not communion. Holy distance is distance for the sake of communion. It does not protect personal space but seeks to share it with others.

A holiness that maintains distance but not direction is no holiness at all. A God who is other than the world but also seeks to keep the world at bay is not a holy God, which is to say no God at all. Only a God who is both other than the world and utterly for the world is a holy God. Likewise, only a human who is both other than the world and completely for the world participates in God's holiness.

The distance and direction of holiness imply two other essential dimensions of it: openness and vulnerability. To seek communion with an other requires openness to the other. In turn, to open oneself to communion with an other is to risk rejection—unrequited love. Surely God knows these truths better than anyone does! A holiness that entails both distance and direction therefore must also entail both openness and vulnerability.

Some of these ideas are a bit complex. So, when I try to explain them to undergraduates who don't have a background in theology, I use the metaphor of a kiss. A kiss, whether platonic or romantic, is a beautiful expression of communion. It is the coming together of two others—the traversing of distance in a moment of communion. This definition of a kiss implies that it is only possible because it is preceded by distance. Without distance, there can be no kiss. Similarly, there is no holiness without distance or otherness. *There is no holiness but relational holiness—* holiness that exists in relation to others.

However, as we have already established, distance is not enough. A kiss is preceded not only by distance, but also by one party leaning into that distance. Similarly, according to our metaphor holiness cannot simply be the distance that precedes a kiss. It entails leaning into that distance for the sake of communion. Without a leaning into the distance, there can be no kiss. Similarly, there is no holiness without leaning into the distance for the sake of communion with the other. *There is no holiness but directional holiness*—holiness that exists for the sake of others.

When we lean into a kiss, it is important that we don't traverse the entire distance ourselves. That's a serious breach of social protocol! We do not take a kiss by force; we open ourselves to receive it. We invite it. A kiss that is taken is not a kiss—not really. A true kiss must be received in reciprocation, a common leaning into the distance that separates us. Without an unforced invitation to the other, there can be no kiss. Similarly, there is no holiness without respecting the space of the other in an open invitation to communion. *There is no holiness but open holiness*—holiness that warmly invites others without coercion.

When we lean in for a kiss, when we traverse distance and thereby extend an invitation for intimacy, when we open ourselves to others by moving toward them, we become vulnerable. Anyone who has not been met half way after leaning into a kiss can testify to this claim. To lean into the distance between oneself and an other is at once to invite communion and to risk rejection. If there is no vulnerability to rejection, there is no true invitation to an other for communion. Without vulnerability, which is necessitated by openness and respect for the other, there can be no kiss. Similarly, there is no holiness without the risk of rejection by the other. *There is no holiness but vulnerable holiness*—holiness that risks the invitation for communion in full abandon.

A kiss requires distance, leaning into that distance, respect for and openness to the otherness implied by that distance, and vulnerability to the other that might reject the invitation to meet within that distance. These aspects are all required of a kiss because a kiss represents communion that can only burgeon out of the distance implied by otherness. A kiss is a unity that only distance renders possible.

Holiness requires all the same elements. It must be preceded by distance, for it requires being set apart from an other. It must include leaning into that distance, for being set apart is a vocation for the sake of the other. It must be lived out with absolute respect for and openness to the other, for the vocation of holiness (which is love) cannot be forced. Finally, it must entail risk and vulnerability, for in abandonment it invites communion with no guarantees of receiving it.

In conclusion, I offer two practical reflections.

First, like a kiss, holiness requires reverence for the otherness of the other. One who claims to be holy must never seek to maintain that identity by denigrating others. One who is holy never prays, "God, I thank you that I am not like other people: thieves, rogues, adulterers . . ." (Luke 18:11). The only way to maintain an identity of holiness is to be different from others for the sake of others. Holiness that is purchased at the cost of another's dignity is sacrilege. Thus, when Christians seek to establish their own superiority by demeaning non-Christians, they only succeed in demeaning holiness itself.

Second, like a kiss, holiness is costly. The one who claims to be holy must risk leaning into that which is utterly foreign for the sake of communion. For all the talk of holiness entailing purity and cleanliness, the one who is holy must be willing to get his or her hands dirty for the sake of others. To fail to do so is to adopt a façade of holiness akin to the priest and Levite who ignored the man in the ditch in the Parable of the Good Samaritan, thinking it was better to remain pure than help a stranger in need. When Christians are more worried about maintaining their own status of "holy" than feeding the poor, clothing the naked, protecting the vulnerable, and freeing the oppressed, they degrade holiness for the sake of setting their conscience at ease. Holiness is evident in a willingness to get into the ditch with the marginalized, not in a preoccupation with our own purity.

Ryan Patrick McLaughlin is currently a visiting assistant professor in the Religious Studies Department at Siena College. He has published two books: Christian Theology and the Status of Animals *and* Preservation and Protest: Theological Foundations for an Eco-Eschatological Ethics, *as well as several articles in the field of animal theology and ethics.*

Holiness Living as Journey

Timothy B. Whetstone -Espada

J.R.R. Tolkien's epic tale involves two main characters: Frodo Baggins and his companion Sam. Shortly after setting out for their quest, Sam is frozen for a moment and says, "This is it . . . If I take one more step it will be the farthest away from home that I've ever been." Then Frodo recalls how Bilbo Baggins always used to warn that, "it's a dangerous business, Frodo, going out of your door. You step into the road, and if you don't keep your feet, there is no knowing where you might be swept off to."[402] The *road* takes the hobbits from the familiar to the unknown. They are tested, exposed to dangers and yet, encounter unimaginable beauty in new places, people and experiences.

Life brings with it a journey that at times is quite dangerous. Not necessarily perilous but dangerous nonetheless—filled with ambiguity, doubt, struggles, darkness, and choices—where this is it moments, and one more step, may take us further away from what we find familiar. In truth, it may be the furthest away from home we've ever been.

Scripture tells of a monumental story that takes place in the 13th century BC involving a young man named Joshua who is called by God to lead the Israelite nation into Canaan. This land was promised by God centuries earlier to their forefathers—Abraham, Isaac and Jacob. After nearly 500 years of being slaves, homeless and landless, traveling to the Promised Land was an immense transition fraught with anxiety.

The book of Joshua tends to be less about the person Joshua and more about the God of Joshua. Joshua 1 reminds us first and foremost that God is with us. God promises Joshua not only land, but also His presence, "As I was with Moses, so I will be with you; I will not fail you or forsake you" (Joshua 1:5).

Yet, how can we step without *losing our feet?* These *next step* moments are often less about *if* we'll take them and more about *how*. Even though cruelty and darkness exist in our world—which is never God's plan—He has not abandoned us. We can trust that "every place that the sole[s] of [our feet] will tread upon . . . [Yahweh] will be with [us]" (1:3). We can know that, even if we stumble, God will continue to "direct our steps" (Proverbs 16:9). We can faithfully surrender to

---

402. J.R.R. Tolkien, *The Fellowship of the Ring* (New York: Ballantine, 2012).

the One who "won't let us down . . . won't leave us" (Deuteronomy 31:8, MSG). And we can cling to the promise that God never gives up on us. It's more than a promise, however. It's an invitation into a relationship and one that will transform us if we, let ourselves be "pulled into a way of life shaped by God's life, a life energetic and blazing with holiness" (1 Peter 1:12, MSG).

This life of holiness is less about morality (right or wrong behavior) and primarily about a relationship with the One who is Holy. A most basic scriptural meaning of *holy* or *holiness* (qadosh- Hebrew, hagios-Greek) is "set apart" or "dedicated" to God—simply, to belong to God. God desires for us to belong to Him, "I will be your God, and you will be my people" (Leviticus 26:12; Hebrews 8:10). As believers who respond to His presence in our lives, we dedicate ourselves to God as ones belonging to Him. Our lives are then shaped by God's holiness. Subsequently, a cyclical movement helps nurture these "blazing holiness lives" because "without holiness no one will see the Lord" (Hebrews 12:14b).

We are called into relationship not only to know more *about* God who is Love and who is Holy, but also to *know* Him intimately with all our being. John Wesley remarked that "knowing God . . . is not simply a matter of cognitive knowledge; it necessarily involves experiential or transformational knowledge."[403] Wesley's emphasis was not on a propositional knowledge but a transformational love relationship that enables us "to love the Lord [our] God with all [our] heart, soul, mind, and strength" (Matthew 22:37).

A lifestyle of holiness begins with God. And God, who revealed Himself through Jesus the Christ, must be at the core of who we are. In order to have Christ at our core, we must be in relationship with Him. This relationship is rooted in prayer. Prayer is not a mechanism but a relationship where we are nurtured and grow to know God and love God (1 John 4:8, 16). It's most certainly something we do, but it must become more. Prayer must become a part of who we are. As we surrender ourselves and ask, "Lord, teach us to pray," we begin to see the heart of our Lord—His mission of reconciling creation (2 Corinthians 5:19; Colossians 1:20) and to experience His holy transformation in our lives.

In Joshua 1 we read how God establishes a relationship of presence with His people. He challenges them to nurture their relationship through prayer and being intimate with His word. "Know the law; then meditate on the law" (Joshua 1:8). *Prayer* (a relationship) and *Scripture* (His Word) then become vehicles of transformation with God. Scripture speaks of this in Psalm 1, "Blessed are those . . . who delight in the law of the Lord and meditate on his law day and

403. M. Robert Mulholland Jr., "The Wesleyan Doctrine of Scripture (As Contrasted with Fundamentalism)" in *Square Peg*, Al Truesdale, ed. (Kansas City: Beacon Hill, 2012), 31

night. They are like a tree planted by streams of water, which yields its fruit in season and whose leaf does not wither—whatever they do prospers." This prayer relationship nurtured by His word is truly a love affair with the Lord.

Out of this love affair (prayer relationship), we are moved to more—to worshiping the One true fulfillment of the law: Jesus our living Word. We gather regularly to praise in all circumstances *because He first loved us* (1 John 4:19). We value corporate worship, yet are not limited to such. In fact, our very lives become expressions of worship through His transforming power in us. Paul reminds us, "God helping you: Take your everyday, ordinary life—your sleeping, eating, going-to-work, and walking around life- and place it before God as an offering" (Romans 12:1, MSG). And yet we're still moved to more.

"Obey the word . . . **act** in accordance with all that is written" (Joshua 1:8). In other words, *serve!* God has invited us into relationship—to know Him so intimately that our natural response is to love and serve Him and others. We hear God call us through His words, "Follow my commands," or as Jesus beckons, "Follow me!" This has always been a dangerous call as it has meant: caring for the sick, touching the untouchable, forgiving the unforgivable, and even loving the unlovable—our enemies. The message remains the same today.

Os Guinness once said, "First and foremost we are called to Someone, not to somewhere or someplace."[404] It's this Someone—Jesus—who invites us into relationship and enables us to love and serve. Service flows out of our prayer and worship-filled lives because God is *with us,* enabling us to live lives of faith and action in Christ (James 2). Through our union or dwelling with Jesus, we participate in the life of God (John 14). As such, we can say that in Christ, God's holiness is our holiness.

Yet, this does not make everything in life easy. In fact, there will be those who will "stand against us" (Joshua 1:5). But we can trust in a faithful God who in His grace is present and empowers us to be prayer-filled, worshipful, and service-oriented kingdom agents. Ultimately, these are not steps to a certain type of Christian life but instead a way of living out a mysterious holy faith. That's the funny thing about a mystery; there's no notion that we have everything figured out. Thus, we always remain open to the adventure of the *next step.*

Just as it was with Frodo and Joshua, this journey is not in isolation. Together we become a people, a fellowship, who move from prayer to worship, to service, to prayer, to worship, and so on. By His power we not only pray His will and His kingdom come on earth as it is in heaven (Luke 11), but also actively participate in it.

---

404. Os Guinness, *The Call: Finding and Fulfilling The Central Purpose of Your Life* (Nashville: Zondervan, 1998).

So, take that next step *further than you have ever been* in confidence that He who is Holy is calling you into holy relationship and will enable you to live a life of holiness.

Timothy B. Whetstone-Espada serves as University Chaplain & Director of Chaplaincy Ministries at Point Loma Nazarene University. Previously he has served in various ministry roles including Disaster Response Coordinator, church planter in several cities, as well as a missionary in Italy, Singapore, and Alabama. He is a husband and father of three young children. Tim loves soccer, the great outdoors, hanging with his family, and always good conversation, a good book, good music and a great cup of café!

Holiness as a Way of Death

Tara Thomas Smith

What you finally must decide—regarding the doctrine of holiness—is whether the body of Jesus is a tremendous threat or a tremendous hope.

Of course, the body of Jesus has always posed a problem for good religious folk. From Levitical prescriptions to Stoic renunciations, the only thing worse than the flesh, it seems, is dead flesh. Christians—and particularly we of the Holiness persuasion—have fared no better with this damned body.[405] To be holy must surely mean to be above all matters of the flesh, all things which are cursed by God, all *sin*.[406]

However: the body of Jesus.

The crucified and dead body of Jesus was and is a stumbling block to religious folk, and it's plain stupid to everyone else (1 Cor. 1:23). What are we holiness people going to do with a corpse? The trouble, you see, is that the fullness of the revelation of God occurs right here. It's a revelation which cannot be charted or analyzed, but only met and received, and only then when I plunge entirely into this broken body. The trouble, you see, is that there is nothing I can do to initiate or sustain or acquire or invoke or otherwise possess this encounter. The trouble is that God's revelation *is* Godself freely given in the man who hangs cursed on a tree.

A doctrine of holiness which forgets this body of Jesus is not more than a doctrine of wholeness. Such a doctrine leaves in its wake a church obsessed with positive attitudes and behavior modifications, one which must hand-wringingly concern herself with drawing circles of demarcation in varying degrees of circumference relative to the cultural whims of the world. In short, a doctrine of wholeness might—*might* effectively wash clean the outside of any number of cups (Luke 11:39), might replace a few rounds of Prozac, might even fill the vacancy left on Oprah's couch, but it will never encounter the holy God who is pleased to dwell in the body of Jesus.

Holiness as Participation

To be holy means to be separate. Simply that. Although the word has acquired—as words have a way of doing—all sorts of added adornment (e.g., to

---

405. "Cursed is everyone who hangs on a tree." Galatians 3:13, NRSV; (cf. Deuteronomy 21:23)

406. "For our sake, he made him to be sin who knew no sin." 2 Corinthians 5:21

be holy is to be good, righteous, pious, blessed, sinless, virtuous, etc.), the word itself brooks no rival: it means only to be separate, consecrated, set apart. In the Hebrew Scriptures, we learn that God is holy because God is separate. God is *other* than what we are.

Yet from here comes the impossible call, "You shall be holy to me; for I the Lord am holy, and I have separated you from the other peoples to be mine;"[407] that is, "be holy, for I am holy" (Leviticus 20:26). If God is holy because God is *other*, then in what sense can human beings possibly be holy? Is holiness adorned like a well-fitted mask? Do we common folk mutate into something other than human at the moment of entire sanctification?

It might help here to begin thinking of what it means to know a person and how that is different from knowing a fact or a thing.[408] Consider this: I might tell you that I have a friend who is not very tall, with auburn hair that is sometimes curly and sometimes straight. I could explain to you that she enjoys cooking for friends, conversations about things that matter, and anything related to sunflowers. I could tell you about her job, her husband, her kids, her preferences, and her dislikes. But even if you had known all of these things about my friend before you met her—the very things which you might later claim as examples of the way you know her—you would not yet say that *you know* my friend; only that you know *of* her. This is because you have not in any sense participated in a relationship with her. She has not revealed herself to you, nor you to her.

So there is a knowledge of persons that is different from a knowledge of things. At an instinctive level, we speak of knowing Cathy or Brandon or Jill differently than the way we speak of knowing the Chicago Transit Authority or the quadratic equation or the alphabet. I know *things* based on what I do to obtain knowledge of those things (*I* see, *I* taste, *I* discern, *I* extrapolate). But I know my friend or my husband or my children or any other person as she reveals (or refuses to reveal) herself to me and as I participate (or refuse to participate) in that same communion. The richness of my knowledge of a person is not funded by acquisitiveness—however robust—but by solidarity and participation. And in this way we realize that every relationship is always at its core an act of faith. That my friend exists in some meaningful way in reality is not for me to know or to doubt, but to live in the light of.

So it is with holiness.

To be holy is not to be spoken of in the manner of *things*. It is not an acquisition. We do not obtain holiness as we obtain a new bicycle. We do not achieve holiness as we achieve first place in a marathon. Rather, we become holy as we participate

---

407. Leviticus 20:26; (cf. Leviticus 11: 45, 19:2, 20:7)

408. Cf. Kaufman, Gordon. "Two Models of Transcendence: An Inquiry into the Problem of Theological Meaning," *The Heritage of Christian Thought: Essays in Honor of Robert L. Calhoun*, R.E. Cushman & E. Grislis. Eds. 182-196, 1965.

in the holiness of God, as we come to know God where God reveals Godself to us. And where does God reveal Godself to us?

The Body of Jesus

We must say this, in the too-brief time we have together, you and I: surely there can be no mistake that the body of Jesus is: what we call the crucified man on the cross, is what we call the holy church, is what we call the poor of the world: the hungry, naked, aliened, and imprisoned. We come to know God—to be made holy—only in the body of Jesus, and the body of Jesus is to be found where God is resurrecting the dead and the damned and thereby gathering his church.

The resurrection is that singular, historical, freely given encounter of Father-Son-Spirit in the world. It justifies—resurrects, fills with the life-giving Spirit—the entire history of Jesus and of the Israel whose lineage is so carefully traced to him. The resurrection is also what justifies the entire *proceeding* history of Jesus and the people who are grafted into him through baptism into his body, the people that he gave himself over to and continues to give himself over to in the life of the Spirit.

The event of resurrection teaches us that the fullness of God is pleased to dwell in the body of *that one*, the dead Nazarene peasant, that this body is where we find God to be known for all time as God-for-us. And therefore, the event of resurrection teaches us that God is pleased to reveal Godself as present to us in the world in the body of *that one* who stands broken before us: the hungry, the thirsty, the stranger, the naked, the sick, the prisoner. And praise be to God, *that one* we will always have with us (Matt. 26:11).

What then, is to be said about the doctrine of holiness? It is not a thing to be strived after or acquired—as if one can strive after dying. It is not an achievement in which to boast—as if one can boast in a dead body. It is not a level of purity or cleanness to which we aspire—as if purity and cleanness can abide the bleeding Jesus. It is not a delicate way of life we must protect from those who would blaspheme—as if anything more blasphemous can be found than the cross.

What is finally to be said is that all hope of holiness must be found in communion with the body of Jesus, gathered as the church, poured out in love to, among, with, and on behalf of the broken and dying bodies of this world. In all these things we are more than conquerors through him who loved us (Rom. 8:33-39).

Tara Thomas Smith is Co-Pastor with her husband Brett at Winamac Church of the Nazarene in northern Indiana. Tara's pastimes include professional thinking, falling down a lot, maintaining hardcore nerd cred, and being subtly delightful. She enthusiastically endorses her two children, Miles and Macey.

Pulling Up a Chair to the Wide and Long Table
Christa Klosterman

On Wednesday mornings at 9 am there is a standing invitation for clergy in my town to gather at the local coffee shop to discuss the week's lectionary passages. As one who preaches mostly from the lectionary, I have made it my habit to go as often as my schedule allows.

Since it is a lectionary group, I usually join with the local pastors from mainline denominations. The differences between us enrich us rather than distract, for our goal is to inspire in each other a deeper engagement in the weekly passages. Most Wednesdays we are successful.

On one particular Wednesday morning recently, the Old Testament text for the week was the Holiness Code found in Leviticus 19. I decided that would be my main text for the coming Sunday. My mainline clergy colleagues were quite surprised to find that morning that I found something worthy to preach from Leviticus' strange rules. But knowing that members of the Church of the Nazarene are holiness people, they asked me to share my insights and thoughts about that Old Testament holiness passage.

While I was willing to share my insights in the conversation, I was also aware of the sinking feeling inside of me that they probably weren't going to be thrilled with what I had to share. Studying the passage in the previous days had reminded me of all the holiness reading and preaching I had heard in the past from numerous Nazarene mentors and preachers. My study on the passage inspired me, but the thought of sharing my findings with those who didn't emphasize holiness did not.

I shared anyway. I relied on my denominational background as I put these peculiar Old Testament rules in the context of a wider holiness understanding. I echoed my holiness teachers and pastors before me. I spoke of the call to be odd like God, to reflect the divine image in our living, to embrace the call to be who we were always meant to be from the beginning. To be holy as God is holy is to recover that image of God imprinted on us in the fullest form by being merciful and compassionate like God is. To be holy, I said, is to mirror the character and nature of God's self-giving love.

When I finished, the Presbyterian minister next to me said, "That is a beautiful description."

"Odd like God. That really sums it up," said the Episcopal priest.

The Lutheran pastor wrote down a few notes.

And I left the coffee shop that day with a new and broader vision for our holiness message.

In the weeks since that particular morning, I have wrestled some with the inferior feelings that rose within me when those outside our tradition asked what holiness people thought about holiness passages in Scripture. It was an automatic response to be apprehensive and hold back. The sense of inferiority that rushed over me was something I was almost taught to expect from those outside the holiness circle. Over the years I had inferred that our humble beginnings and our deep commitment to holiness was for us, but I was also led to expect to be dismissed by those other groups with a wider base and more denominational history. I had figured that holiness was just something for members of the Church of the Nazarene, a distinctive that wasn't worthy of taking outside our close-knit family.

What I experienced that day, of course, was quite the opposite. The thoughtful response I had to offer was well received by those who do not focus on holiness to the extent that members do. Those clear lines we drew in the past between denominations based on their distinctive doctrines have become quite blurred. The posture that once had us separating ourselves from the others has begun to shift to a more humble posture where our diversity can actually enrich us. We're beginning to learn that we have much to learn from others. Therefore, members of the Church of the Nazarene have much to offer the wider Christian world when it comes to holiness, and we ought to rethink our habits in our conversations with the whole Church.

As members of the denomination, we are quite comfortable talking about holiness among ourselves, but we have this apprehension about dialog beyond our group. Somehow, we began to think, as I did, that they don't want to hear it, that we will be dismissed, and that we can just engage in conversation on other topics. Sometimes, we haven't found any reason to talk much beyond our denominational circles. We've kept our gift of understanding holiness (and I do think it is a gift) all to ourselves, when really it is a gift to be shared.

Perhaps it is time to pull up a chair at the wider table of Christian conversation and offer the blessing of our holiness message. We need not be arrogant or demanding, but simply bring the best we have to offer that others might be enriched by this notion that we really can reflect the divine image, that God really does enable us to take his character on ourselves, that the world might be transformed. Perhaps we just need the vision to see that we have something to offer the wider church, that not to show up and offer our gifts is to hoard them selfishly.

There are all kinds of ways to show up at the table of wider Christian conversation. It can happen in more formal and global settings, but it can also happen in those local gatherings where the pastors from a variety of denominations show up to partner and dialog with each other. Wherever Christians show up to talk, we holiness people need not feel a sense of inferiority. Instead, we can offer the gift of holiness we've polished and wrestled with for so long.

We also ought to show up as those with something to learn. As we offer our contribution to the larger Body of Christ, let us also remember that we aren't the only ones who have a handle on this call to holiness. Just as we have gifts to give to the wider Christian community, so we also have some gifts to receive from the wider Christian community, even when it comes to holiness.

If we are willing to listen and receive, we just might be pushed to think of the holy life in ways our sister denominations have explored and polished over the years. As members of the Church of the Nazarene begin to wrestle more deeply with the holy call to justice, perhaps there is something for us to learn from those (especially in the mainline denominations) who have devoted themselves to doing justice over many years and in a variety of ways. Perhaps they can show us the pitfalls and best practices, the exegetical background and theological rationale for seeking justice in ways that will help us learn and grow. Or as we work to discern God's voice in living the holy life, perhaps we can learn about discernment from Quakers or Catholic spiritual directors. The wider Christian community has also been gifted by the Spirit and has the ability to enrich us.

If we who are members of the Church of the Nazarene are deeply committed to holiness—and I believe that we are—then we must admit that holiness is not just for one small sect in the Christian tradition. It's meant for all followers of Jesus. We holiness folk haven't always lived this way, and that's unfortunate. But it doesn't need to dictate the future.

Perhaps in these post-modern days, as the lines of distinction between Christians blur and the need for each other increases, we can learn to join the table of conversation. We can come to that wide and long table both as those with a gift to offer and as those who have much to learn from the wisdom and insight of others as we try together to live lives that reflect the *Imago Dei* in the wider world around us.

Let the conversations begin!

Christa Klosterman is an ordained elder in the Church of the Nazarene, currently on special assignment to two United Methodist Churches (Fruitland, ID and Ontario, OR). She likes preaching, camping, good books, connecting conversations, and being an aunt. Most days she thinks pastoring two churches is better than one.

Social Holiness as Embracing Difference

Wm. Andrew Schwartz

John Wesley and Tina Turner are sitting in a bar. Tina Turner asks, "What's love got to do with it?"

John Wesley replies, "Everything!"

While this imaginary encounter might leave you wondering what John Wesley was doing in a bar, John Wesley's central emphasis on love is widely noted. As Mildred Bangs Wynkoop contends, "Love is the dynamic of Wesleyanism."[409]

This should come as no surprise, given the importance of Scripture in Wesley's theology and the centrality of love in Scripture. When Jesus was asked which of the commandments was the most important, he replied, "'Love the Lord your God with all your heart and with all your soul and with all your mind.' This is the first and greatest commandment. And the second is like it: 'Love your neighbor as yourself.' All the Law and the Prophets hang on these two commandments" (Matthew 22:37-40).

As Wesley notes, however, this call to love is something everyone approves, "but do all men practice it? Daily experience shows the contrary. Where are even the Christians who 'love one another as He hath given us commandment?' How many hindrances lie in the way!"[410] Wesley continues, "The two grand, general hindrances are, First, that they cannot all think alike; and, in consequence of this, Secondly, they cannot all walk alike; but in several smaller points their practices must differ in proportion to the difference of their sentiments."[411] In other words, the greatest hindrance to loving our neighbor *as we love ourselves* is that our neighbors aren't ourselves. Our neighbors are distinctly "other." Put another way, the great hindrance in fulfilling the call to love as Christ loves is "difference"—different opinions, different practices, different cultures, different religions, different political views, different moral stances, the list goes on.

Of the characteristics that mark the 21st century, pervasive plurality is dominant. As technology advances, the interconnectedness of all things becomes more and more apparent. Globalization, the interplay of cultures and peoples on

---

409. Mildred Bangs Wynkoop, *A Theology of Love: The Dynamic of Wesleyanism* (Kansas City, MO: Beacon Hill Press, 1972), 21.

410. John Wesley, Sermon 39, "Catholic Spirit," *The Works of John Wesley*, 3rd Edition (Grand Rapids, MI: Baker Books, 1996), 493.

411. Ibid.

a global scale, means a shrinking of the world. The era of isolationism is over. The era of multiplicity reigns.

But difference is not a new phenomenon. Differences in the way that people understand the world, in the way that we live in the world, were—even in the time of Wesley—unavoidable. Wesley states, "It is an unavoidable consequence of the present weakness and shortness of human understanding, that several men will be of several minds in religion as well as in common life. So it has been from the beginning of the world, and so it will be 'till the restitution of all things."[412]

Unfortunately, we are far too quick to reject difference. No doubt it comes from a deep desire for logical consistency and the assumption that our views are true. Wesley acknowledged this, "Every man necessarily believes that every particular opinion which he holds is true; (for to believe any opinion is not true, is the same things as not to hold it)."[413] And, if we begin by assuming that "my view" is the right view, then it stands to reason that those views different from my own are false. Our proclivity to such arrogance is deeply rooted. Wesley himself asks, "Who can tell how far invincible ignorance may extend? or (that comes to the same thing) invincible prejudice?—which is often so fixed in tender minds, that it is afterwards impossible to tear up what has taken so deep a root."[414]

Instead of self-centered absolutism, Wesley supported a humble perspectivism, in which one holds to the perspective that seems right for oneself (for we can do no better), all the while acknowledging our proclivity for error, "Yet can no man be assured that all his own opinions, taken together, are true. Nay, every thinking man is assured they are not . . . 'To be ignorant of many things, and to mistake in some, is the necessary condition of humanity.' . . . He knows, in the general, that he himself is mistaken; although in what particulars he mistakes, he does not, perhaps he cannot, know."[415]

In light of this epistemic humility, Wesley urges that we be careful not to force our views upon others (even though we believe them to be true), "Every wise man, therefore, will allow others the same liberty of thinking which he desires they should allow him; and will no more insist on their embracing his opinions, than he would have them to insist on his embracing theirs."[416] Now this doesn't mean we stop trying to convince others to agree with us. Discourse is still imperative. Certainly, Wesley continued to preach and teach what he considered to be the right views on God, morality, and religion. Rather, we are simply to treat others as we would want to be treated—to insist only to the extent that we would want them to insist.

---

412. Ibid.

413. Ibid.

414. Ibid.

415. Ibid.

416. Ibid.

Wesley is not suggesting some form of relativism by which all perspectives become true, nor is he advocating for a self-absorbed absolutism by which only "my" views are true. Actually, it's not really about truth at all. As Wesley notes, "Religion is not opinion: no, not right opinion, assent to one or to ten thousand truths . . . Right opinion is as distant from religion as the east is from the west."[417] Rather, it's about how we treat each other. It's about relationships. It's about loving our neighbors as ourselves. It's about holiness.

Wesley famously states, "The gospel of Christ knows of no religion but social; no holiness but social holiness, 'Faith working by love' is the length and breadth and depth and height of Christian perfection."[418]

Holiness, like love, is relational. Accordingly, social holiness is a matter of loving our neighbors as ourselves. As Wesley exclaims "'Holy solitaries' is a phrase no more consistent with the gospel than holy adulterers."[419] Social holiness is love manifest.

In the early years of Methodism, this call to social holiness took the general form of caring to the poor, marginalized, and oppressed. However, in today's dynamic pluralistic context, social holiness must also include embracing differences in the way prescribed by Wesley. We must look at these "others" and say together with Wesley:

> Do you show your love by your works While you have time as you have opportunity, do you in fact 'do good to all men,' neighbors or strangers, friends or enemies, good or bad . . . if thou art but sincerely desirous of it, and following on till thou attain, then 'thy heart is right, as my heart is with thy heart.' 'If it be, give me thy hand.' I do not mean, 'Be of my opinion.' You need not: I do not expect or desire it. Neither do I mean, 'I will be of your opinion.' I cannot, it does not depend on my choice: I can no more think, than I can see or hear, as I will. Keep you your opinion; I mine; and that as steadily as ever. You need not even endeavor to come over to me, or bring me over to you. I do not desire you to dispute those points, or to hear or speak one word concerning them. Let all opinions alone on one side and the other: only 'give me thine hand.'[420]

To do so, we must accept, as Wesley instructs, that we are in error. We must recognize that true religion is not about right opinion. We must remember that

---

417. Wesley, Sermon 55, "On the Trinity," *The Works of John Wesley*, 3rd Edition (Grand Rapids, MI: Baker Books, 1996), 493.

418. John Wesley, *Hymns, and Sacred Poems*, viii.

419. Ibid.

420. Wesley, "Catholic Spirit," 495.

God continually works in different contexts and that this work is to be affirmed and celebrated.[421] No doubt, the diversity we encounter in the 21st century is of a different degree than Wesley's time. However, as John Cobb reminds us, "In his own situation [Wesley's] views pushed forward the frontiers of toleration, and even support, of those who are different."[422]

What this means for social holiness in the 21st century is a radical embracing of difference, rooted in love. Social holiness means embracing members of the LGBT community. who often struggle to find a place in Holiness congregations. Social holiness means embracing those with whom we have theological and political disagreement, letting go of labels like liberal and conservative, fundamentalists and heretics. It's not good enough to simply "love the sinner and hate the sin." Instead, we must put aside all judgment and acknowledge that "Though we cannot think alike, may we not love alike? May we not be of one heart, though we are not of one opinion?"[423]

When it comes to these "others," these whom we have rejected as false, mistaken, and in error, Wesley boldly calls us to maintain our beliefs while respecting difference in love, "No man can choose for, or prescribe to, another. But everyone must follow the dictates of his own conscience, in simplicity and godly sincerity. He must be fully persuaded in his own mind; and then act according to the best light he has. Nor has any creature power to constrain another to walk by his own rule."[424]

To be holy is to be in loving communion with God and others. And while the main obstacle in fulfilling this call to love is difference, the solution (according to Wesley) is to look beyond difference to see the person in whom God is actively at work. Social holiness means, in part, liberating others from our judgment and humbly recognizing our own imperfections.

I suspect Tina would agree.

Wm. Andrew Schwartz is a Ph.D. candidate in philosophy of religion and theology at Claremont Graduate University, and Managing Director of the Center for Process Studies. He holds an MA in Philosophy from Claremont and an M.A. in Theology from Nazarene Theological Seminary. An active member of the Wesleyan Theological Society, Andrew's academic interests include comparative philosophy and theology, Wesleyan theology, and religious pluralism.

421. John Cobb, *Grace and Responsibility: A Wesleyan Theology for Today* (Nashville, TN: Abingdon Press, 1995), 145.

422. Ibid, 150.

423. Wesley, "Catholic Spirit," 493.

424. Ibid, 496.

Holiness as an Integrative Element of Christian Life

Ánderson Godoy Salguero

Like many Latin Americans, I was born in a Catholic Christian family, and, like most Latin Americans, this did not mean much to me. It was when I was sixteen years old that I "became a Christian" in a Church of the Nazarene in Bogotá, Colombia. One of the first things I learned at church was that a Christian was not supposed to be like other people. Furthermore, now that I had accepted Jesus, my goal was to "convert" others.

Before long, I learned that I was not just a Christian but also a Nazarene. I was told that as a member of the Church of the Nazarene I was "called unto holiness." Since this was all new to me, I tried to get a definition of holiness from my leaders and friends at church. Though they said various things, they all seemed to agree on one thing: holiness is the call of God to set me apart. I was in the world, but I was not from the world any longer.

As a new believer, the one thing that became clear to me was that Christianity, in general, and holiness, in particular, required me to be radically different from others. This idea was reinforced when I went to Bible College and learned that holiness is the *distinctive* doctrine of the Church of the Nazarene. In other words, if there is any doctrine that differentiates us from other Christian groups, that is the doctrine of holiness. Now, after 10 years of studying and working in theological institutions of the Church of the Nazarene, I see more of the complexity behind this simple declaration that we should be different.

Holiness can be a complicated topic in Christian life and theology. Theologians have written book after book trying to understand holiness and to make holiness more understandable to others. (You are holding one of those attempts in your hands now.) The problem is that not everyone is as equally inclined to read volumes trying to figure out what members of the denomination mean when we say that we have a "distinctive doctrine." Sadly, this lack of serious investigation often results in accusations of snobbish Christianity or, even worse, in an actual Christian snob who thinks of him or herself better than others.

It is true that misunderstandings give place to conflict, but it is equally true that unclear declarations give place to misunderstandings. Let me then be clear. Holiness *is not* the distinctive doctrine of the Church of the Nazarene; Holiness is (or should be) part of the life and doctrine of every group that call themselves Christians. "True," some may say, "holiness is not the distinctive doctrine of the Church of the Nazarene, but *entire sanctification* is." I am sorry to disappoint you again, but the truth is that even this Wesleyan theological understanding of holiness is held by a significant number of denominations other than ours.

Since unclear declarations give place to misunderstandings, allow me to be even clearer. The moment in which holiness (or a particular understanding of it) becomes the criterion to say, "I am different from you," is also the moment in which a wall is built between people and relationships are damaged. This is not an authentic expression of holy living for it takes holiness as a distinctive, discriminating, and hierarchical element of Christian life. Instead, the opposite should be true. Holiness must be the common, unselective, and unranked reality of those who partake in Christian life in the Church of the Lord.

But let us not be unfair. The idea of holiness as a cohesive element of Christianity and not as a one of division has been difficult to grasp not only for members of the Church of the Nazarene but also for Christians in general. If one takes a look at the history of the Church, there have been plenty of occasions in which a so-and-so group thought they found the ultimate understanding of Christian life and decided either to force others to become like them, or to forbid them to do so. Regretfully, we must admit that there is an ample tradition of using Christian principles, and especially the life of holiness, as elements of separation and not as elements of integration. However, this must change.

Am I saying then that there is no benefit in denominations? Am I suggesting that members of the denomination are exactly the same as any other Christian group? Of course not. I love my denomination, and I thank God for letting me know him in this church. Denominations are important for they offer different perspectives of Christian life and speak clearer to different personalities and cultural backgrounds. I happen to believe that as long as you pour good coffee in it, any mug will do the trick.

There are plenty of traits that give the Church of the Nazarene a defined identity, and a commitment to holiness is just one of those. My plea for we members of the denomination of the 21st century is for us to understand that *to be called unto holiness is to be called unto unity in recognition of human frailty*. It is only by recognizing that *we all* have sinned that the call to a holy life makes sense at all.

This is especially important in our increasingly multi-cultural and multi-religious settings. I had the privilege of receiving theological formation surrounded from people of different cultures in Latin America and Asia. The one thing that impacted me the most was the seemingly inverse proportion there is between talking of holiness and the practice of holiness. Groups that spend much time and effort in describing their holiness often do so in an attempt to prove how superior they are from the rest. In contrast, people who are in constant interaction with other groups, and who are willing to learn from them, needless explanation of holiness and tend to focus more on its practical application. This is especially true in places where Christians are persecuted. When becoming distinctive is a disadvantage, or not even an option, then unity and love in action become the best expression of Christian holiness.

I do believe that the Church of the Nazarene has something to say to the world. The world needs to be reminded that holiness is possible here and now. Purity of intention, wholehearted devotion to God, and the certainty that one does not have to be slave to the power of sin, are desperately needed in the today's Church.

Nevertheless, I also believe that zeal for holiness is not enough by itself. Holy people know that apart from God there is no hope, and because of that, they have nothing about which to boast. The call of holy people is not to show their distinctiveness, but to understand their very own frailty, and to be strengthened by honest and open relationships with God and others.

It is through holiness that we understand *we are humans after all*. We are one with those who love the Lord and want to follow him. We share the strength that comes only from God to his Church; we are one in strength. But we are also one with those who struggle, with those who do not know, or prefer to ignore. We are dust of their dust; we are one in weakness.

That is precisely the beauty of holiness as an integrative element of human existence. The call to holiness reminds us of our brokenness as human beings. It reminds us of the ongoing tension as we share life with others and see in them who we were, who we are, and who we are becoming. But even more, it is by the call of holiness that we understand our purpose and final destination, that we can go to no other for only God has words of life.

Years have passed since I committed my life to Christ. Now, I have a wife, and I have just started serving in a country where Christians amount to just 1% of the population, and where the membership of the Church of the Nazarene is in a steady decline year after year. I do not need to tell the people here that I have a distinct doctrine. That is exactly what they think of me, and that is one of the reasons why they want little to do with my religion. If, on the other hand, I go around telling the few other Christians in this place how distinct my beliefs are, there is a good chance that I will be left alone. And in the extreme case that I would insist on my distinctiveness with my wife, I might not have dinner tonight.

This is not a call for rebellion. This is just a matter of common sense. Focusing on the integrative aspect of holiness is a survival strategy for the Church of the Nazarene, especially in multi-religious settings. This is a call to tell non-believers that we are as human as them, that we struggle as they do. This is a call to tell fellow Christians that we, just like them, believe in the power of God and his desire for the redemption of creation. This is really a strategy for thriving, more than surviving, both now and into the future.

Ánderson Godoy Salguero is a Colombian graduate of South-American Nazarene Theological Seminary and Asia-Pacific Nazarene Theological Seminary. He and his wife Janary serve as missionaries for the Church of the Nazarene in Japan. Ánderson is currently writing a thesis on Japanese theologian Kosuke Koyama and is very interested in practical theology, interculturalism, neuroscience, photography, juggling, and several other unrelated fields.

The Beauty of Holiness:
Changing our Rhetoric
Jacob Lett

Since beginning my journey in Church of the Nazarene academia about 10 years ago, it has been my experience as a student, professor, and researcher that our rhetoric surrounding the topic of holiness has been that of defense or change. In the midst of our important discourse, we have left many uninspired, confused, or indifferent towards holiness. Therefore, in this essay, I would like to briefly introduce to our conversation the *theological aesthetics* of Swiss Catholic theologian Hans Urs von Balthasar and express how his framework might be important to changing the ways in which we discuss holiness.

Though unknown to most evangelicals, Hans Urs von Balthasar (1905-1988) was a man of immense intellect and extraordinary gifts. Having written over one thousand books and articles, Balthasar is considered by many to be one of the most influential figures in 20th century theology.[425] Henri de Lubac famously said that Balthasar is the most cultured man of his time.[426]

Balthasar did not enter formal theological studies until after he had already completed a doctorate in German literature. While finishing his dissertation, Balthasar felt called to enter the priesthood. Soon after, he entered the Jesuit novitiate, which required him to study two years of philosophy and four years of theology. Reflecting on his time studying theology, Balthasar wrote, "My entire period of study in the Society was a grim struggle with dreariness of theology, with what men had made out of the glory of revelation. I could not endure this presentation of the Word of God. I could have lashed out with the fury of Samson. I felt like tearing down, with Samson's strength, the whole temple and burying myself beneath the rubble."[427] Balthasar was known to sit through theology lectures with his ears plugged, while reading through material more interesting like the early Church Fathers.

Balthasar sought to transform modern theology by reintroducing the theme of "beauty." In his grand 16-volume work, the first series of 7 volumes titled

---

425. For a more detailed biographical sketch of his life, see: David L. Schindler, *Hans Urs von Balthasar: His Life and Work* (San Francisco: Ignatius Press, 1991).

426. Henri De Lubac, "A Witness of Christ in the Church: Hans Urs von Balthasar," *Communio* 2.3 (Fall 1975).

427. Hans Urs von Balthasar, *Introduction to Erde und Himmel: Ein Tagebuch. Zweiter Teil II: Die Zeit der grossen Diktate by Adrienne von Speyr* (Einsiedeln: Johannes Verlag, 1975), 195.

The Glory of the Lord attempts to develop Christian theology from the loss of the three transcendentals. In other words, he is attempting to complement the "true" (logical) and the "good" (ethical) with the "beautiful" (aesthetical). To explain his intent, Balthasar states:

> The introduction will show how impoverished Christian thinking has been by the growing loss of this perspective which once so strongly informed theology. It is not, therefore, our intent to yield to some whim and force theology into a little travelled side-road, but rather to restore theology to a main artery which it has abandoned. But this is in no sense to imply that the aesthetical perspective ought now to dominate theology in place of the logical and the ethical. It is true, however, that the transcendentals are inseparable, and that neglecting one can only have a devastating effect on the others.[428]

According to Balthasar, a world without beauty causes the good to lose its attractiveness and the true to become incomprehensible. In order for truth to be reasonable, it must be beautiful. In order for goodness to be just, it must be aesthetical.[429] By robbing the spiritual senses of their need for color and contour, for taste and fragrance, theology has robbed knowledge of its mystery and robbed good works of their power.

Balthasar was not arguing for some mere sentimental, romantic, or self-indulgent concept of beauty. Beauty in particular is love, and love is ultimately Christ, the archetype of all forms of knowledge. Balthasar states, "What is here called an 'aesthetic' is therefore characterized as something properly theological, namely, as the reception, perceived with the eyes of faith, of the self-interpreting glory of the sovereignly free love of God."[430] The love of the incarnate Word can be so enticing that it draws us under a spell much like a work of art can captivate our senses and imagination.

Much more can be said about this, and I encourage the reader to explore Balthasar's book, *Love Alone is Credible*, for a good introduction to his theological aesthetics. Now, however, we must ask how does Balthasar's work relate to the theme of renovating holiness? It has been my experience in the Church of that Nazarene that as we continue to examine our entire sanctification statement, defend past experiences, and develop new standpoints, we are losing our listeners in a confusing trail of semantics and dogma. As we are discussing what we

428. Hans Urs von Balthasar, *The Glory of the Lord* (San Francisco: Ignatius Press, 2009), 1:9.

429. Balthasar, *Glory of the Lord*, 1:18-19.

430. Hans Urs von Balthasar, *Love Alone Is Credible* (San Francisco: Ignatius Press, 2004), 11.

mean by "entire" and the difference between American-holiness and Wesleyan-holiness, many in the younger generation are simply leaving to local communities of faith with less baggage.

As our culture transitions into postmodernity, I wonder if Balthasar's aesthetical lens has something to offer us. Perhaps there is a compelling nature to holiness that gets lost in the constant battle of defending or improving our doctrine. Though we will always need to reformulate dogma to the cultures that surround us, would we be wise to add a mystical, aesthetic quality to our discourse? Can we embrace the truth that the Triune love can capture a person in such a way that is not possible to utter with human words? Perhaps our holiness theology could display itself better in the subtle light of poetic metaphor rather than the blinding glare of rational conceptualization.

Please do not hear me saying that changing and improving our doctrine is not needed—far from that. Rather, I would like to encourage us to think as much about the culture created by our rhetoric as we do the content of our doctrine. To put it another way, Balthasar states, "The site from which love can be observed and generated cannot itself lie outside of love (in the "pure logicity" of so-called science); it can lie only there, where the matter itself lies—namely, in the drama of love. No exegesis can dispense with this fundamental principle to the extent that it wishes to do justice to its subject matter."[431]

In a world infused with grace and bathed in love, holiness holds an intrinsic value, a Triune beauty that leaves its beholder craving it. To close, Balthasar's bold prose seems fitting:

> Beauty is the last thing which the thinking intellect dares to approach, since only it dances as an uncontained splendor around the double constellation of the true and the good and their inseparable relation to one another . . . No longer loved or fostered by religion, beauty is lifted from its face as a mask, and its absence exposes features on that face which threaten to become incomprehensible to man.[432]

Jacob oversees all ministry field experience and teach theology and mission courses at MidAmerica Nazarene University. Also, he is the Pastor of Cross-Cultural Mission at College Church of the Nazarene in Olathe, KS. In his free time, he is pursuing a Ph.D. at NTC, Manchester. His research is on Hans Urs von Balthasar's doctrine of atonement.

---

431. Balthasar, *Love Alone*, 82.

432. Balthasar, *Glory of the Lord*, 1:18

Holiness Is for Everyone
Keith Davenport

How are people talking about holiness? Are people who visit a worship service or small group at the local Church of the Nazarene able to observe that holiness is important to the denomination? Do church board members and small group leaders get excited teaching about the intricate workings of entire sanctification?

If one were to measure the extent the Church of Nazarene believes in holiness by the amount of talking its members and active attenders engage in on the topic, one would likely notice some telling statistics. Our discussions may even suggest that holiness is primarily only for a small number of members of the denomination (such as professors, pastors, and denominational leaders), because they are often the only ones to have well-informed or enthusiastic conversations about holiness.

This reality, however, is not consistent with the beliefs of the Church of the Nazarene. As a denomination, we believe that holiness is for everyone. Lines like "Be holy" (Lev. 19:2) or "It is God's will that you should be sanctified" (1 Thes. 4:3) are not meant for a select few. No, the hope of holiness is the hope that all followers of Christ can be not just forgiven of their sins, but freed from them as well. The invitation to be made holy is one for all followers of Christ. Holiness is for everyone.

Therefore, everyone should have the opportunity to engage in meaningful conversations about holiness. Conversations deepen understanding. The more people talk with one another about the specifics and details of sanctification, the more they can learn from the experiences and education of others. The more that a person learns about holiness, the more she is able to experience it. The more he experiences it, the more comfortable he feels talking about it. And so the cycle restarts with more conversations, more learning, more experiencing, more living out, and then more conversations and so on.

This notion that conversations are important to a local congregation is not new. Pastors and church leaders have found that in order for an issue to be important to the ministry and life of the church, it has to be a regular subject of both formal and informal conversations in the church. For example, Victory Hills Church of the Nazarene of Kansas City, Kansas regularly talks about church planting in board meetings and worship services. In the span of ten years, this same congregation has assisted in planting eleven new congregations. Likewise, Bethany First Church of the Nazarene in Bethany, Oklahoma engaged a new paradigm for missions by forming a lasting partnership with Swaziland. BFC talks about their Swaziland partnership in their worship services, in small groups, and on their website. Because of its healthy model, the BFC Swaziland partnership has inspired doctoral studies and similar partnerships in other congregations. Conversations shape belief and practice.

The Church Universal is increasingly recognizing that local congregations should be active in "theologizing." The Anglican Church in the Kansas City metropolitan area recently launched the St. Mellitus Theological Centre, an institution dedicated to theological education intentionally geared toward lay people. St. Mellitus' maiden voyage into the theological arena featured N.T. Wright giving a lecture series called "Theology for Everyone."[433] The name was adopted from a commentary series known as the "For Everyone" series.[434] This commentary series was especially written for the average church attender, not the seminary professor or graduate. In Wright's keynote lecture, he made clear that, for the Apostle Paul, the way in which the early church would stay united and obedient to God was through practicing theology together. If the Church of the Nazarene wants to stay united and obedient to God, if holiness really is for everyone, then the entire church must be engaging in the conversation.

In the same way that Paul encouraged the early church to work out its theology by talking it out, the church today ought to continue to work out its theology of holiness by having intentional conversations about it. The local congregation can learn much more about holiness by talking through the major issues of the doctrine, such as the tension between crisis and process. While using modern day language might be helpful in introducing the doctrine, using biblical and theological terms creates a fuller and deeper understanding of the doctrine that is not possible with only the contemporary substitutes. With formal and informal conversations in the local church, all Christians, regardless of their formal theological education, will be able to explain what sanctification is and how it is both a part of and different from salvation. The more a person knows, the better he or she can understand the experiences he or she has in life.

This deeper level of knowledge of how God desires to work in the life of a Christian brings the person closer to God. As Saint Anselm said, theology

433. N. T. Wright, "Theology for Everyone," Lecture, Double Tree Hotel, Overland Park, KS, March 25, 2014.

434. N. T. Wright, *New Testament for Everyone*, 18 vols. (Louisville, KY: Westminster Knox, 2011).

is "faith seeking understanding."[435] Creating opportunities for dialogue about holiness is a way to practice theology in the local faith community.

I found this reality to be true in my experience as pastor of Faith Church of the Nazarene in Lawrence, Kansas. The church had had very little interaction with the denomination in the several years before my arrival and had lost its identity as a Church of the Nazarene. The most helpful way for us, as a community of faith, to reconnect with the Wesleyan tradition was to talk about it. As a distinct doctrine of our denomination, the doctrine of entire sanctification was at the forefront of these conversations. Our dialogue started with sermons on holiness. It continued with Sunday School, built around the Articles of Faith.

As the church continued to grow, others continued the conversations. I continued to plan both individual sermons and full sermon series specifically about entire sanctification throughout each year. Sunday School teachers began choosing for themselves curriculum about holiness. People were responding to the invitation to sanctification. As people desired to become members of the congregation, sanctification became a major talking point in membership classes. Eventually people asked for special meetings (over a soda or coffee) just to talk more about holiness in depth. The church even spent some Sunday worship services dedicated entirely to small conversations about sanctification in place of the typical sermon.

Holiness is for everyone. Engaging the entire congregation in conversations about holiness through small groups, sermons, classes, and conversations nurtures a healthy culture in the local church. If the local church is to do theology together, we need local pastors and lay people to lead the charge. Equipping the congregation with the ability, vocabulary, and purpose to do theology together as a community is essential. This may mean leaders having more conversations about holiness as well. Words like "sanctification" and "perfection" are biblical words that we can explain in understandable ways. Even the word "entire" can be explained in ways anyone can understand.[436] Conversations develop pastors as much as lay people. Holiness is for everyone.

The more a person learns about holiness, the more he or she can experience holiness and understand this experience. Developing this culture of conversation will create unity and momentum for the Church of the Nazarene as a holiness denomination by inviting more people to be sanctified and to participate in developing an understanding of holiness. Using and teaching key theological

---

435. Alister McGrath, *Christian Theology: An Introduction* (Malden, MA: Blackwell, 2001), 44-45.

436. See Keith M. Davenport, "Sanctification as Prescription" in *Conversations on Holiness*, Keith M. Davenport, ed. (Kansas City: Beacon Hill, 2013), 23-32.

terms help keep the deepness of the doctrine intact. Holiness is for everyone, so let us help everyone talk about it.

Keith M. Davenport is editor of Conversations on Holiness *(2012). He is a graduate of Olivet Nazarene University and Nazarene Theological Seminary. Currently, he serves as Manager of Student Activities and Leadership Development at Johnson County Community College in Overland Park, Kansas. Keith and his family attend Christ Community Church of the Nazarene in Olathe, Kansas, where Keith leads the college ministry.*

Being a Holiness Denomination in a Post-Denominational Age:
Exploring Social Holiness Narrative Threads
Nell Becker Sweeden

Faced with denominations that are seemingly irrelevant and ineffective when it comes to global realities of poverty, hunger, lack of clean water, human trafficking, etc., many young Christians have exited and are exiting the structure of the denomination, not to mention the Church and Christianity entirely.[437] As courageous entrepreneurs, community organizers, and quiet Christians committed to action, many post-denominationals have started ecclesial gatherings and conversations, non-profits, and churches that seek to alleviate suffering, come alongside marginalized persons, and combat injustice around the globe.[438] In this essay, I'll explore Wesleyan-holiness identity narratives amidst twenty-first century post-denominationalism in the context of an emerging awareness of global injustice and commitment to Christian social engagement, especially among young people ages 18-30.

Reflecting on the decline of denominations in twenty-first century America, Russell Richey's assessment is apropos, "Might the problem, the cause, lie in the collapse of denominational purpose and in the loss of a real reason for hanging together?"[439] Thus, in a time when many are leaving, the Church must rediscover why we gather together. I propose a way forward for denominations in examining, uncovering, and re-telling their theological identity narratives with

---

437. The phenomenon of post-denominationalism reflects Christians of all ages who have exited or are exiting the structure of the denomination. While in the future this exodus may have the potential to spark reform, at present post-denominationals find that program-driven structures of denominations are located "far beyond the actual lives of the faithful." See James R. Nieman, "The Theological Work of Denominations," in *Church, Identity, and Change: Theological and Denominational in Unsettled Times,* ed. David A. Roozen and James R. Nieman (Grand Rapids, MI: Eerdmans, 2005), 625. Additionally, the unprecedented growth of young people self-identifying as religiously "none" is closely tied to other trends estimating that nearly one in five (or 18%) adults under 30 have left the religion of their upbringing and are now unaffiliated. See Pew Forum study on "Religion Among the Millennials" February 2010. http://www.pewforum.org/Age/Religion-Among-the-Millennials.aspx (accessed May 30, 2013). See page 4 of full report.

438. Witness organizations like Cupcake Girls, slaveryfootprint.org, Q ideas, Invisible Children, Love 146—not to mention larger Christian parachurch organizations like World Vision, Sojourners, etc. For an interesting description of the socially conscious orientation of younger evangelical Christians, see Gabe Lyons, *The Next Christians: Seven Ways You Can Live the Gospel and Restore the World* (Colorado Springs: Multnomah Books, 2010).

439. *Church, Identity, and Change: Theological and Denominational in Unsettled Times,* ed. David A. Roozen and James R. Nieman (Grand Rapids, MI: Eerdmans, 2005), 34.

new complexity and transparency. Collective identity is conjured up in gathering and shaping life around stories. Stories are not merely descriptive but prescriptive. As John Inge suggests, "Stories give us a way to walk."[440]

Wesleyan-holiness denominations have multiple narrative strands as part of their histories, and at least two holiness strands of origin. For the Church of the Nazarene, the twentieth century marked an era of personal piety and holiness, of the second crisis of (instantaneous) sanctification—drawn out of the nineteenth century American Holiness Movement narrative strand. The twenty-first century, in turn, has become the era for recovering John Wesley's understanding of personal holiness. In light of the socially-conscious turn among young people, however, I suggest that denominations also must press further to uncover the threads of John Wesley's social holiness—that is, his passion and action for social transformation through holiness of heart and life. This is a complex story in and of itself, yet perhaps in rediscovering and retelling this storyline, young people may begin to find a "storied place" in which to gather and journey forth.

Tracing Threads of Social Holiness

John Wesley creatively arranged ways for himself and the people called Methodists to care for vulnerable persons suffering from poverty in eighteenth century England. The impetus for social holiness, for Wesley, arose quite simply out of the Christian commitment to love God and neighbor. According to Wesley, the poor were those who lacked the necessities of life, while "whoever has sufficient food to eat and raiment to put on, with a place where to lay his head, and something over, [was] *rich*."[441] Wesley strictly advocated for *all people* to take responsibility in helping their neighbor no matter their own condition.[442] Wesley modeled his own principles of earning all he could (including soliciting large contributions from the wealthy), living in extreme thrift so as to save all he could, and giving generously to those he encountered living in need.

Wesley's mission to offer holistic transformation in Christ was creative and multifaceted. He organized schools for both children and adults, providing education for the underprivileged.[443] The schooling was offered free of charge for families in need, and children were often given clothing and meals.[444]

---

440. Inge, *A Christian Theology of Place* (Burlington, VT: Ashgate, 2003), 107.

441. Wesley, "The Danger of Riches (1781)" in *John Wesley's Sermons: An Anthology*, ed. Albert C. Outler and Richard P. Heizenrater (Nashville: Abingdon Press, 1991), 453.

442. Richard P. Heizenrater, Ed. *The Poor and the People Called Methodist* (Nashville: Abingdon Press, 2002), 30.

443. Ibid., 51-52.

444. Ibid. Also see, Manfred Marquardt, *John Wesley's Social Ethics: Praxis and Principles* (Nashville: Abingdon Press, 1992), 83-

Wesley also made use of technological advances in printing of the late seventeenth and early eighteenth centuries to establish a broad spectrum publishing program.[445] The goal was to provide the poor with books that would complement his preaching and provide instruction on life issues. Such books included theological primers such as *Imitation of Christ* by Thomas à Kempis as well as his own book, *Primitive Physic*, which included home remedies for illnesses to help those who could not afford health care.

Committed to the biblical mandate to visit and care for those imprisoned, Wesley regularly visited prisons and advocated for better conditions for prisoners, including foreign French, Dutch, and American prisoners.[446] He urged Methodist societies to visit prisoners and to collect money in order to supply proper clothing, food, and mattresses for them.[447]

Wesley also explored micro-loan programs and work cooperatives to help struggling merchants and manufacturers initiate earnings through small businesses. [448]

Wesley's Methodist successors also continued this legacy in social holiness. Confronted by injustices of slavery and poverty of nineteenth century America, communities of Methodists and other Wesleyan denominations intentionally focused on addressing these needs as a part of their holiness identity and mission.[449] The Wesleyan Methodists under the influences of Luther Lee operated an Underground Railroad station in Utica, New York. The Salvation Army began out of William and Catherine Booth's motivation to bring salvation to persons struggling with poverty and hunger by providing for their physical and spiritual needs. Benjamin Titus Roberts' outspoken criticism of pew rentals and other discriminatory practices that favored rich over the poor together with the failure of the Methodist church to stand against slavery would initiate Free Methodism. And Phineas Bresee's commitment to the poor through the Peniel Mission urban outreach in Los Angeles, California would mark the beginnings of the Church of the Nazarene.[450]

Conclusion

In recovering the narratives that make up our Wesleyan-Holiness heritage, we discover a people committed to action that fostered individual and social

---

445. Marquardt, 57.

446. See John Wesley, *Journal* (October 15, 1759), *Works* [BE], 21, 231 (See also October 24, 1760, [BE], 21, 285).

447. Marquardt, 83.

448. See John Wesley, *Journal* (November 25, 1740), *Works* [BE], 19. 173).

449. Donald Dayton, *Discovering an Evangelical Heritage* (New York: Harper & Row, 1976).

450. For this summary of Wesleyan-Holiness denominational narratives, I am indebted to the work of Jamie Gates and the Wesleyan Holiness Consortium's collaborative unpublished white paper on Human Trafficking as the new abolitionist movement.

transformation. Their commitment to holiness manifested itself in growing together in Christ and in tangibly living out God's love and mercy to those around them, particularly those most marginalized and neglected in society. As a holiness people, we only recover this aspect of our heritage *in part* when we return to our identity narratives.

Clearly, we must also embody this identity through our holy actions as manifestations of the "good news" of Jesus Christ before a watching world. Such actions are nurtured in and by the life of the church. Thus, embracing our multiple narrative strands, we must also embody our heritage of social holiness in our individual lives and families, in small discipleship groups, in our local congregation and neighborhood, and even in our commitment to point to God's reign globally.

What if our churches looked like communities of Christian responsibility sharing a commitment to service, living simply, combating individualism, and making wise consumer choices because of our deep care for those whose lives are affected by our actions? What if each of our Wesleyan-Holiness denominations invested themselves within the larger Wesleyan matrix (and even the Church at large!) in partnership in order to respond globally with unified voice, shared resources, and joint action against oppression and injustice? Perhaps then our churches and denominations might reflect anew the tangible embodiment of the ways of Jesus, our Lord, who gathers us into his global Body to live out hope in the midst of a broken world.

Nell (Ph.D., Boston University; M.Div., Nazarene Theological Seminary) is Assistant Professor of Theology and the Richard B. Parker Co-chair in Wesleyan Theology at George Fox Evangelical Seminary in Portland, Oregon. In addition to Wesleyan theology, Nell's areas of scholarship include contextual theology and ecclesiology. She also consults for Nazarene Compassionate Ministries. In her spare time, she bikes, hikes, and runs with her family.

Welcoming New Tents:

Inviting and Empowering Global Engagement with Holiness Theology

Myra Oomit

The recent history of my geographical origins started back in the American South, when itinerant preachers of various calibers would attract crowds of townsfolk to their tents for a dose of salvation or deception. One weekend, a young man who much later became my grandfather took exception to one visiting preacher's admonitions calling parents to bring their children to have the demons beat out of them. Dozens of children were brought to "find Jesus" at the end of a rod. Following a disagreement with the town deputy over the need to address these nefarious activities, my grandfather decided that if preachers had the freedom to twist the gospel to beat children *en masse*, then his knife had the freedom to liberate the "revival" tent of its structural integrity. He soon severed enough ropes to end the ordeal, and in the ensuing exodus, my grandfather slipped back to the family farmhouse.

Around midnight, a taxi pulled up with a message from the sheriff explaining that the deputy had procured a 90-day warrant for my grandfather's arrest. However, if the deputy could not find his culprit before the warrant expired, no arrest would be made. Thus, it came to pass that my grandfather left the farm, met my grandmother in another state, and started a new family story of which I am a part.

Since following God's calling to my husband's homeland in Asia, I have remembered this story of origins and new beginnings in my struggles to listen, adapt, and express my faith in ways my neighbors and family can appreciate. Try as we may to dress, speak, think, or feel as if we were from someplace else, our origins are immutable, irreversibly shaped by those who came before us. But we choose how to interpret our origins and how to forge new paths from these starting points.

As members of the Church of the Nazarene have sought to set up a single theological camp uniting a global church around holiness and Christian perfection, we have struggled to account adequately for contextual realities. I suggest empowering indigenous holiness theologies (IHTs) as one way to address fruitfully the varied contextual origins of members worldwide while retaining our distinct emphasis on holiness of heart and life. Listening to IHTs can help us discern where to cut non-essential ties to our origins to make room for new tents in our theological camp, allowing us to become a truly global holiness community built on the historical foundations God has laid for all of us.

What Are Indigenous Holiness Theologies?

As members of the Church of the Nazarene attempted to recognize and to empower the global church through the process of internationalization, denominational policies have made repeated references to indigeneity and indigenous churches. The term "indigenous" reflects authentic origination in a particular location, a sense of organic nativeness as opposed to artificial imposition by foreign influences.

Many mission texts of recent years have discussed indigenous theologies as a sign of a mature indigenous church. An "indigenous theology" is a type of contextual theology born of a particular people group's authentic "faith-reflection based on the Christian gospel amidst [their] indigenous culture."[451] This Spirit-led theologizing involves reinterpreting indigenous life and Christian Scripture in light of one another.[452] The laity plays a prominent role in this process, helping identify the "enduring gospel" that "takes seriously the condition of ordinary people who suffer in [their] society."[453] Reading Scripture and context in this way impels incarnation of the gospel message into indigenous flesh and blood. Indigenous churches in any context must be given freedom to contextualize the message of Scripture boldly for the sake of their vitality and mission. Indigenous theologies can then serve as transformative leaven within the broader indigenous society as well as within the global church family.

For congregations in the Church of the Nazarene to develop authentically indigenous *and* authentically denominational theologies, they must be invited to engage boldly with biblical holiness and Christian perfection. The results of this kind of engagement are a variety of context-specific indigenous holiness theologies (IHTs) that help the Church of the Nazarene develop a global view on how God is working out holiness among the denomination's people.

Being Where We Are From

As the preservation of a historically-rooted identity marked by holiness has been a persistent concern for members of the Church of the Nazarene, the very

---

451. Jhakmak Neeraj Ekka, "Indigenous Christian Theology: Questions and Directions in Making," *Bangalore Theological Forum*, 39 (2007): 105.

452. Ibid, 117.

453. John de Gruchy, "Revisiting Doing Contextual Theology," *Journal of Theology for South Africa*, 141 (2011): 26.

concept of inviting the newest members to take a crack at re-articulating our denominational theology would likely produce a degree of anxiety for many within the church. Risk is inherent in this process.

However, dangers that are more significant lie in not empowering and listening to IHTs. IHTs encourage each of our communities to recognize the riches of God's activity in where we are from without forcing us to pretend we are all from the same place. We all share in many parts of the same great story, but we also have unique testimonies to share. Stifling these stories impoverishes us all. Furthermore, we must realize that all churches have active theologies and naturally seek to contextualize in efforts to address questions arising in context. All churches try to make sense of the work of God through their own indigenous history.

How a denomination allows its distinctive identity to be approached will determine how deeply incorporated it may become in the self-theologizing process of its newest member communities. For members of the Church of the Nazarene, this means that advocating simple acceptance of "non-negotiable" doctrinal positions on holiness may lead to superficial commitment to these formulations while the active theologizing of the local church finds different emphases. Though holiness reflections may arise, they may be forced into borrowed terms, leading to awkwardly foreign incarnations. However, prayerfully inviting our newest brothers and sisters to let the Holy Spirit lead them into expressions of holiness and Christian perfection most meaningful in their contexts may be the only way of advocating the true integration of our denominational emphases into the very DNA of local churches' indigenous theologies.

Indigenous churches can be invited to incorporate resources from the global Church of the Nazarene family into the reading and application of Scripture. Because the non-dominating presence of outside resources is a vital component for healthy development for indigenous theologies, offering distinctively denominational resources during the indigenous meaning-making process can lend a uniquely denominational as well as uniquely indigenous character to these contextualizations. Each distinctive context and the guidance of God's Spirit will determine how these resources from the denominational landscape can be employed to build indigenous theological tents on the common ground of God's work of holiness.

Strategies fostering IHTs must advocate genuine listening, giving indigenous Christians opportunity to share their witness and to gain insight from others within the global Church of the Nazarene family. In sharing with one another and listening to one another, the process of indigenous holiness theologizing is facilitated in multiple settings as churches encourage and challenge one another to interact meaningfully with their global and local contexts. In being free to be where we are from, we who are members of the Church of the Nazarene as a global body may find more clarity about where we as a holiness people are going in our unfolding future.

The Global "Camp Meeting"

Intentionally inviting IHTs to drive our denominational discussion of holiness means recognizing the Nazarene camp in ways we may find unusual. I have heard it said that we will never know we are pickles if we spend our whole lives in the brine. Taking a step back from our context allows us to view how it has "formed and flavored" us, to identify places of God's powerful movement in our unique stories.

For instance, we can observe that Wesley's theology was shaped in no small part by his contemporary "social and economic conditions."[454] The Methodist fervor for serving the marginalized and the "millennial rhetoric" that went hand in hand with many expressions of the hope of holiness flourished in the midst of "America's quest for a virtuous republic" following American independence and into the mid-19th century.[455]

Similarly, the environment of camp meetings that hosted instantaneous experiences of entire sanctification for many early members of the denomination emerged within particular socio-political and geographical conditions in the United States in the nineteenth century.[456] Early holiness mores responded to a specific cultural setting in early twentieth-century America, forbidding activities representing social ills in that context.[457]

In these ways and many others, the ongoing revelation of holiness that has shaped many members of the denomination indigenous to North America has taken form within particular contexts. As those who have dominated the direction of holiness conversations in the church learn to relinquish unequal power in holy love for the global church family, we all need to learn to discern which parts of our theological camp are God's good news that can find incarnation in various

---

454. Wes Tracy, "Economic Policies and Judicial Oppression as Formative Influences on the Theology of John Wesley," *Wesleyan Theological Journal*, 27 (1992): 30. Cited 1 August 2013. Online: http://wesley.nnu.edu/fileadmin/imported_site/wesleyjournal/1992-wtj-27.pdf.

455. Timothy L. Smith, "John Wesley's Religion in Thomas Jefferson's America," in *The 19th-Century Holiness Movement Volume Four* (Kansas City, Mo: Beacon Hill, 1998), 32.

456. Stan Ingersol, Harold Raser, and David Whitelaw, *Our Watchword & Song: The Centennial History of the Church of the Nazarene* (ed. Floyd Cunningham; Kansas City, Mo.: Beacon Hill, 2009), 35.

457. In-Gyeong Kim Lundell, *Bridging the Gaps: Contextualization among Korean Nazarene Churches in America* (New York: Peter Lang, 1995), 4.

contexts and which parts are pieces of our own indigenous stories that are not required to be integrated into everyone else's.

Distinguishing gospel from contextual interpretation will be a difficult, even painful process for which we will require God's strength and guidance. Let me be clear that we are not talking about merely altering what holiness looks like outwardly to suit a particular context. IHTs do not simply "broaden our rules" or set translated hymns to indigenous instruments. IHTs interpret biblical holiness through particular native languages, evolving worldviews, cognitive schema, and spiritual-religious histories we will not all share. Acknowledging IHTs means recognizing that terms used to discuss the denomination's holiness theology probably will not translate precisely. In empowering IHTs, we will need to try much harder to communicate with each other and to understand the depths of what God is doing among us. Through such holy communion, our church will find God's revelation in a holiness that is not supracontextual but multicontextual as the unique insights and contributions of all members of the Church of the Nazarene are brought into the conversation surrounding our distinct theological heritage.

Welcoming new indigenous tents into our camp meeting has important implications for the Nazarene holiness camp. We must humbly build temporary structures on holy ground. God has blessed us with a distinct calling to be holiness people. To develop on that foundation, we have all received particular resources and materials. We have woven in parts of our contexts when pitching our theological tents here. We want our theologies to be like the good tent revivals of old: places where visitors were attracted from all the surrounding area and holiness of heart and life was empowered by God's Spirit.

We run into trouble when we insist one particular tent is a castle that cannot be moved, and that the words proclaimed from within it must undoubtedly ring with the good news of gospel to whoever hears. There is no room for these kinds of tents in our Nazarene holiness camp if the whole global family is to live together in this space. We may need to cut the ropes on such tents and pray for healing in the spaces such syncretisms have overrun.

Starting from our common theological heritage and trusting in the same Spirit who gave that to us to lead us forward into our common future, we all can build theological tents that reflect God's work of holiness in our midst and from our own places of origin. We should not forget to give and to receive hospitality as we all move from tent to tent to listen and share testimonies of the power of holiness. May God give us ears to listen as we discover our holiness identity anew.

From the same stock as a tent vandal from the South, "Myra Oomit" is a millennial who became what the Church of the Nazarene interestingly calls a "tentmaker missionary" in a sensitive area of Asia. The pseudonym Myra Oomit signifies a personal past in an English language-dominated culture (Myra—English name derived from "myrrh") and a future family among culturally diverse communities (Oomit—Translated "hope" from Turkic languages of Asia). Myra has an MA in Theology from an educational institution in the Church of the Nazarene.

Assessing the Conversation

Thomas Jay Oord

If you have read every essay in this book or most of them, you might feel like you have eaten 100+ course meal! This book is not a feast. It's a holiness binge! The contributors offered plenty of thoughtful material to digest.

Josh and I knew that Xer and Millennial leaders in the Church of the Nazarene had interesting and important things to say about holiness in general and the holiness tradition in particular. These essays prove us right. We are happy to have these contributions now in print. Not only they are important, but we also hope they bear fruit and spark discussion.

As I read through the essays in this book, I saw connections and identified recurring themes. That's the typical way I read books of this nature. Some of the arguments I encountered surprised me. But because I am a Generation Xer and often teach Millennials as a professor, I expected most of the arguments in this book. Diversity reigns in these essays and among these leaders.

When reading, I often found particular ideas, proposals, or themes. Various threads run through this book, although the essays offer clusters of unity amid the diversity. In what follows, I identify dominant themes in the book's essays. Of course, my short summary cannot account for every idea, proposal, and insight. More can always be said. But I attempt a birds-eye view by identifying what I consider the prevailing themes in these essays.

Here are ten dominant themes:

1. Diversity reigns.

I am impressed with the diversity of these essays. It's a smorgasbord of assorted subjects, emphases, and perspectives. If these essays are any indication, Millennials and Xers do not think holiness is one-size-fits-all!

When assembling this group of writers, we asked many non-North American members of the Church of the Nazarene. Some accepted our invitation and were able to submit essays. Contributors come from all the continents (except Antarctica, alas!) and about three dozen world countries. We also sought gender and ethnic diversity. While we could always improve on this score, we think the book is far better than most of its peers in this respect.

When inviting, we did not assign topics. On their own, essayists chose the diverse set of issues you find in these essays. The result is a smorgasbord of great insights and proposals pertaining to holiness.

After reading these essays, I have little doubt that a person's cultural, social, and geographical location influences how she or he thinks about holiness. We may all read the same Bible and be members of the same denomination, but our diverse experiences shape our understanding of holiness. Holiness is at least partly contextual.

Millennials and Xers seem to be saying that healthy diversity should be expected and accepted in the holiness tradition. As the denomination moves ahead into its second century of existence, it will likely have to work at accounting well for diverse issues and voices. Shutting out voices will not make for a healthy denomination.

2. The Bible still matters.

Essayists in this book promote biblical holiness, even when they do not explicitly refer to the Bible. Some emphasize the biblical witness more, of course. But current denominational leaders who may have worried that Millennial and Xer generations think Scripture is irrelevant should worry no longer. The Bible matters.

I find it interesting, however, *the way* in which essayists use Scripture in these essays. Earlier in the denomination's history, it was common for preachers and writers to find in the Bible numerous examples of secondness, the number two, etc. Many thought these passages provided evidence for entire sanctification as a second work of grace.

If the essays in this book are a good indication, Millennials and Xers don't look to Scripture in that way. Instead of finding second or instances of two, essayists point to particular biblical themes they deem important for understanding holiness. The scriptures that they cite in their essays rarely concern a second definite work of grace.

And this leads me to wonder . . .

3. What is entire sanctification, and what role does it play?

You might think a book on holiness written by leaders in the Church of the Nazarene would include numerous essays promoting and appreciating the phrase "entire sanctification." But relatively few essays in this book use that phrase explicitly in a positive sense. When the phrase is used, most writers mention the confusion it carries.

I'm not sure what to make of this. A big part of me is not surprised, because I rarely hear "entire sanctification" spoken in the numerous Church of the Nazarene worship services I have attended. I only hear the phrase at district assemblies or used by scholars trying to explain what they mean by it. (And scholars don't agree among themselves.) As these essays indicate, most people are confused by the phrase and what it entails.

If the Bible matters to Xers and Millennials, which it does, and if only one major biblical translation uses the phrase "entire sanctification" and only in one passage, then using biblical language does not lead one naturally to the phrase. This doesn't mean we need to throw it out. But the absence of the phrase "entire sanctification" in the Bible does account for some of the confusion.

I think we are seeing a significant shift in the holiness tradition. Young leaders in the Church of the Nazarene are not rejecting holiness or dismissing the multiple ways holiness might be understood. These essays witness to the importance of holiness in this emerging generation of leaders. In these essays, we find young leaders today speaking often of living a transformed life or being devoted entirely to God. They speak of God's holiness. In particular, the idea that love is the heart of holiness is present in many essays. (I'll explore issue this next.)

Use of the phrase "entire sanctification," however, seems to be fading. A major reason for this fading is the confusion the phrase elicits. Millennials and Xers use other terms and phrases, although some of those mean what previous generations meant when they talked about entire sanctification. These 100+ essays may be making explicit a shift that perhaps has been largely unnoticed for some time. The phrase "entire sanctification" is fading from use.

4. The issues of love are paramount.

Second only to my awareness of the diversity in this book's essays was my awareness of the frequency essayists talked about love. Love plays a central role in Xer and Millennial understandings of holiness.

In one sense, the emphasis upon love as the core of holiness represents a conservative trend in the Church of the Nazarene. After all, several hundred years ago John Wesley identified love as the heart of holiness: "No true Christian holiness can exist without the love of God for its foundation."[458] The denomination

---

458. John Wesley, "Minutes of Some Late Conversations between the Rev. Messrs. Wesley and Others: Conversation III," *The Works of John Wesley*, 3rd ed., T. *Jackson, ed.* (London: Wesleyan Methodist Book Room, 1831, 1872. Reprinted: Grand Rapids: Baker Book House, 1978), 8:290.

has long embraced Wesleyan theology; at least, most of its theological scholars have embraced it.

In another sense, however, believing love is the core notion of holiness represents something new. Scholars might point to Mildred Bangs Wynkoop's book, *A Theology of Love*, which she wrote in the 1970s, as an important precursor to the current link many see between love and holiness. Wynkoop went even so far as to equate holiness and love.

In recent decades, many of the denomination's theologians have stressed the centrality of love for understanding sanctification. A little book I co-wrote with Michael Lodahl, *Relational Holiness*, has made a difference here. Diane Leclerc's denomination-commissioned text on holiness, *Discovering Christian Holiness*, emphasizes love as well. Other influential theologians in the denomination regard love as the heart of holiness.

5. Community counts; relationships are relevant.

Many suggest that community and relationships are central themes for understanding what some call our postmodern age. The philosophy of modernity is often criticized for being individualistic and thinking of life as disconnected. Many now seek a relational view of reality and the essential relatedness of community.

Xer and Millennial essayists in this book stress the importance of local community, church relationships, and group accountability. Many essayists say this generation sees a strong communal component to holiness. The power of church—community relationships and the life of the tribe—is a common theme.

Some essayists capture this focus by calling for renewed emphasis upon community practices, including the sacraments and other means of grace. Discipleship is crucial. Such practices in community prove crucial for developing the holy life. Holiness as understood by many Xers and Millennials is far more than personal decision. With John Wesley, they seem to believe holiness is a social endeavor.

6. It's more about process than crisis.

For decades, people in the holiness movement have been discussing the roles of crisis and process in sanctification. The discussion is nuanced and complex. But it comes down to whether one believes sanctification is best understood as happening in a moment of decision or through a process of growth. Most people affirm both crisis and process, of course. But most also either implicitly or explicitly emphasize one more than the other.

Millennials and Xers writing for this book do not resolve the process vs. crisis debate. But in their essays, the majority points more to a process or growth-in-grace understanding of holiness. They speak about continual cooperating with God, increasing in Christlikeness, ongoing spiritual transformation. In these essays, process dominates.

In light of the emphasis among Millennials and Xers upon holiness as ongoing transformation, and in light of their lack of emphasis upon holiness as second definite work (see #3 above), this generation of holiness leaders might prefer the word "furtherness" instead of "secondness" when thinking about their views. "Spiritual formation" also points to this continual need for transformation. Whatever the language, these essays stress the ongoing life of holiness.

7. Other Christians are holy too.

One way to understand the diversity within Christianity is to identify particular traditions and movements. The Church of the Nazarene is the largest organized group—denomination—emerging from the so-called "holiness movement." Not surprisingly, the movement gets its name from its special emphasis upon holiness, although what holiness entails was and is diversely understood.

Those growing up in the holiness movement have been tempted to think the Church of the Nazarene has the corner on holiness. Judging by many essays in this book, however, Xer and Millennial leaders care also about how other Christian traditions and movements understand holiness. Many essayists call readers to appreciate the traditions, practices, and ideas of denominations other than the Church of the Nazarene.

My sense in reading these essays is that Millennials and Xers have an expansive vision of the Kingdom of God. They recognize the great value and depth of other traditions, without negating the importance of the Church of the Nazarene. This may also reflect the decreasing emphasis young Christians place on denominational boundaries.

8. There's still a credibility gap.

Even in John Wesley's day, many struggled with the discrepancy between how some Christians claimed holy living should look and the actual way holiness people lived. Some theories of sanctification did not match the actual practice of sanctification.

Mildred Bangs Wynkoop described this discrepancy as a "credibility gap." Many holiness folk claimed to have lost their sin nature, for instance, but the way these folk lived their lives suggested they were still engaged in sin. Others claimed sinless perfection but failed to explain convincingly what Christian perfection involved.

In this book, Xer and Millennial essayists emphasize the importance of lived experience. Holiness must be practical, applicable, and possible. It may also be difficult, and it may mean acting in countercultural ways. Christlike transformation requires breaking ingrained propensities toward sin and developing habits of life-giving love. In sum, Millennials and Xers seem to seek a realistic rather than utopic Christian life.

9. Being holy means engaging culture.

From its inception, those in the holiness tradition have cared about social issues. Many essayists in this book carry on this concern, some even addressing the same issues holiness leaders of yesteryear addressed. The sanctified life has a strong public component.

For instance, some writers renew the denomination's early push for women to serve in leadership roles. Others call for greater personal discipline or abstinence. Essayists express the importance of caring for the poor. Xers and Millennials care about helping people break addictions and live healthy lives.

We also find Xers and Millennials in this book addressing social issues rarely addressed in the early holiness tradition. For instance, some speak out against nationalism, arguing that allegiance to Christ comes before allegiance to nation. Others say being holy means being environmentally responsible. I also find young holiness leaders engaging the issues of homosexuality to a greater extent, with greater depth, and with different views than leaders of yesteryear.

I'm struck by the general approach many Xers and Millennials have toward popular culture. While not accepting it uncritically, they view it more favorably than holiness leaders in the early and mid-20th century. Many engage popular culture without simply castigating it, actually believing they can learn something positive from the world in which they live.

10. Hospitality is the way of holiness.

The final theme I find often in these essays is identified by a few as "hospitality." Many essayists preach the importance of openness, care, and charity toward those who think differently than the essayists themselves. They welcome the stranger, both in the literal and ideological senses of "stranger."

I see a connection between hospitality as a key form of holiness and the first theme I mentioned above: diversity. Millennials and Xers in various cultures of the world seem more aware of differences. These differences may be social, linguistic, ethnic, ideological, religious, or something else. We live in a multi-faceted world.

In this context, essayists appeal to love as the way to engage well those who are different, in whatever way, from themselves. Many seek shalom. And promoting the love of shalom means being hospitable.

Conclusion

Well, those are the dominant themes I find in this book. Of course, you might think some themes I failed to mention are also important. I am not pretending my list is exhaustive.

Josh and I would love to hear your thoughts on the essays. So send your thoughts to us. (For instance, post your ideas and contributions on the Renovating Holiness Project Facebook page.) Even better, share them with others. Some are already planning to use this book in their Sunday School classes. We hope this book sparks numerous holy conversations on holiness!

Times continue to change. That's not new. These essays represent some of those changes in the Church of the Nazarene. In them, I find both a return to concerns of yesteryear and a call for the holiness tradition to address the issues and language of today.

May these holy conversations deepen and widen our view of holiness, incorporating both old and new issues, as we all follow the charge to be holy as God is holy.

Amen.

Thomas Jay Oord is Professor of Theology and Philosophy at Northwest Nazarene University, Nampa, Idaho. Dr. Oord has published more than 20 books and 100 articles on various topics in theology, philosophy, culture, and science. He serves on several academic society leadership committees and blogs on a variety of subjects at thomasjayoord.com. An avid photographer and backpacker, Oord spends much of his leisure time in the beauty of the outdoors. He and his wife, Cheryl, have three daughters.

WANT MORE COPIES OF
RENOVATING HOLINESS?

Go to:
WWW.RENOVATINGHOLINESS.COM

- Read blog essays from our contributors and supporters.

- Check out other books by our contributors.

- Download our group discussion guide for free.

- Purchase single books.

- Get discounts for bulk orders.

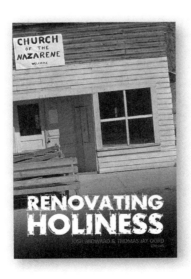